GW00771509

The Autobiography of an Education

Part Two (1972 -1982)

The Inner London Education Authority (ILEA)

Sir Peter Newsam

GreenLea Books

Published by Greenlea Books, Pickering YO18 7QL

Printed in Britain by CPI Books 2014

ISBN: 978-0-9929948-1-5

Acknowledgements

Front cover: I am saying goodbye to the Education Committee on leaving the ILEA in 1982. This was the first and last time I was invited to speak to that Committee. Normally, officials were seen but not heard during its proceedings.

I record with gratitude that much of the material used in this book was collected together as part of an unpublished study of decision-making in the ILEA supported by the Leverhulme Foundation in 1992/1993.

The documents cited in this volume are all available from the London Institute of Education Library.

I would like to acknowledge the love, friendship and help of the very many people who are not mentioned in this book but who, throughout my life, have encouraged me to make something of it from my earliest days to the present. Writing books is not my métier, so I am particularly grateful to Michael Simons, for many years director of the English and Media Centre, for steering this one so carefully to port.

Contents

Introduction

Politicians regularly keep and publish diaries. So we learn from day to day what they say they have been doing or thinking. With the Official Secrets Act somewhere in the background, civil servants rarely do that; local authority administrators, for whatever reason, almost never. What follows is a contribution towards filling that gap. In Part I of this autobiography of an education, I gave an account of what I learnt, how I learnt it and then applied it from my earliest years. It ends with my leaving the education service of the West Riding of Yorkshire at the end of 1971.

Part 2 begins with my appointment in 1972, at the age of forty four, to the Inner London Education Authority (ILEA). My account is not intended to be an objective or in any way a complete account of the events that occurred during the period I describe. It is certainly not intended as a how-to-do-it manual on educational administration. Its aim is to describe, with documentary evidence wherever that still exists, how the mixture of theoretical understanding and practical experience I had earlier acquired had identifiable consequences during my time, first as Deputy Education Officer and then, from 1977, as Education Officer of the ILEA. It describes how things were done. How things might have been done better or otherwise is for others to consider.

In 1982, at the age of fifty four, I accepted an invitation from the then Home Secretary, Sir William Whitelaw, to become Chairman of the Commission for Racial Equality. As my direct involvement in educational administration ended then, though not my interest in the subject, so too does this account of my experience of it. To that somewhat abrupt ending, I have added some reflections on how, in my perception, the structure and purpose of the English education system has changed since the Education Act of 1944. That was three years before the London County Council published the London School Plan. This set out the Council's detailed proposals for the future of more than a thousand schools that it maintained in Inner London.

Chapter 1: Appointment as Deputy Education Officer to the ILEA

On 19 January, 1992, I took up my appointment as Deputy Educations officer at 10% below the job maximum of £8,958. To this the person appointed would 'normally proceed over a period of 3–4 years'. The role of Deputy was defined in the appointment particulars as follows:

> The major function of the Deputy Education Officer is to be able to deputise for the Education Officer as required across the whole field of the latter's responsibilities. He must share with the Education Officer, subject to his final direction and in close personal contact with him, the administrative responsibilities for the whole service and for the representation of the ILEA on national bodies'. The particulars went on to say that the Deputy was 'expected to exercise a co-ordinating function in relation to the work of the separate branches and to work in close cooperation with the Chief Inspector, who is of equivalent rank to that of the Deputy.'

Finally, the particulars explained that the Deputy would no doubt be given special responsibility for some parts of the service, but added: 'It will be necessary for account to be taken of the previous experience and particular interests of the new Deputy as well as of the new Education Officer and it is not proposed to specify in advance what particular sections of the service should command the special attention of the Deputy.'

Having said that, the particulars did do a little specifying in advance: 'The Deputy Education Officer is to be expected to represent the Authority on various outside bodies including those at national level. The new Deputy may expect to have to devote up to a third of his time to outside representation of this kind.' And about 90% of his store of patience, the particulars might have added had the author chosen to be frank. Again: 'He will be asked to act as Chairman of the Divisional Officers' Conference' and he will be responsible 'for finance and the clearance of reports with financial implications, and for representing the Education Officer at the Finance Sub-Committee'.

What the particulars could not be expected to explain was what was to be done if the Education Officer chose not to have regard to views the Deputy might express on areas of the service where that Deputy had 'previous experience' to offer or 'particular interests to pursue'. Nothing, would have been the answer to that. Internal disagreement amongst ILEA officials was for the Education Officer to sort out. The Authority did not concern itself with domestic disputes.

In 1972, the ILEA was the largest local education authority in Western Europe and larger than any school district in the USA, other than New York. With a population of 2.8 million, there were over 420,000 pupils on the roll of the 1,200 schools it maintained; more than 460,000 full-time enrolments in over thirty Further Education Colleges, including students in eight Colleges of Education; about 60,000 members of ILEA-run Youth Clubs and another 180,000 enrolled in ILEA-funded Voluntary Clubs; and some 250,000 enrolments in Adult Education Institutes: about 18% of adult education students in the whole of the United Kingdom. The Authority also managed the funding of as many Higher Education students, through five aided Polytechnics and other institutions, as the University of London. It employed more than sixty thousand people. These figures illustrate the fact that the ILEA dealt with education, as it used to be said, from the cradle to the grave. Schools play a disproportionately large part of the account that follows because it was with schools that I was personally most concerned. Others took the lead in further and higher education and in other areas of the ILEA's work where my principal role was often to prevent other people from getting in their way.

The salary of £8,062 which the Deputy Education Officer was paid in 1972 related to the Education Officer's salary of just over £12,000 and a revenue budget of £175 million. The 1970s were a period of runaway inflation. By 1982, the figure for the revenue budget was just over £700 million but, so far as expenditure on schools was concerned, had been reduced in real terms in response to falling numbers. Salary levels in 1972 have to be multiplied by between ten and fifteen to be roughly comparable with those in 2014. The ILEA was administered from County Hall, on the other side of the Thames from parliament, and through ten divisional offices, each concerned with individual London boroughs or, as the map on the next page indicates, in three instances with two of them.

I was to discover early on that the constitution of the ILEA almost invariably defeated commentators hostile to its existence. In April 1972, a pamphlet appeared entitled 'No choice but to go'. This declared that, in the ILEA, 'the paid officials decided policy' and the Authority 'had no representatives directly appointed to it'. The first assertion was wholly mistaken. Policies could only be acted on by officials after decisions made by ILEA committees on which both political parties were represented. The second assertion was equally incorrect. Unlike any other education Authority in England, forty members of the ILEA were directly elected to it as councillors of the Greater London Council. The Authority consisted of these forty members and of thirteen others, appointed from amongst their elected members by each of the twelve inner London boroughs and the City of London. It was only the Authority, consisting of these fifty three elected persons, that could take decisions on the annual budget or propose changes to legislation or deal with other such constitutional matters. The Authority's Education Committee included a further twenty one 'added' members to the fifty three elected ones. In 1972, this group of members included people, such as Lady Plowden and Professor Vaizey, with experience or expertise on educational matters to offer. Five teacher representatives were included within this group of twenty one added members.

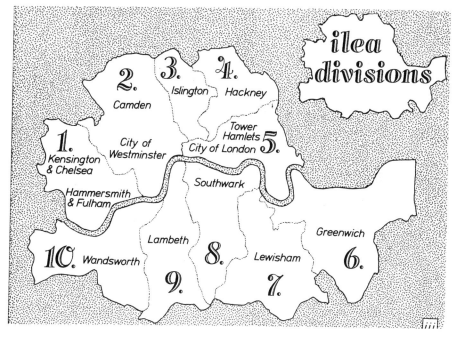

During my first weeks at the ILEA, I began a task which I had not nearly completed when I left just over ten years later: finding my way to and, as often as possible, into the 1,300 or so educational institutions for which the Authority was responsible. Finding my intellectual bearings was just as difficult. It is impossible to think sensibly about the future of any large organisation without some understanding of its past. What it has been and has now become suggests how it might develop. Amongst the documents I looked at initially was a recently published A History of Education in London 1870–1970 by Stuart Maclure. This account was later extended to 1990 and remains the most accurate and perceptive account of the achievements, in turn, of the London School Board, the London County Council (LCC) and, from 1965, of the Inner London Education Authority. A second document I consulted was a lecture to head teachers given in 1947 by Dr A G. Hughes, the then Chief Inspector of the LCC, the ILEA's predecessor. The lecture was entitled 'Some Reflections on the London School Plan.' 1947 was only two years after the end of the war. Food was still rationed, the country was almost bankrupt and over five hundred of London's schools had either been destroyed or were still suffering from serious forms of bomb damage. The lecture described what the LCC hoped to achieve in the years to come, but it was the following paragraph that struck me most forcibly:

> One danger of planning for the future is that it tends to divert the attention of administrators from present needs. But let us not overlook the solid achievements of the past three years. Here are some of them: fees abolished in secondary schools; the school leaving age raised to fifteen; the number of State scholarships doubled; the Council's major scholarship scheme, comprehensive and generous before the war, still further expanded; maintenance grants for all needy pupils over the age of eleven; 150 London pupils going to public boarding schools each year from homes which make it impossible for them to benefit fully from a day school education; three camps open from March to November; greatly increased facilities for pupils to hear good music and see good plays; financial help for school clubs and societies, and for holiday journeys as well as for school journeys in term time; travelling expenses, free milk, cheap dinners; a new scheme to help pupils to learn to play musical instruments; the purchase of original works of art for schools; the replacement of the junior scholarship examination by a simple test, devised externally it is true, but marked by the schools; more weight given to parents' wishes in regard to secondary education, and much more weight to teachers' estimates to the point, at age thirteen, of the abolition of the junior technical scholarship and the supplementary scholarship examinations; easy transfer from one type of secondary school to another at any time; the staffing of the new secondary schools improved on an average almost to the pre-war secondary school standard of 1:22; freedom to widen the school curriculum, for example, by teaching a foreign language; secretarial assistance; the establishment of five experimental secondary schools.

In 1972, it was a humbling experience to read Stuart Maclure's account of the London education service which had developed since 1870 and of the LCC's achievements in the immediate post-war years that Dr Hughes had described in his 1947 lecture. If we could achieve anything comparable in the next few years, I concluded, we would be doing remarkably well.

My arrival at the ILEA coincided with two important policy initiatives. In 1971, Dr Briault, the previous Deputy, had been appointed Education Officer and, apart from the day-to-day management of a huge education service, was simultaneously embarking on both. The first was later to be given the title 'An Education Service for the

Whole Community' (ESWC). The second, following from an Education Committee decision in 1970, was to end, by 1980, selection at 11+ at any schools maintained by the ILEA and the development by then of a full range of comprehensive secondary schools. Meanwhile, two existing policies were being worked through. The first was a review of the thirty-six further education colleges. The second was a survey of more than eight hundred and fifty primary schools and, in the light of population changes, to determine which were to be enlarged and which, if any, should be closed.

An Education Service for the Whole Community

The ESWC project had been maturing in Dr Briault's mind during his fourteen years as Deputy to the previous Education Officer, Sir William Houghton. The task now was to prepare a document to put to the ILEA's political leadership. Expenditure would be involved and the document would have to be convincing to have any hope of gaining sustained political support as well as that of the thousands of teachers, lecturers and others whose efforts would be needed if the enterprise was to succeed. So it was that, just before taking up my appointment as Deputy Education Officer, an unwelcome appointment in the higher reaches of the administration I was later to discover, I had been invited to a meeting of senior ILEA administrators and inspectors at Eastbourne. They had assembled to look at the first draft of what was to become the Education Officer's report to the Education Committee on the ESWC. I arrived just before dinner and recall standing at the top of the stairs and looking down at my future colleagues, only two of whom I had previously met. The fourteen senior officers and inspectors were casually conversing. The men were in dinner jackets and their ladies in long dresses. Between them, I later worked out, the twelve men and two women administrators and inspectors had nearly two hundred years' experience of London education. I had none. Nor had I had anything to do with urban education elsewhere; nor, for that matter, had I ever worked in a Labour-controlled education authority. Of more immediate consequence, as I had not been advised to bring a dinner jacket, I found myself somewhat socially adrift.

At the age of sixty, Dr Briault had no time to waste. The retirement age was sixty-five so he had only a few years in which to set London's education service on a new path. It was understandable that he wanted long-standing and trusted colleagues around him; understandable too that, as I was not such a person, I was left to find my own place in the system. Apart from the miscellaneous functions referred to in the appointment particulars, my principal role, as in the case of the American Vice-President, was to be one heartbeat away, temporarily at least, from the top job itself; but Dr Briault, other than for a few weeks shortly before he retired, was never ill and was seldom away. Despite the 'sharing responsibilities' bit in the Deputy's job description, I had not been given direct administrative responsibility for anything except finance and the chairmanship of regular meetings with ten experienced and often disgruntled Divisional Officers. For the first time in my career as an educational administrator, I felt isolated. I was near the top of a huge administrative structure but not an effective part of it. As Deputy in the West Riding, my room had been next to Sir Alec Clegg's. We were in close, daily, head round the door, touch. In London, my room was on a separate floor from the Education Officer's and I had to negotiate a place in his over-loaded diary to make appointments to see him. So I had no idea what he was doing from day to day or which of my colleagues he was seeing or what he was then saying to them. During the week, I was caught up in a series of time-consuming meetings to which I could contribute little useful. Everyone was being polite but that was the truth of it. One consequence of this lack of direct involvement in the administration of the ILEA was that it left me time to visit schools and other institutions. These visits had important consequences.

After some six months in and out of London's primary and secondary schools, with occasional visits to several special schools and further education institutions, I was nearly overcome by a sense of alarm. This had two sources. On secondary education, everything I had learnt about educational administration and had experienced as a teacher told me that the drive to create comprehensive schools, though efficiently conducted, was seriously flawed. If pursued, it would be damaging to some of the best secondary schools in London and would not replace them with the right kind of school anyway. It deserved to fail and almost certainly would. The second main source of unease concerned the primary schools. In some parts of London I found a few good ones but, in other areas, I had visited schools that were facing difficulties not of their own making and seemingly close to collapse. No one seemed to be doing enough to help them. I had other concerns also, but these two were the main ones.

Meanwhile, the Education Officer was pressing ahead with both the major initiatives to which he and the ILEA were committed. 'An Education Service for The Whole Community' (ESWC) was a hugely ambitious project that had three elements to it. The first was straightforward: all institutions maintained by the ILEA, from nursery class to the five polytechnics, had to continue to improve what they were offering to those for whose education they were directly responsible. Second, all these institutions were to recognise that they had a responsibility for the welfare of students and pupils in other ILEA institutions as well as in their own. In that connection, they were to get to know and, whenever appropriate, to work with those other institutions. In particular, schools and colleges had to stop seeing their premises as for their use alone. Issues such as the long-standing arguments between schools and the adult education service, which used those schools in the evenings, now had to be resolved. The third element of the initiative was the crucial one. This was Dr Briault, a powerfully effective administrator, at his visionary best. He had spent a professional lifetime teaching individual children, inspecting individual schools and now had major responsibility for all that was happening in the hundreds of institutions and for the thousands of children and adults within those institutions. But what of the people who had left school at fifteen or, in the case of older ones, at fourteen and had never gone near an educational institution since? Most of them paid taxes and even if they did not, Briault believed that the Authority had a duty towards them too. So he was now asking everyone in the Authority's service – teachers, lecturers or administrative staff – to share a common purpose. They were to see themselves as members of a single, inner London wide, education system, serving the interests of all the people living or working in London. In that capacity, all were to share in the drive to re-engage with as many as possible of the thousands of people who had left school as soon as they could and since had had no further contact with any form of education or training. It was with this third element of the initiative in mind that Dr Briault's report set out who these missing thousands were. What he was asking now was not just for people in the education service to do things differently but, far more difficult, to think differently about what they were doing or failing to do, achieving or failing to achieve.

Three things were needed for the success of the ESWC initiative. The first was an administration with the required political backing and a sufficiently determined and competent staff to set the Authority on a new path. Dr Briault and his immediate colleagues had the necessary political support, experience, determination and ability to do that. The second requirement was time. Any administration can devise proposals for substantial change in a few weeks or even over a weekend, but changes on the ground, requiring human beings to adjust their thinking and behaviour to effect those changes, take far longer. For the initiative to succeed, sustained development for up to ten or more years might well be necessary. Dr Briault, the driving force behind the initiative, had only five. The third and most important requirement for the success of ESWC was for the changes it required to take place during a period of calm. A huge education system needed to be free to concentrate its efforts on achieving its principal aims rather than having to respond, at unpredictable intervals, to sudden, substantial, challenges to settled structures and even to its very existence. Only in this way could some thirteen hundred institutions manage to sustain the effort necessary to give practical effect to the additional responsibilities they were being asked to assume. Yet it soon became apparent that stability was the one thing on which the Authority could definitely not rely.

The ESWC report, sixty pages long, was issued by Dr Briault, as Education Officer, rather than in the name of the Authority. When published on 9 October 1973, a copy was sent to every teacher and lecturer in the Authority's service. The ideas behind Dr Briault's initiative were supported by grants enabling cooperation between institutions of different kinds to be given practical encouragement. By 1977, 207 such projects had been undertaken in an effort to reach out to the missing thousands. Perhaps as important, a wide range of institutions had by then got used to talking to each other, often for the first time, across entrenched institutional and professional boundaries.

The ESWC programme was well supported, somewhat at arms' length, by the ILEA's Education Committee. It had its successes but it was eventually overtaken by other matters pressing on the Authority. To that extent, its results fell short of what

Dr Briault had hoped to achieve. I admired the thinking behind what Dr Briault was trying to do but took little part in the enterprise itself. This was partly because no one asked me to but mainly because it was difficult for a newcomer to contribute usefully to this initiative without the detailed knowledge that Dr Briault and his immediate colleagues had acquired over many years. In 1947, the London School Plan had set out one vision of the future for schools in Inner London. In 1973, Dr Briault set out an enlargement of that vision, incorporating wider aims and a far wider range of institutions, from nursery schools to the five aided polytechnics and the adult education service. No one person or publicly accountable set of people has since been in a position to do anything comparable or seems likely to be in the foreseeable future.

Ending 11+ selection in ILEA secondary schools by 1980

The second major policy to which the Authority was committed related to secondary education. This became my main concern over the four next years, so the account that follows reflects this. Soon after the local government elections of 1970, ILEA's newly elected Labour administration had called for plans to create, by 1980, the fully comprehensive secondary school system envisaged by the London County Council in 1947. Why had this not been achieved over the past twenty-three years by a predominantly Labour-controlled London County Council and then, since 1965, by the ILEA which replaced it? Part of the difficulty in London lay in the acute shortage of London's own money that the government allowed the Authority to spend even to repair its buildings. Replacing more than a few of its secondary schools with the type of building necessary to create the kind of comprehensive schools the Authority believed to be necessary had been impossible. Compared to the school buildings I had seen in Yorkshire and elsewhere, many of the secondary school premises in London verged on the ruinous. In one secondary school, I had found myself helping a science teacher lug a large basin of hot water up to a science laboratory that lacked a tap to provide it. Another difficulty was the changing political position nationally. Altering the nature of any individual school, for example by ending academic selection at it, required the consent of the Secretary of State of the day, who might be opposed, as several were, to any such changes. It so happened that the change from Conservative to Labour control of the ILEA in 1970 coincided with a change from a Labour to a Conservative government in that same year. That made any move requiring an end to selection at 11+ within London particularly difficult.

To a newcomer to London, the contrast between the ILEA and what had happened in the North and West Ridings was immediately evident. In 1965, the Conservative North Riding had embarked on widespread consultations on the future of its secondary schools. In 1968, it had put forward proposals for a fully comprehensive set of schools. Labour was in control nationally and had approved the County's proposals. In the West Riding, Labour was in control of the council between 1959 and 1967 and the Conservatives between 1967 and 1974, when the County ceased to exist. During the years to 1972, while Mrs Fitzpatrick chaired the Conservative Education Committee, selection was ended at Harrogate secondary schools after widespread discussion there. Later, the national position was such that no further changes were possible in Ripon or Skipton, where selection still continues more than forty years later. In the ILEA, slow but steady progress had been made up to 1970 but, in that year, the newly appointed Secretary of State for Education was Margaret Thatcher – the educational equivalent of a full stop.

Despite the unfavourable political climate nationally, the response of Dr Briault and a small group of ILEA officers, led by Miss Clarkson, was rapid and thorough. For planning purposes, the thirteen Inner London boroughs within the ILEA were divided into four quadrants. In quick succession, four Green Papers were produced, one for each quadrant. These documents set out the demographic facts of the secondary school population. ILEA's research department produced ten year school population forecasts, updated each year, of remarkably consistent accuracy. These indicated that the secondary school population would be rising with the raising of the school leaving age in 1974 but that the size of the age group entering secondary schools, the crucial age group when deciding the increases or decreases in the number of school places required, would have begun to fall by 1980. This was as far as anyone could then see. The Green Papers deployed the educational arguments for a reduced number of schools, to be achieved by the closure of some, the enlargement of others and amalgamations affecting yet others. Other than on denominational grounds, a fully comprehensive secondary school system would require the ending, by 1980, of selection into any secondary school maintained by the Authority. To put the matter another way, if a school maintained by the Authority was still selecting pupils by that date, the Authority would thereupon cease to maintain it.

Central to the thinking of the Green Papers was the requirement that the comprehensive secondary schools to be developed each had to have an entry of at least 240 pupils a year (eight forms of entry, with thirty pupils in each form). In certain circumstances, seen as a second best alternative, schools could have a reduced entry of 150 pupils (five forms of entry). Here the problems began. Most of the forty-five grammar schools then in inner London had an entry of about ninety pupils a year (three-form entry), though a number of very good grammar schools were even smaller than that. This meant that there were only two ways a London grammar school could become part of the fully comprehensive system proposed. The first was to increase in size as an individual school. The second, in the absence of the new building necessary to achieve this, was to amalgamate with one or more other schools to achieve at least the minimum size required for a comprehensive school. If neither of these things were possible or proved unacceptable to the governors, a voluntary aided school, which nearly all London's grammar schools now were, might choose to leave inner London and re-establish itself in an area where new secondary school places were needed and money was available to build them. They could do this with such assistance as the ILEA could offer. Subject to the agreement of the local education authority concerned, they could develop either as a comprehensive school or as a grammar school. If none of this proved possible, the Authority would cease to maintain the school. As a voluntary aided school owned its own site and premises, it could then either close or remain in London and become a fee-paying independent school.

ILEA politicians had a healthy sense of self-preservation. Although the drafts of the Green Papers had been seen by the Policy Committee, the Introduction to them by Sir Ashley Bramall, the Leader of the Authority, made it clear that any proposals made were those of the Education Officer, not of the Authority: 'I want to emphasise that, quite deliberately, we left Dr Briault to make his own suggestions as the first stage in the consultative process. The elected members of the ILEA are in no way committed to any of these suggestions; we shall make up our minds only when the full round of consultations is completed.' Nothing could have been clearer than that.

So far as the ILEA was concerned, the thinking about comprehensive education, underlying the alternatives set out for discussion in the Green Papers, was a modified version of what had been proposed in the London School Plan of March 1947. That Plan was a remarkable document, both administratively and as a source of educational ideas. Few better documents have been published since. In the 1947 lecture already quoted, Dr Hughes had summarised the LCC's thinking on secondary education as follows:

> There has been so much debate on the Council's revolutionary proposals for secondary education that is not necessary at this stage to reiterate the arguments. It is, however, necessary to emphasize that the Council's comprehensive high schools will be English schools, and not copies of Scottish or American schools. Equally, they will not be three schools (modern, grammar, technical) in one building. They will be integrated communities providing a social life and a very large element of classroom education common to all. The schools will in fact help to spread a common culture, a culture that will enrich the lives of everybody, and to some extent be independent of the kind of work people do or the incomes they earn. The comprehensive high schools will not, however, ignore the vocational interests of their pupils. It will be necessary for them to do everything possible to safeguard the high academic standards now associated with the old-established secondary schools, for on these depends the recruitment of our professions. Equally necessary will be the development of advanced practical courses, and comprehensive high schools may be expected to develop technical and commercial as well as academic subjects, each at sixth form level, reaching an advanced standard and exerting a bracing influence on the work of other parts of the school. The uncommon man with high academic or practical aptitudes will not be neglected. Thus, as the plan says, 'A great variety of courses will be organised, each course designed according to the abilities and aptitudes of the pupils and the ages at which they are likely to leave school. From such an education it

is hoped will flow in time a healthy mutual regard and understanding between persons of different kinds of ability with far-reaching effects on the cultural, industrial and commercial life of the nation and on the social life of its people.' Living in a revolution must often be uncomfortable, and some of us will suffer the pangs of seeing excellent schools losing their identity. If, however, we keep our vision clear, living in a revolution need not be unhappy; it can be exhilarating.

It will be seen that the London School Plan was designed to deal decisively with a problem that remains unresolved nearly seventy years later. By means of their all-encompassing curriculum, the new secondary schools to be developed would provide secondary education for all, the central theme of the 1944 Education Act, in schools that admitted pupils up to the age of eighteen. This would end the separation of academic from vocational courses as the required curricular diversity was to occur within individual institutions rather than between them. To provide the variety of courses proposed, the new comprehensive High Schools would have to be large. The London plan envisaged 103 such schools, sixty-seven of them County schools and thirty-six of them Voluntary schools, many of the latter denominational ones. Each school would admit some 300 or more children a year, leading to a total number on roll of about 2,000 pupils, aged between eleven and eighteen.

Dr Briault had entered the LCC's service as an inspector in 1948, one year after the London School Plan was published. Neither his thinking nor that of the political leadership of, in turn, the LCC and the ILEA, had altered fundamentally since; so it was this approach to secondary education that permeated the Green Papers, the term used for the documents distributed for consultation . By the 1970s, experience since 1947 suggested that a comprehensive school did not have to be as large as the ones proposed in the London Plan to be able to offer a curriculum broad enough to enable the academic and vocational elements of the curriculum to be brought together in a single school. 'Vocational' was taken to include what was elsewhere described as 'technical'. An entry of 240 children a year was therefore the size prescribed in the Green Papers. I was slow to recognise that this size of school was not seen by long-serving senior ILEA officers and inspectors, or indeed by most of the Authority's elected members, as one of several ways of providing comprehensive education, it was seen as defining the nature of comprehensive education itself. Anything else would be a botch and the ILEA was not interested in botches.

In 1972, in different areas of inner London, the secondary school system was in a state of transition. Several types of secondary school existed. Of the 219 secondary schools, forty-five were grammar schools. There were about fifty large schools, such as Kidbrooke, Mayfield, Holland Park, Hampstead and Crown Woods, which could fairly be described as comprehensive, both in terms of providing the all-encompassing curriculum proposed in the London School Plan and in the sense of recruiting a fair proportion of children of all abilities. Many of these schools had been developed on ample sites on the fringes of Inner London where new housing estates had needed new schools. Finally, there were over one hundred secondary schools which were, in practice, though not always in name, secondary modern or 'other' schools, to use a term then in use for secondary modern schools trying to develop into comprehensive ones.

The planning principle behind the Green Papers was straightforward. It was to create by 1980 something as close as possible to the schools proposed in the London School Plan. Alternative ways this could be achieved and schools of the required size created from the schools that now existed were set out in the Green Papers. On the definition of a school that could be described as comprehensive, the alternative proposals put forward were hardly possible to argue with.

Soon after my arrival in London in 1972, I attended a 'Green Paper' meeting in West London. Just over fifty secondary schools were represented by head teachers and members of their governing bodies. I sat at the back of the hall and listened to what was being said around me as well as from the platform. As I did, I became increasingly uneasy. My conclusion was that the core proposal for a number of amalgamations would prove unacceptable to many of the grammar schools involved. In effect, it would destroy them. Over the ILEA as a whole, many of the forty-five grammar schools had traditions stretching back over a hundred years. Combining them with other schools, often in different buildings, to achieve the required size would lead to an upheaval and loss of identity which appeared to them, reasonably enough it seemed to me, to amount to closure. Yet few of the grammar schools were in a position to enlarge themselves sufficiently to achieve the minimum size required. Most were on already overcrowded sites so that, even if the money for new building could be found, they would never be able to reach anything like the size Dr Briault had said, and the Authority had agreed, that a school needed to be to be accepted as comprehensive one. The alternatives were dire. If the size criterion were to be enforced, many of the voluntary aided grammar schools, which owned their own sites and premises, might decide to sell up and leave London. They would then be taking with them some of London's best qualified teachers, particularly at sixth form level. Grammar schools which did not do that would either have to be closed or, if they thought they could survive as such, stay in London and become independent fee-paying schools. In either case, they would be making no further contribution to the education of many of the children for whose education the Authority was responsible. In short, as my visits to some of the grammar schools confirmed, the proposals seemed likely to prove unacceptable to many of them, educationally damaging to the quality of education in Inner London or, if closing schools became necessary, increasingly likely to be prevented by the Secretary of State.

So what needed to be done? For the first time in my professional life, I found myself directly opposed to the thinking of the administration of which I was a part and, so far as I was aware, of the political leadership of the local education authority in which I was working. What was being proposed directly conflicted with everything

I had learnt and cared about in secondary education, as teacher and educational administrator, over the previous twenty years. I agreed wholeheartedly with the thinking behind the London School Plan for secondary education. It was far ahead of its time. But I did not believe it was now possible, even desirable, to put that plan into effect. The London of the 1970s had become very different from that of the disciplined, wartime, 1940s when the plan had been devised. Several of the long established comprehensive schools I had visited were working well but, in other parts of London, demographic changes and the restless movement of both pupils and staff meant that some of London's largest secondary schools were seriously unsettled. At one boys school, described as comprehensive but, in terms of its intake, hardly more than a huge secondary modern school, the head had asked me not to walk down a certain corridor. From the level of noise coming from it, I could understand why. At another such school, I had seen a boy pick up a plate of hot food he had just been handed and throw it straight back into the face of the dinner lady who had passed it to him. On the other hand, the grammar schools were largely unaffected by these unsettling demographic changes and the movement of staff and pupils associated with this. Parents of pupils in the grammar schools, when they moved to areas surrounding inner London, were usually keeping their children in those schools despite the extra travelling time this involved.

My conclusion was that the comparatively stable, well-qualified and well-established teaching staffs of London's grammar schools had to be kept together and encouraged to stay in London. How was this to be managed? My own teaching and administrative experience had convinced me of the damaging consequences for most children, in any area, caused by selecting some of them to different schools at the age of eleven, so I fully supported the Authority's decision to end that. But I had far more relaxed views on school size than those set out in the Green Papers. Just before leaving the North Riding in 1966, I had been asked to produce the first draft of a response to Anthony Crosland's circular 10/65. Neither that circular nor the North Riding's response to it had anything to say about school size. More directly on the question of school size, I had later spent time in Settle High School, a comprehensive school in a rural part of the West Riding. It had about three hundred pupils in it because that was the number of children there were in that area. It was an excellent school. I, for one, would have been happier to send a child of mine there than to some of the much larger schools in London, including the one my children attended, notwithstanding their impressive curriculum offer. With this experience behind me, by the time I reached London, I was also convinced that secondary modern schools, defined as schools which the three quarters of the age group who did not reach the standard for entry to a grammar school were required to attend, though some had excellent teachers in them, were not schools to which parents who had aspirations for their children would ever be content to send their children. Parents not prepared to send their children to secondary modern schools included just about everyone working in County Hall, politicians and officials, such as myself, alike. Secondary modern schools were schools for other people's children. There could be no place for them in the London of the future.

It seems necessary to add, because some believe otherwise, that there was no hostility towards the grammar schools amongst any of my colleagues. On the contrary, most of them had been to grammar schools, had taught in them and thought well of them. The problem lay with the fact, for it is a fact, that grammar schools necessarily create secondary modern schools down the road. It was these that were increasingly seen as the problem.

After less than a year in London, I was questioning the fundamental assumption underlying the Green Papers: that a school could not be comprehensive if it had an entry of less than two hundred and forty pupils a year; or one hundred and fifty in exceptional circumstances. It seemed important to discuss these issues, though my opinion on them had not been invited. My problem, which I was finding increasingly irksome, was that, as Deputy Education Officer, I had no direct responsibility for secondary – or indeed for primary – education in the ILEA; or indeed for anything much else other than finance and chairing sometimes fractious meetings with divisional officers. I had been side-lined.

What follows is not an objective account of the disagreements that arose over the next eighteen months. It is one person's account, from one person's perspective, based on a selection of the documents that one person retained, of interactions that ultimately determined the structure of secondary education in inner London. It is an account of how and why the ILEA eventually found it necessary to abandon, without always admitting to itself that it had, arguably the single most important element of the London School Plan. That plan was not abandoned because its thinking was flawed. Little better thinking has been produced since. It was abandoned because the changing demographic, social and political circumstances of London in the 1970s had made the London School Plan of 1947 impossibly difficult to implement.

The first three documents set out below are an account of the controversy that took place in March 1973, just over a year after my arrival. The first related to one of the four quadrants of the ILEA where Green Paper proposals were being debated. It was for discussion on the following day when the five people, of whom I was not one, who were handling the drive to create comprehensive schools were meeting to discuss the progress so far made. Apart from the Education Officer and the Chief Inspector, the three others present were the Assistant Education Officer for Schools, the Assistant Education Officer responsible for all building programmes and the Staff Inspector for secondary schools. As the first document, in particular its paragraph 5, anticipates much of what eventually happened later, the heading is in bold. The temptation to re-write some of the document'ss infelicities has been resisted.

From the Deputy Education Officer. Secondary Review (Camden, Islington and Hackney) 22 March 1973

Notes for meeting on 23 March with the Education Officer, Dr Birchenough,

Mr Braide, Mr Bowie, Mr Rogers

1. I think it may well be possible to end selection in Camden, Islington and Hackney in 1974: in other words to make this year's transfer process the last of its kind.

2. At present, we are trying to do too many things at once:

    (a) End selection

    (b) Improve unpopular schools

    (c) Secure balanced entries

    (d) Establish schools of sufficient size to enable a full range of courses for children of all abilities

    (e) Plan sensible sixth forms for the future

    (f) Relate what schools are doing to the needs of the community and to involve the community in the work of the school

    (g) Increase the proportion of mixed schools

    (h) See that voluntary schools are reduced in the same proportion as county schools

3. In a static situation there are good grounds for adhering to the Authority's general policy of uniform treatment afforded to all parts of its area. In the present state of flux, I suggest the opposite. As early as possible this summer, before the end of the Green Paper consultations for Divisions 1-3 (Camden, Islington and Hackney) I believe we should commit off-programme money to John Howard/ Clapton Park and declare that we are ending selection in Hackney in 1974.

4. Dr Briault's original formulation of the problem made it clear that there is no chance whatever in Camden and Islington of all the schools remaining open and being effective 11-18 schools in 1980. Many are by no means effective now. Hence the proposals for a series of amalgamations. There seem to be three reasons why there is no real prospect of these amalgamations occurring:

    (a) 1980 is itself an arbitrary date. In a rapidly changing situation it could well be that the schools created would themselves not be effective a few years later. Enormous effort is now being required to reach a state which would essentially remain insecure.

    (b) The experience and wishes of many teachers is against making an effort of this kind. Many have been through previous amalgamations and found them profoundly disturbing to staff and pupils alike. My own view, necessarily superficial, is that a number of schools are too precariously established to carry through the amalgamations proposed without seriously damaging effects on the children within them. In difficult conditions, the only way to amalgamate is to enlarge a securely staffed school by introducing new kinds of pupil at eleven, thereby giving the staff and pupils time to adapt. This is the method adopted elsewhere in the Authority and now suggested for John Howard/Clapton Park. The sudden putting together of one set of eleven to sixteen year olds with another such group to create a largish entity is not acceptable. Nor is the idea of stopping entries to popular schools while the process is taking place. Parental feeling at the point of transfer is too sensitive for this.

(c) There is a positive wish for smaller schools. It is possible to regard this as a rationalisation of a wish on the part of staff or parents to stay in existence as a school. But the claims for the smaller school in the inner city cannot so easily be set aside. We have to address ourselves to the problem of what is best for most children. If it is only the abler children who are thought to suffer in the smaller school we must look for ways of improving this and analyse what it is about successful small schools which take children of all abilities, and there are some, which enables them to succeed.

5. The Green Paper discussions are going on throughout the summer. There is a risk of fixed positions being adopted by the various people carrying out these discussions. Hence the need for us to make up our minds quickly what direction we wish these discussions to take. We need to try and co-ordinate the responses to the Green Paper into a set of coherent suggestions to which the Authority could agree. I have set out below the best compromise I think we have any chance of achieving; I do so in the form of a request that the Authority might receive from schools, parents and the general public in the area:

(a) Let all the children stay in the schools they now attend.

(b) Let all the schools in the area move towards balanced entries in September 1974. The three-form entry grammar schools of Camden, Highbury Hill High, Central Foundation and William Ellis should take an entry of between 100 and 120 pupils each.

(c) Co-operative sixth forms between schools which wish to take part should be created in the area. The first of these VI Form Centres should be created at Islington Green, which should stop accepting pupils in September 1974 to make room for the sixth formers who would subsequently be moving in. As soon as possible thereafter, sixth formers from the area, including some of the three form entry schools mentioned in (b) above, would begin to move to the sixth form centre to leave space for the enlarged entries to the 11 to 16 part of these schools.

In outline, this is the proposal which the Authority might receive. It provides for the ending of selection, mixed sixth form education throughout the area, schools which could be to some degree community based, the prospect of balancing entries and a minimum of disturbance to pupils already in school.

The meeting on 23 March was a frosty occasion. Only Bill Braide and Dr Briault spoke to my note. They did so dismissively. The small schools being suggested, they declared, could not be comprehensive in any meaningful sense of the term. Such schools would simply be secondary modern schools with no chance whatever of providing the broad, academic/vocational curriculum required to meet the needs of children of all abilities and interests. Besides, the Education Committee had already agreed with the principles on which the Green Paper proposals were based and there was no reason to suppose that its members would change their minds at the first sign of difficulty. It was irresponsible to argue otherwise.

My colleagues were right in supposing that small schools could not be like the schools envisaged by the London School Plan. I was well aware of that. But the London of 1973 was becoming increasingly unlike the London that had existed in 1947. Had no one noticed that? At the meeting itself, I had found the manner in which my arguments had been rejected disturbing. My colleagues' unwillingness even to question a crucial element of the Authority's policies in the privacy of the Education Officer's room was still more depressing. I was particularly irritated by the assumption, uniformly made by ILEA administrators who had only worked in London, that experience acquired elsewhere had little relevance to the circumstances of inner London. The typewritten note, dated 26 March, addressed to those present at the meeting on 23 March, conveys the mood in which it was written:

> One could express this in various diplomatic ways but essentially it was decided that if suggestions of the kind I have put forward were received from the teachers, parents and governors of Islington and Camden, they would not be welcome. The reasons for this are important. The objection is not that it would be impossible to achieve agreement on the lines I proposed – that is not something that can be decided sitting round a table in County Hall – but that it would be undesirable to try. Several reasons were advanced for this; all of which I find unconvincing:
>
> ### (a) The 11–16 part of a small school
>
> It is said that entries of about 110 into the 11–16 part of a school must, in principle, mean that the children would be deprived of something essential to the education of 11–16-year-olds. But we are committed at John Howard and elsewhere to entries of 150 which are supposed to support a sixth form. Is it really plausible to say that an entry of 110 is totally unthinkable when a sixth form is being otherwise dealt with by co-operation between VIth Forms or a Sixth Form Centre?
>
> If anyone doubts that schools with entries of 110–120 can offer a widel range of opportunities for 11–16 year olds it is a matter of getting into a car and visiting some. I am all the more certain of this given London's generous staffing: we could staff our 110–120 entries like other people's

150 entries. Against the fact that London schools have fewer than their share of the ablest children, I would put the benefit to the less able of being in smaller communities. It is no use having fine facilities if the pupils do not turn up to enjoy them.

In particular, the notion that a second language could not be managed or that housecraft and so on would suffer cannot really be sustained. What is a major education authority all about? Is it really being said that if we asked, for example, the Staff Inspector for languages to create, possibly by intensive exposure to the language at some point in a school career, excellent second language opportunities, he could not do so? If we are talking of show-pieces, it is comprehensive areas rather than individual comprehensive schools that we must learn to develop and we could lead the way.

In thinking of small schools, the minds of my colleagues immediately turn to schools like William Blake. But assume the end of selection. Assume you are building on a stable grammar school staff with high morale and you have a different proposition altogether. It was said that I was proposing secondary modern schools. In reply I would compare what might be created at Central Foundation, Highbury Hill High, Camden Girls and so on with Islington Green, which I would close. I believe three group ones (i.e children in the top 25% of the tests at 11+) have chosen to transfer there this year. Our present proposals assume the closure of Camden (which is what amalgamation in a Parliament Hill/William Ellis complex in practice means) and the preservation of Islington Green. Who really is creating or preserving secondary modern schools?

Finally, I believe that small schools are showing how staff and pupils can combine in new relationships which I believe the Authority wishes to promote.

(b) Sixth Form possibilities for small schools

Obviously a great deal of thinking would be required about the nature of a Sixth Form Centre. It is on this that I would wish to focus the thinking of teachers and others during the summer. The problem: how does one offer to everyone in Camden and Islington the prospect of first rate Sixth Form education for their children? The essence of the Centre is that the small schools, some of them very prestigious, would propose it. Their pupils would form its core. Larger schools would have no immediate need to join. Nobody is dragooning Highbury Grove, for example. On the best free enterprise principles, that school might well wish to retain its present arrangements.

I believe that a move from Islington and Camden of the kind I have suggested would have a profound effect on what is happening elsewhere in the Authority. Size of school, for example, determines our whole attitude to the voluntary aided denominational selective schools. Smaller schools combining for Sixth Form work could bring forward the end to selection very considerably. It should cause us to moderate our present enthusiasm for enlarging the Roman Catholic schools in south London to 900 places. It could affect what we are saying and what is being said to us in Hammersmith, Kensington, Chelsea and Westminster. Schools could stay in their present premises, where we have put all the Raising of the School Leaving Age money, and combine at Sixth Form level. And do so quickly. And so on and so on.

The William Blake School referred to was a secondary modern school in Wandsworth that was causing concern. Soon after this minute, Islington Green, officially described as 'comprehensive', to which only three pupils assessed as of grammar school ability had been admitted in the previous year, was preserved. A group of local parents, including a youthful Professor Maurice Kogan, Bruce and Anne Page and others, decided to send their children to the school. They acquired an outstanding head in Margaret Maden, who later became the first head of what was later to become the Islington Sixth Form Centre. For a time, the school became an example of what can be done, in a socially and economically diverse urban area, if influential parents use that influence and persistence to enable an equally forceful head to transform the work and reputation of a school.

There was little hope that this second note would be more likely to convince my colleagues than the first, but there was a constitutional as well as a personal point at issue. Where were the political leaders of the ILEA in this difference of opinion about the way one of their key policies was being conducted? Admittedly, the Education Committee had fairly recently authorised the Education Officer to publish a set of proposals for putting that policy into effect. So they were aware of what those proposals were. These probably conformed to their own convictions and certainly did to the professional advice they had consistently received over many years. But ought not other ideas to surface and at least be argued? It was on this issue that a personal point arose. If my opinions on what the ILEA was trying to do were to be disregarded, what was the point of my being there? Accordingly, on the same day as that second minute, I sent a manuscript note addressed only to Eric Briault:

Dear Eric,   26 March 1973

Islington, Camden and Hackney

There are three reasons why I believe matters cannot rest as they have been left and that the point of view I have been expressing should be conveyed to the Leader.

First, I believe that what I am saying would command the support of most of the teachers in the area. Perhaps this is not in dispute but, if the point is to be disregarded, I would wish to explain to the Leader why I think it should not be.

Second, although I hesitate to refer to that well-worn tide in the affairs of men, I believe that major change could be brought about within the next few months if we seize the opportunity. In my view, selection could be ended far sooner than in our tireder moments we sometimes suppose. My reading of the pattern of the future may be mistaken. This is a matter of political judgement and, again, this is why I believe the Leader should be aware of my views, even though these are not shared by my senior colleagues.

Finally, there is a personal point, which falls into two parts. We are all committed to ending selection at eleven. Now evidently, and you could argue irrationally, I put this higher in my order of priorities than do others. But over the next few years selection at eleven is going to remain a crucial issue for the Authority and it must be established quickly whether I am seriously out of step. If I am, the implications are personally very serious indeed.

The second part of the personal point is this: I believe one main function of a deputy is not to make life difficult for his chief. But I also believe it is one other main function to point out when a mistake is being made. Now, rightly or wrongly, I believe you are misreading the present and the way forward and that an opportunity for an unstoppable drive to end selection could be lost. So I am asking to sit round a table with you and the Leader to talk this through. What was it Cicero said to a young colleague? 'For God's sake disagree with me, so that there may be two of us.'

My note was acknowledged by Dr Briault by being returned to me with a little tick at the top to indicate that he had read it. He had added no comment. This arrived at the same time as a letter from Bill Braide that referred to our earlier meeting. This was intemperately expressed. Phrases such as 'we could not hold up our heads again' and even 'over my dead body' peppered the text. It was an extraordinary letter to receive from an experienced, very able, highly regarded and usually friendly and unruffled colleague. I had touched a nerve. I kept this letter in the same folder as the other documents now quoted but, at some point in the months that followed, it disappeared.

After reflecting on what had happened, I reached four conclusions. The first was that, when my initial minute had been rejected, my immediate assumption that my colleagues were either stupid or that I had not explained myself clearly enough was mistaken. The truth was that my colleagues were by no means stupid and had understood immediately what I had been saying; they simply and vehemently disagreed with it. Schools of the minimum size required by Dr Briault in the Green Papers were not seen as one form of comprehensive school; such schools were taken to define the nature of comprehensive education itself. I had learnt from R G Collingwood, many years earlier, that it is impossible to debate with a definition. One either decides to accept it or one does not. I did not. For their part, my colleagues were unwilling to depart from what Collingwood described as their 'absolute presupposition' about the nature of comprehensive education. A presupposition does not derive from fact and is not influenced by fact. Like a pair of irremovable green spectacles, it determines the colour of what the wearer sees. So what my colleagues saw was a newcomer to London, with little experience of education in a large city and with no responsibility for secondary education, suggesting that they should now abandon a fundamental element of the London School Plan for comprehensive schools: an element that had underpinned their own work and that of many politicians, inspectors and administrators since 1947. No wonder they were as angry with me as I was with them.

My second conclusion was that my colleagues were not going to change their minds. What hope was there then for the opinions I had formed about the condition of many of the primary schools I had been visiting? These, often unflattering, opinions were certain to be quite as unwelcome as my ideas on the way secondary school re-organisation was being handled.

My third conclusion concerned the way the ILEA dealt with problems and, indeed, with myself as a newcomer. I recalled what Alec Clegg had said to me soon after I had arrived in the West Riding. 'In a month or two', his exact words were, 'tell me what you think are the worst six things that we are doing in this outfit.' The implication was clear. For newcomers to be allowed to challenge settled practices was essential for the health of any organisation. Yet, recognising that I might be a person who could contribute to the ILEA's thinking about education did not seem to be part of the ILEA administration's intellectual furniture.

My fourth conclusion, as important as any of the others, was that I disagreed with the ILEA's whole approach to planning in the shifting demographic and other circumstances within which London's schools were increasingly having to function. The Authority's frontal attack on problems seemed to have succeeded in the past. But the re-structuring of London's Colleges of Further Education was being achieved in what seemed to me to be a far better way. Close and expert discussion with all the colleges involved was quietly taking place. No plans had been published in advance, as they had been in the Green Papers affecting secondary schools. Area by area, educationally and financially stronger entities were being created with full professional support from the staff of the institutions affected. The number of colleges was being reduced in consequence. The transformation was being brilliantly managed by a team of no more than five well-respected inspectors and administrators. Meanwhile, in relation to school structures, now and increasingly in the future, I believed the frontal approach, with detailed Green Papers produced in advance for consultation, would fail. It was not the only way of effecting change. Para 5 (a) of my original minute of 22 March, 'let all the children stay in the schools they now attend', indicated how the first stage of what they wanted to achieve might be accomplished. A few years later, I described that approach as an example of 'the lock gate principle'. In contrasting it with attempts to implement complex plans articulated in advance, I put the point this way.

> Why have radical educational ideas, from all different political directions, made so little headway over the past forty years? It has to do, I believe, with a failure to understand the workings of a lock gate. Consider a boat that has to be raised twenty feet to go upstream. To the uninitiated, this seems impossible; in practice, behold the lock gate. The way to go upstream is this. The boat is brought to the first lock gate. There follows some brisk twiddling of wheels. The first gate opens, in goes the boat, and the gate is shut tight behind. More wheel twiddling ensues. Bubbles and froth appear within the lock but up goes the boat, unswamped, to the new level. A final twiddle of the wheels and out comes the boat and the beer and the sandwiches. But what happens if both sets of lock gates are suddenly opened with a grand, rhetorical, manifesto-induced, flourish? Precisely. 'Whoosh' comes the water; the boat is rocked violently and sinks without a trace. In this respect, that boat is like almost every radical post-war educational policy.

So the issue was not just about particular policies for secondary or primary education; it was about the whole way the top management of the ILEA thought about its work, its unwillingness to allow any challenge to received opinion and the, in my view flawed, planning methods it persisted in adopting in trying to bring about the changes it wanted to make. These settled habits of thought seemed impossible for one person to shift and too frustrating to live with for long. If my views were not anything the ILEA's senior managers were interested in, failure to gain a hearing when I believed I had important things to say was quite as unacceptable to me. Accordingly, rather than hover about on the fringes of ILEA's policy-formulation process, I decided to leave. Having taken that decision, I told Eric Briault that, as I was so far out of step with my colleagues, I would be looking to leave the ILEA as soon as a suitable opportunity arose. I had a mortgage to pay and children to feed, so I did not intend to resign until I had somewhere suitable to go to. I then told the Leader, Sir Ashley Bramall, whom I had so far rarely met, that I intended to leave. Both he and Dr Briault received the news with equanimity.

Enter Mrs Irene Chaplin, Deputy Leader of the Authority, to whom I had not yet had a chance to speak about my leaving. On the Sunday morning after I had spoken to Sir Ashley, the quiet of Blackheath was shattered by an unmistakable mixture of noises. At the front door was Mrs Chaplin, loudly addressing her husband in their two-seater outside while simultaneously banging away at the door-knocker. Once inside, she addressed me at the top of her voice. 'We were just passing by,' she announced, 'and I am here to tell you that this business of leaving us has to stop!' The bare-faced improbability of that 'just passing by' took me aback. Mrs Chaplin lived in Bloomsbury and you do not 'pass by' a one-way street in Blackheath on the way to anywhere. But it was encouraging that she had taken so much trouble to ask me to stay. After further thought, that is what I decided to do.

In deciding not to leave London I had also decided something else. So far, I had been careful to comply with the conventions that applied within the ILEA. It was not open to a Deputy Education Officer in the ILEA to give advice directly to the Leader or to other members of the Education Committee, either at a meeting of a committee and most certainly not at any informal meeting, if that advice differed from that given by the Education Officer; so I could not express my opinions in that way. But I did not intend to lose the argument about the future of secondary education in inner London. It was too important for that to be allowed to happen. The immediate problem was the way the administrative leadership of the ILEA thought. Any direct effort to convince Eric Briault to change what he and others were committed to doing would fail. But there was nothing in the Authority's conventions which prevented me dealing with that problem indirectly. So I took to visiting schools and exchanging opinions with head teachers and senior staff. Only by doing that could I be sure that my arguments about school size would be supported by teachers in the grammar schools who would be willing and confident in their ability to be able to teach children of all abilities.

What finally convinced me that London's grammar school teachers of one subject could transfer their skills, if they were so inclined, to teach children of other abilities was one where I watched Miss Charlesworth, of Highbury Hill High School, teach Latin. Two things struck me about what she was doing. The first was that she was teaching Latin rather better than I had done. The second was that, though quite close to retirement, when I discussed the possibility, she assured me that she would be quite prepared to teach English to children of other abilities if asked and, indeed, would welcome the opportunity to do that. I became convinced that a gifted teacher, such as Miss Charlesworth and others I encountered on my visits, provided they were interested in doing so, could motivate any children and handle any teaching problems that would arise in a small secondary school admitting children of all abilities. Such schools had been made to work well outside London. The notion that there was something about London's children or its teachers that made that impossible was obviously absurd. But how could the debate be moved forward? There was only one way to find out. At one stage, Mrs Butcher, headmistress of Highbury Hill, asked me whether there was any point in her Governors putting a suggestion to the Authority that their school should be allowed to stay in its present premises, slightly enlarged if possible, and to admit an all-ability intake. My reply was that it was open to the school's governors to make any such suggestion. I was personally in favour of it, but naturally could not predict what the Authority would make of it.

The Labour Party's victory in the 1974 General Election provided the impetus needed. That happened just as the implications of falling numbers within the ILEA were becoming more evident. The latest estimates of future secondary school numbers indicated that the fall in numbers would be continuing well beyond 1980. The need to end selection was becoming urgent. Why was this so? When, as in inner London, selective schools and a number of comprehensive and secondary modern schools co-exist, the effect of a diminishing age-group on each type of school is not a matter of educational or political opinion. It becomes a matter of arithmetic.

Consider the following. Expressed in approximate numbers, in 1977, an 11+ age group of close to 32,000 would be entering ILEA secondary schools. That 32,000 would contain 8,000 children in the top 25% of the ability range, eligible for entry to a grammar school. If some 4,000 of that 8,000 went to the forty-five grammar schools, as would be the case in the ILEA, that left another 4,000 to be distributed amongst the remaining schools. To create a fully comprehensive school, defined for this purpose as one with a full share of children in that top 25%, that 4,000 could have a further 12,000 below that ability level added to it to create an intake 16,000 to comprehensive schools with a balanced intake. With the 4,000 going to grammar schools added to those 16,000, in 1977 there would then be an intake of 20,000 going to grammar or comprehensive schools. The remaining 12,000, as a matter of arithmetic, would have to go to secondary moderns, defined as schools with no or very few entrants in the top 25% of the ability range.

In practice, in London that 16,000 entry to comprehensive schools could be increased to about 18,000 of the entry going to schools with sufficient entrants in that top 25% to be described as comprehensive. This would leave about 10,000 of the year group of 32,000 going either to what might be described as secondary modern plus schools, containing a handful of entrants in the top 25% of the ability range, or to secondary modern minus schools, with most of their intake in the bottom 50% or even the bottom 25%, of that range. A few years earlier, ILEA's Research Department had shown that the London school most badly affected in this way had 75% of its pupils in the bottom 25% of the ability range. Badly damaged secondary modern schools of this kind, routinely described by hostile politicians and elements of the Press, who assumed that any school that was not a grammar school could therefore be described as a 'comprehensive' one, as 'sink' comprehensives.

To sum up: in 1977 there would be an intake at eleven of about 4,000 to forty five grammar schools, of about 18,000 to some ninety schools that could be described as more or less comprehensive and of about 10,000 to between seventy and eighty schools which, however described, would in in practice be a form of secondary modern school.

But what would happen when the 11+ age group fell to 24,000 in 1982, as was being predicted in 1974? That would lead to just 6,000 children in the top 25% of the age group transferring at 11+. If the grammar schools remained, 4,000 children would still be admitted to them. That would leave only 2,000 such children to be distributed amongst the remaining schools. In practice this would mean that many, perhaps most, of the ninety or so schools that, in 1977, had been fully or nearly comprehensive in their intakes would, as a matter of arithmetic, revert by the early 1980s to becoming some form of secondary modern school. Demography would have undone the efforts the LCC and the ILEA had made since 1947 to develop an increasing proportion of its schools as comprehensive ones. It was as serious and as inevitable as that. Unless action was taken to prevent this, many well established London comprehensive schools would be becoming secondary modern ones. That was the iceberg towards which many London schools were heading.

Soon after the Labour Party's victory in the 1974 General Election, the new Labour Secretary of State asked all local education authorities to submit proposals for the re-organisation of their secondary schools on comprehensive lines. But what were the ILEA's proposals to be? A draft response for the Education Officer to put to the Policy Committee was circulated amongst senior officers and inspectors. Those drafts are missing but Dr Briault's advice in the Green Papers on the minimum size of a comprehensive secondary school was unchanged. The effect of falling numbers was nowhere set out. The draft mentioned that a request had been made by Highbury Hill High to be allowed to remain at about its present three-form entry size and admit children of all abilities. Dr Briault's draft recommended that this request be rejected. My reaction was to produce an acerbic alternative draft. I was aware that my paragraph by paragraph comments on the draft prepared by my colleagues would not find their way into the Education Officer's report, for it would be a report signed by him that would go to the Policy Committee. But my comments constituted advance notice of what, if given the opportunity, I might be saying on that occasion. They restated my opposition to what was, in effect, a proposal to close Highbury Hill High and my repeated arguments on the question of school size and what small schools could offer. The tone of my comments on the Education Officer's draft report reflected my anger at the way my arguments were being kept away from that Committee:

> I do not regard it as self-evident that an enormous breadth of options in the fourth and fifth years of secondary education is desirable. There are arguments both ways. 'The tendency of larger comprehensive schools to offer a wide choice of courses to pupils broke down many points of stability. Groupings of children changed radically each period, staff could not get to know groups of children as effectively and vice versa, room changes abounded throughout the day and the very framework of security disappeared for just those children who needed it most'. My quotation is from a 1972 report by West Riding secondary school heads on problems not of the curriculum but of 'violent indiscipline in school', a phenomenon not confined to London.

> It is significant that there is no paragraph on the opportunities small schools afford. There are arguments in favour of comparatively small groupings (500 or so pupils) for the 11–16 age range, provided their sixth form arrangements can be supplemented in some way. It is important to recognise that eight forms of entry, for example, does not guarantee sensible self-contained sixth form arrangements, as an analysis of London's present experience would quickly show.

The headmaster of the largest school in England made the case for small linked groups recently (TES 17.5.74 'False syllogisms of size' – John Sayer). Referring to the 'halls' at Banbury': With about 500 pupils, they each have their own head, deputies, secretary, caretaker and all the other tokens which make them an identifiable school for their pupils.'

Alec Clegg made the same point in his farewell remarks to West Riding teachers in March 1974: 'I believe it is much sounder for a school of 1700 or 1800 to be divided into 'houses' which are virtually separate schools, each of some 500 pupils bridged across the top by a VI Form of 200 plus.' Before the irrelevance of anything outside London is advanced as a reason for ignoring it, I would wish to argue, having taught in Oxfordshire and worked in the West Riding, that the need to take care of group sizes is greater in London than in either of the other two places and the resources, of finance and inspectorate skills, to support organisation of this kind are also greater.

Having repeated my belief that the proposed plan for creating comprehensive schools would fail and that we would still have selection at 11+ in London in 1980 and beyond, I went on to argue:

To continue selection into the 1980s, as now seems likely, is flatly contrary to the Authority's declared policy and will increasingly damage those of its schools that now most nearly approach being comprehensive. Furthermore, it leaves the Authority with the difficult and intensely unpopular task of ceasing to maintain selective schools in accordance with an uncertain time-table and in an equally uncertain political climate. In effect, this means a long and drawn-out war of attrition. It is true that the Authority would be consistent about the kind of school, defined in terms of minimum size, that it would be prepared to permit. But it is more important that the Authority should be right and carry people with it than that it should be consistent. The heart of the problem is whether effective comprehensive education could be achieved by means of co-operative arrangements between schools, many of which would be small. Perhaps it is becoming increasingly unwise, in dealing with urban education, to try and deduce the quality of an institution from its form.

I managed to insert a few comparatively minor changes to the document that finally went to the Policy Committee at a meeting held at Chelsea College. In the days when reports were typed and then put through a copier, the presence of scissors and paste insertions was made evident by light black lines at the joins. This was in such contrast to the usually tidy version of reports to the Policy Committee that there was some speculation amongst the members about where the different bits had come from. Perhaps for the first time, the fact that there were serious differences between senior officials became evident to some leading members of the Committee. The extent to which this was then only half suspected by Sir Ashley himself was revealed years later in a letter to me, dated 25 August 1994:

Rumours were floating round the principal floor about disagreement between you and Eric (emanating I imagine from the personal assistants), but I did not realise quite how serious it was. The question of small schools did, of course, surface at the famous meeting in Chelsea College.

As that Policy Committee's meeting determined the future shape of Inner London's secondary education, what happened at it needs some explanation. Dr Briault had many other problems to deal with on that Policy Committee's agenda, so he may have given little thought to the paragraph about Highbury Hill School. He might reasonably have been rather irritated by my comments on his draft but would have considered it inconceivable that the committee, against his advice and, if called upon, that of the Chief Inspector, would agree, contrary to the committee's own consistent decisions over the years, to make an exception in favour of one small grammar school in Islington that could not possibly be described as comprehensive. My position was different. I was entirely focused on that one paragraph in the many documents the Committee had before it. Everything I cared about secondary education in London depended on the Committee agreeing with Highbury Hill's request to be allowed to end selection, stay on its present site and admit an all-ability entry.

The Policy Committee's practice was to reach decisions on the various options put before it without spending much time in debating them. So it would be a matter of a fairly quick yes or no to Highbury Hill's request. During the Committee's discussion of the document on creating a comprehensive set of schools in London, I was sandwiched rather uncomfortably between Dr Briault and the Chief Inspector. When we came to the paragraph about Highbury Hill, the point was made by Dr Briault that it would be most unwise, at this late stage, to alter the principles on which a complex review was being undertaken. But before the meeting, I had made it known to one leading member of the committee that I had visited the school and spent time there. I was certain that this would lead to my being asked whether I had any comment to make on the school's suggestion. When asked that question, as I was, I knew it would be pointless to express outright disagreement with the Education Officer. So I did the opposite. I said that I agreed that, as Dr Briault had said, it would be unwise to embark on any large scale alteration to the principles on which the Authority's plans were based, but what was at issue here was an experiment relating to a single school. An experiment was just that. The arrival of some rather different eleven year olds in a couple of years' time would be most unlikely to damage the education of children now at Highbury Hill. If it showed any signs of doing that, the experiment could be discontinued.

That statement was theoretically correct but far short of being frank. I was certain that such an experiment would become almost impossible to reverse; but I thought that, in the circumstances of this particular meeting, it was for someone else to point that out. Public Notices would be required to end selection at Highbury Hill and a second set of Public Notices would be required later if that decision were ever to be reversed. Furthermore - and this was the crucial point – if one small grammar

33

school was allowed to survive, far below the minimum size Dr Briault had declared was necessary for a comprehensive school, any threat to cease to maintain other grammar schools that wanted to do the same would become both practically as well as politically impossible. I already knew of several famous grammar schools, including Camden School for Girls,that would far prefer to stay on their own site and end selection than to become entangled in complex arrangements for amalgamations with other schools, nearly always on split sites. Dr Briault made no comment on my remarks so, after a brief discussion, the Committee agreed to accept the proposal from Highbury Hill's governors and moved on to the next item on the agenda. At one level, I knew that I had not behaved well but, in ignoring every piece of advice I had offered them, neither had some of my colleagues.

That Policy Committee decision late in 1974 ended the debate about the future shape of secondary education in inner London that had remained unresolved for the twenty seven years since the London School Plan of 1947. Nothing was said at the time but, as soon as he had time to reflect on what the Committee's decision made inevitable, Dr Briault will have known that the vision of what London's secondary schools might become, so lucidly set out in that Plan, which he and his colleagues had worked hard over many years to develop, was over. From then onwards, he looked carefully at new proposals as they came forward but left the day to day discussion with members about how to proceed to me. It was at this stage that, for the first time, I began to address minutes on secondary re-organisation directly to leading members. Meanwhile, other pressing problems were arising to which Dr Briault needed to apply his formidable administrative skills.

From September 1974 things moved fast. Grammar school governors began to write in to say they would prefer to stay at about their present size and end selection rather than be required to become larger. The Catholic diocesan authorities supported that approach. That led to a second crucial decision on secondary education in London. This took the form of a statement by Mrs Garside as Chair of the Development Sub-Committee. On 4 March 1975, she then announced that, from September 1977, the Authority would cease to maintain any secondary school that was still selecting pupils at the age of eleven. At the following meeting of the Education Committee, the Leader of the Opposition, Mr Vigars, challenged her on whether she had indeed made such a statement. Mrs Garside then confirmed that she had.

There is no documentary evidence on how that crucial decision on the date to end selection moved from 1980, the date set in the Green Papers, to 1977. My version of what happened is that, at some point early in 1975, I was in the Leader's room on some matter not relating to any date for ending selection. He took a phone call from what I then took to be the Sunday Times. During the course of that telephone conversation, Sir Ashley mentioned 1980 as the date by which a comprehensive system would apply throughout the ILEA. There was no reason for him to depart from the 1980 date that had been proposed in the Green Paper consultative documents. There had been no further discussion, at the Policy Committee or elsewhere, on any proposal to change the date for ending selection, though there ought to have been. But the projected fall in secondary school numbers had, by early 1975, made it necessary to revise the assumptions on which I, for one, had been working in 1973. On the new figures, 1980 was a dangerously long time to wait. Thoughts on this were exchanged with Mrs Garside, recently elected to replace Mrs Chaplin as the Authority's Deputy Leader. As I recall – and in 2006 Mrs Garside confirmed – the suggestion that 1977 rather than 1980 should be the date for ending selection was made in a hasty conversation between us that took place in the corridor outside the Leader's room in County Hall. That 1977 date evidently coincided with her own views as well as with ideas being expressed to her by some of her colleagues, amongst them Caroline Benn and Tyrrell Burgess, both added members of the Education Committee but not on its Policy Committee. It is because decisions of that kind have such political risks attached to them that the notion that education could ever be taken 'out of politics' is so wide of the mark.

Any decision to end selection by a given date was extremely risky. A number of things, from court cases to the rejection of particular proposals by the Secretary of State, could make a date as early as September 1977 impossible to achieve. But although trying to end selection at forty five grammar schools so soon would be difficult, it was just possible. On the other hand, failure to end selection by then meant that it would be arithmetically certain that an increasing number of existing comprehensive schools would be becoming secondary modern ones.

A few weeks after Mrs Garside's statement that selection to schools maintained by the ILEA would cease in September 1977, the importance of what was at stake was put to the test. As he looked at the amount of work that had to be done to end selection by then, Dr Briault concluded that the risk of failure was too great. To end selection by September 1977 meant that parents would need to know, by December 1976 at the latest, what kind of secondary schools they would be able to send their children to in the following year. At a meeting with the Leader, in the early summer of 1975, at which some leading members and I were present, Dr Briault argued that too much had to be done too quickly to meet the December 1976 deadline and that the date for ending selection should be changed from 1977 to 1978. He was right to be concerned at the risk of failure. That was a very real possibility; but I disagreed with his conclusion. We were now at a point where I could express my views openly. I said that postponing the ending of selection for a year might be even more risky. It would lose the forward momentum which had been developing and which major organisational changes always require to avoid stalling. During the discussion, the Leader's uncertainty became evident. Where there was an obvious difference of opinion between the Education Officer and his Deputy, for him openly to side with the Deputy could have far-reaching consequences that he would be anxious to avoid. Suddenly, John Harwood, the Leader's personal assistant, who was not at the table with the rest of us, placed a piece of paper in front of Sir Ashley. None of the rest of us had seen it. The intervention of a personal assistant at a meeting where the Education Officer was giving advice to the Leader was unprecedented. Harwood's single sheet of paper provided figures similar to those that I had been using. It showed the increasingly damaging effect on existing comprehensive schools of retaining selective schools at a time of sharply falling numbers. Having this document in front of him meant that Sir Ashley did not have to decide between the Education Officer and his Deputy. Harwood's note was confined to facts, so it left the Leader free to decide what to do about them. After checking that there was no disagreement about those facts, Sir Ashley concluded that the 1977 date for ending selection should stand.

At some impossible now to verify date in 1975, there was a residential meeting of primary and secondary heads from Lambeth. These gatherings tended to be social as well as educational occasions. Wine, purchased by those attending and not the ILEA, flowed. After dinner one evening, the mood became jovial. Those assembled were entertained by a song sung by two grammar school headmasters: Martyn Reed, the author of the song, and John Phillips, headmaster of Battersea Grammar School and soon to be the first head of Furzedown comprehensive school, later renamed Graveney. The District Inspector, backed up the vocals by dancing about in the background.

This is what the heads sang to the tune of the *Vicar of Bray:*

> In good King Robbie Butler's reign
> The children of the nation
> Were put in schools at plus eleven
> According to their station
> The teachers too into three parts,
> Like Gaul, were thus divided,
> For so on high it was ordained
> Instruction be provided.
> And this is law I will maintain,
> Though changes come much faster,
> That who in the D.E.S shall reign
> I'll be a loyal Headmaster.
> Then in the year of '65
> A comprehensive order
> Said, 'Three in one you all shall be
> From Dover to the Border.'
> We teachers all this new made law
> Received with acclamation;
> So resolute was our intent
> To stay in education.
> The well-laid plans of mice and men
> Go frequently awry, sir,

> And in the reign of Maggie T.
> This law did not apply, sir;
> We looked to right, we looked to left,
> With vile procrastination;
> Yet stoutly maintained our intent
> To stay in education.
> At length Reg ruled the DES.,
> (No sitter he on fences)
> He too laid down all schools should be
> Henceforward comprehensives.
> So once more with united voice
> We yelled with jubilation:
> 'Through thick and thin we'll save our skin,
> And stay in education.

The author was a little astray with that 'comprehensive order'. Circular 10/65 had been a request to local education authorities, with no statutory force, to submit plans to create comprehensive schools. Some did so quickly, some after lengthy delays, some never. As for Reg Prentice not sitting on fences, that was accurate enough. Not long afterwards, he hopped right over one and joined the Conservative Party.

In 1975, sub-committee meetings were, for the first time in any major local education authority, open to the public. The photo below is of some of the members at the first such meeting. Mair Garside is chairing the meeting and Eric Briault is looking pensive. Others mentioned in the text include myself, Bill Braide, Sir Ashley Bramall, Harvey Hinds, Caroline Benn, Margaret Morgan and George Carter, NUT representative on the committee.

Events moved fast on secondary re-organisation during the last months of 1975. On 6 August 1975, the best-timed building programme of the decade was announced by that under-estimated Secretary of State, Fred Mulley: the special programme for assisting re-organisation (SPAR). This programme made it possible for selective schools to manage a comprehensive intake by marginally enlarging themselves or adapting their premises. When term began in September 1975, ILEA officers, heads, staff, governors and architects moved fast. Thirty-six building schemes were submitted and, with an alacrity never subsequently repeated, the Department of Education and Science approved the programme on 22 December that year.

As so many re-organisation schemes, some of them very complex, were at different stages of development, it was impossible for the politicians and many of ILEA's own staff to keep up with what was happening. At any one time, there were probably only three people in the ILEA who knew exactly how things stood: the head of the ILEA's planning section, Dorothy Clarkson, Mair Garside and myself. What follows is an extract from one of the hastily written notes intended to keep leading members, administrative and inspectorate colleagues in touch with what was happening:

Secondary re-organisation (Deputy Education Officer) 16 December 1975

Where have we got to: and where are we going?

(1) Where we have got to
Number of schools. On 1 January 1975, the ILEA maintained 199 secondary schools. The number it maintains can change in four ways: it can increase by the creation of a new school or it can decrease through amalgamations, through closures or through moves away from London.

New schools: There has been one new school in 1975: Thamesmead.

Amalgamations: During 1975, twenty-five secondary schools, including fifteen selective schools have either amalgamated or agreed plans to do so. One effect is to reduce the number of schools to be maintained by thirteen.

The fifteen grammar schools involved in amalgamations, with their non-selective partners in brackets, were then listed.

Tracing back to the origins of London schools is often complicated by name changes. For example, Battersea Grammar (boys) joining Rosa Bassett (girls) to become Furzedown (mixed), later renamed Graveney. On the other hand, Grey Coat CE (girls grammar), on being joined by St Michaels CE (Secondary Modern mixed), stayed as Grey Coat CE (girls comprehensive). One amalgamation that had been provisionally agreed by the governing bodies concerned, with details of timing and accommodation needs still to be sorted out, was between Marylebone Grammar School and Rutherford. This later led to controversy.

Closure or ceasing to maintain: The four schools are:
Emanuel
Godolphin and Latymer
Colfe's
Strand
(Strand closed; the other schools were voluntary aided and decided to remain in London and develop as independent fee-paying schools)
Leaving London
Parmiter's
Mary Datchelor

Parmiter's re-established itself as a comprehensive school in Hertfordshire. During the course of arrangements for Mary Datchelor to establish itself outside inner London, the Chairman of the City Company concerned, with whom I had had detailed discussions about its future, sadly died. The Company declined to enter into any further discussions about the future of this excellent school for girls and decided to close it. This was a serious loss to London education. The Labour Group's formidable Chief Whip, Miss Elsie Horstead, was an old girl of the school and did everything possible to save it.

There could be some variation between these categories but between them they lead to a reduction of nineteen in the number of secondary schools the ILEA will be maintaining. Secondary numbers have not yet fallen and a planned reduction of nearly 10% of the schools is a fair achievement at this stage.

Comprehensive partnerships.
Twenty-four selective schools are involved in VI Form partnership arrangements with ten non-selective schools. These were listed.

Note on ending selection: Selection is being ended in the following ways:

Selective schools in amalgamations	15
Closing (3 becoming independent)	4
Leaving London	2
In comprehensive partnerships	24
Total	**45**

(2) Where are we going?

The implications in 1976 and 1977 of carrying through initiatives undertaken in 1975 are considerable. It is not only the forty-five selective schools that are at issue. As mentioned above, a further ten schools are associated with selective schools in amalgamations. Other changes, which require radical rethinking within a school, are not listed: e.g. Quintin Kynaston becoming mixed, the effect on non-selective partners (e.g. Parliament Hill in relation to changes at William Ellis). If some or all of these changes are included, it will be seen that more than fifty-five secondary schools are facing immediate changes and that there are a further thirty where the staff can be expected to be preoccupied with some important variation in their way of conducting themselves.

The consequences for the use of inspectorate time are evident. I believe we should confine our efforts over the next two years to two things:

(a) Overwhelmingly the more important, to make the changes now initiated really work;

(b) To deal decisively with the six problems set out below. Others could, of course, be added but any new initiatives should be weighed for their effect on carrying through existing ones successfully.

Six secondary problems, involving eleven schools

Here followed a list of eleven schools, each in premises built before 1900, three of which were to close, four to be amalgamated to become two and four on which decisions were to be made after further local discussion. In the end, as part of a programme developed during 1977, all eleven schools, in practice though not always in name secondary modern schools, were closed. The incorporation of two of these schools into Holland Park School proved far from straightforward. It did not help that the headmaster of one of them, Isaac Newton, was an active teacher representative on the Education Committee. Furthermore, during some previous election campaign, undertakings appeared to have been given by Labour candidates that schools in North Kensington would be kept open, despite an increasing lack of children willing to attend them. I had not been aware of these undertakings. Confronted by this intelligence at a meeting of the Policy Committee, after a moment's hesitation, I suggested that it might be fair to interpret any such undertaking as one to keep 'a strong educational presence' in the area. This, I declared, we would certainly do. My suggestion had been greeted by a few seconds of silence before the Leader enquired, in his cool forensic manner, what exactly I meant by this strong educational presence we were to keep. As I had only just thought of the phrase, I had no idea yet what it might mean. This caused a certain amount of mirth when that became obvious and I was invited to return with a proposal that could be defended in public.

> To these problems could be added various ideas for mixing schools (e.g. Sir William Collins, a boys school, later to become a mixed school as South Camden Community School). If we settle these problems during 1976, so that they can be brought to some conclusion in 1977, we will have done well. And during 1976 we would be identifying and examining further matters to think through in 1977. These suggestions, if carried out, would bring down the number of secondary schools by at least a further five and we should probably aim at continuing to reduce by about five schools a year. This is manageable provided we do not at the same time commit ourselves to the contradictory policy of trying to prop every school up.

> As a general point, the fewer secondary schools we have the longer the distances pupils will have to travel to those we retain. This strengthens the case for more mixed schools.

What this note indicates is that, even with the most up to date information available, predictions about what had to be done in the comparatively near future seriously underestimated how much more would be needed. The suggested reduction of five schools soon became eleven. Re-organisation on the scale now being undertaken required close, day by day, attention to administrative procedures. It left no room for mistakes.

Between January and November 1976, the date by which we needed to have settled which schools would be admitting children in September 1977, a great deal had to be done quickly. In January 1976, Mr Mulley, the Secretary of State, agreed to come across to County Hall to discuss how the ILEA's plans to develop a comprehensive system were going. The crucial problem we needed the Secretary of State to grasp, although he obviously could not be asked to fetter his discretion in relation to any individual school, was that delay on his part in approving or deciding not to approve the Section 13 (of the 1944 Education Act) Notices required to change the character of a school (e.g. by ending academic selection to it) would be fatal to the Authority's plans to end selection by September 1977.

These Public Notices had to go through several stages. The first stage required them to be published in the right places and to contain accurate information, by which the Authority would later be bound, on how exactly, year by year, the change proposed would be managed; in particular, where the pupils would be accommodated at each stage of the process. It was crucial to get the form of each Notice right. Any mistake and an objection to one within two months of their publication would be likely to be upheld and the whole process have to be gone through again. There was only one person in the ILEA with the experience and precision of mind to ensure that no objection to the form of any of the sometimes complex Notices the ILEA had to publish would be upheld: Miss Dorothy Clarkson. At one stage, she was moving from one flat to another but found it impossible to take the time off to complete her move. For six months, at considerable financial cost and huge stress to herself, she was caught between the two. Every Friday evening she left County Hall with a brief case bulging with documents. Throughout the year, she made not a single mistake. So if it is ever asked who made the detailed statutory arrangements, with faultless accuracy, affecting the future of so many London secondary schools, in such a short time, with the consequences of anything going wrong so serious, the answer is Miss Dorothy Clarkson, later MBE.

The second stage began when the Notices expired after two months. The Authority then received copies of all the objections that had been sent to the Secretary of State and had to provide responses to each of them. This might lead to further to-ing and fro-ing if the Department officials concerned thought the Secretary of State needed more information (or, as we suspected in one instance, the official concerned was simply ill-disposed) before deciding whether or not to uphold the objections received.

The final stage was the approval, rejection or amendment of the proposal by the Secretary of State. In its actions, including the information it could give to the public, the ILEA could not anticipate the Secretary of State's decision; so timing was crucial. Ending selection in September 1977 meant that parents of children transferring to secondary school then needed to know, during the autumn term of 1976, which schools they could apply for. So the risk of missing this timetable, if anything went wrong with the Section 13 Notices or if Mr Mulley or his officials proved dilatory, was serious and ever present.

The thrust of the hurriedly dictated note that follows was to give three ILEA members the information enabling them to stress to the Secretary of State, who was coming to County Hall next morning, the vital importance of reaching decisions quickly on proposals for structural change. Hence the urgent tone of the following extracts from the brief for that meeting, addressed only to the Leader, Mrs Garside and Mr Hinds:

ILEA Secondary Schools – Creating a comprehensive system 15 January 1976

The first part of this note concerns the Section 13 timetable. The second deals with some of the work that lies ahead on a number of 'other' non-selective schools and related problems. Section 13 Notices will sometimes be involved here too.

Part 1: The Section 13 timetable

1. We have looked back at the last thirteen schools for which schemes have so far been approved. The shortest S.13 clearance took four and a half months from the date of issue, the longest ten months. The average was eight months; but Camden Girls School has already taken a year.

2. We have 34 S.13 Notices to clear within 1976 to be safe in ending selection in 1977 and to prevent parents fretting. Clearly, we won't get the Divisional booklets, printed this September, right.

3. For five schemes the objection period has expired: for six schemes the objection period is still running: for thirteen schools Notices have been authorised by Sub-Committee and should be issued shortly. For ten schools Notices have yet to be agreed.

All the schools were listed in the briefing note. Members would have personal knowledge of each of them.

Notes on S.13 procedures.

The timing problem for Emanuel illustrates our difficulties. We answer the objections. There is a pause. Then more questions. It is the nature and timing of these that can be disconcerting. We understand why the DES feel that the Secretary of State and the Department must be protected and be seen to have had regard to every objection made. But objections made after the final date for objections contained in the Notices?

Camden Girls illustrates a second problem which could crop up again, particularly at some of the RC schools. The site is very sub-standard. But the school will be admitting a hundred children a year, only slightly more than it admits now. Yet there has been a flurry of correspondence recently about how serious we are in intending to improve the site. This we are genuinely trying to do. The DES problem is that they expect all kinds of legal objections to any decision made. But there ought by now to be some form of check list which the DES could employ as soon as any proposal reaches them. I see no reason why they should wait for the expiry of the Notices to clear their minds on the nature of the proposals themselves, if they find these obscure.

Similarly, it would help if HMI would visit and consider a proposal, at least in a preliminary way, very early on; and will they please not move HMI just when they have achieved some understanding of our problems? Bill Francis suddenly disappeared.

These notes are written in haste and ought not to give the impression that anyone in the DES is being dilatory or unhelpful. But we ourselves would have ground to a halt long ago if we had tried to continue the very full briefing of members, early morning meetings, Policy Committee discussions on the wording of reports and so on, with which we started. No one can deal with thirty four Notices in one year in the way they used to deal with three or four a year.

Finally, we really are in trouble over the September 1976 starters. Parents are asking, Divisional Officers are having to give shifty answers. Literally, every day is significant now.

Part 2: Other problems of secondary school re-organisation

There are twenty-two small non-selective schools that have to be brought within the comprehensive system or, in a few instances, closed: (22 schools named)

Some of these schools will pose no great problem; e.g. the three RC schools underlined are part of a respectable comprehensive partnership. Others can be dealt with similarly. But some can't. We are in the process of working out a timetable for these schools and are supposed to report to you by Easter – after having consulted all and sundry. We will do what we can but I hope the DES will watch our efforts with understanding. S.13 Notices will be needed, our latest advice tells us, when schools widen their entry. So, again, we have not much time to settle matters before September 1977. There are at least nine other schools caught up in amalgamations, sex-changes and so on. We can be seen to be looking at these during 1976. This will help morale but, even in my most optimistic moments, I do not think we will be able to settle them all this year.

Three general points:

(a) The DES (and Mr Mulley referred to this when the EO and I went over there with you) appear to believe we are not closing secondary schools. They should count each January and see how many we have left. I calculate that re-organisation will bring down the number of secondary schools we maintain by nineteen. I estimate a further four or five schools a year for the next two or three years. It is fair to count amalgamations because the resultant form entries will be down and premises will be released.

(b) Within ILEA, we mourn the fate of list B of our re-organisation submission (a list of other secondary schools that urgently needed improvements). There has been some internal fuss at the DES about the large share ILEA received and I do not think we will get more. But it might be useful to go through the items. Something may turn up.

(c) It is the shift in attitudes that is taking place, which takes just as much planning as organisational change, that we have reason to be particularly pleased with. I hope the visitors will return to the DES as convinced as we are that the weight of teacher thinking has now swung behind a 1977 start to a comprehensive system.

There was no such thing as 'amalgamation' recognised in the Education Acts that then applied. The only ways to combine two schools were to close one and simultaneously enlarge the other or to close both and simultaneously create a single school out of the two previous ones. In practice, what the ILEA never did, after closing one, was to require all its pupils physically to move across into the other. To do that, in the circumstances of Inner London, would be rather like sending a torpedo into an oil tanker. The only amalgamation that went wrong, because at the last moment the governors decided to object to what they had earlier agreed to, concerned Marylebone Grammar School. In his autobiography, *The Turbulent Years*, Kenneth Baker, the local MP, described the ILEA's attitude towards the school as follows: 'The ILEA, led by Ashley Bramall, decided to strike the school down. It was to close and the boys were to go to another school known in the neighbourhood for its violence, vandalism and poor standards. It was an act of vandalism based on bigotry. I vowed I would do everything I could to bring an end to an Authority where dogma took precedence over good education'. In fact, the ILEA had never proposed to move the boys then at Marylebone Grammar School into another school. They would stay where they were as the intake to the new school developed down the road in suitably refurbished premises. Kenneth Baker's failure to understand what the ILEA was proposing, then and later, was total.

While the formal arrangements for the preparation and publication of Notices were taking place, I was visiting grammar schools and attending meetings of parents and governing bodies. Three kinds of school had to be dealt with. One small group of voluntary aided schools, none of them denominational, were opposed to making any change to their selective admission arrangements. They preferred to remain in their own premises and become fee-paying schools. They did not want to enter into any discussion on their decisions. With rare exceptions, they were already socially as well as educationally selective, with parents who were sufficiently wealthy to pay fees. The ILEA, in order not to disturb the education of the children already in those schools, decided to pay their fees until they left their sixth forms. A second group, mainly consisting of Catholic grammar schools encouraged by forceful diocesan directors, agreed to enlarge their mission and accept catholic children of all abilities. A third group consisted of undenominational, voluntary aided, grammar schools. These schools, mostly established up to one hundred years ago, often had parents who were fearful that their children's education would be damaged by any change. Such worries were often reinforced by governing bodies, strongly influenced by and often led by devoted alumni of the schools concerned.

In dealing with this third group of schools, it soon became evident that most parents, as opposed to governing bodies, were only really concerned with the interests of their own children. At any potentially hostile meeting , I had learnt to avoid any apparent attempt to persuade. I would begin by confirming that no child now at the grammar school would be required to move from it. Having made sure everyone grasped that, I would go on to remind the meeting that the new intake of eleven year olds would not begin until 1977. By then, I would add, every pupil now in the Sixth Form would have left the school. After talking round that point for a few moments, I usually found that a number of parents, presumably those with children then in the Sixth Form, had begun to drift away from the meeting. I would then spend time musing on the effect of a rather different entry of eleven year olds in 1977 on today's fourteen-year-olds, who would then be entering the sixth form. How disturbed would those sixth formers be by these eleven year olds? This had not been a problem elsewhere, I could assure the audience, but did anyone think this would be a serious problem? Few parents thought it was. This was the point at which to announce some good news. The Department had allowed the ILEA to replace this or that bit of decayed building at the school and replace it with a new something that the school's architect would now start designing. By the time we reached the effect of the 1977 eleven year old entry on children now at the school who would then be fourteen, I would concede that they would notice the arrival of these newcomers. But did anyone think they would be bullied by these eleven-year-olds? On one occasion, my leisurely removal of different layers of anxiety was cut short. The head boy of William Ellis, a leading grammar school in Camden, rose to his feet before I had a chance to say anything and made a powerful speech in favour of opening the school to all comers. He was absolutely confident, he declared, that the staff of the school and the boys now there would make a success of anything they put their minds to. This went well. He was applauded and my rather laboured approach could then safely be foreshortened.

His speech was one that any Labour Secretary of State could have made from 1997 onwards had they had the courage to make it. None had.

The whole issue of secondary education, the ending of selection in Inner London and the termination of direct grant to a number of leading schools in London and elsewhere kept the newspapers busy in 1976. In that same year, Sir Keith Joseph, then in opposition, offered the following thought: 'The blind, unplanned, uncoordinated wisdom of the market is overwhelmingly superior to the well-researched, rational, systematic, well-meaning, cooperative, science-based, forward-looking, statistically respectable plans of government.' The flight from reason and its application to human affairs that this pronouncement reflected was ill-received in Inner London, where the disastrous educational consequences of letting things rip in the face of rapid economic, social and demographic change were everywhere apparent. But Sir Keith, brilliant in so many ways, had as yet no practical experience of education or, indeed, of anything much else.

Although heavily engaged in administrative matters, I continued to visit schools and colleges. In doing so, at some point late in 1976, I acquired a black eye. I had been attending a fashion show at the London College of Fashion, just off Oxford Street. I was sitting in the front row, paying close attention to the young women as they stomped down the catwalk. At one point, my eyes were fixed on the girl in front and not on the one just behind her. The latter was showing a vaguely Caribbean dress and had been equipped with a large bunch of bananas. As she advanced along the catwalk, she had been peeling off single bananas and throwing them into the audience. When she reached where I was sitting, she repeated the process. This time the single banana refused to detach itself, so the whole bunch, too heavy to travel far, arrived on my forehead before I had time to duck. This caused happy laughter all around the audience and led to my black eye. In the office next morning, my explanation of what had caused it was greeted with polite but barely concealed disbelief.

Members of the ILEA's majority party were kept informed about developments in secondary education; so too were the leaders of the minority Conservative Party. Their emphasis tended to be on what was now happening in the secondary schools rather than on their future structure. On 14 September, Mr Vigars, Leader of the Conservatives, put down the following motion for debate in the Education Committee on the following day: 'That the Schools Sub-Committee do ascertain the schools which, by reason of serious undersubscription, poor examination results or other factors, are cause for anxiety; and consider the steps to be taken to remedy the situation.' Hence this rapidly composed briefing note to Sir Ashley on that same day:

Brief for the Leader from DEO   14 September 1976

Mr Vigars must know that the Schools Sub-Committee is already engaged on this and has been for some considerable time. One initial point of clarification: it can be a mistake to regard under-subscription as an automatic cause for anxiety any more than finding a school has too many children in it is an automatic cause for rejoicing. Demographic changes, the location of schools, their accommodation and so on have their own effects. You may wish to mention a few examples:

(a) George Green's. Here we have an excellent five-form entry school which is already over-subscribed. If we only had the building, we could happily accommodate a six-form entry. But if, for any reason, we had built eight forms of entry, the location of this school might have meant it was under-subscribed. This would have had no implications whatever for the quality of the school's work.

(b) Numbers entering a school can be affected by what is happening down the road. Newly formed comprehensive schools are sometimes guilty, if that is the word, of causing problems for their neighbours. For example, over-subscription at the newly created Clapton Comprehensive Girls School (as John Howard came to be called) caused some under-subscription elsewhere. So too did the over-subscription at Central Foundation Girls School when it became comprehensive and at Lewisham Girls when it too enlarged and began to take a fully balanced intake. Success has its consequences. It will be increasingly important in the next year or two, as numbers decline, to keep a sense of proportion: a school cannot fill itself with children that do not exist. Above all, we do not want to have schools which are overcrowded when there is no need for them to be. Nor do we want others touting for custom to avoid the reproach of not being over-subscribed.

(c) It is, of course, recognised that reduced demand for places at a particular school may be a symptom of something serious that needs examination. On the secondary side, so far as the activity of committees is concerned, there is a particularly careful look at this by the Transfer Section. Indeed, they have called for a report in the following terms: 'That the Education Officer do report on the options open to the Authority in tackling the problems caused by the fluctuations in demand for schools reflected by parental preferences, especially in the light of the ending of selection in 1977'.

(d) That last phrase in the Transfer Section's reference is particularly important. I have referred to the problems caused when parents have access to newly created comprehensive schools. We have a large number of these beginning in September 1977, some of them with not many places to offer. This will make it particularly difficult for supply and demand, if one is to look at it in these terms, to balance at each individual school. In this situation, it will be particularly unwise to suppose that something is automatically wrong if a school is under-subscribed or particularly right if it is over-subscribed, though we will have to look very carefully at the reasons behind both conditions.

The Transfer Section referred to was a special section of the Schools Sub-Committee. It was skilfully chaired by Tyrrell Burgess. In great detail, members looked at what was happening to the pattern of parental preferences at every secondary school. The transfer system that developed was simple for parents to understand, applied over the whole of inner London and, year by year, raised the proportion of parents obtaining a place for their child at the school they nominated as their first preference to slightly above or slightly below 86%. This was a considerable achievement in an urban setting with a wide choice of schools (mixed, single-sex, large, small, denominational, non-denominational, voluntary aided, voluntary controlled or county, with various combinations of these characteristics) for which parents could express a preference. Many years later, this wide choice of schools, in London as elsewhere, came to be described as a 'one size fits all' system. This reflected a total lack of understanding by the people using the phrase about the nature of the schools they believed themselves to be describing.

Towards the end of 1976, it became evident that, barring something quite unpredictable, such as court cases going the wrong way, selection at all Inner London secondary schools would indeed end in 1977. With a few exceptions, the process of re-organisation had not been conducted with ill-feeling, though there were natural anxieties on the part of schools having to deal with far-reaching changes to the way they conducted themselves. Nor had parents taken to the streets to preserve the 11+ examination. During the period between 1975 and 1977, Public Notices were issued for thirty-nine re-organisation schemes, involving forty-eight secondary schools. Only eighteen of these schemes were the subject of statutory objections by a local authority or by ten or more local government electors. At a time when almost any change affecting education in London led to public meetings, deputations and, too frequently for comfort, sit-ins, this was a remarkable achievement.

By December 1976, the projected numbers or children entering secondary schools in early 1980s indicated that more schools would have to close to avoid a long tail of schools gradually providing less and less for their pupils as they moved towards collapse. In 1972, the ILEA maintained 219 secondary schools; by January 1975, that had become 199. In September 1982, a few weeks after I had left the ILEA, there was an entry at 11+ to 159 secondary schools. Hence one reason for the title of a talk I gave in 1983. The title, 'Revolution by Consent', reflected the fact that reducing the number of secondary schools by sixty over a decade had not led to major parental, teacher or pupil disturbance.

There were two decisive moments in ending selection to inner London's secondary schools in 1977. The first was the Policy Committee's decision, in September 1974, to allow one small grammar school, initially as an experiment, to take an all-ability intake while remaining at a size far below that previously accepted as a minimum. The second, in March 1975, was Mair Garside's decision, later confirmed by the Education Committee, that set September 1977 as the date by which selection would cease at any school still to be maintained by the Authority. The first decision required the Authority to accept that changing circumstances had made it necessary to abandon, however reluctantly, the LCC's vision of a secondary school system that would end the rigid distinction between 'academic' and 'technical and commercial' courses. This was bitterly disappointing for some of my colleagues who had devoted themselves over many years to making that vision a reality.

The second decision was to set an early date for ending selection. This required a willingness to take a serious educational and political risk to enable London's secondary schools to withstand the potentially disastrous effects of falling pupil numbers. The GCSE results in 1983 indicated that ending selection in 1977 had not led to any fall in standards. On the other hand, ending selection did not, as some had hoped but I had never supposed, put an end to there still being a number of poorly performing schools in some parts of London. What ending selection did was to prevent an otherwise inevitable increase in the proportion of schools in that condition. When some of us visited New York late in 1976, we saw in the policed corridors of some of the schools in the Bronx what London had, for the most part, managed to avoid. What ending selection to inner London's secondary schools did was to establish a secure platform on which the badly needed improvements to secondary education in inner London could be built.

The belief that nearly all of London's grammar schools were, at some stage, 'destroyed' by dogmatic politicians is still held in some quarters. The fact is that the forty five grammar schools that existed in London in 1972, on ending selection in 1977 and with rare exceptions, in one form or another still exist in 2014. Nearly all of them are heavily over-subscribed and are successful, academically and in other ways that can prove just as important. The parents who send their children to what were once grammar schools would rightly regard it as ridiculous, as well as offensive, to be told that that their schools had been destroyed rather than preserved and, wherever the site made this possible, had been encouraged to expand. These schools were and remain some of the best in the country.

Chapter 2: Primary education and appointment as ILEA Education Officer

The particulars sent to candidates for the Deputy Education Officer post had explained that the Authority was embarking on a 'comprehensive review' of inner London's primary schools: their size, physical condition, location and, in relation to the areas they served, sometimes their future. This review was well under way when I arrived in 1972. It was administratively led and was being expertly conducted. I had little to contribute to that process. What was or was not happening inside the primary schools was not part of the review. It was over this that disagreement with my colleagues about the state of many of London's primary schools came to the surface. Between 1966 and 1970, as Assistant Director for primary schools in Cumberland, I had four years' experience of spending most of my time in primary schools or working with teachers at those schools. I had got to know some of those teachers and those schools really well. Later, as Deputy to Sir Alec Clegg in the West Riding of Yorkshire, I had seen fewer primary schools but, in both local authorities, I had been able to observe levels of achievement against which I could measure anything encountered in London.

As Deputy in the ILEA I had no formal responsibility for primary education. Nor had anyone shown any interest in opinions I might have formed on the London schools I had visited. The line of responsibility for primary education went from Miss Burgess, an able administrator who had never taught, to Bill Braide, whose responsibilities included over a thousand primary and secondary schools. It then went directly up to the Education Officer. The inspectorate, through the Chief Inspector, also offered its advice to Dr Briault directly. Positioned on the sidelines, I had access to minutes on primary school matters as they moved between those administratively responsible for them.

The background to the flurry of minutes that began in February 1974 was that, when I arrived, the ILEA maintained over 850 primary schools. I had visited, in the sense of spending a morning or afternoon in and out of their classrooms, only about forty of these. With few exceptions, I had been unimpressed and, at times, alarmed by what I had seen. To an observer from outside, most compared badly with those of Cumberland and the West Riding. In some parts of London, many of the schools managed to be both dull and undemanding. In others, any form of stability was lacking and the children's education suffered accordingly. I summed up my reaction to what I had seen in a speech some years later:

> Perhaps the single most important idea of the early and middle years of the 1970s was the absolute and overriding need to arrest or, in some cases, forestall a decline, at times seen as a potential collapse, in the quality of key elements in inner London's education service. I do not believe anyone can understand what was or what was not done by County Hall in the 1970s unless they are prepared to enter into that dominant perception. Consider the condition of inner London's primary schools. In the early 1970s, the verbal reasoning scores, imperfect measure though these be, confirm what was otherwise apparent. Despite the huge disruption of the 1939–1945 war, London's tradition of good elementary education, arguably about the best in the country, was initially maintained. That tradition survived the break between primary and secondary schools at the age of eleven, to which the 1944 Act gave legislative force. In the early 1960s, inner London children, on leaving primary school, were still doing considerably better than the average for the rest of the country. But it was in the late 1950s that four things began to change the performance of inner London's schools.
>
> First, there was a move out of London of some 500,000 people, many of them skilled workers with their above average performing children. They were moved as part of what now looks like the planned dereliction of the inner city, but was then designed to reduce acute housing stress through the development of new towns or estates on undeveloped land on the edges of London. The people who moved out had jobs. They wanted gardens for their children. Those that stayed behind were often unable to move because they were poor or did not have jobs; so they stayed and tried to bring up their children, often on their own, in crowded flats or in temporarily provided accommodation.
>
> The second move was inwards. Into the empty spaces, in particular to meet the needs of London's hospital, transport or other services, came individuals and families actively recruited from overseas. The numbers coming in were fewer than those leaving but, a factor of permanent significance, with those leaving London went many of the jobs, from furniture making to small scale engineering, that had given the inner areas of London much of their economic strength.

The story is familiar so far. If that is all there had been to it, the educational problems would have been manageable. But the educational consequences of demographic change were compounded by a third factor. An experienced and stable teaching force might have been expected to manage the change in population; even the influx into the schools of thousands of children with not a word of English. But just as parents and children moved out in large numbers and over a comparatively short period, so too did many experienced teachers as part of that wider movement out of London. In the late sixties and early seventies, in several hundred of London's primary schools, continuity of instruction, built up over a hundred years of experience by some of the best teachers in the country, was close to collapse. School after school, for term after term, was left with one or two senior teachers in charge and with a constant succession of young products of the Colleges of Education: inexperienced, ill-prepared for inner-city education and, above all, ill-paid and ill-housed. In their thousands, they stayed for a few terms to enjoy the non-teaching aspects of London and then, understandably enough, returned, slightly shell-shocked, as I put it at the time, 'back home to mother', somewhere well away from London.

There was a fourth factor. This was vividly brought home to me on visiting a Hackney primary school in 1973. For the number of children on roll, the school seemed to have an ample supply of teachers. So what was the problem? Not only were those teachers moving but so too, even more disturbingly, were the children. At any one point, 300 pupils on roll were a snapshot of almost double that number who had moved on and then off the register in the previous twelve months. Not so much a school, I found myself thinking, more a whirling, thrown together, ever-changing collection of children and adults with a day-to-day existence reminiscent of a reception centre. Tidy staff pupil ratios devised in quiet offices in County Hall hardly seemed appropriate to this and many other schools in a similar condition.

By the mid-1970s, the system was moving forwards again. The teachers were taking hold. The Authority, in its turn, was doing all it could to hold teachers in London. The aim was to make conditions there good enough to persuade them to stay, if only for another term or two. Staffing ratios were improved and generous ancillary help was supplied. Quite calculatingly, to avert prolonged crisis, the ILEA bought a degree of stability. In this it, at least partially, succeeded; but the consequences of some of the arrangements then made were long-lasting.

The reasons for what was happening seemed clear. In the late 1950s and during the 1960s, the 'inner city' problem had been created in inner London. As part of its response to the Plowden Report of 1966, the ILEA's Research and Statistics Branch had responded to these new circumstances. It had identified ten factors associated with the schools or the family circumstances of children attending them that needed extra resources of staffing or money within what the Plowden Report described as

'Educational Priority Areas'. The ten factors identified, expressed as percentages of the children affected at each school, were as follows : males in the family in unskilled or semi-skilled occupations; children in households of six or more persons; children living in households of more than 1.5 persons per room or in households without an inside WC; pupils receiving free school meals; pupils absent during first week in May; recent immigrants in the school; pupils in the bottom 25% of the ability group and, particularly important, the proportion of teachers in the school who had been there for less than three years and of pupils who moved during the year.

On these criteria, in 1966 one school, already mentioned as most in need of help, had a percentage of 68% of recent immigrants, 75% of its pupils in the bottom 25% of the ability group, 83% of teachers in the school for less than three years and over 55% of pupils moving during the year. Down the list, the hundredth school had over 35% immigrants, nearly 50% in the lowest 25% ability group and about 70% of its teachers at the school for less than three years. In some schools, a high proportion of these transient teachers only stayed for a year or less. At a time when the national percentage of pupils receiving free school meals was 5.1%, in London the first school on the list had a percentage of 29.5% and the hundredth school of 13.5%. The criteria for being entitled to free school meals were then far stricter than they later became.

Child poverty, though an important factor, was not the main problem faced by the London's schools in the greatest difficulty. Children in even the poorest family in a stable society in Cumberland or Yorkshire or the London of the 1950s, provided they had enough to eat, were not overwhelmed by their situation. In the 1960s and early 1970s, the worst problems in London arose at schools in which a high proportion of children suffered from multiple forms of deprivation and were constantly moving from one school to another because of housing problems and were then being confronted by teachers equally on the move. Later, to these factors associated with disadvantage were added the percentage of children who did not speak English at home, those with a single parent and those in the care of a local authority.

As no politician or journalist sent their children to the most damaged of London's primary schools, their condition largely went unnoticed by the Press. That the decline in average performance was not steeper and, by 1974, was beginning to be reversed, was a tribute to the sometimes desperate struggle of comparatively few experienced London headteachers and their senior colleagues. Theirs was a notable achievement, insufficiently recognised at the time and since. Easily the best way to improve matters would have been to persuade able teachers to stay at their schools and to recruit some better ones. But precisely the opposite was happening. In the early 1970s, the number of newly recruited teachers to London had risen to three thousand a year. Many were barely competent. Whereas before the war the LCC had recruited only a few of the highest graded college leavers to staff its primary schools, the ILEA found itself having to recruit, as well as a few promising ones, newly trained teachers graded by inspectors as low as 7 or 8 on a 9-point scale. This was acutely depressing.

The ILEA's Research and Statistics Branch, throughout my years at the ILEA, was led by first-rate people. All primary school leavers were tested in English, maths and verbal reasoning. The results of the verbal reasoning tests were closely related to those of the English tests and were produced annually. These were standardised tests, applying over the country as a whole and were supervised by the National Foundation for Educational Research. The table that follows shows the results for pupils transferring to secondary schools in 1972. These results only became known in 1973. They were more than five points down on the national score, whereas in 1960 they had been three points above it. In 1973, no one could be certain that the fall had been arrested.

Graphs of system-wide average performance can conceal as much as they reveal. In London, many primary schools had remained largely unaffected by demographic changes. They had retained most of their teachers and continued to perform well above the national average. Conversely, the performance of the worst affected schools was far below the figures shown on the graph. It was this that was so alarming. It has to be recognised that the performance scores of eleven year olds, appearing on the graph for a particular year, show the effect of what had been happening to those children, often elsewhere than in England, in earlier years.

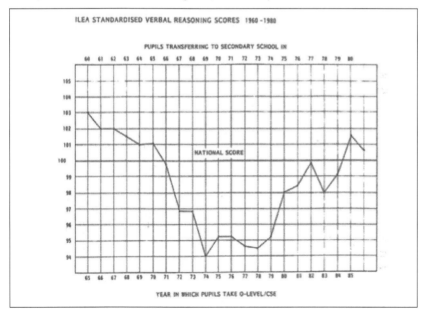

One immediate problem seemed to be, as I looked at the 1973 figures, that no one at County Hall was sufficiently aware of how bad things were in some of the schools or, if they were, had found ways of dealing with the problem. Where, for example, were the inspectors? At some of my visits to schools, the District Inspector for that Division came with me. I was immediately made conscious of the divide that existed in London between inspectors and administrators. In the LCC and now in the ILEA, administrators were seen by inspectors as people who knew how to deal with committees and whose job was to provide what the schools needed. Administrators dealt in quantities. It was for inspectors to deal with qualities. Inspectors alone knew about what was happening in schools and how to assess their quality and that of their teachers. In the ILEA, administrator and inspector were taken to exist in parallel universes. Only in one person were quantity and quality thought to exist together. That person was the ILEA's Education Officer. As his deputy, I was perceived by some long-serving inspectors to be firmly positioned on the administrative side of the divide. That this was not how I had seen myself in Cumberland or the West Riding and was not how I now saw myself in London caused unease when this became apparent. As it soon did.

There were three ways in which primary education in the worst affected parts of inner London could be helped to improve. The first was to recruit a large number of effective teachers and then to persuade them to stay in the schools where they were most needed; the second was to do everything possible to arrest the movement of children from school to school as their parents tried to find somewhere to live; the third was to use the inspectorate or teachers chosen by them to work with schools to help them manage their problems better. Unfortunately, both the quality of the teachers recruited and the movement of children between schools were not factors the Authority could do much to control. That just left having people from outside the schools to help improve what was happening inside them. My own visits told me that, in some of the least effective schools, things as obvious as a lack of interesting books for children to read, that teachers had been too busy with other problems to deal with, could quickly have been sorted out by a visiting inspector who knew what he was doing.

An important weakness in the Authority's approach to primary education, it appeared to me, was that the London schools inspectorate, mostly able and hard working, were nearly always subject and secondary school based so far as their own experience and interests were concerned; yet they were acting as inspectors of both primary and secondary schools. Too many inspectors visiting primary schools, I came to suspect as I went round them, did not get much beyond the head's study. London was confronted, in some districts, with far greater difficulties than had existed in Cumberland or the West Riding yet its response to those problems, although these had been clearly identified by the Authority's Research and Statistics branch, had been relatively ineffective. It mainly took the form of inspectors asking administrators for extra resources to be given to schools rather than ensuring they had access to people who knew enough about their problems to help them use the resources they already had more effectively.

The Educational Television Service (ETV)

Persuading colleagues that something needed to be done about this was not easy. I was particularly concerned at the use – or misuse – of London's Educational Television Service (ETV). This sent out black and white television programmes at fixed times in the day. Video recording was in its infancy so everything had to stop if a particular programme was to be watched. My reaction to the effect of this was indicated in a somewhat tactless note to the Education Officer, with a copy to the Chief Inspector, about a primary school I had visited in Islington in February 1974:

> **Hanover School.** Here are some necessarily superficial reactions to a brief tour round the school:
>
> The school has a 'good' intake and sends pupils off to most of the acceptable schools in the area. But it is all rather dull when it ought to be fizzing. This is where ETV comes in. The set stands in the middle of the library. If you want to watch ETV, you stop reading.
>
> My difficulty over ETV is, at this stage of this particular school's development, that I think it has no real part to play. It is just another thing tacked on. All the advisory panels in the world and the technical skills in programme making are not going to cause this school to think through its problems. This needs people on the spot and, until the people on the spot have done their job, extra resources, extra teachers and so on will do very little to help.
>
> This is my problem with ETV in the primary school. I see how it could be of enormous value to both teachers and children. But, as things are, I see how it could be the reverse. I would be seriously worried if Hanover watched ETV more than it does, run as it now is. And – though this can only be an impression – there seem to be too many schools like Hanover. Far from being trendy they seem to have a peculiar deadness about them.
>
> Of course, within Hanover there are some good young teachers, no doubt. No doubt someone who understands what our good primary schools are doing could go in and find growth points. They could make their excitement known. They could try and transmit this to the head. They could think of ways to develop it. In a year or so they could transform the school. They could help the work of that school transform the work of others in the neighbourhood. And so on. All these things could be done, but they have not been and, until they have, what can ETV possibly do to help? I know how dangerous it is to generalise from a superficial acquaintance with a few schools but what that acquaintance tells me is that some of the fundamental conditions under which educational television can be a success in primary schools are missing from London and that it will take more than video recorders to put things right.
>
> I may be wrong about this school; but the essential question remains. Do

the people who know most about primary education really believe that the way forward is through centrally organised operations, such as ETV, or do they not? My own view is that the next thing to ensure is that every primary school has regular access to someone who understands and can support the best primary practices. This is not so at the moment. More regular help needs to be given on the spot. If we have to choose between the development of central services and the development of local ones, my money would go on the latter.

The Education Television Service, as I discovered at about this time, had been created and developed by Dr Briault himself when he had been Deputy Education Officer. There was no response of any kind to this minute from either of its recipients. What I really believed, but did not at this point think it wise to say directly, was that, though the original idea behind ETV was far-sighted, it was now becoming an expensive prop to schools which could not think of anything better to do with the children. I was equally unimpressed with any contribution the inspectorate might have been making to improving what this particular school, with a 'good' intake, was managing to achieve.

The next document on primary education that I retained, though it is evident from the text that I had been sending others, was written a few weeks after the declaration by Mrs Garside that selection to secondary schools would end in September 1977, so I had a great deal else on my mind. I was responding to a draft document from the Chief Inspector in which he suggested that one or two advisory teachers be appointed to help schools deal with children who had special needs:

Advisory Section on Special Needs – Experimental Project 11 April 1975

In my view, the draft report of 10 April 1975 is both admirable and mistaken. It is admirable in that it clearly defined the nature of the proposed experiment and the most sensible way of conducting it; it is mistaken, in my view, for reasons which I have repeated like a Cato for two years.

It is no use conducting experiments, providing little bits of support, unless the elementary problems have been tackled.

To repeat my repetitions and take the primary schools:

(a) In order to provide proper cover for the primary schools one needs a knowledgeable person spending about one day a term in each school, talking through problems, watching new staff, suggesting new possibilities, encouraging, and so on.

(b) In London terms, this means about one person to about thirty schools or sites. This enables the person to spend more than one day a term in some schools, to take part in in-service work and to have a cold occasionally.

(c) We have not got this minimum cover in London. In some areas we have not got it by a mile. Until we have, a good many of the extras we offer, in the form of specialist services or help, are unusable. Unless the matter is tackled energetically, it will get worse. Over the next two years, District Inspectors will increasingly be drawn into secondary school problems: re-organisation and VI forms particularly.

The main job is to make sure our schools are the kind of places in which children can learn with security. To quote Bullock: 'There is no mystique about remedial education, nor are its methods intrinsically different from those employed by successful teachers anywhere. The essence of remedial work is that the teacher is able to give additional time and resources to adapting these methods to the individual child's needs and difficulties.'

Our duty, it seems to me, is to advise members that the pressing need is to establish quickly the minimum inspectorate support required. Unless this support is in place and effective, extra resources and experiments may give us the appearance of being active and forward-looking. The reality will be otherwise.

This set of comments got nowhere so, on 9 May 1975, I wrote again to the Chief Inspector, with copies to the Education Officer and others:

Support for Primary Schools

This note brings together the thoughts expressed in my minute of 11 April and the experiment suggested in the report to the Advisory Section on Special Education.

My analysis of the problem briefly is: (here I repeated the points made on 11 April). My suggestion for consolidation would be to move to a position where there are at least two primary inspectors in each division.

The main functions of the area-based primary inspectorate would be:
- to spend sufficient time in schools to know them really well
- to help schools think through their aims and practices
- to transmit the best practices from one school to another
- to ease transfers of staff from one school to another when rolls fall differentially
- to identify in-service training needs within and between schools, including the needs of probationers, and to work through teachers' centres to see these needs are met
- to have particular regard to transition from one school to another, including concern for the first year's work in secondary schools
- in general, to be accountable for the quality of work in the schools.

Still nothing happened as a result of these minutes. They read oddly to anyone acquainted with events in London at the time they were written. Why no reference anywhere to the crisis at William Tyndale school? The answer is that I was unaware when I wrote them that there were any problems at the school. As the Auld Report later recorded, groups of the school's managers had by then been in County Hall meeting the Chairman of the Schools Sub-Committee, Harvey Hinds. A report had been written by the District Inspector pointing out that there were serious problems at the school, that its numbers were declining and that, at some point, the infant and junior schools might have to be amalgamated. Mr Hinds had discussed the report with the Chief Inspector and the Staff Inspector for primary schools. Both had decided that the best way to deal with the problem was to leave it to the District Inspector to enlist any specialist help he thought was needed. Neither of these two senior inspectors had visited the school to see for themselves what was happening there.

When I learnt of it, I found this failure by leading inspectors to visit a school that was in trouble inexcusable. Mr Hinds had eventually asked the Education Officer to consider combining the infant and junior schools, which shared a building. On 11 May 1975, two days after the minute quoted above, this suggestion for amalgamation was on the agenda of the Officers Co-ordinating Committee. I attended this meeting and heard for the first time that there was a school called William Tyndale and that there were problems there. The District Inspector gave his report on the amalgamation proposal. Given his report's lack of urgency or the information that Mr Hinds had been seeing unrepresentative groups of managers, Dr Briault conveyed to Mr Hinds the Committee's opinion that the two schools should be left as they were for the time being. From that time on, events rapidly escalated but there was no discussion at County Hall, with myself or others, until matters reached the national Press. The managers, encouraged by Mr Hinds, wrote to say, with copies to the Press, that they wanted an enquiry into the school. Mr Hinds then held a meeting on 2 July with managers and the staff of the school. No ILEA officials were present. On 10 July, the Schools sub-committee resolved that there should be an ILEA inspection of both schools, followed by a public inquiry to deal with wide-ranging issues, including the respective rights of school staffs and their managing bodies. The inspection of the junior school then took place. It was hampered by the absence of the headmaster and six teachers, who had decided to teach a group of children off the school premises. Only sixty-eight children were at the school on the day the inspectors arrived to inspect it.

The public inquiry opened on 27 October 1975. It was not until nine months later, 10 July 1976, on the publication of Robin Auld QC's report into events at the school, that I and others learned the details of what had been happening. That inquiry was still being conducted at the time of the minutes that follow. They arose out of a draft report from the inspectorate which explained that inspectors were believed to spend one quarter of their time each term in the schools for which they were, in some way, responsible. What were they doing for the rest of their time? Apparently, they were heavily engaged in different forms of teacher training and, to be fair, there were good reasons for this. For example, if the problem with physics teaching in secondary schools was found to be that too many teachers of physics did not know enough physics to teach it properly, there was little point in inspecting them. What those teachers needed to acquire was a better understanding of physics; and the same problem applied to some other elements of the curriculum. Meanwhile, time and effort was not being systematically spent on primary schools because, with a few notable exceptions, too many inspectors, in my view, knew too little about how best to help them.

No doubt the arithmetic in the draft referred to would later have been sorted out; perhaps because the supposed visits related to a year rather than to a single term, but my irritation with it when it landed on my desk, even as a draft, will be evident:

Note to the Chief Inspector (copy to EO)   16 February 1976
Draft Report on the Inspectorate

Hedged about with whatever qualifications you like, paragraph 30 shows what is wrong. Even at the arithmetical level, the Emperor's clothes are missing.

a. take a school term to last 64 days (actually 190 in a full year)

b. ¼ of 64 is 16

c. so, on average, (some better some worse) a District Inspector is said to spend 16 full days a term visiting schools.

d. how many schools does each DI have? Leaving out special schools, it averages out at fifty-five primary and ten secondary.

e. each primary school is said to average two DI visits and each secondary 4.5 visits a term. That equals 110 primary visits and 45 secondary: 155 visits in all. Hot work for 16 days, just under 10 visits a day.

f. Assuming five hours in which a school is visitable and no travel time in between them, each visit lasts about half an hour. Which is what some outsiders sometimes suspect!

g. now, of course, no one can properly visit a primary school, in the sense. of becoming involved in its thinking, in less than half a day. Which puts the arithmetic in para 30 in perspective. The figures must either be misleading (seriously overstating the number of visits) or the quality of the visiting must be thoroughly suspect (confined to a few minutes). Or both. Or the proportion of time spent visiting is wrong. But even if this were doubled, visits would only average an hour.

The implications of paragraph 30 are far-reaching. How far do they explain what the problem is in, for example, Hackney's primary schools? And how are to set about dealing with this?

To make sure the point was registered, on the next day off went the following.

Note to Chief Inspector (copy to EO)   17 February

Draft inspectorate report

Perhaps you would just add this to my previous note. It's not too grimly serious. I have looked up Kay's instructions to the first HMI in the early 1840's. In each half year, 22 five-day weeks (they worked six days but left one for writing up reports), or 110 days were for visiting schools. On 80 days, a single school would be looked at. On 30 days, two could be fitted in. So in each full year, 140 schools were each visited twice, 80 for two full days, none for less than one full day.

Assume our present productivity to be half that of the ancients. In some way, each inspector with full time responsibility for a group of schools ought each year to be able to give 70 schools (slightly over the present District Inspector load) the same service that Kay's inspectors gave 140: ie visit each school, for at least a day, twice in the year. That is my starting point.

I think this is where we differ. I do not regard this inspection process (regular and at proper depth) as just one amongst other functions. It is the function, to which others are added if they are not detrimental to its exercise. And not added if they are.

The essence of the matter is that the work should be done sensitively and thoroughly. Who does it is less important. It may be that some existing DI's would rather do other things, feel they know what is happening without having to look regularly, and so on. In such cases, by agreement, others can carry out the function. There is no harm in that; but it is not a matter of individual decision, in my view, by DI's whether the work is to be done; how and by whom is for discussion. The whether ought not to be. That is policy.

I am back on reordering of thinking versus incrementation. In arguing for extra primary inspectors, I have never supposed that tacking a few more bodies on to the machine would of itself achieve much. It is only by reordering thinking that one does this. Within two years we want a system which makes it virtually impossible for someone to enter a school and:

 a. find a class of eleven-year-olds busily and silently colouring in an illustration of une glace during a French lesson.

 b. see hardly a book in a third year junior class of an Educational Priority Area school whose products fill the remedial department of the receiving secondary schools. There were five 'helpers' in the school.

I could go on. To conclude: if proper inspection were to be established the Authority would suddenly feel small. Any LEA feels small when you can ring a person up and ask how things are in the top juniors at a particular school and the person at the other end knows because he has seen them, talked to them and discussed them with their teacher. Nothing less will do and it can be done. We have enough people to do it.

All this has implications for the 'monitoring' apparatus we are busy erecting. This looks like a horrendously inefficient way of trying to find out what is happening, like putting our noses up against a frosted window to see what's going on inside. I am in favour of knocking boldly at the door and joining the party.

Later in 1976, with the strong support of Leila Campbell, then chairing the Schools Committee, the proposal for a primary schools inspectorate, operating within the existing District Inspector arrangements, was accepted. The primary inspectors were was paid for by reducing the number of advisory teachers that individual members of the inspectorate had found it useful to recruit to support them in their work. Some excellent appointments were made to the new Primary Inspectorate, mostly from first-rate head teachers. Barbara MacGilcrist, for example, later became the ILEA's Chief Inspector and subsequently, to give her full title, Professor MacGilcrist, PhD, OBE, Deputy Director of the Institute of Education at London University. From my perspective at the end of 1976, the ILEA now had sufficient people in place to begin to improve the quality of education in London's primary schools.

The Christian Schiller Lecture

There is a negative air about these minutes on primary education in London. If I did not particularly like what I saw, what did I think would be better? It was a year later before I expressed views of my own for which documentary backing has been retained. On 11 February 1976, Christian Schiller died. I did not hear of that until some days after the flurry of minutes quoted above. He was one of the truly great members of Her Majesty's Inspectorate. His particular concern was with primary education. In writing of him later that month, Sir Alec Clegg entitled his article 'Rigour and Inspiration' and went on to say, 'I still think that Christian Schiller may be rated by history as the most powerful influence to be exerted on the junior schools of Britain after the first world war.' So, to fast forward for a moment, it was in September 1977, when the newly formed primary Inspectorate was just beginning to make its influence felt and I had been Education Officer for some months, that I was invited to give the first Christian Schiller memorial lecture.

The lecture reads oddly today. It was given before the days of the National Curriculum, SATs, literacy hours, targets, Key Stages, attainment levels, league tables, Ofsted and the perceived need for lesson plans. None of these were things I had been required to deal with during my own years as a teacher. My remarks indicate, in general terms and to an audience which included parents and others interested in education as well as teachers, how I then understood what primary school teachers were or ought to be doing. Here follow some extracts of what I then believed and said:

There are two foundation stones on which our primary education has been built. The first derives from the observed facts about the way children develop. All children are not the same and individual children are not the same at different times in their development. What we offer in schools has to take account of this. It is as simple as that. The consequences, however, are by no means simple. In order to take account of individual difference and development over time, the teacher has to acquire skills in observation. These skills have theoretical underpinnings and there can be argument about the relative value of the various teaching methods put forward. But formal or informal, progressive or whatever the opposite is, knowledge and understanding of the individual child underlies skilled intervention – and skilled intervention is the teacher's task. Observation is at the heart of child-centred education. For the life of me I cannot see anything controversial or imprecise in that.

There are five points I want to make on observation and the intervention that follows. First, I do not know the medical or logical term to describe blockage by theory but it is a mistake to be too easily diverted from the simple act of attentive looking. Behold the child with impossible handwriting. Out comes the theory that illegibility is in some way the consequence of a whole catalogue of disadvantages occurring hundreds of yards from the school. So what can you expect? But the immediate problem – and you will guess I have real incidents in mind – is that the child is one of those left-handers who has reached, without correction, a particularly convoluted stage of pencil-holding, all made infinitely worse by a tiny stub of pencil. Now we can all of us help a child hold a pencil sensibly and provide a usable pencil, even in these hard times. But not if we don't notice what is needed. That's my first point. The biggest improvements we will make in our primary schools in the next few years will not be by doing complicated new things, but by doing simple things better.

My second point is that effective observation requires classification. We have to be wary of the consequences. But we must not let the idea of teacher-expectation determining a child's performance sink so deep in the consciousness that it becomes an immovable part of our intellectual furniture. As long as we are conscious of a problem we ought to have the wit consciously to avoid it. And there is one particular confusion to avoid. Because careful observation leads to classification and classification, it is thought, leads to trouble, the argument is reversed and classification is avoided by a deliberate effort not to notice difference. 'They are all children to me,' it is said, but the phrase and the goodwill behind it cannot be used to avoid tackling that child's need (mustn't label him a failure), or widening that one's scope, (mustn't let him think he's something special). We must not base our procedures on systematic myopia, however kindly meant.

My third point is that notions such as experience and activity need to be handled with care. It is one thing to say, following Dewey, Piaget and others, that at least at some stages in a child's learning all learning is grounded in experience. It is another thing to assume that all experience leads to learning. It does not. There are a thousand ill-prepared museum visits to prove that. Some experience, I would argue, is positively anti-educational. If the mind – a child's or an adult's – does not actively grasp and order what is presented to it, it may well happen that no trace of the experience remains. Which reminds me; in this wider sense, activity does not always require anyone to move about. Activity – intellectual activity – is the contrary of passivity and can occur when sitting at a table – or when bounded in a nutshell, as Hamlet put it – as well when engaged in some task that requires movement. Experience needs to be planned and selected. As Dewey once wrote: 'The central problem of an education based on experience is to select the kind of present experiences that live fruitfully and creatively in subsequent experiences.'

My fourth point is that it is not true that placing the child in the centre of a teacher's concerns is so impossibly difficult that only a few teachers of rare quality can attempt it. Any reasonably conscientious person can improve in awareness of others; and there is nothing soft or casual about the process. Intelligent and sensitive observation is a demanding business.

Finally, the work of observation that I have been describing is not all that is implied in child-centred education; but it underlies it. Through Hadow to Plowden and others, the scope of observation has widened. From the individual before us we have moved to think of that individual child in the wider setting that surrounds him, his home, his language, his culture. That awareness does not make a teacher into a social worker, just into a better teacher.

The second foundation stone on which our practices are built reflects the fact that education is taking place within western society and in the 1970s. The education we provide is therefore concerned with the intellectual and other values underlying our society; with moral values; though not necessarily with a particular set of religious beliefs; with an awareness of the context within which we are living, historically, geographically and politically and, running right through all this, the recognition that all children have an equal right to the full development of what they are or can become.

A second element in what we do relates to the here and now. It includes the basic skills our children need to acquire and what they need to know. It is within this element that we work at the changing curriculum.

So much for the two foundation stones on which we have built our primary education. There is rigour in each. Within the first, which requires knowledge of the child and his learning, the teacher is the fully independent professional. Within the second, there are wider issues and a partnership is at work. Society's values and the curriculum, what children need to learn and be able to do, are not solely for teachers to determine.

Nor, may I add, do I believe they ought to be in the sole or dominant charge of a local group of managers, parents or others, however selected. There are such groups through whose fingers the values of western society could slip rather messily to the floor. That is why the idea of education as a national service locally administered is not just an empty phrase. Society at large has to ensure the continuation of its values in the institutions it maintains.

The art of running a school, or a group of schools or of dealing with an individual child is to use what we build on the first of the foundation stones, our understanding of children, to support and enhance what we build on the second, the values and knowledge which, as a society, we want these children to acquire.

Several things make this difficult. There are those who ignore the child. They start, perhaps, from the curriculum and assume, on analogies from industry, that there is a definable end product: the educated child. People of this cast of mind think mainly in terms of the measurable and are particularly interested in the pursuit or enforcement of minimum standards. 'I am going to school today to enforce minimum standards' sounds well enough the first time if you say it briskly enough. But repeat it slowly three times and it goes off a little.

Over 100 years, HMI have done their best to deal with this last group of people by explaining what they know and have seen; thereby helping to avoid the notion that setting standards and testing their achievement somehow causes a general improvement in educational outcomes. The Senior Chief Inspector, Miss Sheila Browne, recently quoted Matthew Arnold in 1869 describing the over-employment of tests. He said 'it has two faults: it tends to make the instruction mechanical and to set a bar to duly extending it. School grants earned in this way – by the scholar performing a certain minimum laid down beforehand – must inevitably concentrate the teacher's attention on the means for producing this minimum, and not simply on the good instruction of his school. The danger to be guarded against is the mistake of treating these two – the producing this minimum successfully and the good instruction of the school – as if they were identical'. Very wise. Some hundred years later Christian Schiller put the same point rather differently: 'If a minimum of attainments is fixed such that it is in the power of all, it is demonstrably irrelevant to the vast majority and of no practical value. If a minimum is fixed such that some only can reach it, it must demonstrably be beyond the powers of the rest and its imposition will undoubtedly lead to a distortion of their powers. In my view the goal of a minimum of attainments is incompatible with continuity in the process of learning.'

That is what I call having the last word and it brings me to my conclusion. Christian Schiller is gone. Nevertheless I am hopeful in two quite different ways. In unsettled times, the role of HMI is becoming increasingly important. Miss Sheila Browne's address to the Council of Local Education Authorities this summer deserves to be widely read. What she had to say reminded us that there is a continuity of tradition running from Arnold, through Michael Sadler and Christian Schiller to the present day. The essence of that HMI voice is that it reflects and has at all times defended the balance I have been trying to describe. It applies the values and the intellectual skills of the civilisation of which we are a part to the observations of trained observers; and publishes the result.

My second ground for confidence is personal. It rests on the consciousness, derived from observation, of the quality that is being reached in our primary schools when teachers have a vision of what can be achieved. We all know such schools. We see the way the children live and learn in them; we see the pride they take in that learning and the high standards they achieve; we see the teachers who know their children and who use that knowledge to intervene in the development of each so that their confidence and skills are enlarged and their prospect of further development widened. Increasingly, we see parents sharing in this co-operative enterprise. Above all we see balance; teaching and learning built on the two foundations I have been describing: both deeply grounded in the values and scientific, empirical, approach of Western Europe. And in seeing these schools and the developing tradition of primary education in this country I am confirmed in the view that the direction in which our primary schools are moving is fundamentally the right one.

The reference to HMI in this talk reflects the high opinion of their expertise that was widespread at the time and I shared. From my years in Cumberland and since, I had valued their advice and I now admired what the Chief Inspector was now saying and doing. My remarks about primary education, made in 1977, may appear to have an air of complacency about them. If so, they were concealing deep concerns about the condition of many of ILEA's primary schools.

To return to the ILEA of 1976, what I did not realise, until the Auld Report was published on 1 July of that year, was that my view of what the functions of the inspectorate were differed from that of the ILEA's Chief Inspector and, it later became apparent, from that of some other members of the inspectorate. Paragraph 49 of Auld's Report read:

> The Authority's Inspectorate does not regard its prime function as being the inspection or checking of the quality of education being provided in the Authority's schools. The Inspectorate sees its main role as being the giving of advice and support to teachers in the schools. As Dr Birchenough, the Chief Inspector, put it in evidence to the Inquiry, the role of the Inspectors in checking the quality of education provided is only a secondary function; the quality control has largely devolved to the teachers themselves.

This was not my view of what the Inspectorate should be doing, though I later developed more sympathy for the role of the inspectorate in directly trying to bring about school improvement. Under the 1944 Education Act, local education authorities had a statutory duty to ensure that 'efficient instruction and training' was being provided in the institutions it maintained. If it was not the primary duty of the Inspectorate to provide assurances that the Authority was fulfilling its statutory duty, who else was there to do the job? The difference of perception involved here remained to be resolved.

The Camden School for Girls Summer School

To return to secondary education: the problem of ensuring high quality sixth form education in a comprehensive future remained a preoccupation throughout 1976. One idea for improving matters proved surprisingly easy to put into effect. In 1975, I had visited the summer school run by Camden School for Girls. This consisted of an intensive study of classical Greek. The school's headmistress, Carol Handley, was a classical scholar and her husband was professor of Greek at London University. The summer school was an eye-opening experience. At school, I had been taught Greek over a period of about five years from the age of eleven. I had not enjoyed the experience; nor had I learned much Greek. The sixth formers on the summer school, on the contrary, seemed to be thoroughly enjoying themselves. They were hard at it all day and had to be bundled reluctantly out of the school late in the evenings. Assume ten days of the summer school and ten hours of Greek a day, and it really seemed to amount to something like that. That made one hundred hours. The eye-opening bit for me was that, by the end of the summer school, the sixth formers grasp of Greek was, with one or two exceptions, far better established than mine had been after five half-hearted years of learning it. Motivation, good teaching and concentration of effort had combined to achieve this.

The idea of offering the experience of a summer school to any ILEA sixth formers who wanted to take part in one originated with a note to the Assistant Education Officer and the Staff Inspector for secondary schools, but apparently not to the Chief Inspector or the Education Officer:

NOTE to Mr Venvell (copy to Mr Jagger)   8 April 1976

SUMMER SCHOOLS

This is just a note to summarize what we have discussed at odd moments:

1. In summer 1976, the Camden classics summer school takes place. Perhaps all three of us could drop in so we have some views to share thereafter.

2. In December 1976 it should, saving elections, be clear that selection to secondary schools will end in September 1977.

3. In summer 1977, the idea is for there to be divisional summer schools.

The money will have to come from the centre, the impetus can only come locally. No impetus, no summer school.

4. Broadly, after the summer term examination period, the idea would be to aim at people about to enter the second year of the VI Form. Question: for two weeks or one?

5. A summer school would:

a. offer an intensive course in one or more areas of study to each person attending. Question: ought the work to be confined to one area only for each individual?

b. aim to introduce each individual to a level of work not yet achieved or, in some cases, even contemplated

c. introduce participants to the possibilities open in higher education

6. Those involved would include:

(a) Sixth Form teachers. One object would be give opportunities to teachers to discuss their work together in a concrete way. The summer school would be a form of in-service training.

(b) Our own Colleges, Institutes, Polytechnics and, no doubt, some University Departments. One or two institutions might take a particular interest in one Division, for example.

7. I leave it that you will discuss together whether to proceed and how. Then please speak.

In 1977, that broad offer was made and, both then and in the following years, summer schools were attended by an increasing number of London's sixth formers.

At some point in May, I learnt that Eric Briault was retiring at the end of 1976. I had never bothered to find out exactly how old he was and he had never indicated that he would be leaving that year. I was not at all sure that I would be able to do his job well enough but was quite sure I would not want to remain as deputy to someone the Authority thought could do it better. So I duly filled in the forms when the post was advertised and nominated two referees: Sir Alec Clegg and the Chairman of the Haberdashers schools. I was subsequently appointed Education Officer to the Inner London Education Authority on 13 July 1976, three days after the publication of the Auld Report. The salary was £16,128, excluding the London Weighting of £472. 'Any salary progression', the appointment letter went on to say, 'is, however, subject to the constraints imposed under Government pay policies'. There was no question of performance-related pay in those days. The appointment was to run from 1 January 1977, the day after Dr Briault's retirement; but it was from mid-July 1976 that the tone of everything I wrote began to change.

After the committee had appointed me as ILEA's Education Officer, I stayed behind for a few minutes to have some further discussion with members of the appointment committee. I then went along the corridor to speak to the other candidates, all of whom were colleagues of long standing from other local authorities. I recall feeling relieved rather than elated. At least the future seemed clear and secure, though it turned out to be neither. But any inflated sense of self-satisfaction tended to evaporate quickly in County Hall. As I reached the waiting room in which the other candidates were sitting, I found that Sir Ashley had got there before me. 'So you see', I heard him tell them, with rather more emphasis than I found reassuring, 'it was really a case of the devil you know . . . '.

The New York Urban Coalition

Later in the year, while still Deputy Education Officer, an opportunity arose for me to join a small group of Teacher Centre wardens, plus Alan Radford, a District Inspector, and Anne Sofer, an ILEA member, on a visit to New York. The purpose of the visit was to look at some of the initiatives being taken by the New York Urban Coalition. On my return to London, I wrote a report to the Policy Committee on aspects of what we had seen and learnt from our visit. In the extracts below, I refer first to the New York education system as 'under strain'.

> There is a movement of skilled workers out of the City. In the past few years, several of the largest corporations have moved from New York, taking with them jobs and an important part of the revenue base on which the City's finances depend. In general, lack of planning in New York and the presence of it in London have had proportionately about the same effect in reducing the number and nature of the jobs available in the City.

The comment on London planning derived from my view that many of London's inner city problems had been created by well-intentioned planners. They had successfully encouraged the movement of large numbers of stable families from inner London, including many of its best teachers, to new developments in the suburbs of London or in new towns elsewhere. Unfortunately, in their enthusiasm, they had given insufficient thought to the problems they had left behind for others to deal with.

The view of ethnic minority communities in New York, in some areas increasingly becoming the majority, was that education, dominated by white educators, was failing their children. Parents were determined to hold the schools to account. The argument was not conducted in theoretical terms. I described an occasion in 1968 when eighty three teachers had been cornered in a school hall:

> The lights in the auditorium were then switched on and off and the teachers were told from the crowd that if they came back to the district they would be carried out of it in pine boxes. As the crowd was armed with sticks and wore bandoliers of bullets, the teachers could hardly shrug this off as hyperbole.

Looked at in 1976, the New York notion of a school differed from the London one:

> Subject to all the usual cautionary remarks about the limited value of

generalisations, it can be said that whereas we ordinarily think of a school as something organic, with a life of its own, the New Yorkers think of it more as a vehicle for delivering a curriculum to its passengers, the children. There are four main components of a school: the premises, the curriculum, the teachers and the children. In New York, the emphasis is on the two former. The schools, despite all the surrounding hazards, seem cleaner than ours; the curriculum is looked after with equal care. Each Grade has its fully worked out curriculum within which there is room for experiment but to which there is no approved alternative. Given the fixed points of the premises and the curriculum, the importance of the individual teachers diminishes somewhat. To return to the metaphor of the vehicle, teachers are seen as interchangeable parts of the machinery. If one teacher/part goes or is moved, any other teacher qualified in the grade can take his place; so the recent high incidence of movement of teachers between schools in New York is not thought as damaging as it would be here.

In considering the New York response to the attacks on the system by community groups, I commented:

1. Partial decentralisation of the schools was the compromise finally reached, but the determination of parents and others to make teachers accountable for the achievements of their pupils remains unabated. Elementary schools, for example, are annually and publicly ranked from 1 to 800 in terms of the scores achieved in reading and other tests.

2. A difficulty has been and remains that the measurable outputs of a school, and therefore those for which a teacher can be held accountable, are few in number and limited in their scope.

3. Under these strong external pressures, teachers have tended to confine themselves to areas where their accountability lies. Within schools, the heavy concentration on the skills required to score well in the standardised tests is everywhere evident. What is not evident is that this concentrated effort has been accompanied by any improvement either in the test scores or in the standards these purport to measure.

One afternoon, Alan Radford, Anne Sofer and I attended a meeting held by New York's Board of Education (see photo on the next page).

The tense look on my face had arisen because there were growing signs that the meeting was about to be brought to an untimely end by an angry group of people already starting to surge towards the platform. The surge succeeded and the meeting ended abruptly. Apparently, this happened quite often but casualties were rare.

During our visit, we had a chance to look at the efforts being made to improve the education of minorities in New York. 'Minorities' had already, in much of New York, become majorities. Whereas in 1960 63% of the school population was defined as white, by 1976 the proportion was 34% and still falling. Black Americans and newcomers from Hispanic countries, in approximately equal numbers, had become the true majority. We were impressed by the risks being run in London if some of the lessons from New York were not learned. I was made aware of this when talking about London's response to the arrivals from overseas which we were now dealing with. I was interrupted by the New York's Deputy Chancellor, Bernie Gifford, a brilliant product of Harlem and then Harvard. He asked if he could continue with the remarks I had been making. He then did so, anticipating what I was about to say with remarkable accuracy. When asked how he had managed that, he replied that he had just been repeating what he had being saying in the mid-1960s but no longer did. Any form of colour blindness, he told us, would not work. Needs were there, both in the majority and minority communities, but those needs were not always the same. The sometimes different needs had to be identified and then met. The consequences of ignoring this would be dire. The New Yorkers left us in no doubt of this.

During the visit, we saw the effect of teaching children arriving in New York with little or no English, at least for some of the time, in their mother tongue. We watched a class of recently arrived Italian children being taught in English by a native Italian speaker. They were being taught something about the Mediterranean in the simplest possible language. The class appeared to be a dull and unresponsive lot, slumped in their chairs and unsmiling; very much like a group of English children of the same age being taught something boring on a warm afternoon towards the end of term. Suddenly the teacher lost patience. He addressed them in a rapid burst of irritable Italian. The children sat up. He fired questions at them in Italian. Hands shot up, faces became animated, smiles appeared, the lesson crackled along with everyone alert and trying to get a word in. The children were transformed. When I got back to the Harvard Club that evening, I wrote down a single sentence to take back to England: 'No one has the right to deprive a child of his intelligence.'

A visit to High School Redirections illustrated the effect of dealing with disruptive pupils in places away from school – in this case the top floor of a deserted warehouse – in circumstances where their relationships with teachers were good enough to enable them to resume some form of education. There they were, these sometimes dangerous 'disruptives' who could not manage or be managed in a conventional school, sitting at their desks, some in overcoats for the place was barely heated, and getting on with a variety of tasks they had negotiated with their, uniformly friendly, teachers. None of the disruptives now seemed to feel the need to disrupt. Their teachers appeared to have found ways of connecting with each of these young people and enabling them to succeed in their own way. Continued experience of failure, at school or elsewhere, does not make an individual better at failing. Far from inducing that individual to improve; more often it reinforces failure.

We spent some time looking at what was being done to help the lowest performing children, not always the poorest, in one of the High Schools. We found a small section of this school very different from the rest. The two rooms used by these failing children were attractively carpeted. Books were everywhere. The whole atmosphere was quiet and relaxed, quite unlike the noisy and busy, police-controlled, corridors in the main part of the school. The school day was not separated into different lessons. The activities the, mostly black, young people were engaged in during what, in England, we thought of as the integrated day, were very similar to those in some of the small primary schools I had visited in Cumberland. The logic of the arrangement was clear. As the aim of the extra money was to help a particular group of pupils reach the standard of other pupils who did not receive the money, to know whether the money was having that effect meant that the group receiving that extra money had to be taught separately. So pupils not in the group thought to need extra help were not allowed into their two rooms or permitted to use the excellent stock of books on display there. We did not find this, admittedly logical, way of ensuring that differential funding led to differential improvement attractive, though test results showed some signs of its having that effect. It was also possible, we concluded, that putting the best teachers in charge of children who most needed good teaching would be just as effective as the extra resources these children were receiving. In many London schools, wherever the best teachers were, too few of them seemed to be in the schools or in the parts of a school that most needed them.

Finally, one main purpose of our visit was to look at the idea of an urban coalition. In reporting later to the Policy Committee, I quoted remarks made by the first Chairman of the New York Urban Coalition in 1969:

> After the divisive and distressing riots of the summer of 1967, it was

apparent to many leading citizens, including Mayor Lindsay, Andrew Heiskell, and A. Philip Randolph of New York City, that government had largely failed to deal effectively with those conditions in our cities that in great part gave rise to the riots. Such private efforts as existed already, some of them excellent, were, in total impact, inadequate. Why not then, it was asked, try and pull together the enormously diverse energies and talents of the private sector – business, the neighbourhood communities, labor, foundations and religious and educational organisations – in a concerted effort to make improvements in the situation, if only to get a dialogue started once again.

In my report, I went on to say:

> It is impossible for an outsider visiting New York not to be impressed with the energy these extra-governmental forces have, in combining together in an effort to, as they put it, 'improve the quality of life in this city'. In a sense, New York is two stages ahead of London. The degree of criticism of New York education, for example, has been very much greater than anything yet seen in London. That is the first stage. The second is that it has been accompanied by a range of positive moves by agencies outside the education system, of which the Urban Coalition is a foremost example, which we have also not seen in London.

Examples given of the Urban Coalition's recent initiatives were:

> The development of mini-schools. These are schools within a school where the emphasis is on close relationship between teacher and pupil, often coupled with a central point of interest; for example, a mini-school where the particular emphasis was on the performing arts or on one of the local industries

> The creation of school-based planning teams. These include members from the school's whole 'constituency', in particular, parents. Their purpose is to ensure that what happens in an area of the curriculum or for a particular group of children is grounded in the considered acceptance and support of all who may be affected

> The idea of 'magnet' schools; for example, a High School into which a neighbouring industry (e.g. the aircraft passenger transport industry) makes a major contribution to the school in terms of the skills of their own staff: geography, mathematics, languages and so on. The effect of this on attendance and the proportion of pupils going on to Higher Education has been considerable.'

My report to the Policy Committee concluded with four matters which I thought it might be useful to explore further. These were not framed as recommendations for debate; just as suggestions to be considered:

> 1. ways of improving the data base on which the Authority's planning rests.

2. new approaches to the problem of reconciling accountability with an improvement rather than an impoverishment of what actually happens in schools.

3. how to extend our present efforts to teach minority and non-English speaking pupils to the limit of their potential.

4. whether New York's idea of urban coalition – a combination of interests and institutions whose object is to move beyond sporadic criticism of the public services to a serious effort to help improve them and therefore the quality of life in the City itself – has any part to play in London.

The first three are thoughts that apply within ILEA. The fourth raises wider, deeper and, in the long term, perhaps even more important issues.

So much for the written record. The visit proved important both in what it suggested might be possible in London but also in what it warned us to avoid. On the positive side was the whole 'can do' attitude, of which the Urban Coalition was just one expression; another was the boldness with which the problem of disaffected young people was being tackled. High School Redirections, for example, engaged with a group of young people, several times the size of anything we would have contemplated in London. In general, there was the readiness to put ideas into practice. Final decisions in an education service the size of Greater London were taken by seven people: one from each of the five boroughs of New York and two appointed by the Mayor. In practice, the core of the decision-making element of the ILEA consisted in about that same number of people.

What New York convinced us we needed to avoid was giving teachers a motive for doing the wrong thing. That was what the New York school system, in our view, often did. One reason for the sheer dulness of much of the teaching we saw there was that it required teachers to concentrate on lifting a proportion of the pupils above a prescribed standard. This was the mistake that Matthew Arnold, HMI as well as poet, had drawn attention to nearly one hundred years earlier. Its effect was to direct the teacher's efforts on the pupils just above or just below the prescribed standard at the expense of pupils with no prospect of reaching that standard or, just as worrying, those who were already well above it and needed no further attention from the teacher to reach it. At the back of the New York classrooms that we spent time in, we regularly met the very dull and the very bright fooling about together and learning very little.

Listing the elementary schools, on the basis of standardised tests, from one to eight hundred was not helpful either. It did not do much for parents in the Bronx, in school number 780 there, to tell them that if they could afford to live across on Staten Island, they might have had access to school number 100. The effect of the list on schools towards the bottom of it, already dealing with intractable problems in unsettled communities, was to encourage them to do the wrong thing: in this instance to get rid of their most troublesome and low-performing pupils. Schools knew well enough that the obvious way to improve average performance in the tests, on which schools in New York were being judged, was to rid themselves of the children who did worst in them. Yet these were the children that most needed their help. Like several other thoroughly bad ideas, these two were later imported to England from America by impressionable but inexperienced British politicians or their equally inexperienced advisers.

Shortly after returning from New York, as the future Education Officer, I sent a note to Sir Ashley Bramall. I had no idea how Eric Briault and Sir Ashley communicated with each other. Their offices were close to each other on the floor below mine. As I only went to see either by invitation, all I knew was that, in relation to his political colleagues, Sir Ashley's title of Leader meant just that. So the importance of rapidly establishing sound relationships with him was obvious. But how was this to be done? One thing I had learnt from my ventures into logic at Oxford was that any question determines the form of its answer. So it was important only to ask Sir Ashley questions that had answers I might be in a position to supply. With that in mind, I decided to set out, somewhat informally, my suggestions on what I thought the Authority ought to concentrate on doing in the following year. If any of my suggestions did not go down well, they could quietly be withdrawn. Outright rejection, by Sir Ashley or by anyone else, of any definite suggestion I made as Education Officer, as I had learnt from Frank Barraclough over a decade earlier, was something I intended to avoid from the outset. A related consideration, learnt from Barraclough's report to the North Riding Committee on circular 10/65, was to leave out anything, however important I believed it to be, that I was not yet in any position to deal with. So there was to be no mention of the special schools, the future of the Stoke D'Abernon Teachers' Centre, the whole way in which the Authority's budget was put together, the future of the ESWC initiative, relationships with the London boroughs or the role of the Inspectorate; and there would only be a brief mention of the Education Television Service, on which I had been casting an increasingly cold eye.

Finally, my note was designed to prevent the huge overload of work from which Eric Briault had, in my view, suffered as Education Officer. So there were to be no dates, details or undertakings of any kind put forward at this stage. The way to avoid breaking a promise is not to make it in the first place. After suggesting to Sir Ashley what I thought we needed to be doing, I needed to know, as soon as possible after taking over in January, what he and his colleagues wanted to add to – or perhaps subtract from – my list of suggestions.

Anyone with experience of local or national government will not get beyond the first paragraph of my note to Sir Ashley without wanting answers to a series of questions. What do the words 'us' and 'we' convey about the relationship between a future administrative head of the education service and its political leadership? In particular, what is this about 'policy lines', for are not these simply a matter for the politicians to devise and for their officials to implement? In that connection, why is there no reference to existing policies, manifesto commitments and so on? And what of the tone of the note? Is this the way officials were in the habit of writing to the political leadership of the ILEA? Although the note itself shows signs of haste, it was written with more care than at first may be apparent. Here it is, exactly as it was written, with explanatory notes to explain what might otherwise remain obscure.

Note to the Leader   ILEA: 1977   26 November 1976

1. Next year, it should be possible for us to launch five or six initiatives. To attempt more is probably to achieve less. At the same time, we have to leave space – thinking and organising time – to respond to about the same number of initiatives from outside ILEA. My own suggested list of initiatives is in para 2; likely impulses from outside or other pressures upon us are in para 3. As always, the problem is going to be to avoid overloading the system by embarking on schemes we cannot carry through; so I hope we can settle the main policy lines fairly soon.

2. ILEA initiatives

(a) Improvements in Primary Education

This is my main personal interest. I would like to make a report on this, the first that I put forward in January. The report would include what we know about standards and how we propose to improve them. In particular, it would deal with the work of the ten new inspectors. Amongst other things, I want to make it clear that they should spend a full day during next year in every school for which they carry some responsibility. This remains to be finally agreed with the Inspectorate themselves. The effect of the inspectors' work next year should be to enable me to put up a full report on primary education at the end of 1977. I see my job as giving this activity impetus and stopping other people getting in the way (working parties and so on). It should not take a great deal of administrative time. We now have the people in post to shift the system upwards provided they are not diverted from their task.

(b) High-quality work in our comprehensive schools

We have kept very quiet on the progress of re-organisation because essentially we have been trying to do two things:

First: make sure the 1977 entry is properly dealt with, first of all in the primary schools and, secondly, at the receiving end in the newly-formed comprehensive schools, including some of our existing 'comprehensive' institutions. The big worry is that some of our schools will fail to respond to the change in their entry. The Inspectorate are engaged in trying to get this right. I am writing an article in Contact soon to try and help this along.

Second: improve the quality of sixth form education. There is absolutely no reason why we should not produce the best range of opportunities in the U.K. We have the institutions and the people here to do it. It has been heavy going with some of our schools but our aim has been to involve, in particular, some of the leading grammar school teachers in new thinking about what can be done at sixth form level. Partly this is to prevent any backsliding on their part; but largely it is to ensure that their skills really are fully incorporated into the comprehensive system. As things have been moving rather slowly, we are trying to get the Camden heads to shock some of the others into emulation. Dr Conway is trying to get some form of summer school going in 1977 so that we can display the range of opportunities open to children at sixth form level in our schools and, perhaps almost as important, give our sixth form teachers the experience of working together that I have referred to. No doubt someone is going to describe this as elitist but I believe we must move quickly to a position where if you want first-rate sixth form education London is the place to go for it. Again, this will not need a great deal of administrative time: we have an inspectorate team that can bring this on.

The reference to Dr Conway, a distinguished head of the Jewish Free School in Camden, is an illustration of the 'economical with the truth' approach with which administrators working in a political context are familiar; although a distinguished Cabinet Secretary was later criticised for his frankness in pointing this out. As the minute of 8 April 1976, quoted earlier, indicates, Dr Conway was not trying to get sixth form summer schools going entirely on his own initiative. He was being encouraged to do this from County Hall. Why not say so directly? Because if the Leader or, more probably, some element amongst his colleagues objected to the idea, Dr Conway might have to be asked not to pursue the idea further. But at least the Education Officer would not have had a proposal turned down: and having proposals turned down did not, in my experience, make for efficient administration. Fortunately, in this instance, the idea of summer schools, as an extension of what the Authority could offer to highly motivated sixth formers, was welcomed; so a proposal to develop them, with much of the preparation already completed, was immediately supported. The first summer schools were up and running in the summer of 1977.

(c) Race Relations and Children of Minority Groups

Now our schools are becoming more stable, we need to know who is in them and what we are doing to help them. I am clear that we are not doing enough for our ethnic minorities. The report by HMI on their work in Brixton will not show us in a particularly good light and the initiatives we have taken there are already insufficient. They leave out the crucial point: the quality of what is happening in the schools themselves. A whole number of things need to be put together: finding the teachers who are working effectively, supporting them with proper resources, looking again at where responsibility for dealing with the whole problem rests, and so on. To take the last point, our present arrangements of one or two inspectors is an example of our incremental approach whereby we identify a problem and then appoint someone to deal with it. What is needed is a re-ordering of our thinking.

This whole area of work, which I believe to be crucially important for the Authority, will take a great deal of time and effort and will lead to a number of people being upset within this building and outside it. Rather like the transfer issue, unless someone gets hold of it firmly and soon I do not believe the various threads will be brought together or that anything much will actually happen.

The general thinking behind this paragraph had its origins in the first rate analytical work of the ILEA's Research and Statistics Department. Teachers and ILEA officers and inspectors were alike agreed that we were now getting better at managing the demographically different school population that had been developing. The facts indicated otherwise. The urgent need to find ways to deal with this derived from that New York visit some of us had made in 1976. It led to a report to the Education Committee in 1977 and the development of new section of the inspectorate. This in turn led to the appointment of the ILEA's first inspectors from London's ethnic minorities.

(d) F\HE Re-organisation

It looks as though this should be completed during next year. There is a whole range of suggestions that will have to be discussed soon which I will not trouble you with here. Considerable administrative time will be taken up; mostly Mr Bevan's.

(e) Re-organisation of the EO's Department

In general, I believe the way the system works is going to be more important than the forms through which it is administered. Again, I believe that distributed administration carries with it certain strains which one can partially reduce but cannot remove entirely. So the improvements we make will not be dramatic. Nevertheless, I believe the administrative system we have or will move to is perfectly adequate to deal with the four major issues outlined above. Any re-organisation proposals will take a great deal of administrative time. One of my main concerns will be to see that it does not inhibit the other initiatives which, frankly, I believe to be of greater importance.

In fact, a series of re-organisation proposals proved even more difficult, took longer, were more time-consuming and, in some quarters, far more controversial than I had expected.

3. Other matters which will impinge upon the work of the ILEA

(a) the Taylor Committee and its findings (School governing bodies)

(b) Warnock and its implications; (Special Education)

(c) development of our ways of monitoring standards

(d) advance preparation for budgetary problems – the future of ETV and so on

(e) development plans for primary and secondary education and our use of accommodation.

Early in 1977 the extent to which unforeseen events impinged on the programme of work sketched out in this minute became evident. Fortunately, the proposals made in earlier paragraphs were sufficiently few to avoid the need to abandon any of them.

> Apart from (c), with which Dr Shipman will be concerned, (a) and (b) will be very much for our new people, Mr Stubbs and Mr Brighouse, to carry forward. I believe we are only going to get real results if they take a fresh look at these problems and go at them hard. Certainly, this is what I will encourage them to do even if it means having to re-think some of the policies the Authority has comparatively recently adopted. You will at least wish to see the options.

As their later careers indicate, it seems unlikely that any Chief Education Officer could have found himself with an abler deputy than John Bevan, already in post, and being about to encounter Bill (later Sir William) Stubbs and Tim (later Sir Tim) Brighouse as his immediate colleagues. The remark 'you will at least wish to see the options' would have been correctly understood by Sir Ashley as Education Officer language for saying 'you will almost certainly *not* wish to see suggestions for re-thinking policies the Committee has recently adopted but you may be receiving advice suggesting reasons for doing so.'

Finally, what am I supposed to be doing? I shall be doing what I can:

> (a) to provide the impetus on the primary side [2(a) above, (not time-consuming)]
> (b) pulling together work on re-organisation of the department (time-consuming) with colleagues, in particular Mr Bevan
> (c) dealing with our national commitments; working with the Director-General and with leading GLC colleagues (unpredictably time-consuming).
> (d) working with leading members (as required).
> As I see it, the heads of branches, at deputy level, will be operationally in charge of their areas of work unless I specifically reserve some element of this to myself. This will mean that they have more direct control of what they are doing than any of us do now. A part of my role here, it seems to me, is to act as a person to whom leading members go if the direction the administration is taking is in some way unsatisfactory to them.

The reference to heads of branches at deputy level reflected a major change in the way the administration was to work over the next five years. A free-standing Deputy, such as I had been, with no direct responsibility for any branch of the service, left him with too much time on his hands. Deputies, particularly if they are younger than their chief and ambitious, need to be kept busy. John Bevan, with a complex task of dealing with the whole of the Further and Higher education system, was First Deputy. He would take over if ever I was away, which I occasionally was, or ever ill, which fortunately I never was. One of the two new senior officers to be appointed, both later raised to second deputy level, would look after schools and the other be responsible for the whole general purposes area, including finance. These three would deal directly with the chairmen of committees and draft the reports going to those committees. Every Monday morning, with the Chief Inspector and with no substitutes allowed, the four of us would meet as a Senior Officers Group to sort out any problems between areas of responsibility, consider new developments and, in general, ensure that no batons were being dropped as the weeks went by. The purpose of this was to avoid the Education Officer being overwhelmed or, just as troublesome, become overwhelming as the sole ultimate source of decision-making on the officer side.

The physical separation of the Education Officer, in a large office on a separate floor from his senior colleagues, could not be avoided without disturbing the Education Officer's close relationship with the Leader, whose office was just down the corridor. Systematic and regular meetings between the senior officers group, with the unfortunate acronym of SOG, at least meant that, if anything went wrong, it would be clear with whom responsibility rested. It also meant that, as these meetings were held regularly, there was no need for the sometimes lengthy minutes between senior officers, such as those I had written during my time as Deputy. Communication at the top became shorter brisker, and usually oral. As for my acting as the person to whom leading members came if they wanted something done, this required members to ask me or my deputies to have a problem dealt with rather than try and tackle it on their own with some other members of staff. This is what Harvey Hinds, intent on avoiding the Education Officer, had done with disastrous consequences for the reputation of the ILEA and for himself. With rare exceptions, these arrangements worked well and applied to relationships with members of the majority and minority parties alike.

My minute to Sir Ashley led to a brief discussion between us. His approach was that I should get on with the suggestions I had made and he would meanwhile decide with his colleagues what other things they wanted done. The London Labour Party manifesto had only detained us briefly. Sir Ashley had drafted most of the section dealing with education himself. Helpfully, he had only committed the ILEA to doing a number of things that he knew we were already doing.

Dr Briault, ILEA's Education Officer 1971 - 1976

In this one-sided account of some of what happened during my time as his Deputy, it seems right to leave the last word with Eric Briault. That requires scrolling back a year to explain what follows. In 1975, a potentially damaging problem had arisen. As part of the arrangements for enabling selective schools to take a comprehensive intake, some schools moved from their existing premises to larger re-developed ones. This needed money and, if the school was a voluntary aided school, a proportion of that money had to come from the governing body. On this occasion the school was voluntary aided and, was to move from its overcrowded site in Spitalfields to the remodelled premises of a girls school that was closing. Before deciding to go ahead, the governing body wanted some guarantee that, if the timing of the sale of their premises did not coincide with payments that had to be made for the work of adapting new premises, the Authority would contribute up to £1 million to be paid back when the sale of the school premises finally occurred. This made obvious good sense to the senior ILEA officer concerned, who was an expert in building matters but not in the law of education. The move had to be completed quickly and the risk of the Spitalfields premises not being sold for far more than the sum being guaranteed appeared small. The officer sent a note to the Chairman of the Development Sub-Committee recommending Chairman's action to authorise a contract that included this fall-back clause. The Chairman, on that advice, signed the requisite order and the GLC contracts department drew up the necessary contract. This was then duly signed and sealed. The officer concerned, who had been clearing his desk in anticipation of this, later that week left the Authority's service for a senior post in Scotland.

The arrangement itself had seemed simple common-sense. Unfortunately, common sense is an unreliable guide to what is lawful. So when the Spitalfields premises remained unsold and the governors needed to pay their builders, they sent a letter requesting the payment of the £1,000,000 due to them in these circumstances under the terms of their contract. The letter caused consternation in County Hall. The arrangement that had been made was clearly ultra vires. A local education authority had no power to make capital payments for building at a voluntary aided school. The proposed payment was one the Authority's Comptroller of Finance would refuse to make and it was he alone who could sign the cheque. The governors were invited to come to County Hall to discuss the problem. We had difficulty in detaching them from their coats. The meeting that followed was led on our side by a formidable Scottish lawyer. The deputation from this long-established grammar school included a High Court Judge and two QCs. The meeting was unfriendly. The QCs waved the contract in front of us. They were furious on being told that the money specified in the contract could not be paid. The High Court judge took over. This ended with our agreeing with him that there was no doubt about what the Authority had contracted to do. But there was equally no doubt that we were unable to do it, even if taken to court.

After a complex set of discussions with the District Auditor and the Department of Education and after several months of to-ing and fro-ing, we arrived at the solution with which we had begun. If the governing body was prepared to change the status of the school from voluntary aided to voluntary controlled, in the process giving the Authority a majority on the governing body, the promised payment could lawfully be made. Otherwise it could not. The irritable flow of documents was dealt with by Fred Hogben, possibly the last ILEA employee to arrive at the office each day attached to a bowler hat. In the end, the governors agreed to the change in the status of their school and what the Press, with London's Evening Standard to the fore, would have trumpeted as a major public scandal had it become public knowledge, was avoided. At a time when the William Tyndale affair was making headlines, that was just as well. The problem here was that a Committee Chairman had been put at risk by allowing herself to be persuaded by an ILEA official to bypass the usual procedure for dealing with contracts of this kind. Had she kept to the rules, with which she was familiar, the legal flaw in what he had suggested would immediately have been picked up. The necessary rescue operation had been time-consuming and, at times, unpleasant to deal with.

Eight days before the meeting of the Committee which was to appoint his successor and in the knowledge that I was a candidate, Eric Briault wrote me a letter. He sent copies to the Leader and Deputy Leader of the Authority, two persons who would be directly involved in the appointment. The letter was carefully worded. Canvassing for an appointment was strictly forbidden under the Authority's Standing Orders; hence his apparently casual reference to his letter as one 'which I dare say you will be surprised to receive.' Scrupulous as ever, he was making it clear that I had no knowledge of the letter in advance. Whether I deserved such magnanimity after I had given him such patchy support over the previous five years is another matter. I have removed the name of the school but here is what he wrote:

> Dear Peter,   5 July 1976
>
> I feel I must place on record my deep appreciation of and great admiration for the way you have dealt with this matter. Since the time, about a year ago, when you and I first became aware of the situation in which we and the Authority had been placed, the problems and complexities have been seen to be immense. After we had reported on the matter in the early autumn, you offered to handle subsequent action personally and I most gratefully accepted that offer. You have succeeded in keeping all the complicated aspects under full and careful consideration by all the interests concerned without its becoming a matter of public dispute, as it might well have done, and you have helped the governors in their present decision while doing everything possible to explore a solution they would have preferred. I am aware of the immense amount of your time this has taken and even more the severe pressures involved. I can only say that I and the Authority are fortunate to have had you and your special skills in negotiation and personal relations to do it. I am sending a copy of this letter, which I dare say you will be surprised to receive, to the Leader and Mrs Garside.
>
> Yours very sincerely,   Eric.

The heading given to the next chapter of this book is 'Education Officer'. For the years I have so far been describing, Eric Briault was that person. The best and fairest account of him, as a person and educational administrator, is contained in a privately printed document written on his retirement by his friend and colleague Bill Braide. Appropriately, he called it A London Man, for it was in London that Eric Briault had taught, become a leading inspector, then Deputy Education Officer and finally Education Officer to the ILEA. Only fifty copies were produced. Mine is in the Library of the Institute of Education. My own public appreciation of Eric Briault's achievements had to wait until I wrote his obituary in the Association of Education Committee's weekly publication, Education, on 26 January 1996. Here are a few paragraphs from what I then wrote:

> Dr Briault brought to his years at the centre of inner London's education service a rare combination of academic distinction, educational understanding and administrative skill. Above all, he brought absolute personal integrity. That, as Education Officer, he might occasionally be mistaken was conceivable; that he would ever be other than honest and direct in what he said or did was not.

> Briault had far more to offer than administrative skills of a high order. Beneath a cool, controlled exterior lay depths of personal commitment. That commitment was most notably expressed in his 1973 Report to the Education Committee: 'An Education Service for the Whole Community'. In that report he asked of the education service, of every part of it: whom are we failing to reach and what can the different elements of the service, working co-operatively, do to remedy this?

> With generous support from senior ILEA politicians, Briault urged London's education service to tackle the issue of educational and social exclusion, not in theory but in practical ways which the Authority had committed itself to support. So it was that, for the first time in London's educational history and almost certainly for the last, from nursery school to institutions of higher education, there was a sustained effort to reach out to the missing thousands.

> The political tides of the 1980's swept away much of that thinking and nearly all of the initiatives that sprung from it: but the vision remains and, when all allowance is made for the contribution of others, that vision for London and the values that informed it were Eric Briault's.

> In these days of short-term contracts and fragmented education services, the notion of a person of first-rate ability devoting thirty years, first as an inspector and then as a leading administrator, to one great city may seem strange. But in that respect, as in other more personal ones on which I have barely touched, those who worked with Eric Briault will know how much has been lost. With a mixture of admiration for that over-arching achievement and sadness at its passing, I suspect that we also have to recognise that we will not look upon his like again.

Nor will we. Hence the sadness of the Shakespearean echo in that last sentence. Six years before Eric Briault died, London had become, as it still remains some twenty five years later, the only great city in the western world without its own education service.

Education Officer (1 January 1977 to 31 August 1982) Chapter 3: 1977

On the way into County Hall, on the morning of 1 January 1977, the difference between now being the Education Officer of the ILEA, rather than its Deputy, felt huge. There was little logic in this. During November and for much of December, Eric Briault had been taking accumulated leave. Earlier in the year, he had been unwell and away from the office for several weeks. Towards the end of December, he had cleared his desk and his room was now empty of all trace of him. I had been in and out of that room nearly every day to be close to the office staff. They had continued to deal with incoming paper and problems as though nothing was about to change. Nothing of mine had been moved downstairs into that large wood-pannelled room. Briault was still inner London's Education Officer, ultimately responsible for the running of the complex system he had managed with such assurance, still there to be phoned or to be asked to decide. In those last few days, I did not phone and there had been nothing for him to decide. But I knew where he could be reached; and it was during that time that I came to acknowledge how much the London education service owed him for his integrity, his skill and commitment.

As I moved through the outside office, through the waiting room and into the room that was now unquestionably mine, the sense of oppression lifted. There was so much to do. So I was soon back in the outer office, asking someone to help me shift the desk against the outside wall. Rather than talk from behind a desk, I wanted to be able to swivel round and speak directly to anyone entering the room. But did I really know what the ILEA's Education Officer spent his time doing? I had accompanied Briault to public meetings, watched him deal with committees, heard him give talks to teachers and others, but had no idea how, when or in what terms he communicated with his colleagues or with leading members of the Authority. Nor had I done more than glance at the way the role of Education Officer was defined in the Authority's Standing Orders. It was with these that elected members and officers alike had to comply. So, on that first evening, I took a copy home. In a slightly later version that reflected the addition of two new Second Deputy posts to the existing Deputy Education Officer post as chief officers, this is how the Education Officer's job was there defined:

ILEA Standing order: The Education Officer shall:

1. be the head of the Authority's service, the chief executive and chief administrative and co-ordinating officer, the leader of the team of chief officers;

2. be the principal adviser to the Education Committee and sub-committees on matters of professional, administrative or managerial educational policy with responsibility for securing co-ordinated advice to enable members of the Authority (a) to decide the Authority's objectives, policies and priorities and (b) to monitor and control the implementation of policy and the use of resources and ensure consistency of the department's proposals with the Authority's policy

3. advise the Education Committee and sub-committees on all major questions of organisation and on questions of staff management including the distribution of functions across the Authority's service.

4. be responsible for securing the professional and managerial effectiveness of the Authority's teaching staff throughout the Authority's service.

5. notwithstanding the identification of powers and duties ascribed to Chief Officers in the sections below, have the right to intervene in and report separately to the Education Committee and sub-committees on any of the services provided by the Authority.

The most important section of this job description was in 2. This made four things clear: that the Education Officer was the adviser to the Education Committee as a whole and not just to the majority party; that he had to secure co-ordinated advice (hence Dr Briault's dislike, which I rapidly came to share, of having dissenting views presented to committees or to leading members by ILEA staff); that his advice was intended to help members 'decide the Authority's objectives.' In other words, the Education Officer was to share in the policy making process, though decisions would, of course, ultimately remain those of the Authority. Finally, the Education Officer's department was expected to have its own proposals to make but had to ensure these were consistent with whatever the Authority's policies were, so far as these had been articulated.

Sir Ashley Bramall was a lawyer and took documents such as Standing Orders seriously. His interpretation of these was that it was not open to him directly to tell the Education Officer what to do or say; only a committee of the Authority could do that. Nor could other than routine decisions be taken in private. There had to be an item on some agenda, seen by members from the Opposition, for any important decision to be reached and then acted upon. What then of reports made to and agreed by the Policy Sub-Committee (from now on 'the Policy Committee')? The Policy Committee consisted solely of members of the majority party and was not open to the public. It met fortnightly. It had great power but no executive function. It considered, commented on, asked for more information about, and formed a view on recommendations contained in draft reports from the Education Officer on issues later to be considered at public sub-committees on which both political parties were represented. In a letter to me, dated 25 August 1994, when the ILEA had ceased to exist and I was writing about the conventions that then applied, Sir Ashley wrote this about reports to the Policy Committee: 'the convention which I tried to establish was that, since papers were the Education Officer's, the sub-committee could not amend them, but it could decide anything it liked instead of the recommendations in the paper or it could return a paper to the Education Officer asking him to add to it or remove things from it.' I can recall many occasions when the Policy Committee asked for something to be added to a report, and it was. What I do not recall is ever being asked to remove from a report anything that took the form of an option that a committee of the Authority was to be invited to consider.

The definition of the Leader's role in the Authority's Standing Orders was altogether less precise than that of the Education Officer. It read:

> **Leaders**,
> The members of the Authority or Education Committee so chosen by the largest party on the Authority shall be known as the Leader and Deputy Leader of the Authority and/or Committee and members so chosen by the second largest party shall be known as the Leader and Deputy Leader of the Opposition.

No specific executive functions, in relation to the Education Officer or of any other kind, were ascribed to the Leader in the Standing Orders.

The pages that follow are not intended, even at a superficial level, to be a how-to-do-it manual of educational or other forms of management; they are intended to provide examples of how, effectively or otherwise, what I had learnt in various capacities over the years, was applied to a set of problems with which I became involved as Education Officer.

The decision-making process within the administration itself was something that had to be settled early. Before becoming Education Officer, I had read a fair amount of management literature, mostly emanating from the USA. I was particularly interested in views on the role of Chief Executive expressed by Peter Drucker and, in his own somewhat anarchic way, by Robert Townsend of Avis. So far as finance-related management systems were concerned, I had read the Department of Education's publication 'Output Budgeting: Education Planning Paper No. 1' with care. It had not been rapidly followed by Paper No. 2, I noticed, so I took this to be about the last word in departmental thinking on the matter. With Karl Popper's falsification principle in mind, I had spent a day in a School of Management library trying to identify efficient businesses, defined by the movement over time in their share prices, which had developed similar management systems and had then abandoned them. Why had they done that? On looking for their reasons for jettisoning various forms of output management system, I found these sufficiently compelling to suggest that the ILEA should not adopt any such a system in the first place. A straightforward zero budgeting system, starting from what the legislation required the Authority to do and working up from that, seemed easier to manage and quite as effective.

On the nature of the Chief Executive function, I had experience of two ways in which that could operate. The first consisted of leadership by a single person, whereby no one in an organisation was in any doubt about who was in charge of it. Frank Barraclough of the North Riding was just such a person. His deputies came and went; he remained in total command. The role of Gordon Bessey in Cumberland had been similar but less forcefully executed. The West Riding, a much larger organisation than the North Riding or Cumberland, had worked differently. As Sir Alec Clegg once told the Education committee, 'you have two Chief Education Officers for the price of one and two thirds.' By this he meant that he had made his Deputy, Jim Hogan, directly responsible for a whole range of activities in which Sir Alec, though formally responsible, played no active part.

Until 1971, the ILEA appeared to have operated something close to a two person Chief Executive system, with Sir William Houghton, as Education Officer, and Dr Briault, as his Deputy, sharing responsibility for running the system. Towards the end of this period, Sir William was not in good health and Dr Briault had become increasingly responsible for an increasing amount. Sir William collapsed and died in the office shortly before he was to retire. On being appointed Education Officer, Dr Briault had seen no compelling reason to share a defined number of responsibilities, which he was already carrying out satisfactorily, with a newcomer, such as myself, of uncertain competence. So, in administrative terms, since 1971, the ILEA had had a single Chief Executive: Dr Briault, dealing directly with colleagues responsible for defined elements of the administration of the education service. One consequence of this, in my perception, had been a seriously overloaded Chief Executive. Another was that, on my arrival as Dr Briault's Deputy, I had few specific responsibilities other than to manage the Authority's budget and to hold the sometimes prolonged and fractious meetings with the ten divisional officers. That left me with too much time on my hands and no established mechanism for making my sometimes unwelcome opinions known on matters where I had 'experience and particular interests', to quote the words of the Deputy's job description.

Many explanations were later produced to explain why the problems at William Tyndale School were not dealt with earlier. My view was simple. There had been an inspectorate failure to deal with the matter or, when it had found itself unable to do that, to give the Education Officer immediate and accurate first-hand information and advice on what to do next. With so many other matters requiring his attention, Dr Briault had seen no reason for any urgency. This had reinforced my view that the ILEA was too complex an organisation for the Education Officer to act as a single person chief executive, even when that person was as knowledgeable and experienced as Dr Briault, which I certainly was not. Nor did I believe in deputies with too little to do; so 1977 began with what was, in effect, a two person Chief Executive. It consisted of myself and John Bevan, who was responsible for just about everything outside the school system. Two new senior appointments, in the form of Tim Brighouse and Bill Stubbs, were made and each had defined responsibilities for important elements of the education service. Before long, this was recognised and their posts raised to second deputy level. That led to four of us at the top of ILEA's administration and left me with more time to exercise a general oversight of what was being done. It had the effect of ending, within County Hall at least, the notion that senior administrators, other than the Education Officer, dealt only with quantities. Any idea that Tim Brighouse and Bill Stubbs, with experience of teaching and administration outside London where such distinctions were not made, were not capable of assessing, with the inspectorate's help, the quality of education in the institutions for which they had responsibility was implausible. Their arrival meant I now had time to deal with the Authority's relations with a wide range of bodies which the ILEA chaired or on which the ILEA was represented. Chairing the regular meetings with the Directors of social services in the London boroughs was one such morale-sapping occasion; attendance at lengthy and usually rather pointless Burnham Committee meetings on teachers' salaries was another. I also answered all letters from MP's, responded to articles in the Press, met deputations from the public and dealt with teachers and their unions in the Standing Joint Advisory Council. At these meetings, the unions argued fiercely amongst themselves and, for light relief, unitedly with me. Through my membership of the Director General's Management Board, I also kept in touch with Chief Officers of the Greater London Council, whose departments provided the ILEA with a wide range of services. The new arrangements left me time to visit schools and other elements of the Authority's service and to remain in close, often daily, contact with the elected and added members of both political parties on the ILEA itself.

I had begun the year with a clear idea, on the lines of that minute I had written in November 1976 and had discussed with Sir Ashley, of what I wanted to concentrate on doing as Education Officer. But almost as soon as I had settled into my new room, unfinished business landed on my desk. It looked like an unimportant matter but the Authority was surrounded by a largely hostile Press. Journalists from many different papers lived in London, so they liked their news to be local and acquired without the need to travel far. Journalists relish a row, so even a small story could lead to banner headlines if the news was bad. Good news was rarely found worth mentioning.

On this occasion, a potentially contentious problem concerned the use of school premises for an election meeting held by the National Front. The practice had been for the ILEA to give priority to election meetings over the existing use of school premises for educational purposes, such as adult education. This had caused trouble recently when a National Front meeting was held at a school in the middle of Lambeth. It was assumed by angry local residents and parents, most of whom were of West Indian origin, that the Authority was supporting the National Front by allowing it to hold an election meeting in 'their' school, as they understandably saw it. The legal position was that, if the premises were not being used for educational purposes, the National Front or any other legally constituted political party had to be allowed to use a school for an election meeting. Angry local people had written to the Permanent Secretary of the Department of Education asking him to instruct the Authority to ban the National Front from using the school. He had naturally declined, but the row had simmered on. On 7 December, on one of his last visits to County Hall, Dr Briault had initialled a draft report asking for approval to change the Authority's way of dealing with its premises at election times. In future, it would no longer automatically cancel the use of its premises for educational purposes to give priority to election meetings. On 23 December, 1976, the head of the General Purposes Branch, when he might reasonably have been expected to be thinking about Christmas, had added a note to the draft that Dr Briault had already approved:

> In my view this report is incomplete without some reference to the difficulties which could arise over priorities between educational users and election candidates in the use of school halls. If the practice is changed and problems do arise in the GLC elections next May, and this must be considered a strong possibility, the Education Officer is in an exposed position because he will have withheld information from the sub-committee which has been asked to take a decision on the matter.

Yes, and by May I would be that Education Officer. But was it not an opinion that there might be difficulties rather than information that there would be that was being withheld? A new Education Officer could afford to any lack such opinions, I concluded; so I scrapped the report and sent a note to the Leader on 17 January:

> Candidate's rights to use school premises for election meetings are set out in Sections 82 and 83 of the Representation of the People Act for parliamentary and local government elections respectively. In each case, however, there is a sub-section which says that these rights do not authorise any interference with the hours during which the school premises are used for educational purposes. It has been the practice, nevertheless, for a number of years to give precedence to the use of a school hall for an election meeting over its normal educational use. This would usually be for an adult education institute class. I see no real reason for this practice and, unless you wish otherwise, propose to discontinue it.

Do you agree, please?

The Leader initialled back 'yes'. This meant that, if anything went wrong, it would not be his fault; it would be for me to justify the defective advice I had given him. I had not, of course, reminded him of the Lambeth issue, nor did I ask him whether he wanted me to ensure that there was rather more badminton taking place in certain school halls than previously. It is unhelpful for an official to invite a politician to answer a question to which that politician cannot safely provide an answer. There did not seem much risk of anyone taking offence at these changed arrangements, but later someone did. Tim Brighouse, soon after his arrival, found that the National Front had applied to use a school in Lambeth for an election meeting on an evening when, it so happened that, as at a number of other local schools, some badminton was going on. Their application was refused and we were off to the High Court. Tim was worried about an appearance there but Sir Ashley reminded him that he was not engaged in a confessional and would probably be all right. Fortunately, the National Front did not turn up at the hearing, so he was.

The priorities I had set out in my minute to the Leader of the previous November were almost immediately again disrupted by a far larger problem. Later in January, I was suddenly informed by Hugh Harding, Under Secretary at the Department of Education, that, with one exception allowed, the nine Teacher Training Colleges maintained by the Authority but funded by the Department, were either to join neighbouring Polytechnics, if suitable ones were prepared to accept them, or to close. Generous terms were proposed for staff made redundant during this process. Where was John Bevan? Ordinarily, it would be for him to deal with matters of this kind, but he was still involved full-time in disciplinary procedures affecting the staff of William Tyndale School; so recommendations on what to do were left to me to put to the appropriate ILEA committees. Big problems can be easier to solve than small ones. It was immediately agreed by the College Principals when we met that there was no point in arguing with the Department. They determined the number of teachers to be trained and that was that. After a brief and uncomfortable meeting with all concerned, it was left for me to recommend which College would be the one to survive on its own. With the intended closure of Stoke D'Abernon in mind, though not yet mentioned to anyone, I decided to suggest that we should preserve Avery Hill in Greenwich. This had reasonably good residential accommodation for staff conferences. The premises of Furzedown College, it had occurred to me, could also be used to solve another problem. During a single afternoon visit to the College with John Phillips, headmaster of Battersea Grammar School, we agreed that the amalgamated school of which he was to be the head, since called Graveney, could, if suitably adapted, be created on the Furzedown College site. How on earth the College had been allowed to acquire the thirty four pianos we counted on our way round it was something we found puzzling.

During these first weeks as Education Officer, it appeared to me at times that I was having to run the whole administration of the ILEA single-handed. Bill Stubbs and Tim Brighouse arrived during January but neither had any experience of London and needed time to settle in. As Deputy, John Bevan was engaged full-time in an Employment Tribunal, lasting several months. George Andrews, head of the Teaching Staff Branch, was similarly preoccupied so it was not until 9 March that the senior officers' team was in place and I was able to relax.

In my first year as Education Officer, I had three opportunities to express views on what I believed were the main developments which the Authority might wish to consider or to which it was likely to have to respond. The first opportunity consisted of an interview given to the Authority's in-house magazine Contact. The article appeared early in January and gave me a chance to articulate views on a wide range of issues, including my perception of the role of Education Officer. Articles of that kind do not change what thousands of teachers and other staff either think or do; but they can influence a few of them and can give even a casual reader some idea of what the Education Officer is trying to do and how he wants to do it. The heading in bold of the article in Contact, 'Mobilising Precision', was well chosen by the Editor. My responses to the questions put to me included:

> It is sometimes said of a large Authority that it is remote and vague. It has no business to be either. Its strength, like that of a major hospital, lies in its ability to mobilise precision. Its weakness can lie in allowing size to become a state of mind. In a small Authority, where you are close to the ground, you can identify needs quickly. Then it's rather like having a tooth-ache on a Sunday. You are alone with the problem. Outside the ILEA, I've often had to recognise that there was little point in identifying needs that there was no chance of satisfying. There are no such inhibitions in London. Everyone here assumes, properly enough, that it is the Authority's business to try and meet each and every educational need as it arises. That's not always possible, of course, but we can continue to improve the speed and effectiveness with which we apply our wide-ranging resources.

Talking of the primary schools and their problems:

> It is not that Inner London hasn't a number of highly effective primary schools. I've seen many outstanding ones and so conclude that excuses based on the supposed deficiencies of London's children are misplaced. I agree with the 'Right to Learn' group of teachers on this. If the children at - but I mustn't mention names - are learning happily and well then it cannot be right for a neighbouring school to remain wrapped in a form of sociological determinism which convinces at least some of the staff that nothing much can be done with theirs.

The prospects for comprehensive secondary schools in London:

> Now that the organisational issues are moving into the background, I expect to see alternative approaches within the comprehensive system.

Understandably, during the long years when our comprehensive schools were developing alongside the grammar schools, certain orthodoxies became established. These were very necessary and will continue to provide the central tradition of comprehensive education. But I would expect the grammar schools, with their own long-standing traditions, to change the nature of comprehensive education in London as well as to be changed by it themselves. For example, some of the new comprehensives are small, so they are thinking of ways of approaching education which don't necessarily imply an enormous range of options in the fourth and fifth years. They don't see this as a weakness. Nor do I. A Brussels sprout is not a failed cabbage. Each has its valuable qualities and has no cause to be diffident about them. Breadth of choice is highly desirable, but depth may be even more so. The two are not incompatible and we will have to see how parents respond to what is offered. Nothing will stop some people saying that the ILEA is developing a system which has no individuality and frowns on diversity. The reverse is true, as parents will find out when they visit schools to decide on their children's future over the next year or two.

On the future:

I am sometimes accused of taking an over-optimistic view of the future. I say 'accused' because confidence in the future, confidence in the fact that, between the noisy extremes, most people are working hard and effectively to improve the quality of education, is thoroughly unfashionable at the moment. For more than 2,000 years some of the best minds in Europe have applied themselves to education's main themes. Now there are signs of fatigue. Somehow, I hope we will be able to raise the level of the debate over the next year or so.

How is this to be done?

Initially, perhaps, by refraining from exclusive reliance on 'either/or' types of argument and working on some which say 'both'. For example, take the declaration of faith a head once expressed: 'All can walk part of the way with genius.' That stops people either supposing the whole aim is to sort, give marks to or concentrate exclusively on the differences between children or from veering to the other extreme of saying that it is only what children have or can undertake in common that is permissible. We must develop both ideas: that which children have in common and that which distinguishes them, one from the other. Having to hold two ideas in our heads at the same time should not defeat us. Sometimes it seems to.

On the end of a period of expansion and change:

My own view is that institutional change may have gone faster, sometimes in convulsive leaps, than the rate at which conscientious people can reasonably be asked to adjust their thinking. Change can act as a stimulant but, like other stimulants, too much too quickly can have unpleasant side-effects. Profound changes, which are now what are called for, have to be thought about and worked through over a period of years.

On the nature of control over the school system:

> If something or someone is going wrong, I am all for saying so directly. But I do not see myself as sitting all-wise on the apex of some organisational tripod. That's a disagreeable posture. It didn't lend much clarity to the remarks of the priestess at Delphi, I recall.

In conclusion:

> I come back to the importance of identifying needs. My instinct is always to look for what is happening well and to make sure it is promoted and extended. There are many hundreds of able and energetic people in London's education service. They need the means and the support to enable them to carry out their work effectively. My job is to try and help them do just that.

Those final sentences summed up what I took to be the ILEA's approach to the institutions it maintained. Within the parameters of the statutory requirements that the Authority had to meet and of the Authority's own regulations deriving from that legislation, the role of the administration was to support schools and colleges in their efforts to work effectively. Such an approach did not leave room for any attempt to 'control' the day-to-day management of any school.

The image of a Brussels sprout not being a failed cabbage was one I had used a few weeks earlier at a meeting of primary school heads. Some of the schools were, by London standards, rather small and believed themselves to be particularly at risk of closure at a time of falling numbers. Anyway, the remark went down well with that particular audience and 'a Brussels sprout is not a failed cabbage' was soon to be found on lapel badges which an enterprising head of a small school produced and distributed to parents at his and other schools of a similar size.

My second opportunity to offer views on the response I believed the Authority wanted to see to the ending of selection to secondary schools in September that year arose towards the end of January. Of the suggested priorities I had put forward to the Leader on 26 November 1976, the most pressing was to do everything possible to ensure that both primary and secondary schools responded efficiently to the different intake of children that the secondary schools would be receiving when selection at 11+ ended in September 1977. So the article for Contact, that I had earlier told the Leader I would be writing, now had to be written. The version published in Contact in January was based on a talk I had given the previous December in Camden. It was addressed to all ILEA primary and secondary schools heads. As in that minute to the Leader in the previous December, the article opened with a 'we' rather than a 'you', to which it moved in the second paragraph:

Developing comprehensive education from September 1977 – what needs to be done?

I hope we are going to think of 1977 not as the year when something stopped – when selection into Inner London secondary schools ended – but as the year when something started: a major effort to upgrade our whole secondary system. Inner London has about 10,000 teachers in secondary schools which do not select and a further 1,500 in those which at present do. In 1977, the two join forces. It seems to me incontestably true that together these 11,500 can provide the skills and experience needed to create a system that is fully and effectively comprehensive. This may sound a bit like Blucher coming to the aid of Wellington at a tricky point in the battle of Waterloo. So be it. The important fact is that this campaign has to be won jointly too: the campaign to preserve and develop high quality education that is open to all, which all are encouraged to use to the full, wherever they come from and whatever future they plan for themselves.

September 1977 is not just a matter of redistributing children. Out of the two traditions that will be coming together – the long-standing grammar school tradition and the rich and newer tradition developed in the best of our comprehensive schools – a new entity has to be created. It will not be administered or legislated into existence. How then is it to be done and by whom? Forgive the Kitchener finger pointing straight at you. There is nowhere else it can point. In particular, it is you that each one of those children transferring to secondary school next year will need. Having said that, I am diffident about offering further suggestions for September 1977. There is no shortage of back-seat drivers. But at least something of what you hear over your shoulder may be useful and in that hope I would like to say four things: the first two to primary heads and their staffs, the second two for secondary consumption.

Some 30,000 children will transfer to ILEA secondary schools next year. They need to be as well prepared as they possibly can be. Each one of them. So, please, will every primary head satisfy himself or herself personally that every child in this year's transfer group has acquired, to the limit of that child's ability to do so, the skills needed in his or her new school. I can hear the chorus of, 'Easy, it's already being done'. But it isn't. It is in some schools but it isn't in by any means all. For by being 'personally satisfied' I do not mean looking over the results of tests, discussing children with other teachers, having a general sense of what is happening, visiting classrooms, and being intelligently aware of who is doing what. I mean something altogether more rigorous. I mean talking to each child about what that child has read or is reading. I mean, where appropriate, listening to that child read. I mean looking at what each child has written. I mean observing what each child can do with number. I mean looking at how he writes that down. I mean becoming directly aware of the level at which each child is working in all the activities the school is undertaking. And I mean continuing this process right through to the end of the summer term. Within the constraints of time and human capacity, that is what I mean by being 'personally satisfied'. I mean one other thing also. Everyone with responsibility for this must try and see that children who ought not to be transferring to secondary school next year will not do so. I refer to children ascertained or about to be ascertained as in need of special education in a special school. Their numbers are small. Their educational needs are great. The effect of inappropriate transfer to secondary school, on themselves and on the school, can be disproportionately serious. Somehow we must reduce the incidence of this. Procedures stick. We must unstick them. For this one year, I would ask you to try this in two ways with the transfer group. First, use the proper channels. Use the proper channels properly. If this doesn't work, you will have to use the wrong channels. Write to me direct. For this one year for this one age-group. That should not crack the system.

There are some times when some things, however detailed, ought not to be delegated. I believe each head's responsibility for the children transferring in September 1977 is one of them. And I will do what I can to help. My main reason for pressing this need for the head's personal attention is that it will benefit the children; but I have a subsidiary reason. The reputation of London's primary schools depends on a number of things. One of the most important is the opinion of professional colleagues elsewhere in the system. No secondary school teacher should have reasonable cause to say that children are being transferred with deficiencies that proper care could have remedied. Secondary school teachers have their own responsibilities which I will refer to later.

So much for the children transferring to secondary school. My second suggestion to primary heads is even more down to earth. Over thirty selective schools will be taking the full range of abilities next year. The staffs of those schools are making notable efforts to prepare for this. It would be ironical and quite unwarranted if it were anywhere suggested of these schools 'they won't be able to manage the slower ones, of course'. Not so. Next year the ex-selective schools will want a full range of applications. Positively the worst thing that could happen would be for parents next year to receive 'I don't think your child is quite up to that school' kind of advice, directly or by implication. That simple mustn't happen. I am sure it won't, but the whole business of advising parents will unquestionably put extra weight on primary heads. The Divisional Officers will do all they can to help; but we all have to acquire new bearings, geographical as well as educational. The school down the road, that has seemed light years away for most of our children, may suddenly have become the one to which they can properly look. Almost without exception, London's grammar schools have opened their doors to all London's children; but they cannot admit those who do not apply.

Now for my two secondary school points. The first complements the one I have just been making. All secondary schools are becoming comprehensive next year, not just the grammar schools. So all schools need to be thinking through the implications of this. Most are, but all should recognise that those already taking a non-selective intake can hope for children who have benefited from the increasingly stable staffing in the primary schools. They can expect an improvement within the intake. They can also expect – all of them – a different intake. My concern is that between us we should not underestimate what children can achieve within a system that is fully comprehensive. This 'different intake' may still need some explanation. As you know, on transfer children are described (but I hope not thought of) as 'above average', 'average', 'below average'. The distribution over ILEA as a whole is 25% above average (Band 1), 50% average (Band 2), 25% below average (Band 3). For administrative purposes, this 'balance' is converted in terms of a form entry of 30 pupils. So the ILEA-wide balance for every group of thirty is 7.5 children in Band 1, 15 in Band 2 and 7.5 in Band 3. As there are no schools with an entry of only 30 children, these fractured children are, in practice, mercifully cured by multiplication.

The consequences of this are here described in the text. One example given is of an eight-form entry (240 pupils) school which would, under this banding arrangement, in 1977 receive sixty-four (not forty-four as it did in 1976) Band 1 pupils and sixty (not sixty-eight) Band 3 pupils. This is the extent of the 'different intake' referred to.

As the Leader reminded me when I showed him the article in draft, the banding system for Roman Catholic secondary schools was based on the performance of children in Roman Catholic primary schools. This was rather better than those in other schools. The text continues:

> The ending of selection is not just something happening to grammar schools. It affects every secondary school, some more, some less, but all in some way. This needs thinking about and higher expectations must be built into that thinking.

> My second secondary point may be a little controversial. In the first few weeks of next autumn term I believe we should avoid any tendency towards what might be called diagnostic dither. Clarity and security provide the best start to the school year. Not all children have felt themselves to be particularly successful in their primary schools. The Authority's description of some of them as 'below average' will not have repaired the poor self-image, as the jargon has it, which some will bring with them. So in that first week or so, it seems to me, there needs to be a positive effort to see that the entrants are busy, that they know what they are supposed to be doing, that they are enabled to do some things well and that they are appropriately praised for doing them well. It is in these first few weeks that insecure, half-revived hopes can flicker and die, or deep loyalties and new habits of work can be formed. Here comes the controversial point. Every stage of education tends to undervalue the one which precedes it. 'What are they doing with those infants?' is the cry coming out of a number

of junior school staff-rooms. Similarly, the secondary schools sometimes wonder what the primary schools have been doing for all those years. My own view, based principally on the standard of written work and on several years of visiting schools to look at this, is that it is rare to find work in the first term of secondary school that equals the standard achieved by the same child in the previous year. This is particularly true where the less able children are concerned.

In the text, there follows a personal example, mentioned earlier, of what had happened when I had tried, as a teacher of eleven-year-olds at Littlemore grammar school, to impress the heads of their primary schools by showing them how well I had been teaching their pupils English during their first year at secondary school. The text continues:

> I had assumed that what the children had produced for me in the first week or so at the grammar school was the best that the primary schools had left them able to do. Quite evidently, it was not. The primary school heads were right to be rude. I can only wish that similar self-doubt would occasionally trouble some secondary school teachers who think the best way to improve the performance of their primary school colleagues is to appeal to the newspapers. Anyway, the point of the story is that teachers of top-year juniors tend to know far more about what their children can do and are often better at insisting upon it than most teachers of first year secondary children. There is nothing surprising about this. For every hour an individual secondary school teacher will spend with a first-year child, the primary teacher will earlier have spent many more. However, the real question is what to do about the effects of discontinuity.

> What I propose for 1977 is that, area by area, any potential flurry of recriminations should be replaced by properly organised meetings. Representatives of primary and secondary schools could usefully sit down together to discuss the experience of the 1977 transfer, not in general terms but with examples of work to look at. This is the way to make progress. These, then, are my four points: primary heads to take a particular look at children transferring next year and then, with Divisional Officers, to think especially hard about the advice given to parents about the new opportunities now open to all children at all schools. Secondary schools to seize hold of the fact that change is not something happening down the road: the ILEA's first comprehensive intake needs fresh thinking and fresh commitment. Finally, given that every effort is made to see that the new secondary intakes start near the level achieved in their primary schools, the strengths and weaknesses of that achievement need proper discussions within the teaching profession itself, preferably during that first term.

> I began by saying that our aim must be to upgrade the secondary system. No one wants to see unreasonable expectations imposed on children; but I believe we are entitled to have higher expectations of the children transferring to secondary school next year than we have had in the past

and that they and their parents are entitled to have higher expectations of us. We have between us the chance to lift the quality of what we offer to a higher plane. That is what we will succeed in doing if we care enough about it.

I showed the article to the Leader to see whether he had any comments. The note he wrote on the top managed to be both untypical and typical at the same time. The untypical bit was the, never to be repeated, so far as I can recall, first word. The typical bit was to point out a mistake I was about to make. He reminded me that the banding formula for entrants to Roman Catholic secondary schools were based on the better than average results achieved in Roman Catholic primary schools. They were therefore differently calculated from those to which I had referred. Sir Ashley's note read:

> Marvellous! My only comment is that on page 4 the example should make it clear that it is a non-RC formula.

So off went the article, duly corrected in the light of Sir Ashley's comment. Only two heads took up my offer to get in touch with me directly if our procedures were sticking in some way. One of them confessed that he was just trying out the system and had no genuine crisis to report.

The working week now consisted of a constant series of interruptions and timetabled meetings. Far too many matters still had to be dealt with by the Education Officer in person because the other party would accept no one else. Admission arrangements to secondary schools were just one instance of that. Formally, for example, admission arrangements to voluntary aided denominational schools were reached after 'consultation' between the governing bodies of the schools and the Local Education Authority. In the ILEA, the Catholic Diocesan Authorities handled the initial discussions with ILEA officers and then transmitted any agreement reached to the individual schools. Admission arrangements to Catholic schools tended to be time-consuming to negotiate but, with rare exceptions, once agreed, the schools kept to them. A feature of these arrangements was that these secondary schools were asked to comply with the Authority's system of banding, designed to ensure that the entries to each school, subject to denominational requirements, reflected a fair balance of ability, so far as this could be measured by tests at 11+. As the following indicates, it was ultimately for the Authority itself, not its officials, to agree or not agree with the arrangements negotiated on their behalf:

> Note to the Leader (copies to Deputy Leader and Mr Tyrrell Burgess) 22 February

R.C Admission Agreements

> I attach a copy of the draft model agreement for R.C schools in both dioceses which finally emerged from our discussions with the Commissions. I think

this wording is the best we can get but I have suggested (and they have agreed) that a further clause − 'The agreement will be subject to review in three years' − should be added. If you agree that the draft is acceptable, the Commissions will write to the governing bodies recommending the model as a basis for agreement with the Authority. As their negotiations with individual governing bodies are not likely to be completed for some months, we propose to write to them saying that it is hoped that they will bear the model agreement in mind when deciding admissions for September 1977.

Tyrrell Burgess, an Added member to the Education Committee, chaired a highly efficient group of members who looked in detail at the way school admission procedures were working each year.

Early in March I had my third opportunity to present views on the ILEA's structure and functions. Elected members, Conservatives and Labour alike, asked for a report from me 'on the organisation of the education service'. It was made clear that my report needed to be comprehensive in scope and produced quickly. In previous jobs, even as deputy in London, I had rarely had to draft lengthy or complex documents. Though the need to have to write such a report was unwelcome at a time when I was myself trying to get to grips with how the ILEA complex administration had been managed by Dr Briault, writing it gave me an opportunity to express views on how the Authority now worked and might wish to develop in the future. So, in the weeks before mid-March, I found myself, over several weekends and with contributions coming in from several of my colleagues, having to produce a report some 6,000 words long. Although preoccupied with this, I still had to be accessible in my office for much of the week, attending meetings and and keeping an eye on what was happening elsewhere. Inevitably, most the difficulties that arose from day to way could not be predicted in advance.

Getting relationships with key members of the Authority right was one thing that had to be established quickly. In that respect, Mrs Chaplin deserves a chapter of her own. Staff appointments were her responsibility and had in the past proved contentious. Although appointments at the level of an inspector were theoretically for Mrs Chaplin to approve, in practice they were left to the administration to handle. When I had been Deputy, one such appointment had caused trouble. It concerned an inspector who had left school at fourteen, subsequently qualified as a teacher and had become an outstandingly good head of a primary school. Not all successful head teachers make good inspectors but, on a visit to Cumberland I had made with this one and his staff, almost as soon as he arrived amongst them, heads and teachers from various Cumberland primary schools were clustering round to hear what he thought about what he had seen in their schools. Amongst teachers, he knew exactly what to do and did it very well. Mrs Chaplin noted his lack of a degree and asked to see him. She was not impressed. She particularly took exception to his London accent. Present at the discussion we had about him, though it had nothing to do with his responsibilities in the ILEA, was Martin Lightfoot, a past editor of Penguin specials on education. Martin was tall, clever and a Cambridge graduate. It sometimes seemed to me that Mrs Chaplin saw in him the son she had never had. He in turn treated her rather as an aunt and addressed her with an easy familiarity that I never adopted. Anyway, as my discussion with Mrs Chaplin continued, Martin had stretched himself out at full length in an arm chair, listening to what was going on. Suddenly he intervened. 'I think the trouble may be, Mrs Chaplin', he suggested thoughtfully, sounding like someone genuinely trying to be helpful to a person struggling with a problem that they were finding altogether too difficult to handle, 'that you don't really much like members of the working class'. This was a devastatingly dangerous thing to say to Mrs Chaplin, in earlier days known as 'the red Miss Marcuse'. The explosion was immediate. As Mrs Chaplin raged at him, Martin looked mildly surprised at the flow of words coming his way. After a while, he straightened himself up in the chair and gracefully offered an apology. Surprisingly soon it was accepted and he was forgiven.

To return to March 1977: the arrangement for the appointment of senior officers or inspectors to the ILEA, 'senior' being defined by their salary level, was that they would initially be interviewed by an Officer Board. The candidates recommended for interview would then have their names and accompanying papers, with others from the long list, sent for approval to the Chairman of the Staff and General Committee: Mrs Chaplin. The convention was that the Chairman would not remove any name from the list of those put forward for interview but could add one or more others. This convention, unwritten as were others in the ILEA, had caused serious trouble in 1976. On that occasion, a name had been added by the Chairman to the ones proposed by the Officer Board but the papers before the committee did not indicate whether that had been done and who that added person was. At interview, this candidate, an ILEA employee, did well. It rapidly became clear that the committee was moving towards appointing him. At this point, Dr Briault had intervened to say that, in his opinion, the candidate was unsuitable and might, indeed, bring the Authority into disrepute. There was a personal problem being dealt with that had not yet been resolved. The Leader and other members of the committee were furious. In terms I never heard before or since, they criticised Dr Briault for placing them in a position to consider a candidate that he was then telling them was unsuitable. They were particularly irritated to have their own preliminary judgement of the candidate overturned in this way. Eventually, when the nature of the problem was indicated, reason prevailed and another candidate was selected. But it had been an unpleasant occasion and could not be allowed to occur again. Hence this note to Mrs Chaplin of 8 March 1977:

> Appointment of Deputy Chief Inspector, (Further and Higher Education)
>
> As a result of the interviews on 2 and 3 March, the officer board, of which I was Chairman and which was made up of Dr Birchenough and Mr Bevan, put forward the following candidates for interview by the Sub-Committee:-

Abrahams G.A.
Hayes   N.D.
Higham   J.
Tranter   A.

I understand from the Chief Inspector that you wish the appointing Committee to see Dr M. If this is so, I trust the clerk will be asked to indicate on the papers that four candidates have been put forward by the officer board and one added by the Chairman. There was a problem about this on a previous occasion, you recall, when members objected to Dr Briault mentioning this at the meeting itself. I naturally want to avoid that happening again. Incidentally, we thought well of Dr M. but he had no experience of, and had formed no links with, the world outside the Polytechnic and would have to start with hardly any background at all. None of us thought that would help us much.

Mrs Chaplin, radical politician though in origin she was, had a preference for senior inspectors who had doctorates from a university she thought respectable but, though forthright in her opinions on this and other matters, was never one to stand on her dignity when well-supported contrary opinions were addressed to her. On this occasion, she simply removed Dr M. from the list.

Amongst other distractions during the month were the Press. It remained important to deal quickly with misleading articles. I wrote such replies myself, as in this letter to the Guardian on 18 March:

> There was a bizarre reference to the ILEA in the article on language teaching in Friday's Guardian. It implied that the ILEA does not think it important to teach modern languages well. Quelle blague! We are well aware that modern languages are not taught well in this country, in grammar, comprehensive and secondary modern schools alike. It needs no HMI report from the grave to tell us this. But we are doing all we can to improve matters. To take one example of that: in July our inspectorate, developing work that started last year, is organising courses in Spanish, German, Russian, Arabic, French, Chinese and modern Hebrew. At the learning end there will be more than 250 ILEA VIth formers. On the teaching side there will be the Polytechnics of Central London, of the South Bank and of North London and the Colleges of Kingsway-Princeton and of Hammersmith and West London. The help that is being offered from Further and Higher Education institutions is a notable feature of these arrangements. The object of our summer courses is to improve the skills of the VIth formers themselves and to enable us to plan new opportunities for language teaching in successive years. The notion that the ILEA is not concerned with high standards in modern language teaching is a fantasy.

These day-to-day commitments that filled my diary in the early months of 1977 made any sustained effort to write difficult. My practice, that year and later, was to write draft reports myself and then invite others to comment on or correct them. I found this easier and more conducive to good temper, as a confirmed tinkerer with the work of others, than asking for drafts on which I would later comment or, more irritatingly for their authors, substantially alter.

The report on the structure and activities of the ILEA that members had asked me to produce turned out to be the longest and most wide-ranging that I produced as Education Officer. On the Conservative side, interest had been expressed in creating some form of borough-based divisional executives, one tier below the Education Authority and its committees. These new committees would consist of locally elected members from each of the inner London boroughs. One effect of the report was to end, for the time being at least, any further discussion about this possibility. On the Labour side, members wanted a clear account of how the confusion of responsibilities between elected members, school governors, ILEA inspectors and administrators, which they believed were responsible for the problems that had arisen at William Tyndale School, were to be avoided in future.

The report dealt with these issues but also with much else. Its third section, on the relationship between the individual and the education service, reflected the way I believed education in London should ideally be delivered. Reluctantly, I soon had to recognise that there was no hope yet of moving far in the direction proposed. The obstacles were too great and the changes needed had to join the lengthening list in my head of 'things that ought to be done but which will not be attempted because to do so would over-extend the system, thereby causing confusion and leading to ultimate failure'. The following quotations are from the three main sections into which the report was divided:

Report by the Education Officer on the ILEA's Administration

Section one: an examination of the Authority's main functions; section two: some suggested improvements to the exercise of these functions and the issue of devolution to locally elected committees; section three: the individual and the education service – suggestions for the future.

Section one: The Authority's main functions

There is a tendency, even within the Authority, to take the exercise of its major functions somewhat for granted. Underlying them all, there are two of particular importance. The first is the Authority's concern, with an underlying statutory responsibility, for the quality of education in the institutions for which it is responsible. The second is the continuing need to interpret locally the changing forms of national policy and, conversely, by the Authority's own direct participation through its members and officers, to try and ensure that that policy takes proper account of the needs of inner London. Within this general framework, the major activities the Authority undertakes to discharge its functions can be defined as those which are of inner London-wide importance and require to be exercised on that scale to be carried out effectively. Broadly, these are the functions ascribed to the Council for Greater London, to use the term then in use, in the 1960 report of the Royal Commission. These activities include: the control and management of capital programmes; the year by year management of the revenue budget; control over the disposition and organisation of educational institutions; central negotiation with teachers; the organisation of major central resources; the management of further and higher education and of adult and special education.

To talk of functions is to talk about what people do rather than the way they think. But in any description of education in inner London, it would be wrong to disregard, however difficult it may be to define, the existence of a specifically London voice in education. It unmistakably exists, just as there is a Birmingham or a Manchester voice reflected in the contributions those cities make to education both within their own areas and nationally.

The way in which, within policies laid down by the Committee, the Authority's administration carries out its main functions can be illustrated from the recent past. I have set out below seven examples which show the scope of these functions:

1. The re-organisation of higher and further education – Between 1971 and 1973, a complete review was undertaken of the 36 maintained technical, commercial and other colleges of further education within the Authority's area. After detailed discussion with students, staff, governing bodies and teachers' associations, a new structure was adopted in 1973 and the present pattern of 24 colleges established.

2. The review of primary schools – this is a continuing process but, between 1973 and 1975, the future of each one of more than 800 primary schools was examined within 120 planning areas and, in the light of changing numbers, denominational needs and the accommodation of each, a pattern of distribution established. This work forms the foundation on which, for years to come, policy can be built.

3. The re-organisation of secondary education – in 1972 the Authority launched, through its green papers, a major effort at consultation. During this process, its proposals were modified. In March 1975, the Authority decided that selection for admission to secondary schools should end in September 1977. At that time, 45 schools in inner London were still recruiting selectively. Plans had been agreed for some but, in just over two years, by July 1976, discussion with all the schools had been completed, proposals worked out and section 13 notices issued.

4. The Special Programme for Assisting Re-organisation (SPAR). On 6 August 1975 the Department of Education and Science announced that the Secretary of State had allocated a sum specifically to assist in the re-organisation of secondary schools. Work had to be started by 31

March 1977 and be completed by 31 March 1978. As soon as term started in September 1975, teams of officers visited to discuss with heads the individual needs of each school. In all, 36 projects were submitted and, on 22 December 1975, the programme was approved. Since then, detailed schemes for each project have been produced and are being carried out within the difficult time and cost limits that have been set.

5. Expansion of nursery education and services to under-fives and their parents – a three-year expansion of nursery education has been undertaken, providing over 100 new classes and schools with more than 4,500 places. Apart from the building programme, co-operative ventures in joining care with education and encouraging parental participation have been undertaken with voluntary bodies and inner London borough councils.

6. Creation of a new careers service – following the Employment and Training Act 1973, the Authority determined to establish a fully qualified service, centrally co-ordinated and directed, but available to young people and employers through local offices. There are now 22 local offices, the central London careers office and headquarters services at Carmelite Street. The Authority has moved further than any other local education authority towards implementing the Act and offering a comprehensive careers service to young people leaving schools and colleges.

7. An education service for the whole community – in 1972, the education officer made proposals for a new initiative to ensure all branches of the Authority's service worked together to reach out more widely than hitherto to meet the needs of inner London's population. These proposals were adopted and widely debated. As proposals, they were and remain open-ended and have a bearing on suggestions made later in this report. 207 individual projects arising out of this report have been supported.

This list puts my own contribution in the five years between 1972 and 1977 into perspective. Only two of the seven examples, items 3 and 4, had been affected in any important way by anything I had done during my time as Deputy. Though I had watched from the sidelines, the rest would have happened when and how it did had I remained in Yorkshire. The remark, in 3, that the Authority's proposals for secondary re-organisation 'were modified', rather than 'constituted an unpublicised but suddenly introduced reversal of policies adopted in 1947 and vigorously pursued ever since', as in fact they had been, was phrased to discourage further debate.

> I believe it to be a matter of fact rather than opinion that, in the past five years under Dr Briault's leadership, the Authority's administration has, within the policies laid down by the Committee, successfully planned and carried through, after wide consultation with the public and the individuals affected, extensive and complex changes in the exercise of

what I have described as its major functions.

The report went on to say on falling pupil numbers:

> Over the next few years, apart from the number of students aged over 18 in colleges, which will be rising, the facts are clear enough. But falling numbers are not just another consideration alongside others; they are the context in which all that the Authority does has to be seen. When conditions are static or enlarging, a process of incrementation develops. Pieces are added on. There is some new building here and a new scheme there. This induces corresponding habits of thought. A problem arises: the instinctive reaction is to appoint someone to deal with it. The new context means that a new principle has to be grasped. When numbers decline the process by which enlargement occurs cannot be reversed. We cannot, as it were, take a snapshot of the future and expect it to remain in place as we plan our way towards it. Inner London has to learn to manage a process. The lesson we have to learn is that henceforth change is likely to require a re-ordering of all that remains. The matter can be summed up in contrasting images. Enlargement can be accomplished by adding bricks to a structure that remains fundamentally unchanged. To reduce is to take a cup full of water out of a bucket whose whole contents are then required to find a new level.

Individuals think, committees find the process harder. Their members are often busy people and find themselves wanting to decide something rather than be required to look at anything in a different way; so it was never clear how far the 'manage a process' principle, as opposed to defining a point in the future and working back from it, was accepted either politically or administratively in some parts of the Authority. What is certain, however, is that it was the administrative principle used to deal, amongst other things, with the sharp reduction in the number of premises used and of the schools using them well into the 1980's. Intellectually, settled habits of mind were slower to change. This was particularly true of a marked unwillingness, amongst some elements in the ILEA's service, to understand and then respond to the changes that were occurring in the inner London boroughs since the London Government Act of 1963. The widespread changes taking place to local government outside London since 1974 had also largely gone unnoticed. The report continued on the theme of falling numbers:

The few figures that follow are selected to illustrate my point; they do not purport to provide a balanced view of a complex problem.

> Live births: Live births to mothers whose normal place of residence is within the Authority's area have moved, from a peak in 1963-4, as follows:

1963–4	1971–2	1972–3	1973–4	1974–5
63,000	38,319	34,588	32,556	31,196

The number of children actually entering Authority schools is affected by net movement out of London. Over the past five years, the number entering school at five has been between 66.6 per cent and 62.4% of the number of live births five years previously.

The primary school population: The number of children in Authority primary schools is:

September 1966   1976   1986 (estimated)

213,356   180,206   118,786

Ten year projections of primary school numbers are necessarily highly provisional. Several of the age groups concerned have not yet been born; nor can sudden increases in inward or outward migration be accurately predicted.

In fact primary numbers in 1986 were nearer 150,000 than 120,000 but, well before then, the forward estimates had been adjusted accordingly. There followed estimates, borough by borough, of the population figures for the whole population of inner London on different fertility and migration assumptions.

The purpose of providing these figures is to establish the point that we are not dealing with a fixed future and in talking of planning and of exercising our main functions it is within this context. It can be put this way: what we doing in 1977 in relation to our picture of 1986 has to be consistent with what 1986 will look like in 1981, which is itself only a few years away. In that context, six examples of how the Authority's main functions might be improved are provided below:

1. Within and between the institutions the Authority maintains, most of the organisational changes, other than those affecting colleges and departments of education, have now been carried out. This and other factors, such as the greater stability of staff, mean that the main emphasis must now be on consolidating the quality of service we provide: on content rather than form.

2. The Authority has to articulate the needs of education in inner London and, as it responds to national policy, contribute to the formation of that policy with those needs in mind. The importance of doing so has never been more evident than it is now.

3. In the absence of major new rebuilding programmes, the Authority faces the prospect of housing a sharply declining school population and a range of other services in a large stock of increasingly expensive to maintain premises, some of which are past the end of their useful life. This is an intractable problem but one that has to be dealt with.

4. Inner London is now a multi-cultural society. The implications for

education are still being worked through. Where language is primarily the problem, we appear to know how to deal with it. It is a matter of applying the right resources to the right places. But there is no similarly straightforward response to cultural pluralism. Our efforts at assimilation do not always succeed and are called into question. Amidst these uncertainties, some children do not perform as well as they should. The Authority's response to this needs to be clarified and its efforts to bring about improvement intensified.

5. In educational and organisational terms, the 16 to 19 age group needs particular attention. Their education takes a variety of forms. Over the next few years, the Authority will have to evolve methods, including new forms of co-operation or organisation, which raise the level of what can properly be offered, efficiently and within the resources likely to be available.

6. The Authority's centrally organised services have themselves to be kept under review. The question that has continuously to be asked of them is a simple one: it is whether we still want to do what we have been doing in the way we have been doing it.

This list of items was not worded in a way to encourage debate. At that stage, as always, it seemed crucial to avoid questions to which there were no answers that I was yet able to produce. For example, in (3) above there is a reference to the need to deal with school places becoming surplus as numbers fell. Projections for primary school numbers had been set out. So the facts were not withheld, but it would have been unwise to encourage anyone to note, for example, that if primary school numbers were likely to fall over the next few years by, say, 30,000 and given that the average size of primary school was about 300, did that mean that a hundred primary schools would need to close and, if so, which schools had anyone in mind? In practice, of course, there were ways of reducing the number of school places, such as removing temporary classrooms or ending the use of some detached buildings, which did not involve the closure of a school, but it would be some time before detailed documents, initially for discussion at the Policy Committee, could be prepared.

In (4), the comment 'Our efforts at assimilation do not always succeed' irritated Barry Troyna, a leading researcher into the education of ethnic minorities. Did the Authority or anyone else, myself in particular, really think assimilation would ever succeed, he asked? For my part, of course not; but there were many people in the ILEA who did believe that. The Authority had yet to make up its mind on such issues. During that process, if they there was to be any hope of persuading anyone to re-think anything, it would be foolish to begin by declaring, without explaining why, that those who were convinced that assimilation was both possible and the way forward were misguided. Officials and elected members were going to have to work their way together to new approaches to such problems. Hence, once again, the 'our' in 'our efforts'.

Finally, in paragraph (6), I had in mind, for example, soon suggesting that the Educational Television Service be closed, at a saving within two years, of nearly £500,000 a year, and that the Teacher's residential centre at Stoke D'Abernon, at which a day's stay cost as much as at a three star hotel, should be replaced by one to be developed at Avery Hill. Why not say so then? Again, there was no point in raising contentious issues of this kind before having ensured an adequate degree of political support and worked out some way of providing satisfactory alternatives to institutions being closed down. It would be several months before we would be in a position to do that.

Section two: Improvements to the Authority's main functions and the scope for devolution

The most important point on main functions was expressed in these terms:

> I wish to re-affirm the principle that it is the administration which is responsible for carrying out formal action or reporting to a chairman or to a committee. At County Hall, it is on the assistant education officer that responsibility primarily rests. It is at this point that judgements have to be made about reference to senior colleagues or to members. This is not a responsibility that can be exercised without full information and, within my department, the main responsibility for providing accurate and informed advice rests on the inspectorate.

The converse of that first sentence, which I had discussed with the Leader, was that if members addressed their concerns to persons other than myself or my deputies, we could not be held responsible for any advice that members then acted upon. This was a somewhat convoluted way of indicating that the William Tyndale saga, during which the Chairman of the Schools Sub Committee had tried to sort out problems at the school with the Chief Inspector without mentioning what he was doing to the Education Officer, or indeed to myself as his Deputy, was not to be repeated. Inspectors were to advise me or one of my senior administrative colleagues on serious problems arising in any school or college. One or other of us would then advise the appropriate committee, or in some instances its Chairman, of the Authority's responsibilities and offer advice on what action might then be taken. One thing that now definitely had to stop, I had made clear to colleagues, was inspectorate advice on individual institutions, to me or to anyone else, which did not depend on direct and recent observation of what was happening there by the person or persons offering that advice.

The report then dealt with the suggestion that there should be more delegation from County Hall to the ten divisional offices or to elected committees in each of the thirteen inner London borough council areas. As specialist staff, dealing with the whole of the ILEA, were not employed in multiples of thirteen, the number of inner London boroughs, it was explained that devolving in this way any function, now performed by three or four people, would be an expensive thing to do. So far as elected divisional committees were concerned, one for each inner London borough council, the history of these elsewhere was explained; so too was the reasoning contained in the report of the Royal Commission on local government in England (the Maud report of June 1969). That report explained that divisional executives, of the kind the ILEA Conservatives had in mind, had two serious defects: they caused both delay and confusion. In illustrating both, as I was unable to improve on what he had said, I quoted remarks that Alec Clegg had made to the West Riding of Yorkshire's Education Committee as long ago as in 1953:

> In one area of the county there were in 1944 seven committees with a membership of 98 and 49 individuals occupied the 98 committee places. The number of committees has now increased to 22 and their membership increased to 228, but the number of individuals serving on the committees remains unchanged at 49. It might almost be said that the same number of people do the same amount of work with almost twice as much trouble and less efficiency than they did before, or that ostensibly the same people do the same work over again but in a different place and at a different time.

A second difficulty was one of overlapping functions. I quoted Alec Clegg again:

> One of the most remarkable facts about divisional administration is that divisional executives and school governors both behave as if the former had considerable control over the latter, which is far from being the case. Furthermore, the local authority itself has certain powers of intervention but it has always proved difficult to establish what is to happen if divisional executive and local authority do not see eye to eye on how matters at an individual institution should be conducted. It is not in the nature of a subordinate committee to refrain from contesting the nature of its status on occasions of this kind.

ILEA members found these examples of the effect of an additional, locally elected, tier in the administration of education discouraging and the move to create any form of divisional executive subsided, for the time being at least.

Section three: The individual and the education service: suggestions for the future

This section suggested a wholly new way for the Authority to operate, starting not from the institutions it maintained but from the position of the people using its services:

> A restatement of the problem – like many other organisations, the Authority tends to place its emphasis on the way it delivers its services. These have been built up over the years and behind each element of the service there is a high degree of professional expertise. As the work that has been carried out over the past months shows, improvements on the

delivery side are not easy to achieve. This suggests a change of emphasis. It is, after all, with the quality of the acceptance that an education service has to be concerned. The point to consider is how the service should look to the individual using it. In particular, the need is to improve access in an intelligible form to what is offered.

After some discussion of what might immediately be done to improve access to the education service, enter what came to be known within the office, with the example of Chairman Mao in mind, as the Education Officer's 'hundred flowers':

> These immediate measures need to be supplemented by changes of a more fundamental nature. When considering the Authority's major functions it was clear that the nature of each function has determined the way in which and the place from which it could most effectively be carried out. That is not so with the services that immediately affect individuals. A divisional office is by no means ideal as a delivery point from the customer's point of view. This being so, it is sensible, it appears to me, to start from the consumer and to consider in what form and over what area the individual wants education services to be delivered. Ideally, services should be accessible within reasonable walking distance of every individual wishing to use them. It is on similar principles that the Authority's 120 primary school planning areas are based.

> The principle I propose is therefore a straightforward one. It is that, in the longer term, the Authority should place accessibility at the centre of its physical and organisational planning and gradually arrange access to or information about its services at a range of educational centres. These centres could be associated with those of other statutory or voluntary agencies and their planning and location would require close co-operation with them. It will be seen that two problems are here being considered together: the Authority's need, in the next few years, to reorganize its stock of premises and this other need to try and improve, in common with other public authorities, ease of access for those who wish to use or play their part in the Inner London services. To adopt the principle of always working for greater accessibility is not to plan to do something extra; it is to decide to do something differently. At present, we plan our change of use of premises primarily for the convenience of those providing a part of the education service. The move needed, year by year, within the necessary changes of use and without other than minor expense, is towards suiting the convenience of those who use it.

> There are already examples within the Authority's area where accessibility could be improved in the way suggested. On average, though the actual figures vary widely from one part of London to another, in each of the Authority's 120 primary school planning areas there will be ten or more Authority premises of one kind or another. These may include a secondary school, a careers office, part of an adult education institute, several primary schools, a youth centre, some college premises and so on.

This indicates the nature of what is possible. Clearly, there is no point in thinking of new, custom-built, premises; we have sufficient building already. The process would take time but could begin immediately. The principle proposed is uniform but would vary in its expression from area to area. In some places, little more would be needed than a place where information could be obtained. At other places, something more thorough -going would develop. But, either way, the movement would be in a direction the Committee wished to travel: towards a closer relationship between the Authority and those it exists to serve.

Somewhere in the back of my mind when writing this section of my report was Sir Alec Clegg's remark: 'the test of an education service is how readily an individual can brush past a rule to a person'. My use of the words 'customer' and 'consumer' would have been unfamiliar in a report to a local authority committee at the time because the legislation was written in terms of the respective duties and rights of parents and public authorities. So far as the schools system was concerned, for example, all parents had a duty to send their children to school regularly and the local authority had a corresponding duty to ensure that there were schools for parents to send their children to and that they did. In other words, the nature of the legislation determined the way many of those involved in the administration of it thought about their work. But everything done had, in my view, also to take full account of and preferably start with the interests, perceptions and preferences of those using whatever education service was being provided.

Elements of this approach were already apparent in the plethora of consultations and public meetings that were a feature of the way the ILEA acted before finally deciding what to do. That approach needed to be systematically extended. The primary school planning areas were, in my view, crucial in achieving that. These planning areas were not created by administrators looking at maps; they had developed over one hundred years of London education. It was year in year out experience which showed how far parents of young children were prepared to walk, perhaps pushing a pram, while taking another child to a primary school; and which roads they were willing or unwilling to allow their children to cross unaccompanied. The precise shape of any of these planning areas changed only marginally from year to year in response to factors of this kind; hence the significance of locating the public's initial access to the education service within each such area.

After a summary of its main points, the report concluded:

> Finally, in implying that I do not believe the problems I have been asked to examine will be solved by moving responsibilities from one set of committees or from one part of the administration to other committees or parts of the administration, I do not wish to undervalue the importance of either. It is simply that I believe the overriding need now is to improve access to the education service by direct means and directly also to raise the quality of the content of education in inner London. Preoccupation with the forms of government may inhibit rather than advance this cause.

It was tiring work to write, at such short notice, a report of this length at a time when so much else was claiming my attention. Perhaps that excuses the reference to forms of government. 'For forms of government', Alexander Pope had written in *An Essay on Man* – and I rather hoped no one would recall – 'let fools contest; whate'er is best administered is best'.

One welcome consequence of the length of this report was that it was a long time before I was asked to produce anything of the kind again. The report did the rounds of several ILEA committees and was finally submitted to the Education Committee by the Staff and General Sub-Committee, chaired by Mrs Chaplin. The report was accompanied by a statement that the Committee 'together with other sub-committees had considered and welcomed the report'. When the report finally reached the Education Committee, on 22 March, 1977, it was simply 'received'. Everyone who wanted to say anything about it had already said it – in some instances, several times over.

One thing the report was careful not to do was to raise specific questions which, for the time being, I was not in a position to answer. The general question I had put forward, in (6) above, was 'whether we still want to do what we have been doing in the way we have been doing it'. Fortunately, nobody asked me to produce a document on the implications of that approach, essentially a form of a zero budget. Three questions arose. First, which were the functions most effectively carried out by schools and which by institutions or organisations, funded by the ILEA, outside the schools? Was the balance right? Second, of those carried out by the ILEA, which and at what level, were the functions the Authority was statutorily required to carry out? Third, of those which were provided at the Authority's discretion, the cost and effectiveness of each had to be regularly reviewed. Were all still needed and, if so, worth the money being spent on them?

On the first question, anything that happened within a school or college was a matter for the head or principal and the governing body to deal with. However defined, efficient instruction had to be provided, but decisions on matters such as the content of the curriculum or whether and at what stage a particular school streamed its classes or required pupils to wear a school uniform, were for the school to take. Inspectors could suggest but it was for schools to decide.

On the second question, there was little doubt about what the Authority was statutorily required to do or provide. For example, responsibility for maintaining schools and colleges included responsibility for acquiring suitable sites, providing buildings and distributing revenue for all schools equitably.

It was over the third question, the wide range of services provided at a level not specified in the legislation, that the Authority had regularly to review what it was doing. These services included a careers service, a special education service, an adult education service, an inspection service, a research department and included the provision and management of residential experience, teachers centres, a youth service and drama, music and dance facilities. To attempt to review all these things at once would lead to confusion, but in the following years, one by one each was.

One problem the Authority had to deal with effectively was the future and distribution of the institutions it maintained. In dealing with an expanding further education system and a simultaneously contracting school system, the fact that the authority owned the premises that both used was crucial. As school premises went out of use, in the absence of new building to meet its needs, further education moved in. The accommodation offered was often barely adequate, but it made expansion possible. Other reviews taking place, such as of adult education and a new form of careers service, required only marginal changes to the accommodation needed.

A major cost to any education service arises from the number of people it employs. That had to be carefully controlled. One thing was evident. In the late 1960s and early 1970s, in order to put a teacher in front of every class, the ILEA had had to appoint a number of teachers well below the standard it had been able to appoint in the past. Identifying such teachers was not difficult. Doing anything about it was. This was partly because the process was itself difficult and expensive. Far more serious was the shortage of suitable replacements. It too often happened that, if an unsatisfactory teacher of a shortage subject needed to be removed, advertisement would produce only two or three candidates, each one of whom might be academically well qualified but already known to be unable to manage in a London classroom. So it often proved better to retain a poor teacher than to risk having to replace that teacher with one known to be even les effective.

By far the most important matter, only hinted at in my report because I was not yet clear on what to propose, was how to improve what was being done to educate London's growing proportion of children coming from overseas or born to parents who had recently arrived in London. The facts were clear enough. Reports from ILEA's Research and Statistics department, vigorously led by Dr, later Professor, Little, made it clear that most of these children started school or arrived in school from elsewhere, performing poorly in all aspects of the curriculum. This was not surprising; but the view generally held and expressed by teachers and others was that, after a difficult few years, schools were now dealing with these educational problems far better than in the past. The evidence suggested otherwise. Always with notable exceptions, newcomers were not catching up. Low performers remained comparatively low performing. Gaps in performance levels that should have been closing were even tending to widen. How much of this was due to what the schools were doing or failing to do and how much to what was happening at home, in the holidays or in the streets? Crucially, what more could be done within the school system to improve matters?

One thing that had to be contested at the outset was that, for example, that boys whose parents originated in the West Indies were, in some way, wired to be troublesome.

Apart from the fact that my father had been educated in Barbados until the age of eighteen, my own observations suggested otherwise. Earlier that year, I had watched a young teacher, on the staff of a girls school, working with a group of fifteen year old black boys from a nearby boys school. It was the disparity of size that struck me first. She was about five foot three and the boys all seemed to be at least six foot high. Furthermore, they were a boisterous lot, pushing each other about and shouting at each other as she entered the hall to take her dance lesson. I need not have worried. She clapped her hands together as she came towards them. In a few moments they were all on stage. It was a rehearsal for a show they were putting on. Lively music was playing. The boys danced and leapt with skill and boundless energy. The teacher was in amongst them, encouraging, directing, as absorbed as they were in what was happening. She was in total command. The boys had all turned up for that class on time, none would have missed it for anything. Noone tried to disrupt it, they were all far too absorbed in the dance to do that. When I mentioned to the young woman as I left that I thought she was an outstanding teacher, she had replied that she did not think she had done anything in the least outstanding. This was just an ordinary dance lesson. 'So maybe it's not what you do, that is so outstanding', I suggested 'perhaps it's what you are as a person that is as important as what you do as a teacher.' It was clear to an observer that it was to her fierce determination that they should succeed that those boys were responding so whole-heartedly.

Confronted by problems on this scale and of this nature, the immediate reaction is to appoint people to deal with it. Yet adding bits and pieces on to a system almost always proves ineffective. What is needed is a redirection of thinking by, as far as possible, everyone within the system. It is that changed thinking which then brings about the necessary system-wide changes in behaviour.

In dealing with the educational response the changing composition of the population of inner London, it might be supposed that it would be the Labour Party that was alert to the need for new ways of dealing with the problems arising and the Conservative Party that was opposed to any special effort to deal with them. This was far from being so in London in 1977, though Roy Jenkins, a great reforming Home Secretary had steered the Race Relations Act through in 1976. Opposition to identifying and then dealing with the underperformance of children from some ethnic minorities, not always directly articulated, came from disparate sources. It came from persons influenced by Marxist thinking. As immigrants were seen essentially as members of the working class, dealing separately with elements of that class was regarded as a typical attempt to weaken the class struggle by means of divide and rule. Persons, including several Labour members of the ILEA who themselves had been refugees, mostly from Europe, and had established themselves in London and had required no special help in the process, in particular, some members of the Jewish community, objected to policies requiring the identification of ethnic or religious differences. For their part, many teachers, particularly in the primary schools, were strongly committed to a 'they are all children to me' philosophy: a conscious decision not to emphasise or even respond to any differences between children. Opposition also came from believers in assimilation as the way forward: seen as the need for newcomers to London to become indistinguishable from existing Londoners. Such people believed the problems that had to be dealt with could not be systemic. They pointed to how well elements of the Indians and the Chinese communities were doing soon after they arrived in London, as opposed to immigrants from the West Indies, Pakistan and Bangladesh. Finally, there was some lack of enthusiasm from administrative colleagues and other well-intentioned members of the ILEA. Recognising that there were problems to which we needed to respond and being aware of strongly opposed feelings about how these could best be dealt with, they were concerned that, with so much else going on - for example, dealing with the consequences of ending selection into secondary schools, reducing the number of schools, trying to retain good teachers and so on - there was a risk of taking on more than we could manage effectively.

In these circumstances, although aware of the inadequacy of this response, it was decided initially to rely on an incremental response, to which there was unlikely to be much opposition; so we concentrated on language classes for those who needed them, the appointment of inspectors and ancillary workers from within the minority communities to help schools in the greatest difficulty. Meanwhile, we tried to increase awareness within all areas of the education system of how much more needed to be done. Finally, a start was made at examining forms of discrimination that might be operating within the ILEA's administration itself. Why, for example, was the ILEA's finance department largely composed of staff originating in the Indian sub-continent whereas so few of them worked- and fewer still were promoted - elsewhere in County Hall? Was it because they were particularly good at mathematics or was it because the poor standard of their written English was holding them back? Probably the latter, it appeared. That raised the question of how those standards of English could be raised and how good a standard of English was really needed, as opposed to being required in terms of examination results, in most of the day to day administrative work in County Hall.

In 1977, too much had to be done too quickly. The one thing that could be relied upon with certainty was that there would be a constant series of interruptions to anything that I, for one, was trying to do. Mrs Chaplin contributed energetically to this problem. I kept having to explain to her that I could not be in several places at once, however much she wanted me to be. She worked full time as an ILEA member. She was everywhere, impossible to keep up with as she hastened from meeting to meeting, usually rather late, with documents flying about from the over-loaded plastic bags she carried them in. The grandly entitled Committee for Local Education Authority Purchases of Science Equipment (CLEAPSE) was one of many local authority committees that Mrs Chaplin chaired. This money-saving body concerned itself with the bulk buying of science equipment for schools and colleges in much of the south of England. As the ILEA was a large organisation, it found itself chairing or having to administer a whole range of such committees. Attendance of senior ILEA officers at such meetings tended to be unenthusiastic and sporadic. Their presence was hardly noticed, their absence resented, particularly if Mrs Chaplin happened to be chairing the meeting. Fortunately, we remained on good terms throughout but she had a habit of peppering me with minutes to which some response was expected. The one I received on 13 June was just one example of this; it took the form of an irritable manuscript scrawl, evidently written at the meeting itself:

> Dear Peter, CLEAPSE
>
> I think it's a bit thick not having the EO represented as he is the Hon Education Officer. IC

The fall in pupil numbers

As my lengthy report to the Authority earlier in the year had explained, the consequences of falling pupil numbers had to be tackled. Action had already taken to reduce the number of secondary schools in the face of the predicted fall in the age group entering secondary schools but there had been no clear statement to the Education Committee about how this was being done. The principles we had been using, an instance of the 'managing a process' procedure I had mentioned in that report, were formally adopted by the Authority in June 1977. To avoid outraged opposition to school closures, which detailed plans covering a wide area, always provoked, we had moved to applying a set of principles, deliberately lacking predicted outcomes, to be applied to decisions about what needed to be done within smaller areas. In an article, published some time later, I described the shift that had occurred since the mid-1970s:

> Re-organisation has taken place in three stages. The first stage was in 1972. Shortly after the future fall in numbers began to become evident, the ILEA divided itself into four and planned the future of the 50 to 60 secondary schools within each quadrant. The procedure was to put out a series of papers explaining the declining demand for school places, defining alternative forms of comprehensive education which it was the Authority's policy to develop, and making proposals for bringing this about within ten years. The plans incorporated some 90 schools, many of them small, voluntary aided, often denominational, grammar schools.
>
> The 1972 proposals ran head-on into three difficulties. The first was the argument about selection versus non-selection at 11+. The second concerned the validity or otherwise of the projections of future numbers. The third can be summed up in a general assumption that 'consultation is a farce: everything is already fixed'. Public discussion of the 1972 proposals brought these difficulties into full flower and made reasoned discussion about the future of individual schools often impossible to conduct. The effect of this was that, after protracted local discussions,

far less was achieved than the logic of the documents deserved. With hindsight, it can be seen that too much was attempted too far in advance over too wide an area.

The second stage consisted of the ending of eleven plus selection between 1975 and 1977. From the administrative point of view, this entailed separating out one thread of a complex planning problem and dealing with it in isolation.

The third and present stage began with a report to the Education Committee in 1977. This set out the five principles on which a review of all the ILEA's secondary schools was to be based. The principles the Policy Committee had confirmed were:

1. The wishes of parents
2. The educational quality of the individual school
3. The degree to which individual schools conformed, or could be made to conform, to high standards of accommodation
4. The distribution of schools (mixed or single sex, county or voluntary, large or small) within an area.
5. The Authority's responsibilities, as an employer, to teaching and non-teaching staff alike.

At the Policy Committee which considered my draft proposals, its members had agreed with these principles after suggesting that the order in which I had placed them, which had not been intended to imply priority, should be changed to place the wishes of parents at the top. So that was done.

It will be apparent that these principles sometimes conflict. A school in excellent premises may be in a difficult to reach location. Alternatively, a popular school may be in irredeemably poor premises. So the search was for the best way forward rather than for the ideal solution. Once the principles for planning were settled, a procedure for consultation was devised. Again, this was a case of choosing the manageable rather than the ideal. Although movement across the boundaries of the ILEA's ten divisions is extensive, planning and public discussion was confined, for the most part, to one or two divisions. The re-organisation process itself was separated into six stages, lasting in all between six and eight months.

This timescale was important. Structural change designed to improve matters in the future is seldom in the interests of the persons or institutions undergoing it. Prolonged debate about proposals for change leads to increased uncertainty and entrenched positions being adopted. So far as parents are concerned, a fixed timetable, clearly announced in advance and limiting debate to one school year in which parents are uncertain which schools would be there for their children to attend, was crucial in preventing, as in this instance it did, widespread unrest. The six stages were:

Stage 1: The Education Officer to distribute, without comment, a straightforward factual paper describing school population changes, the timetable of the review being undertaken and its purpose.

Stage 2: After a decent interval, the Education Officer to prepare a report setting out alternative possibilities for a given area. The appropriate ILEA committee would then be asked to agree that the alternatives could be discussed but, by self-denying ordinance, not to express any view on their merits or otherwise.

Stage 3: The Education Officer and colleagues to discuss this document with staff, governors, parents and the general public and invite them to send in their views by a given date.

Stage 4: The Education Officer then to produce draft recommendations, with his ideas about what should be done, and to circulate these widely to the people whose views had already been canvassed. At this stage, with concrete proposals to debate, local elected members and members of the ILEA committee concerned would, for the first time, become directly involved with the public, usually by means of one or two public meetings, chaired by a leading ILEA Member.

Stage 5: The Education Officer, who had been present or represented at these public meetings, to make his recommendations to the Committee, accompanied by the written comments of those consulted, including any comments on the draft proposals referred to in Stage 4.

Stage 6: With those recommendations before them and a full range of public comments (over 400 pages of them on the last occasion), the Committee to make up its own mind about what to do.

There are four points to make about the way things have gone. First of all, the three obstacles referred to earlier have lost their force. Selection to secondary schools ended in 1977. Issuing and being prepared to discuss a factual paper (stage 1) in advance seems to have cleared away the 'you have all the facts wrong' obstacle. Finally, the 'consultation is a farce' argument has collapsed, since the gap between Stage 4, what the Education Officer originally proposed, and Stage 6, what the Committee ultimately decides, has been there for everyone to see.

Second, the process of planning, with defined stages and an agreed factual base, has led to public comment of a remarkably high standard. Committees and administrators have genuinely learnt from and responded to what has been said to them.

Third, as the decisions finally reached have observably been an improvement on those originally put forward, they have tended to command public support.

Finally, the whole procedure illustrates the planning problem with which we are all becoming familiar. In many areas of the education service, structural change is needed. Yet the best way to prevent change is often to charge straight at the public with a totally coherent, comprehensive and carefully staged plan for achieving it, preferably with photographs. Assaulted in that way, the public digs in to resist. So ways have to be found of enabling large numbers of people to focus on and think together about problems of a manageable size. It is one such way that I have been describing.

It has been a consistent theme in describing my experience of educational administration since 1963 that the most important elements in any report to a committee was often what it left out. In this instance, two obvious things were missing from this account of how dealing with a reduced need for school places was managed. The first is the lack of any statement, private of public, about the scale of the reduction in the number of schools that was likely to be necessary. The second was any reference to the financial consequences of what was being done. On the first point, a reduction in secondary school pupil numbers of some 60,000 was expected during the 1970s. On an average of about 1,000 for each school, that could imply a reduction of about sixty in the number of secondary schools the ILEA maintained. Any suggestion to that effect would have led to banner headlines in the London Press, furious opposition from parents and governing bodies, almost certainly leading to a political retreat into the bunkers. Which sixty schools had anyone in mind, people could reasonably ask? Someone must know. Why was this information being withheld? Consultation was a farce. Everything had been decided already. In these circumstances, many more than sixty schools would start worrying about whether they were one of the sixty and would insist on absolute assurances that they were not. The truth was that neither I nor anyone else could predict, with any degree of accuracy, which schools and how many of them would cease to exist at the end of a genuine exercise in local consultation.

The second thing that was missing was any reference to finance. It was obviously true that reducing the number of school buildings to be maintained would reduce expenditure, as would any subsequent sale of the sites and buildings concerned. The level of savings that might be possible was not difficult to calculate. Unfortunately, any reference to saving money by closing schools would instantly have led to the claim that the Authority was closing them for that reason. The valid argument that reducing the number of half empty schools was strongly in the educational interests of the children concerned would be dismissed out of hand at angry public meetings. So calculations about the number of schools to be reduced and the savings that might follow from that were never presented to any committee or even discussed in any detail with my immediate colleagues. The time to record the level of savings made was in a footnote to the budget documents in the year after they were made. Saving money was not the main motive for restructuring the schools; finding ways to improve the quality of education was. So we focused attention on that aspect of what we were trying to do and made every effort to reach agreement on how best to do that.

Keeping colleagues in touch

With so much happening day-to-day, it was difficult to keep colleagues up to date. On 7 November 1977, I held a meeting with senior ILEA staff. This included administrative and inspectorate colleagues from County Hall but also Divisional Officers and Inspectors. At a time of rapid change, it became particularly important to keep this second group in touch with what was happening at County Hall. The meeting was crowded and held in a County Hall committee room. This was, ill-adapted for the purpose, so there were people behind me, perched on fixed pieces of furniture, as well as in front of me. Unknown to me at the time, my remarks were being tape recorded. Subsequently, the tape had bits blanked out by some cautious individual; presumably because they were inaudible or, more probably, because they were altogether too frank. At this November meeting, I described what was being done about reducing the number of secondary schools the ILEA maintained. I went on to remark, rather too emphatically: 'clearly, the best way to improve the quality of education in London would be to ensure that the least effective hundred schools . . . .' Here I had obviously regretted using any such number and had paused before going on to mumble: 'er, if these schools were simply not, er, to be around'. Even at a private meeting with colleagues, I could not bring myself to use the word 'closed'. The walls of committee rooms in County Hall tended to acquire ears.

My remarks on occasions of this sort tended to be rapidly spoken, full of self-interruptions and often dangerously informal. On this occasion, after describing a number of things we were shortly planning to do, including the move to help schools deal with disruptive pupils, I added, in an effort to be reassuring:

> I have not got anything else up my sleeve. I shall be consulting my colleagues very shortly to see if they have any bright ideas they want to land on us, but I am not aware of any major new areas of development. By that I mean we're not trying to close all the special schools or anything like that. I hardly dare mention (pause, and the sound of some disturbance at the meeting) – that's a joke. In some company, you have to watch it.'(Voice on the tape: 'look behind you'); – 'oh, sorry Marie; that really is a joke!' (laughter)

Not a very good joke, evidently, but even a mention of the idea of closing special schools had disturbed Dr Marie Roe, the Inspector responsible for special education, for this was a time when the recently published Warnock Report had made some people working in and for special schools nervous about their future.

Marie would have had good reason to be disturbed had she known what I really believed should be done about special schools. As it happened, without committing my ideas to paper or discussing them with anyone else, I had already reluctantly abandoned them. My ideas about special schools had been forming well before I had arrived in London in 1972. I then had the opportunity to look at a number of the boarding special schools the Authority maintained. Several of them were in large country houses, spread about the Home Counties. One particularly splendid one had peacocks strutting about in its extensive grounds. The idea was a development of the lock gate principle. There were to be four stages. The first would be to identify, say, three well-established secondary schools. Each would then be associated with one of the residential special schools. No one could really object to that. The second stage, provided the schools concerned agreed – so it was not altogether a joke, Marie – would be to close, in the legal sense, the chosen special schools and simultaneously enlarge and adapt the premises of the associated secondary schools. So a secondary school and what had been the special school would now be a single legal entity with a single, enhanced, governing body. At this stage, no child or teacher would be required to move. All salaries would be protected; so there would be no need for parental, teacher or other forms of panic. There matters would briefly rest. The third stage, at a time and to an extent to be agreed between individual parents and the schools, with any necessary professional advice, would consist of some movement of children between the special schools and the secondary schools of which they were now a part. That movement might consist of the occasional afternoon visit or for such special activities or events as the teachers and parents agreed would be in the interests of the child. Pupils and interested staff from the secondary school might, at this stage, begin to visit the residential school, initially perhaps to do no more than enjoy the countryside and admire the peacocks. The fourth stage could develop over a period impossible to specify in advance. Several things could be expected to happen. There could be growing professional acquaintance, including an interchange of teachers between the staff of what had previously been two schools, accompanied, it may be, by a better career structure for both. Increasingly, to the professionals and parents alike, it would become apparent when individual pupils at the 'special' residential department of the secondary school could benefit, particularly when they were near to leaving school, from some regular attendance at the day school. All pupils in the 'special' department could have carefully supervised, opportunities to do that. As for those country house premises, hugely underused in my view, these could be more intensively used for residential experience, in holiday periods as well as in term time, by day school pupils or Youth Clubs. There could be tents on the spacious grounds as I had seen at Bretton Hall in 1970 during my first day in the West Riding. If the experiment succeeded, some or most of the other thirty boarding special schools the Authority maintained, might join in. So might some of the day special schools be associated with nearby day schools. Many of them would benefit from the wider curriculum opportunities which being included, at arms length if that is what seemed appropriate, in a larger school would make possible.

This idea got no further than this brief remark to my assembled colleagues to the effect that it was not to be pursued. I had regretfully had to conclude that the secondary schools of Inner London were confronted by too extensive changes for any but a very few of the most effective of them to be asked to take on the new responsibilities which would be required. From my perspective, the proposal, like the 'hundred flowers' approach, was an idea well worth pursuing but not at the risk of over-loading an increasingly overburdened system. The essential task for the ILEA, from which it could not safely be diverted, was to do all it could to help the secondary schools make the development of comprehensive education work. Improved residential experience for secondary pupils and a sustained effort to deal with the entrenched difficulty of giving children in special schools, particularly residential ones, sufficient experience of the world which they would later have to enter would have to be left for a future that never came.

My report to the Authority had referred to post sixteen education and training. Eric Briault had reported on the problem in 1968. He had been told that the ILEA was committed to 11–18 schools on the lines set out in the London Plan of 1947 so there was to be no suggestion for any other form of structure. But the facts were disturbing. All over inner London there were schools with tiny sixth forms where not always particularly well qualified teachers were sometimes teaching subject groups of four or five students. This was expensive and, in my experience, educationally unsatisfactory. Sixth formers learn from each other as well as from their teachers. I had certainly found that to be so when I had taught French translation to a group of three students. By the end of term we were becoming thoroughly bored with each other. In the London of 1977, however, given the far-reaching and still continuing changes occurring in its secondary schools, further structural change to them was out of the question, at least until the comprehensive intake had worked its way through the system by 1982. The grammar schools had been persuaded to accept children of all abilities. It had been suggested that forms of cooperation between what might become smaller sixth forms might be necessary, but that was for the future. My view was that the schools would discover this for themselves and would then set about devising ways for dealing with the problem, with financial and other forms of assistance from the Authority.

The approach we invited the Education Committee to ask us to adopt was to be through ensuring that an Authority-wide entitlement for all sixteen year olds remaining in full-time education was put in place. Initially, it was the 'A' level offer that was to be definitely established. This was later to be widened as this note to the Leader, of 4 November, explained:

Budget Motion

16–19 Co-operative work

1. The Education Committee has asked the EO to report by next April on plans which ensure that all secondary schools can provide a minimum of 12–16 A-levels, either on their own or in co-operation with other schools or colleges.

2. Similarly, proper non A-level opportunities have to be provided and

plans for providing these are also called for.

3. At the moment, heads, staff representatives and college representatives are meeting throughout ILEA to work out ways of achieving this comprehensive 16+ offer. Some of the schemes will cost more, in the form of extra teachers, new materials, transport and so on; for example, in the form of another VI Form Centre.

4. This is not all the Authority is doing. This year we ran a series of intensive courses for VI Formers during the summer term. Thirty-eight courses were held dealing with topics that included art, biology, chemistry, child development, classics, computer studies, literature, geography, history, languages, mathematics, music, physics and sociology. In all, over 1,000 young people attended. The reports received show that some of these courses were outstandingly successful in stretching the abilities of the VI Formers to the full. We want to build on this next year and develop further courses and make them more widely available than they were this year. We believe inner London could provide the best VI Form education to be found anywhere and we want to make this available to all who can take advantage of it.

The re-organised Further Education Colleges were ahead of the schools in providing appropriate opportunities for sixteen-year-olds. There were still far too many students of that age who had been persuaded to remain in school sixth forms when they would have fared better in a Further Education College.

I was acutely aware of how inadequate the arrangements we were making were. London was a great city and here we were patching things together when we could have led the country in what we were able to offer to our academically ablest sixteen year olds. How could that be done? On the wall of my room there was huge a map of inner London occupying most of it. Every school and college was marked on it, with different coloured threads linking detached premises and showing what kind of institution it was. As I looked at the map, I could not help also being aware of the location of the leading independent schools situated in inner London or, like St Paul's that my brother had attended, now on the edge of it. Looked at this way, one thing was immediately evident about London. Within it were sufficient teachers of the highest quality to offer, with suitable reinforcements, first rate opportunities to any London child capable of benefiting from their teaching. Where were these teachers? Where, for example, were the teachers with good honours degrees in physics, mathematics and classics now teaching? I had discussed this issue with John Rae, headmaster of Westminster. It transpired that there were more such teachers teaching in Westminster's sixth form than in all the secondary schools of Tower Hamlets and Hackney put together. And the same applied to modern languages. Not all of London's independent schools were first rate but it was obvious that the first thing anyone would recognize, after looking at where many of the best qualified teachers were teaching, was that education in London could never reach its full potential without the active cooperation of the best of its independent schools.

It followed from this that suggesting the abolition of these schools- or proposing financial measures designed to have much the same effect – should stop. Meanwhile, it was damaging and largely a waste of money for taxpayers to pay for numbers of children to attend these schools at the age of eleven or thirteen. It might marginally help the children concerned but would also correspondingly diminish what the schools they came from could offer. The distinguishing characteristic of London's leading independent schools, as it was of others elsewhere, was not what they did for their pupils up to the age of sixteen, though they did that well enough. What was crucially important about these schools, so far as access to university was concerned, was the quality of their sixth forms. It might be desirable but it was certainly not essential for a pupil to have been in one of those schools for the previous three or five years to benefit from those sixth forms. Nor was it necessary to have been selected at the age of eleven to so benefit. The development of Sixth Form Colleges outside London, many of the best of them created from grammar schools, made that clear. Within London, the successful effect of a boys school, such as Westminster, admitting girls to their sixth form or Camden School for Girls, admitting boys to theirs, was further evidence of what might be possible.

The second thing that had to be recognised about the best independent schools was that, far from doing too much, they were doing too little. Unlike most schools in London, they could recruit outstandingly able staff straight from university. I had seen the effect of this though missed experiencing it, when Denis Mack Smith had come to Clifton to teach history during the war. As a brilliant young Cambridge student, declared unfit for military service, he was only a couple of years older than the sixth formers he taught. Yet sixteen of the thirty-seven university awards won by Clifton students in 1942 and 1943 were in history. Given the additional staff they could attract, the best independent school sixth forms in London ought not to have been teaching three or four hundred students each. Well over a thousand students should be what they were aiming at.

The third thing was to suggest how this could be achieved. Suppose, for example, that Dulwich College, where David Emms was headmaster, were to be asked what he would need to increase the size of his sixth form to 1,000 or more and for that part of the school to become be the sixth form college for a wide area of south London. You want new building? Done. Girls to join the sixth form? Done. Effect on other schools, particularly those for girls? Tough; for them sort out. Control over which students to admit? Entirely for you to settle. Money and fees? No fees would be payable for any post-sixteen students at Dulwich, otherwise why should fee-paying parents agree to free sixth form education for others at their school? All sixth form places would be funded by the ILEA, largely out of savings made from discontinuing inadequate and expensive sixth forms elsewhere. What also was needed to ensure that the school could offer, by itself or in association with other institutions, the best possible facilities for dance, drama, music, art and design? London rate-payers would only be interested in funding something that was equal or better than the best being provided anywhere else in this country – or indeed in Europe.

Would Westminster, with John Rae as its head and Canon Carpenter chairing its governing body, both of whom I knew well, be interested? Would Sir Ashley, himself educated at Westminster, think this idea worth pursuing? Where else, amongst some of the best sixth forms in ILEA-maintained schools could we gather together the critical mass of highly qualified teachers able to teach large numbers of young people in sensibly sized groups, able to match the best of anything being done at Louis le Grand in Paris or elsewhere in the rest of Europe? Could the City of London be persuaded to stop grumbling and make an effort to help? Individual City Companies had been doing that for years, but what was needed now was a concerted effort, London-wide. Would a Labour ILEA agree to a development of post sixteen education in a form that would require and be largely paid for by the closure of some of its least adequate sixth forms? Only one leading independent school would be needed to start with. Others would follow. And what ambitious parent would not want to their children to attend ILEA secondary schools up to the age of sixteen with sixth form opportunities like that then open to them?

In 1977, too much was going on elsewhere to move the discussion forward any distance.. The Conservative victory in the election of 1979 put an end to speculations of this kind. Barriers went up and increasingly rancorous relations between government and local authorities, with the ILEA directly in the firing line, took over. From my perspective, of all the things that it was not possible to attempt in the 1970s, engaging some of the best independent schools directly in a drive to provide free access to first rate post-sixteen education throughout inner London was possibly the saddest.

In my minute to the Leader in 1976, I had mentioned that the Taylor Report on governing bodies would be published. Towards the end of 1977, it was. The Report dealt with the composition, powers and functions of school governing bodies. The underlying assumption on which the report was based was that members of governing bodies, as unpaid volunteers, would be whole-heartedly committed to the success of the school to which they had been appointed. There could be no hidden agenda. Herein, so far as Inner London was concerned, lay the problem. There are two reasons why people devote time and effort to become members of governing bodies or indeed of Education Committees. The first is to promote the interests of education, the second is, in one way or another, to damage them. In some parts of London, there were rather too many people in the latter group. It included teachers with extreme views who saw oppression everywhere and took it to be their function to disrupt, overturn or in some other way oppose those who were, by definition, the oppressors. High on the list of oppressors, on this view, were head teachers, people in education offices and unsympathetic Chairmen of governing bodies. So what was to happen, according to the Taylor Committee, if the governing body came under the control of the oppressed and made life impossible for the presumed oppressor-in-chief, the head teacher? More generally, how could the local education authority effectively intervene when a governing body and the head, with or without the support of senior teachers, were at odds with each other? The Taylor report was silent on such matters. As the Authority broadly welcomed the report, which had many sensible things to say, I could not express my concerns publicly. Hence the anonymity of the article published in the *Times Educational Supplement* of 18 December 1977. It was written in haste but, beneath the levity, I was trying to make five serious points: the ease with which a governing body could be taken over if teacher and parent governors of the same political or other persuasion acted together, the uncertain position of the head and senior staff in such a case, the inability of the local education authority to do anything effective to help if things went wrong in this way, the near certainty that the Press would get the story wrong were any dispute to become public and, finally, that if any dispute did became public, that everyone would agree that the local authority ought to have sorted the problem out more quickly.

On 23 December 1977, an article appeared in *Education* which caught my eye. 'Everyone knows', the author wrote, 'what headmasters and chief education officers do'. Really? So far as CEOs were concerned, Professor Maurice Kogan had published what certain leading CEOs had told him that they believed themselves to be doing. But how did they actually spend their time? For my part, whenever I checked what I had been doing during a week, I found it differed markedly from what my office diary recorded that I was supposed to have been doing. Unless the deeply unpopular early morning meetings, favoured by some ILEA members living a short walk away from County Hall, were being called, the day started between 8.15am and 8.30am and went on to 6.00pm or a little later. Often, however, there was a third session. There were 102 such sessions in 1977. These normally lasted until at least 9 pm. On one occasion, when the Policy Committee showed every sign of going on for much longer than that, John Bevan created a useful precedent by rising to his feet, remarking that he had a train to catch and moving swiftly to the door. Henceforth, members of that committee began to cast rather edgy glances in his direction when 10 pm approached. Fortunately, sit-ins lasting into the early hours of the morning had become unfashionable, though I retained the habit of looking carefully, when at any potentially contentious gathering, to detect any sign of a thermos flask or a blanket amongst those present.

During 1977, I gave twenty-seven substantial talks to teachers and a large number of brief ones, such as goodbyes to individuals. To parents, educational groups or people outside the ILEA, there were a further twenty-seven talks and seven brief ones: opening exhibitions of work, speech days and so on. To add to these there were six longish reports to the Education Committee, a few TV appearances, a succession of school visits, countless conversations and interruptions and over four hundred letters. The weekends, other than the twenty-eight spent away from home, were very much part of the working year. No speeches I gave were written by anyone other than myself. Even if only prepared in note form, there usually had to be time spent putting some thoughts down before offering them.

Usually but not always.

On one occasion, while holding a difficult meeting in my office, I was interrupted by my secretary. 'Mr Radford', she explained, 'absolutely insists on having the title of the talk you are giving to the head teachers in his Division later this week'. I had first met Alan when he was headmaster of a secondary modern school in the North Riding in 1963. Alan was a rolled-up sleeve species of inspector and I admired his approach to the schools in his part of London, but I was not pleased to be disturbed and answered briefly. I thought no more about my speech until well on the way to Stoke D'Abernon, where the residential course was being held. The talks given on such occasions were nearly all on the same lines, so I was content not to think about what to say until I had established what the heads wanted me to talk about. On entering the lecture room, I found the assembled head teachers in an unruly state of amusement. The title of my talk was now printed in large letters on the programme that was being waved about in front of me. 'Tell Mr Radford I'm busy' it read.

By the end of 1977, four policies or ideas had either run out of steam or had proved too risky or complex to be worth pursuing.

The first was the Education Service for the Whole Community initiative. This needed a concentration of effort which the rapidly changing shape of London education, with the consequent disturbance to the smooth running of many of its institutions, made it impossible for me to develop as Dr Briault had intended. But the idea of a London education service, in which all had a degree of responsibility for what was happening outside their own institutions as well as within them, remained potent. It was the right idea at what had proved to be the wrong time.

The second, referred to earlier, was the never publicly stated prospect of a gradually managed structural change to some, ultimately perhaps to most, of the Authority's special schools. This would be designed to substitute over-complex movement between different types of school into carefully controlled movement within enlarged existing schools, as and when teachers and parents agreed that this would best meet the particular needs of individual children.

The third idea that came to very little was the 'hundred flowers' approach: shifting public access to education and other related services to some 120 locations in inner London. Each would be within the planning areas for primary schools and so within reasonably safe walking distance for everyone living in that area. The upheavals within the ILEA and the changed relationships with the inner London boroughs that would be required, were altogether too extensive to contemplate.

Finally, I was still a long way from being in a position to pursue the possibility of how and on what terms some of London's most successful independent schools could become part of the structure of post sixteen education in parts of inner London.

On the positive side, elected members had initiated a review of all the sites, including the housing on those sites, owned or reserved, some since the days of the London School Board but mostly since the 1944 Education Act, for use by a constantly expanding education service. Parts of that service were now contracting, so a response to that was now needed. The review, with important social consequences, conducted area by area and in great detail, ultimately led to the release of over three hundred acres of land in inner London and the freeing of more than five thousand houses from blight. This was a detailed, patient, unpublicized and time-consuming initiative, serviced by the Authority's full-time staff but initiated, driven forward and expertly conducted, in meeting after meeting, by a small group of determined, part-time, unpaid politicians.

More generally, the primary schools were becoming more stable and their performance was improving. There had been no headline-grabbing failures, as there had been at William Tyndale, to contend with; though there were still a number of worryingly poor schools and a shortage of experienced teachers to help improve them. Ten primary inspectors, one for each division, had now been appointed to help establish and then encourage good practice. The structure of secondary education had been settled and admissions to the first all-ability intake to secondary schools had been managed with little parental unrest or resentment at any of the schools themselves. The sixth form summer schools had been well-supported and showed every sign of becoming a permanent feature of what could be offered to sixth formers. Late in the year, ideas on how to deal better with pupils who were disruptive had been exchanged with secondary school heads and the necessary financial consequences had been discussed with the Leader. This would enable proposals to be put forward early in 1978. Action was being taken on a variety of ways of responding to the educational needs of ethnic minority communities and a team of inspectors, mostly recruited from those communities, had begun to help schools improve what they and other parts of the education service had so far been able to offer. Steady progress was being made in relating the number and location of schools to the reduced number of children who would need to be accommodated in the foreseeable future.

Much more needed to be done. The internal organisation of the Authority needed attention. Plans for the closure of a number of the Authority's institutions, such as the ETV service and the residential teachers' centre at Stoke D'Abernon, were now almost ready to be put to the Policy Committee. All manner of legislative and other problems would no doubt arise in the coming months but, from my perspective at the end of 1977, there were solid grounds for optimism. The year had begun with John Bevan still entangled in the Tyndale affair and with myself isolated at the head of a huge and, as yet, imperfectly understood administrative structure. By the end of the year, sound working relationships with an experienced political leadership had been established. The senior officers' group, which had initially only included John Bevan and the Chief Inspector, had been joined early in the year by Tim Brighouse and Bill Stubbs. Each of my three deputies was fully capable of taking over anything I was doing if I needed to be away. Together they constituted what Sir Ashley later described as a Rolls Royce solution to the ILEA's administrative structure. Between them, they had managed to solve the problem of the over-burdened chief executive. Life with such deputies became practically stress free.

For much of 1977, day-to-day pressures and seemingly endless committee and other meetings meant that I had rarely been out of County Hall for more than a few hours at a time. One or two visits to see how other education systems in England managed their affairs, even an occasional venture overseas, I began to think, now appeared possible.

Chapter 4: 1978

From 18 January 1978, all letters and documents originating with me, typed or in manuscript, were retained in date order in what came to be known as 'the Black Books'. This happened because I had asked someone to find something I had written soon after I had arrived in London in 1972. I had kept a few documents of that kind, such as those quoted earlier, in my own files and had assumed that someone was keeping the rest somewhere else. Not so. The ILEA had a system whereby all documents presented to a committee were retained permanently in some central filing system. Anything else was destroyed after five years. I had been in the ILEA for six years and no one had told me about this. The result was, in date order, twenty four black bookfuls of my drafts, letters and scrawled notes, weighing down the shelves in my office by the time I left. Henceforth, that means that everything I have said I have written can be checked against what I actually did write. The rapidity and, sometimes, the irritation with which what was written or rapidly dictated will be obvious. I have been tempted to correct the result but, apart from expunging a few names, have not.

As with internal minutes to colleagues, some of the letters to and from my office were handwritten. Apart from the first two letters set out below, four themes from the year are separately identified: new ways of dealing with pupils who were disruptive, my views on aspects of the work of the Authority's inspectorate, the response to industrial action by teachers and, finally, examples of my own relationship with individual teachers.

The first letter in the Black Books was written before the theory that schools have elastic walls had prevailed. Like a bus or a theatre or a restaurant, once a secondary school had admitted and placed on the school register a pre-published number of children, ordinarily defined by the number of form entries of thirty children it could admit, it was regarded as full. There was no appeal against that. The punctuation in the beautifully hand written letter from Lisa, of 18 January 1978, has been left unchanged:

Dear Mr Newsam,

Please can you explain why I cannot attend school. I choose to attend St Martin- in- the-Fields school for 'girls' as I felt it would give me a better education for my future than most schools in my area which is d.O.8. I do not wish to attend Thomas Calton School as I feel it would not be of benefit to my education or future. Please can you help.

Awaiting your reply, Lisa .M.H (age 12)

Letter to Lisa (handwritten) of 21 January:

Dear Lisa,

Thank you for your letter. The trouble is that the school you want to go to is full up and there is nothing I can do to change that, much as I would like to help. You have very good hand-writing, I must say.

The school Lisa wanted to go to was responsible for its own admissions. I passed Lisa's letter on to the headmistress without comment. The headmistress told me some months later that Lisa was doing rather well.

The second letter in the Black Books is an example of a constant feature of educational and other forms of administration. What might have happened but did not can be quite as important as anything that did. For a brief period, London's *Evening Standard* was edited by Simon Jenkins, later of *The Times* and elsewhere. The deputy editor was Richard Bourne. Both knew London well. It was all too good to last. Changes to the paper's ownership and its editors caused the Standard to revert to its traditional disapproval, from which its journalists rarely proved willing to diverge, of all things relating to County Hall. The letter, dated 19 January 1978, was addressed to Richard Bourne. It reflected experience gained in 1976 from that visit to New York:

Dear Richard,

Two things, partly *Evening Standard*, partly ILEA. You will know of the flurry going on at the moment about inner cities. Partnership is the idea now, between various official agencies, the Department of the Environment, DES, Health, the police, the local manifestations of all these people, including the ILEA, borough organisations, and anyone else with some access to the public purse. We are to stop falling over each other's feet in trying to help and to have some money to spend together.

Have you heard of the New York Urban Coalition? I enclose a booklet which describes what it is about and the programme we had when we were over there in 1976. Of course, they are some fifteen years further into the soup than we are over here and they have evolved a very different form of partnership. Never mind the comparative practical effectiveness of the two ideas at the moment. The interesting thing to me is that the insurance companies of New York recognised some time ago that they did not like their buildings burning down; similarly, the publishers had an interest in seeing that children and young adults were able to read. That seemed sensible enough. All these people, with the public authorities, had an interest, as well as the general sense of benevolence, to make them want to improve the quality of life in the city. It is this desire to lift things that seems to be missing here. I may be quite wrong about this but, in London terms, it seems strange that the skills and financial power of the City, to take one main example, have not been mobilised to provide a return on money used for socially acceptable purposes.

For example, they could start by building us a polytechnic – we have the site - and lease it back to us. It would be in the City's own interest to do that. I am putting this badly, but the essential idea is simple. If London takes its future seriously, it has, possibly uniquely amongst great cities, the means to put matters right, or as nearly right as human beings can, over the next twenty to thirty years. Could not the Evening Standard, as the inner London newspaper, hammer home the need for partnerships, at least at the strategic level, which include all the parties that have an interest in London's future? There must be money to be earned as well as spent on this venture, and somehow the will to do this needs to be mobilised.

Here follows a section on the 'comparatively insignificant', in relation to London's problems, contribution the ILEA was making. Papers were enclosed on the improvement in primary school standards; the initiative on multi-ethnic education and its new inspectorate; efforts 'to deal creatively with the disruptives in our midst. The idea of increased sanctions is just too absurd. There is nothing teachers can do to these young people, most of them, which they have not encountered to a far greater degree at home.' Finally, there is a reference to the sixth form summer schools. The letter concludes:

> The future of London has not caught fire imaginatively. The lesson from New York is that the major institutions have got to assume a responsibility and be allowed to assume it. This may all sound rather vague, but it springs from the fact that I do not believe it can be right that the regeneration of London should be left in the hands of public authorities without access to the expertise and financial backing that is here in London already. There are just too many people opting out or not being invited in. In a persistent and articulate way, someone needs to be telling Londoners regularly 'come *on*, come *on*!' The Evening Standard?

Once the potentially brilliant editorial team at the Standard was replaced, so far as the ILEA was concerned, low level hostilities with the London Press were resumed and a never-to-be-repeated opportunity for the leading London newspaper to lead was lost.

Apart from the day to day work of administration, consisting of meetings, large and small, and countless personal interactions, what follows deals with the four main themes already referred to.

Disruption in schools

The first of my 1978 themes was the Authority's response to disruption in too many, mostly secondary, schools. This was becoming an increasingly worrying problem. Late in 1977, I had discussed with administrative and inspectorate colleagues and briefly with Sir Ashley possible ways of helping schools to deal with pupils who were disruptive. Early in 1978, representatives of the secondary schools heads came to see me to ask what the Authority was going to do about this. They had been disconcerted by my initial response. This was that the Authority consisted of elected or coopted members, assisted mostly by men in suits such as myself. In that sense, individually or collectively, the Authority could do little. They were, I suggested, asking the wrong question. The right question was one for me to ask them. Given that the education of all children, without exception, is - and could only be - the responsibility of teachers employed for that purpose, what is it that the heads want the ILEA to provide to enable them to deal, in some educationally acceptable way, with children who disrupt? After a pause for reflection, the heads decided to come back in a few days' time with their ideas about what needed to be done. When they did, they made a series of requests, all of which appeared to me to be perfectly reasonable. After some discussion with my colleagues, I produced the draft for the Policy Committee that follows.

Why do children become disruptive? My view of this had developed over the past twenty years as a teacher and observer of what was happening in classrooms. I had concluded that most truancy and disruptive behaviour were aspects of the same problem. Pupils who are doing well in school and are enjoying that experience do not play truant; nor do they waste time disrupting others when they are there. But when a pupil is getting little or nothing that he finds worthwhile from his presence at school, one obvious response is not to turn up. He becomes a truant. For that same reason, another pupil, when he does go to school, may cause trouble because he can think of nothing more interesting to do when he gets there. He becomes a disruptive. There is nothing surprising about this. Members of Parliament remain in the bar when boring aspects of the legislation, which they may anyway not fully understand, are being debated. They play truant. On other occasions, aware that the Whips Office is keeping an eye on attendance, they turn up at Question Time. Also aware of their own inability to play a useful part in the proceedings, they then behave badly. They attempt to interrupt the speakers by waving order papers about and by shouting in a generally school-boyish manner. They become disruptives.

How can these forms of behaviour, at least so far as they relate to school pupils, be dealt with? The best way to deal with both truancy and disruption is to deal with it immediately. This requires a set of enforceable rules that have to be followed and are. The rules on school attendance are clear. They place a duty on parents to cause their children to attend school regularly. As with any bad habit, the first successful breach of the rules associated with school attendance can establish a pattern. Much the same applies to disruptive behaviour. Unless there is an immediate response to its occurrence, it can quickly become established.

What response? Individual cases make bad law, but before coming to London I had become aware that regulatory arrangements for dealing either with truancy or disruptive behaviour, though necessary, also needed to be administered with understanding. Why is this particular pupil behaving like this? The reasons can sometimes be easily understood and a remedy found. Alec Clegg once told me of a thirteen year old boy, not known as a troublemaker, who had arrived late at school. His form teacher was a young woman who had just arrived to teach at the school. She had asked the boy why he was late. His response had been to hit out at her and begin to run away. He was caught and taken to the headmaster's study. His teacher came too. He was asked why he had he hit the teacher. In many schools, that question would not have been put. The pupil would have been sent home or kept on his own until the end of the school day; then possibly suspended until the parents had visited the school and been warned about his behaviour. This school was different. The Head knew that the boy's father had left home some months ago. He found out that the boy and his mother had had a quarrel that morning. The boy had shouted at his mother and left for school. On the way, he had regretted what he had done and had hurried back to say sorry. His mother had still been angry with him and had not forgiven him. She had told him to get back to school immediately. He had run back to school, still upset about the unsettled quarrel with his mother. He had tried not to be late but was; so when his teacher asked him why he was late, he had lost his temper. He was now very sorry, very unhappy and close to tears. The head turned to the young teacher. What do you think we should do about this? he had asked her. Without replying, she had put an arm round the boy. 'Come on, luv,' she had said as they left the room, 'we'll start today all over again.' His behaviour and attendance had since been exemplary.

Early one morning soon after arriving in London, I encountered an example of the easily avoidable way in which the related problem of truancy can sometimes arise. I was at a nursery school in Lambeth talking to the head teacher. A boy of about twelve had delivered his young sister to the school; but why was he still hanging about outside instead to getting to school himself? I went out to talk to him. He had lost his tie, he told me, and they wouldn't let him into his school without one. 'Well run back home and get another', I suggested. 'I can't,' said the boy, 'my mum would kill me. I've lost one already this term and she'll say she can't afford another.' So there was this boy, stuck in the middle of Lambeth, with no home or school that he dared to go to. What would he be doing for the rest of the day and where would he be doing it? I told him to get to school fast and go straight to the Secretary's office where he would get a tie. I phoned the school, explained who I was, asked the Secretary to produce a tie for the boy and to tell anyone who asked that he had been detained by me. The bill for the tie was to be sent to me at County Hall. But what on earth was that school playing at? It takes two to make a truant and this school had unwittingly been playing its part in creating one.

So one wrong way to deal either with truancy or disruption is not to try and find out why it is happening. A second mistake was to assume, as many still do, that a pupil who disrupts is a particular kind of person, a disruptive, and that a person who does not go to school regularly is a rather different type of person, a truant. In fact, there is often, though admittedly not always, an otherwise fairly ordinary young person who has a reason to avoid going to school or to behave badly when he does. Finding out what that reason is and then dealing with it is what good schools consistently find ways of doing.

Rather than attempt to deal with disruption and truancy at the same time, I decided to concentrate on how disruption, principally a problem in a number of London's secondary schools, could better be dealt with. As its title showed, the notes that follow, dated February 1978, were only a draft of a report to go to the Policy Committee. No doubt it was later amended and improved by my colleagues:

New ways of dealing with pupils who are disruptive   Draft

This report proposes ways of helping schools to deal with children presenting behaviour problems. It is divided into five parts:

The nature of the problem
Present arrangements for dealing with the problem
New approaches
Administrative arrangements proposed
Recommendations

The nature of the problem: A number of children, mostly of secondary school age, behave badly in school. Most are dealt with satisfactorily through a school's own procedures, but some present persistent and intractable problems. The effect of such pupils on a school community or on an individual class can be quite disproportionate to their numbers. There is nothing new about this. I have no evidence that the incidence of bad behaviour in Inner London schools is increasing; if anything, the reverse is true. But it is clear that schools need more help than they are now receiving if they are to find educationally acceptable ways of dealing with pupils who disrupt their own education and that of others.

Disruptive pupils pose a dilemma. On the one hand, society at large and parents in particular have rising expectations of what schools should be providing for children. On that point at least there has been agreement during the Great Debate. It is right that expectations should be high and that schools should do all they can to meet them. But one consequence of the drive for improvement is that schools have become increasingly aware of the effect disruptive pupils can have on the improvement they are

138

being pressed to achieve. As such pupils adversely affect the achievement of others, the easiest way of improving standards in a school may be to rid itself of its disruptive pupils. That is one side of the dilemma. On the other is the school's very proper concern, which the Authority fully shares, that the needs of each individual child should be met. That a boy or girl is disruptive does not mean that he or she is in less need of education, in the fullest sense, than any other child. On the contrary, often the school is aware that the child needs more help than the school itself can give. Hence the dilemma. The presence of an individual child in school may be strongly in the interests of that child but equally strongly against the interests of the wider school community.

Despite the efforts, largely unrecognised, of many teachers and others to resolve the problem, too often the choice is between retaining the child in school, unsettled and unsettling, and suspending the child in the knowledge that this may well exacerbate the problem that lies behind the disruptive behaviour. Such is the dilemma which it is the main purpose of this report to help resolve. There are four additional points the Sub-Committee may wish to consider before deciding how to proceed.

First, disruptiveness is not a simple characteristic of an individual, like having blue eyes or a dark skin; it usually reflects a relationship that has broken down between an individual and the circumstances in which he is placed. Some such individuals are maladjusted in the clinical sense. As such it is education, usually in special schools, to which they are entitled. But by no means all badly behaved children are maladjusted in the formal sense. Most have always been dealt with in ordinary schools and will continue to be dealt with in this way. The special education service must do all it can to see that it deals with all the children it ought to be dealing with; but it is not for special schools and the special education service to deal with the whole problem of bad behaviour. I mention this because, from time to time, criticisms of the service are heard which reflect an unreasonable appreciation of its scope.

Second, given that disruptiveness, at least in part, denotes a broken relationship, it is evident that many schools have been notably successful in establishing relationships, either throughout or in special areas of their work, which have markedly reduced the incidence of disruptive behaviour. The inspectorate has a role here in making known and helping schools to share the experience of effective practice as and when it develops. The aim is to reduce the number of occasions when the relationship between the school and the pupil breaks down. Sanctions such as suspension and corporal punishment, which no one wishes to impose if sensible means of avoiding them can be found, are instances of a relationship which, however temporarily, has broken down. The search is for positive rather than negative educational solutions to reconcile the needs of the individual causing problems with those of the school community.

Third, the implication of this report is that it is the responsibility of schools to deal with badly behaved pupils and for the Authority to support them in this and to provide them with the means to do that. This does not mean that individual teachers should be placed in hazard. I have referred earlier to some pathologically disturbed children in school. Such children need to be identified early and, if such is the finding, educated outside the ordinary school system. I do not think it right that teachers in ordinary schools should be asked, as part of their normal functions, to attempt to contain pupils of this kind whose special needs have been identified but, for one reason or another, have not been met. I intend to do everything possible to see that this does not happen in the future. If existing procedures cannot bring about the changes needed then I will report again with procedures that can.

Finally, later in this report, the Sub-Committee will be reminded that a great deal is already being done, as part of the general work of the Authority on behalf of those with special needs, for children who behave badly. Most of the work is done in schools on the initiative of the head and staff of the schools concerned. For its part, the Authority provides a range of special forms of help to supplement the work of schools. The problem now is to prevent any discontinuity between what the Authority provides and what the schools can themselves do.

Present arrangements for dealing with the problem:
The draft then goes on to describe how the present arrangements for dealing with the problem of bad behaviour were working.

New approaches: The budget strategy for 1978/9 provides an opportunity for the education service of London to make a concerted effort to deal positively with the problems posed by children who behave badly in school. Within the budget, a sum of £1.6 million is available for this. It is envisaged that at least £1 million would be available for the purposes outlined in this report but there would be nothing automatic about this. The Committee would wish soundly-based schemes to be approved with as little delay or administrative intervention as possible. It would wish all secondary schools at least to have the opportunity of joining in co-operatively with others as part of its arrangements. But it would also wish to deal with specific schemes rather than itself devise any uniform scheme throughout London.

Some areas where improvements are needed are already known and I see no reason to delay these. But new ideas or extensions to existing ones can be expected. There is one that ought particularly to be mentioned. Discussions with secondary heads and teachers over the past months suggest that the most pressing need is to develop school support centres. The essence of these is that they are controlled, staffed and resourced by the schools themselves and they provide a place where pupils, some of whom would otherwise have to be suspended, can be required to attend while remaining on the school's roll and in its care. Ideally, I would hope before long to ensure that all secondary schools had available to them a named place where any pupil could go after three or four days if, for any reason, that pupil could not stay within the main school.

If new approaches of this kind are to develop, it is evident that accommodation will be required. Questions of priority are certain to arise. Where existing users of accommodation could reasonably be asked to use alternative accommodation which would not be suitable for support units of the kind just described, it may be necessary to insist that there be a change of use. It requires no great prescience to foresee difficulties here. If the Committee wish to be able to meet the needs of the schools for support centres promptly, these difficulties will have to be faced and the consequences accepted.

Administrative arrangements proposed: This major programme has to be implemented with the minimum of delay. I propose to ask heads to consult with their staff – and where appropriate with their neighbouring schools – on the guidelines outlined in this paper. Following this, any proposals should be submitted to the District Inspectors and Divisional Officers who will be responsible for co-ordinating the submission of the proposals to Schools Branch. As it is likely that some proposals will overlap the existing responsibilities of the administrative branches in my department, one senior officer needs to be given the task of ensuring the programme is satisfactorily co-ordinated and implemented. Accordingly, I have asked the Second Deputy Officer (Schools) to assume this responsibility.

The Finance Officer refers in his concurrent report to the procedures to be adopted in order to ensure that delay is minimised whilst still adhering to the normal levels of delegated financial authority. Monitoring and evaluation of an education development of this magnitude and importance is essential. I have asked the Director of Research and Statistics to advise me on this matter. I shall report to the Committee with proposals.

Recommendations:

The draft leaves a blank here, presumably for discussion with colleagues. Once the recommendations in the report were approved by the Education Committee, Bill Stubbs, as second deputy, became responsible for extending and monitoring the effectiveness of the programme. As some of us had observed in New York in 1976 when visiting High School Re-directions there, 'disruptive' pupils almost always stop disrupting when, often for the first time in their lives, they meet adults who are genuinely interested in them and prepared to listen to what they have to say. A problem that arose later was in trying to persuade young people who were attending school support units, making progress there and not showing any sign of disruptiveness, to return to the school they had previously been attending. I had experienced this problem at first hand. As I was myself travelling towards his school,

I once accompanied a boy, described in the past as a disruptive truant, to the school that had agreed to take him back. We were in the playground but had not yet reached the entrance to the building when a passing teacher saw him. 'Good grief,' he remarked unsmilingly, 'you back again?' The boy turned round and was back out in the street before I could stop him.

Some leading members of the Authority were uneasy about pupils, said to be disruptive, being dealt with in the support units that began to be established. For one thing, they wanted to know how many pupils there were at any one time who had been suspended and were not yet receiving some form of education elsewhere. Establishing an accurate answer to that question was not easy.

Good news suddenly arrived. In 1977, the Conservative GLC had commissioned Sir Frank Marshall, a past Conservative Chairman of Leeds City Council to report on the Labour controlled ILEA. With the aid of a number of expert assessors, in March 1978, his report was published. It recommended the continued existence of the ILEA but made suggestions about the composition of its membership. This support from a leading Conservative was welcome.

Relations with the Inspectorate

A second issue that arose during 1978 was the sometimes uneasy relationship between myself and the Chief Inspector. He was a very able, experienced and knowledgeable person. The problem lay in our different personalities. I would have found it easier it work with someone full of ideas, pressing for this or that to be done to improve London's education service. My role would then be to support what was possible and, when necessary, discourage whatever seemed unlikely to work. But the Chief Inspector's strength was in skilfully implementing existing policies rather than developing new ones. Furthermore, some individual inspectors, for whom he was responsible, were being allowed to cause administrative problems to arise which I believed were easily avoidable. These were then left for me to deal with. That caused irritation, as the tone of some of the following indicates:

Minute to Dr Birchenough (Chief Inspector) 2 February 1978

Language Organiser Hackney

I do not know the ins and outs of this but the general principle is clear enough. If a short-listing is taking place and the inspectorate see an unsuitable candidate being placed on the list there are two things they can do: (1) If it is in their power, remove the name from the short-list or pass the papers to someone who can. (2) Place on record, with you, their objections and the reasons for them *before* the interview. What seems to me quite wrong is to allow someone on to the short-list and then subsequently argue that they are in some way disqualified. We simply cannot manage affairs in that way. I shall be grateful if you will make my views known to your colleagues.

The expression 'I shall be grateful if you will', in ILEA Education Officer language, was a polite way of saying 'I am expecting you to make absolutely sure that'. It had something of an edge to it, as in the penultimate sentence in this note of 20 February about a special school, addressed to the inspector concerned:

> I find myself being informed by the Education Correspondent of the Times that there is to be some form of enquiry into this school. I say I know nothing about it, because I don't. Quoted to me then is a letter from you beginning 'Certain allegations have been made about the school and the Education Officer has ruled that they should be fully investigated.' I am therefore in the position of appearing either incompetent or a liar. In this particular case, I shall be grateful if you will ensure that there is a written report available to me, the Governors and the Chairman of the Schools Sub-Committee. Someone is going to have to assure me that this school is being efficiently run or, if not, that we are doing something decisive about it.

The problems at this school continued during the year and had still not been dealt with decisively. This had to stop. I wrote to HMCI:

> To Sheila Browne,
>
> Senior Chief Inspector
>
> Department of Education and Science   3 August 1978
>
> There has been considerable public discussion about this school. This discussion has both preceded and followed a preliminary inspection into the school which we have recently carried out. I enclose a copy of the report on that inspection. After discussing the matter with the Chief Inspector, Dr Birchenough, I am writing to ask whether you would be prepared to ask HMI to look at the school, either by means of a formal inspection or in any other way you think appropriate. One problem in dealing with this school is that it has not proved possible to carry out a discussion or to set anything down on paper for the governors without the matter being conveyed directly to the Press. This makes it difficult when we are dealing with problems of human relationships as well as with straightforward educational ones. On the other hand, the nature and quality of our own inspection process has been one of the points at issue so there are grounds for asking for there to be an independent look at the school. Hence this letter. If you would like further information about the course of events at the school, we have a file of papers here to which you are welcome to have access.

The whole business of ensuring, under the terms of the legislation, that schools were providing 'efficient instruction', with the William Tyndale affair still fresh in the memory, had earlier in the year led to more pressure on the ILEA inspectorate than had been customary in the past. Hence this note for discussion at the senior officers group (SOG), consisting at the time of the Education Officer, John Bevan, Bill Stubbs, Tim Brighouse and Michael Birchenough:

> Discussion note from EO: The ILEA Inspectorate   29 March
>
> Can some means be found to make the Inspectorate more of a positive force over the next year or so? What I mean is this. The Inspectorate contains a number of distinguished educators. Their influence in whatever they are doing is marked, and examples of it can be seen wherever we look. Collectively, the picture is less clear. The sum seems to be less than the parts. No clear messages get through, certainly to me, about what the Inspectorate believes in, what aims it thinks the Authority should be pursuing and, apart from some minor restructuring, how the Inspectorate itself is to be enabled to do its work better over the next year or so. It may be I am deaf but, if so, someone is going to have to shout a bit. In particular, three questions arise in my mind:
>
>> How is the Inspectorate to show its determination to see that really good teaching is promoted and really bad teaching eliminated? I would like to hear more about the successes – to learn from them apart from just idle curiosity. I rarely do. As for the really bad teachers, I hope everyone is clear that something is to be done about these a` la Mr Morley. First, the documentation needs to be exact, in the interests of the teacher and the ILEA. Second, we need to do everything we can to help these teachers; and record the fact that we have done so. Third, if we do not bring about an improvement, we need to report on that. Finally, when all the effort and reporting has been done, if we are left with a grossly inefficient teacher we must act. There is to be no acceptance that 'nothing can be done'. It certainly cannot be if the preliminaries have not been undertaken.
>>
>> What are the three or four most important things, in schools and further education, that the Inspectorate think we ought to be doing and are not? It is vital that this should be made known. Otherwise, when important decisions come to be made over the next few months, Inspectorate influence will be minimal and this cannot be right.
>>
>> Where are we on in-service training? Has the Inspectorate ideas about the way they would like to see this developing? What do they think of the quality of what is going on, and how it can be improved? Again, I have no clear picture other than that, understandably, any disturbance to the status quo will be ill-received. But do we think we are running a first-rate and unwasteful in-service programme? Please let us discuss.

The reference to Mr Morley, Staff Inspector for modern languages and a newcomer to the ILEA, was to his impressively rapid persuasion of an incompetent teacher of French to resign. The formal procedures for terminating a teacher's contract in the ILEA on the grounds of incompetence were complex, time-consuming and very expensive.

Rightly or wrongly, I remained of the opinion that, though the ILEA's inspectorate included a number of outstandingly able people who ought to be steering the direction the Authority was taking in a whole number of ways, clear messages as to what inspectors thought that direction should be were not getting through to me. Fortunately, my relationships with individual inspectors often concerned educational rather than organisational matters. Alasdair Aston, English Inspector, and I had discussed the possibility of publishing a collection of poems written by London schoolchildren. Alec Clegg of the West Riding had published *The Excitement of Writing* some years earlier and we thought it would be interesting for ILEA children to do something on the same lines. *Hey Mr Butterfly* was duly published and copies were sent to all schools. The Preface I wrote for the book on 17 April reflects a view of teaching English which, in turn, derived from my own experience as a teacher fifteen years earlier:

> Hundreds of books are written about children. This book is a chance for them to say something for themselves. I hope the zest with which they have done so shows through these pages.
>
> The occasion for the book is an exhibition of work from ILEA schools entitled 'The Richer Heritage'. Like the exhibition, the names of the authors of these poems reflect the cosmopolitan nature of inner London; yet many of the poems have a distinctive London feel to them. The age-old, sharp-eyed questioning of the young Londoner is caught in Victoria Pierre's 'Hey Mr Butterfly', from which this collection takes its title.
>
> The finest compliment to pay to the English language is to dare to try and use it to the full. This book is full of attempts to do this. Children can be seen trying to make language work for them, exploring its sense, pressing it to let them say what they want. They are listening to it and looking at it too, noting the shape and texture of words as they appear on the page. There is an unobtrusive teaching achievement here which does not deserve to be missed.
>
> Finally, when all the writing is done, it has to be collected for a wider audience to share. Thanks for this are due to many but above all to Alasdair Aston, ILEA inspector of English.

On the teaching of English, of which I had rapidly fading experience, I was at one with the ILEA's inspectors on the need to combine rigour with imaginative ways of using and responding to the English language. I found some Press comments on the ILEA from otherwise reliable journalists particularly irritating. Hence the last sentence of this letter to the *Sunday Times* on 10 August:

> Your journalist's comments (6 August) on the recently developed London Reading Test are misleading. For those taking it, the test cannot conceivably

'have the same impact on their school future' as the old 11+. The London test identifies children who may need help with their reading when they reach secondary school. It cannot aim them at one school rather than another, which was the main purpose and effect of the 11+.

The team who devised the test was aware that none is culture-free, but it consulted widely before choosing items which, so far as possible, do not handicap children from any one cultural group. The vocabulary used is linked to the books children need to understand in their secondary school. When blanks have to be filled in there are always arguments about the 'right' answer. Your journalist appears to sympathise with the view that it is unkind to mark 11 year olds wrong if they put 'was' rather than 'were' when completing the sentence 'Three girls -- running home.' I disagree. One way of ensuring the underprivileged remain underprivileged is to leave them, on the grounds that they speak like that anyway, with a form of written English which others, employers included, find unacceptable. In particular, the thought that it does not matter what is written because it is only in a reading test seems to me thoroughly unhelpful.

It is extraordinary what a high proportion of people who think schools need not bother about these niceties were brought up in schools and by parents who did.

The mind set of some inspectors still worried me. Their role was certainly to support schools but it was also to report any instances where efficient instruction, for whatever reason, was not being provided. A minute to the Chief Inspector of 5 October on a school, where relationships between the staff were troubled, was rather terse:

> Thank you for sending me the inspector's report. It is interesting but not altogether reassuring. On the top of page 4, the inspector observes that he was not able to judge the quality of work on such a short visit. That is quite understandable. My difficulty is this: much as I want them to exist, I am under no statutory duty to ensure good relationships in the school; but I am under such a duty to ensure that efficient instruction is taking place. Can I assure the Chairman that it is on the basis of this report? If there is doubt about the matter, then I must ask that someone should look at the point specifically: i.e look at the children's work and let me know about the place before half term.

Excitable articles about the ILEA kept appearing in the London Press. The need to avoid giving people looking for trouble a chance to make it made me become somewhat puritanical:

Note to Mr Clyne & Mr Hodson (copy to CI) 12 October

THEATRE IN EDUCATION

Just to sum up what we were saying at our meeting on 5 October. I was reassured to hear that the TIE people throughout London are now being careful about language used in their productions. It is perfectly possible to introduce contemporary themes using acceptable speech. I am not prepared to defend breaches of this convention.

The occasion for this note, principally directed at the senior inspector for drama, was that the head of a girls school had told me that one of her teachers had removed her class from a TIE production on the grounds that several characters were using unacceptably bad language. As a teacher, I would probably have reacted similarly. Meanwhile, I was reminded next day of the excellent work being done by individual inspectors.

Letter to Divisional Inspectors (Mr Long and Miss Jackson)   13 October

Dear Mary and Raymond,
This is just to congratulate you on the splendid report, written and oral, you put to the Sub-Committee yesterday. It was absolutely right and will give added weight to anything either of you choose to say to that Sub-Committee in future. They only need convincing once!

I had no direct knowledge of the way the ILEA inspectorate organised itself but was uneasy about some aspects of it, as this irritable note to the Chief Inspector of 29 November indicates:

Co-ordinating group for in-service training.

This group is meeting on Thursday, 30 November, and I have just seen the agenda. On the minutes relating to a meeting on 5 October, item 4 has caused my blood pressure to rise somewhat. Are we really going to replace that Stoke D'Abernon Advisory Committee with yet another one? Furthermore, is another group to be circulating minutes to this co-ordinating group which, in turn, sends it on to some central group? It is all bureaucracy run mad. Surely what we want is to stop this sort of thing and have a system where an inspector, perhaps with a member of the course, writes a brief note to say if the water is hot, the coffee properly provided, and so on. There is absolutely no reason for teachers to be out of school going round these places and discussing minutiae needlessly. Please do anything possible to stop all this.

Later in 1978, in the face of spirited opposition, the Authority's television service was closed down at an annual saving of some £500,000 a year. In a local authority, savings are the equivalent to the profits made in a public company. The net savings made by closing the television service a year earlier than had been thought possible amounted to many times the annual salary of the individuals who managed its closure a year earlier than I had thought possible. The problem of freeing the Authority from complex contractual provisions relating to the servicing of underground cables to more than a thousand institutions was originally tackled by Tim Brighouse. The closure was accompanied by the transformation of London's Supplies Department. This was housed in a substantial building in south London. In my perception, that Department did not amount to much more than a somewhat down market furniture and equipment store. 1978 saw it beginning to be transformed into an outstandingly successful centre for all forms of media resources, from films and videos to a fine and increasingly heavily used collection of children's books to which teachers from Inner London and elsewhere had access. Leslie Ryder, a member of the inspectorate, was the inspirational driving force behind this development. It was Leslie too who trained a group of media resources officers to work in the schools to enable media resources to be used to good effect. My contribution to this development was confined to preventing anything or anyone from getting in Leslie's way. When, from time to time, something or someone did, he would charge through my outer office and burst into my room declaring his determination to resign. Persuading him not to do that was time-consuming but well worth the trouble.

Closure of the television service led to damaged career prospects for some individuals and, while this was being negotiated, I was not pleased to have an ILEA member telling me of an objection to the closure she had received from an ILEA inspector. Staff had considerable freedom to say what they liked about what was happening around them. Tolerance ruled except when there was interference with advice being given by or on behalf of the Education Officer to members of the Education Committee. Then it didn't.

> Note to Chief Inspector
>
> (copy to Mr Bevan, Mr Stubbs, Mr Hunter) 16 November
>
> Further to my note about an inspector's remark on the ETV Service, may I ask you to remind all your colleagues that the lobbying of members is forbidden under the Staff Code and that any breach of this will be taken as a disciplinary offence. Educational advice comes through you to the Committee or to myself. It is not to express itself in other forms.

Industrial action by teachers

A third important issue during 1978 was the relationship between the Authority and its officials with teachers' associations at a time when national teacher unrest was mounting. Relations between County Hall and leaders of the teacher unions, both at local and national level, for the most part remained good. The crucial need was to avoid misunderstandings. These could lead to positions being taken, by either side, from which neither could retreat. As letters of this kind tended to be circulated to union members, some of whom were convinced that their leaders were in the pocket of County Hall, which they most certainly were not, letters had to be formally expressed. Hence this letter to the Secretary of the Inner London Teachers Association (the London name for the NUT) on 1 March:

Dear Mr Richardson,

I have not yet received the text of the NUT decision following the referral of the teachers' salary claim to arbitration. I understand, however, that there is to be 24 hours notice by each association of any action it decides to take. I am glad to hear of this. Withdrawal of goodwill is one thing, placing the safety of children in jeopardy is another. In this connection, may I ask you to make it clear to your members that the essence of any notice given is that it must be in sufficient time to enable the head of the school concerned to send notice home with the children on the day before anything happens which might affect their attendance at school for some part or all of the following day. Only with such notice can parents take action to secure the safety of their children. That, of course, must be the first consideration, as I am sure you will agree.

As the parent of a child at an ILEA school, I attended an individual interview there at 9.00pm yesterday evening; so I am particularly conscious of the dedicated work of thousands of Inner London teachers. The quality of that work is something which all of us closely involved with the education service wish to see recognized in any way it properly can be. I hope no one doubts that.

In a further letter, on 18 March, I thought I had made it clear to the union leadership that, as free citizens, it was open to teachers not to cross a picket line but that the Authority only paid teachers who did. A new problem had arisen. There was now an agreement between unions nationally (in this instance the NUT and the National Union of Public Employees) not to cross each other's picket lines. The top three officers of the NUT, two of them head teachers of secondary schools, came to County Hall at the beginning of May to discuss the implications of this. We decided to field our top team. To avoid anything which might later be interpreted, on either side, as unclear, I sent out the following note immediately after the meeting:

NUT delegation   3 May 1978

Present

Education Officer, Second Deputy (Schools), Second Deputy (Services), Mr Richarson(NUT), Mrs Fisher and Mr North.

1. NUT wished to discuss the terms of the EO's letter to Mr Richardson of 18 March 1978. In particular, they wanted the ILEA to pay teachers who, respecting the NUT/NUPE agreement, did not cross a picket line.

2. The Education Officer made three points:

i. There was no disagreement over schools which were closed or to which in any other way the teachers had no reasonable access. The teachers' presence and readiness to work would be recorded and salary paid (Paragraph 2 of letter, 18 March)

ii. Where the school premises were wholly or partly open it was for the teachers to register their presence there and carry out such educational work as the circumstances permitted. If, in the judgement of the head, the work could more conveniently be carried out other than on the school premises, he would so inform the teachers concerned.

ii. Teachers who decide for any reason not to enter a school which remained open, irrespective of the presence of children there, would be regarded as absent. As the absence would not be authorised on behalf of the Authority, salary would be deducted (Paragraph 1 of letter, 18 March).

3. On behalf of the unions, the requirements relating to proper notice being given by teachers of any action to be taken by teachers which might affect the children's access to school were confirmed.

Industrial action designed to disrupt the work of schools, as will appear, became more of a problem in the year that followed so correspondence relating to that year is in the chapter that follows.

Groups of parents, when they did not get what they wanted, tended to behave rather more forcefully than in later years. In the summer of 1978, I accepted an invitation to visit Australia to meet, amongst others, the Australasian Association of Institutes of Inspectors of Schools. In the course of my opening talk, I described the changing mood in which education in England, from my perspective, was being conducted. I was able to speak more frankly than when in London about the increasing readiness of people to resort to various forms of violent disruption. This took the form of sit-ins or, in one case, a hatchet, hurled in the general direction of Sir Ashley, fortunately embedding itself in his door rather than in him. At the time, the entrance to County Hall was not controlled in any way; anyone could just walk in.

Day to day administration

Disruption in schools, inspectorate matters and teacher unrest were matters that had to be dealt with throughout the year, but most administrative time was spent in dealing with the day to day matters that arise in any large organization. Robert Thompson's book Up the Organisation, that most readable book on management, had caused me to indulge in rapidly written, often barely legible, manuscript notes to my colleagues about what I wanted them to do. Many of the notes to colleagues were in manuscript and arose out of conversations with Sir Ashley. My handwriting could prove troublesome on these occasions. Only about three people in County Hall were consistently able to read my handwriting and I was not always one of them. So the recipient and I would sometimes have to put our heads together later to try and work out what it was that I had intended to convey. The three notes that follow were written on the same day:

Mr Brighouse from EO (manuscript) 9 May

The Leader wants to write to Len Murray about the NUPE problem. Would you draft a letter to include the following:

1. The nature of our negotiating machinery

2. The nature of the offer we are trying to clear with government departments

3. The NUPE disassociation from this and the consequent inter-union problem

4. The efforts we have made through ACAS to resolve matters

5. The consequences of failing to settle matters: disagreements amongst adults affecting statutory responsibilities towards children.

That's all!

Len Murray was then the General Secretary of the TUC. Sir Ashley was eminently capable of drafting his own letters but a brief Christmas message was all I can recall him sending to schools or colleges on behalf of the Authority. In his view, it was my job to ensure that anything that went out in the Authority's name was legally or otherwise correct. If it proved not to be, it was therefore the administration that was to blame. Letters composed and sent by elected members, himself included, provided them with no such protection.

Mr Stubbs from EO (manuscript) 9 May

1.I undertook to let the Leader know where we are on premature retirement. I spoke to Mr Naylor and he is doing a note but will you see it is discussed with the Leader at some point.

2. As part of the budget ideas for next year, the Leader wants to consider new approaches to providing supply teachers. Please discuss.

Mr Naylor was head of the teaching staff branch. A further manuscript note, sent on the same day, was to Miss Harrison, who was responsible for pupils' welfare. Schools had been asked to put the safety of children as their top priority. What had happened at this one? Senior ILEA administrators were increasingly expected to have the answers to potentially damaging questions before anyone had thought of asking them.

Miss Harrison (copy Mr Stubbs) 9 May

In the Press report today on the death of a five year old in Brixton there is a reference to his school noticing something was wrong. Was it one of our schools? If so, who reported what to whom and what happened next? Please let me have a note on this quickly.

As my note to the Leader late in 1976 had suggested, the report of a committee on special educational needs, chaired by Mary Warnock, would need a response from the ILEA when it was published. I had strong and unconventional views on special education. Members needed to know who to talk to about this and I decided that Bill Stubbs was the right person to take that discussion forward. I would keep out of it and he would let me know what he was doing. Hence the following note, again in manuscript:

> Mr Stubbs   Warnock   16 June
>
> Mrs Garside, with other members, was considering how they wanted to approach Warnock. I leave it that you will be dealing with her directly and keeping me in touch from time to time.

Any settled programme of work was always liable to be disturbed by some form of emergency. In July, a problem at the Metro Club, a North Kensington Youth Club, came to a head. I had not been made aware of a problem there until it erupted. Loud music was being played far into the night. The Club leader found it impossible to close the club at the appropriate time. Having had a knife at his throat when he tried too hard to do that had made this difficult. After complaints from sleepless locals, followed by a noise abatement notice from the local authority, the Ombudsman became involved. The clientele of the club, young, angry and West Indian, refused to quieten down. Closure of the club was insisted upon by local residents. With the Notting Hill Carnival about to take place nearby in a few weeks, the ILEA Youth Service was certain that closure would immediately lead to a sit-in and far louder music still later into the night. Close the club and evict the noise-makers then? The Police had estimated it could take up to two hundred officers to evict the young people, now being joined by an unspecified number of much older people from Brixton. As eviction would almost certainly lead to riot, it was decided to keep the club open and noisy until after the Carnival. It was then formally closed.

The sit-in duly took place and the noise became virtually non-stop. The Ombudsman, to the annoyance of ILEA staff locally and at County Hall, then found against the Authority for failing to prevent the noise by closing the Club sooner. For their part, ILEA staff were sure they had prevented a major disturbance. After the Carnival, the Club was closed. It was immediately occupied by its members. Supplies of anything that could be cut off now had been and the small group now in charge of it agreed to see me to talk over what could happen next. That meeting led nowhere. The club members had clustered round me, all talking at once and ill-disposed to listen to anything I said. After some tense minutes, the young leaders of the club, so far as I know none of them members of the Roman Catholic Church, suggested a meeting away from the club provided that the local parish priest was in the Chair. A few days later, I went to that meeting alone and on foot. A car could invite trouble. At the meeting, I said little. The priest managed to persuade the young people to get rid of the contingent from Brixton, end the sit-in and to accept our offer of other premises. His was an extraordinarily impressive achievement. To that extent, all ended well; but procedural points had arisen and on 6 July I wrote to the official concerned:

The Metro Club

There are three points I would ask you to watch arising out of this affair:

1. The need to keep members informed when clubs are not working well. What is needed here is an early note that can be sent to the Chairman and, equally important, a note recording any conversation then held or decision reached. This is part of a post-Tyndale point, applying equally to Institutes and other bodies we manage, that we must record what we are doing. On this occasion, I cannot contradict the view, strongly held by members, that they were not kept informed.

2. In the Ombudsman's report, one of our officers is quoted as saying (page 10) 'You should know that these complaints have been brought to the attention of both the Education Officer and the MP and I feel certain that both of them will be looking for an explanation from you.' May I ask you to ensure that statements of this kind are not made unless the writer has grounds for believing them to be true? As the Ombudsman's report stands, I am supposed to have known about the Metro noise problem by 2 June 1977.

3. We must watch the character and qualifications of people we employ. I believe an employee in Greenwich and one in Lewisham have worried members. The Leader mentioned the latter to me yesterday. I know nothing about this and I hope someone is not saying I have considered the matter and decided something.

On the same day that this minute was written a manuscript letter arrived from Peter Bradbury, Divisional Officer for Camden The ILEA was divided into ten divisions and relationships between the divisional officers and County Hall, which kept asking them to take on more responsibilities, without extra money or staff, were not always easy. This letter arose after a somewhat frosty meeting I had held with them.

From Peter Bradbury (Divisional Officer)   6 July
Dear Peter,

This is an act of reparation! I am writing to say that I believe the London education service to have been uniquely fortunate in securing you as its Education Officer. I have great admiration for the vision and imagination with which you have begun to rehabilitate the service in its own eyes and in those of the public. The trouble is that the old London hands, so to speak, are a hard-boiled and cynical lot. They view changed perspectives, methods and personalities with suspicious minds, rather like the ancient rustics in the village in which I live. They are, in fact, as I think you have gathered by now, a rather parochial lot - including me. So I do hope that despite criticisms and set-backs, including those from people and interests close to you, you will not become discouraged and disillusioned. We need you – but would hate to have to acknowledge it publicly. And I'm speaking not just for Divisional Officers but for Divisional Inspectors and a lot of heads and parents.

I am sorry that any deep sense of anger and outrage at the pre-Marion Stockley treatment of my division shows through so often. This is not meant *personally* in any way at all and I am distressed to think that you may think it is.

Please don't feel you have to acknowledge this note, and I hope you don't feel I am being patronising. I have an intuition that you may from time to time be going through periods of doubt and discouragement. I hope I have done something to reassure you that, though such feelings are inevitable at times at the top, they are definitely not justified in your case. Yours ever,

Born twenty years later, Peter Bradbury was one of those local government officers who would have been well on his way to becoming a chief executive in the local government structures that had been developing since 1974. I was pleased to get his letter but was not quite as discouraged as he supposed; though perhaps on a rather shorter fuse than I should have been.

I have never believed that adults, or children for that matter, behave better by being shouted at. Hence the form of this letter to Arthur Cummings, Divisional Officer for Lambeth, on 9 August about an individual member of his administrative staff:

Mr David Smith, who leads for the Opposition on the schools sub-committee, spoke to me about Aspen House yesterday. I am asking the Chief Inspector to look further into the matter, but my particular point in writing to you arises out of a telephone conversation which his personal assistant had with an individual in your management section. It is said that the individual concerned was particularly ill-mannered in dealing with the enquiry. I have not taken this as a formal complaint to me but you may find an opportunity to have a general word with whoever may have been concerned about the need to spread sweetness and light over the telephone rather than the reverse!

As ever, Sir Ashley was alert to what was happening in parliament and wanted to be ready with an effective response to any new regulatory requirements. Hence this note to Mr Stubbs and Miss Jenkins of 16 October.

Secondary transfer appeals procedure. The Leader would like a paper to Policy on a suggested appeals procedure. His initial thought is that we should have a central body (like Staff Appeals) rather than divisional ones. He is anticipating, correctly I am sure, the form legislation will take.

One Appeals Committee on school admissions for the whole of inner London rather than ten divisional ones? The possibility of having one for each of more than a thousand schools would have been thought insane. The assumption was that any appeal would relate only to process: whether the admissions process had been correctly carried out; for example, that a child who should have been admitted under a school's published arrangements to this effect had been refused a place although he had a sibling already in the school. What neither the Leader nor anyone else with experience in dealing with admissions could possibly have anticipated was that each school would later have an appeals committee entitled to make a judgement, which no one outside a school can properly make, on whether that school could or could not squeeze in one or two extra children without damaging the interests of those it had already agreed to admit. Sir Ashley must also have noted that the Education Bill was soon to emerge and had spoken to me about it; hence my note to Mr Chanin (General Purposes) on 21 November.

> The Education Bill is, as you know, shortly to be published. By any means in your power would you ensure that the Leader and I have copies as soon as it appears. We have to brief the AMA Education Committee before the end of the month on some parts of the Bill and time will be desperately short.

The hopelessly amateurish way this legislation was dealt with in the Commons is referred to in my address to the Secondary Heads Association in 1979, quoted in the chapter that follows.

The ILEA's relationship with individual teachers

A fourth issue during the year was the Authority's and my relationship with teachers during a period of unrest. The Authority's relationship with London teachers had not changed much since the days of the London County Council, amusingly described by J.G. Ballard, a LCC inspector, in *Things I Cannot Forget*. He there recalls a letter, sent in the 1920s by a LCC official to W.J. Pope, a feisty head of Lewisham Bridge School. The LCC official's letter began:

> Dear Sir,
>
> I am requested to instruct you...

Mr Pope had replied:

> In your letter you say you were requested to instruct me. You probably meant to say that you were instructed to request me...

Mr Pope's point, made in the 1920s was equally valid more than fifty years later. The only direct instruction the Education Officer could give to a head teacher – and he was the only person on whose authority it could properly be given – was if the individual concerned was failing to comply with the law, for example by maintaining a proper register of pupils attending the school, or some regulation, such as the arrangements for admitting pupils to the school, deriving from the duties or powers ascribed to the Authority under that legislation. The crucial distinction, as Mr Pope had pointed out, was between a request to a head to do something relating to the internal management of his school, which that head could properly decline, and requiring a head to conform to the law or to the Authority's regulations arising from its own obligations under the law, with which that head was obliged to comply. The following letter to a well-known headmistress of an experimental primary school, whose premises were designed by the Department of Education's Building Branch, is an example of the delicate balance between the ILEA's administration and the rights and responsibilities of teachers and their professional judgements about what should or should not happen in their school. Dr Shipman, referred to in the letter, was the head of the ILEA's Research and Statistics Branch. To ensure the validity of the carefully designed surveys he conducted, he wanted 100% responses from his sample. My view of testing which had become over-zealous, unlike the simple ones we used in London, had been formed by my own attempt to take the SATs tests used in New York in 1976. I had then found myself arguing with the answers on the grounds that the 'correct' answers, helpfully given at the end of the textbook I had acquired, were often just the dullest. Shakespeare would certainly have been failed for choosing 'darling', instead of 'lovely or 'beautiful', in describing the buds of May. In this instance, I could only request the headmistress to organise the taking of these tests in her school. If she declined to do that, I could require her to allow someone from outside the school to ensure that these tests were taken as they were part of the ILEA's need to satisfy itself that its schools were providing 'efficient instruction'. Miss Kernig, though she still thought the tests were silly, later told me that she had agreed to do as I had requested because I had taken the trouble to write to her.

Dear Miss Kernig, 13 October

Thank you for your letter of 8 October. May I assure you I have read it carefully and agree with most of the thinking behind it. But to take the formal point first: the letter of 12 September was from Dr Shipman and, as you say, he invited your cooperation. My problem is that I am not invited by committees to do things and I do not in turn invite Dr Shipman to supply answers. I have to be rather more direct than that. So, in turn, I have to ask you to carry out this particular test or allow someone else to do that. I am very sorry indeed to have to press in this way.

As to the test itself, I am no expert. The significance of it is that, silly or otherwise, it was used in 1968. Taken over the ILEA as a whole, it will enable us to see how the children's performance in that test has altered over the years. It tests now whatever it tested in 1968 and there really is no other way to make sure, however roughly, of movement over a longish period of years. I believe this to be a protection of the primary system rather than an attack upon it. I would have thought that the recent HMI findings on reading standards in the country as a whole, showing that they have consistently risen since the war, is a good example of that. As a system, there have been mounting pressures on us to institute a whole range of tests. Light sampling over the system as a whole is the best possible antidote to that.

I am sending you an example of the sort of thing that happens when the system cannot otherwise satisfy those to whom it is accountable. There are no examinations of general currency in the USA so they end up with SATs. For questions that can be supplied with more than one answer, I refer you to 321 on page 149. Where would you place this letter I am writing?

Examples followed of multiple choice questions where more than one 'correct' answer seemed possible. My letter ended with:

So the difference between us is that I think we are managing to avoid all this and you think we are moving towards it. By all means let us argue the point at greater length some time but, if I may put the matter − gauchely − humbly − adroitly − fancifully - or patiently, I shall be grateful if you will let Dr Shipman have an answer to his letter.

It was and remains the settled conviction of commentators on schools in England and of politicians that local authorities 'control' schools. Local authorities 'maintain' but do not 'control' schools. What local authorities controlled lay outside schools and followed from legislation or regulations deriving from that legislation. What teachers did within schools was for governing bodies and head teachers to manage under a school's Articles of Government. For example, it was regularly suggested that trendy persons from outside the schools had, in some way, imposed non-streaming on schools. It was never made clear how anyone could have done that, though a local authority could certainly offer opinions on such matters. In an account of London's comprehensive schools published in 1961, London's inspectorate had commented: 'None of the schools bases its organisation upon the impracticable assumption that teaching groups covering the whole range of ability are suitable or desirable'. That was hardly an endorsement of non-streaming. Yet, by the early 1970s, most of the large comprehensive schools in London had stopped streaming in the first − and often in the second − year and thereafter relied on setting for subjects such as mathematics and a foreign language. Schools had adopted this practice because they had to respond to the changing composition of inner London's school population. In many areas of London, the effect of streaming in the first year of secondary education in a large school with an entry of twelve groups of thirty was to fill the bottom four or five classes with, mainly black, boys and the children of recent immigrants to London, many with a poor or even non-existent command of the English language. Those placed in these bottom streams were aware of what the school thought of them and did not like it. The consequences were not confined to the classroom. Disaffection spilled out into the playground and, more damagingly, into the streets and over the week-ends. The understandable reaction to this by headteachers was to prefer setting to streaming and to leave both until the second year of secondary education at the earliest. The notion, firmly held by the ignorant, that changes of this kind arise out of the dogmatic and irrational beliefs of people outside the schools, rather than from the hard-won experience of competent professionals inside them, has proved too firmly fixed in the minds of some commentators on education to be influenced by fact.

Letters to heads occasionally said things like 'this is the legal position or follows from the Authority's regulations so you are required to do or refrain from doing the following'; but such letters were very rare. On one occasion, such a letter was sent to a particularly forceful head who was deeply unpopular with some of the ILEA's political leadership. The head was an advocate of corporal punishment. He was well-supported by many parents and, as I discovered when I visited the school, by a devoted schoolkeeper. They welcomed his firm control of the large comprehensive school which he led. Others admired him too. I had once received a letter from an old lady who lived close to the school. Her life had been made miserable by boys in the school's uniform throwing things over her hedge as they passed by. She wrote to the head. The trouble stopped immediately. She had written to me to say how grateful to him she was. Shortly after the letter below was sent, he applied for the post of national importance and was duly appointed. In writing a reference for him, I was able to cite, amongst other things, the comment of a recently retired headmaster with whom he had worked before he came to the ILEA. It read: 'he is the best classroom teacher I have met during my own teaching career.'

The letter I wrote to the headmaster may require explanation. Admissions to secondary schools were the responsibility of the Authority, except for voluntary aided schools, and not of the head teacher or of a school's governing body. Pupils were admitted to a pre-agreed number of form entries of thirty pupils. That was the number the Authority had decided it was reasonable to ask teachers to teach and it was not thought right that the educational interests of those thirty pupils should be set aside in favour of the one or two more who could be squeezed into each classroom. Once that number was reached, the school was held to be full. There was no appeal against that decision. Parents watched what was happening closely. Provided the published admissions numbers were adhered to and the rules for who got a place were strictly followed, trouble was avoided. The system was seen by parents to be fair. But if it was rumoured that some parents were obtaining additional places improperly, public concern became acute. Hence this unusually tetchy letter of 8 November:

> I understand from the Divisional Officer that you have been admitting pupils to your school and not placing them on the register. I have, therefore, to make two points clear. No pupil is henceforth to be admitted to the register of the school other than with the express permission of the Divisional Officer. Secondly, no pupil should be involved in school activities on the premises unless he or she is a registered pupil at the school or at another school with which an arrangement, such as for Sixth Form cooperation, has been made and approved by the Divisional Officer. Any arrangements to the contrary that you have made must be discontinued.

While on the subject of admissions, there is a further point I must mention. Press statements are notoriously unreliable, but I enclose a newspaper cutting of 20 October. Are the remarks ascribed to you correctly quoted? In particular, I hope the paragraph I have marked is an aberration on the part of the reporter. After the discussion I had with you some time ago about the intake to the school, when I particularly enquired about the possibility of additional pupils and you explained the difficulties, the disparaging remark made about the Authority appears quite unjustified.

Of course, all of us want to do whatever is fair and educationally sound. If you have suggestions about how to improve our procedures it is open to you to put them forward. Suggestions are genuinely welcome; but remarks such as those attributed to you fall well below what I would have expected from a headmaster of your standing. I am sending copies of this letter to the Chairman of your Governors and to the Divisional Officer.

But not, I could have added, being sent to Mr Hinds, the Chairman of the Schools Sub-Committee, whose desire to 'do something' about this particular headmaster was regularly conveyed to me. In the absence of any formal or written complaint, I had to tell the Chairman that, whatever the source of that complaint, the headmaster concerned would have to know what that complaint was and who had made it and then be given a chance to respond to it. A deliberate breach of the Authority's regulations, themselves deriving from the legislation, would be a serious offence, so circulating copies of my letter within County Hall might have led to serious consequences for the headmaster.

The ILEA regularly published system-wide examination results, but left it for individual schools to inform parents of their school's performance. Nothing would convince some critics that the Authority refused to publish results of any kind. I sent a note to Dr Shipman on 21 November:

Examination Results

Mrs Sofer reminded me the other day that we are committed to reporting, in one way or another, the results at different levels; right down the CSE scale as I understand it. Unless I hear to the contrary, I assume this is not proving insuperably difficult.

Finally, one of the most important and contentious educational and social problems the ILEA had to face was not poverty, it was the poor average school performance of some ethnic minority children, including those born in England. The way the ILEA tried to deal with these problems is not dealt with in what follows. The ILEA's approach is described in an excellent MA thesis by a German student at the Queen's College, Oxford. The following paragraphs illustrate the personal issues that arose for me throughout the 1970s in London.

Note to the Leader and Mrs Sofer 4 December

East End Community School (Tower Hamlets)

I met the people running this recently. They are the sort of local group

159

that, under the aid to ten supplementary schools idea, that I hope we will be able to help. I say this not just because we may improve the physical conditions under which these children are being taught, fairly harrowing in this instance, but also because we ought to be able to improve the quality of what these most dedicated people can offer educationally.

By 'educationally' one thing I meant was something as obvious as that the print of the books they were using to teach the children with was far too small, particularly for the very young ones. There was rather more to my visit than that just meeting a man and his wife running, unpaid, a small school for Bangladeshi children at the weekends. A few days earlier, a child of Bangladeshi origin had been seriously assaulted by some local youngsters of school age. I was in a state of sadness and rage about that. While still in that condition, I had visited the school. It was in wretched basement premises, just off Brick Lane, then a far less salubrious place than it has since become. The children welcomed me in the street on my arrival and I spent the afternoon with them. That evening, I went to a party run by some wealthy Bengalis, one of whom I had persuaded to help fund materials for the school. The party was in a fine house in the West End of London. There was music and loud drumming to accompany verses by the Bengali poet, Nazrul Islam. He had been a soldier in the British army and had led the resistance against some of the cleaning tasks that he and his fellow soldiers had been required to perform. That evening, still disturbed by the damage done to that child and by what I had seen off Brick Lane, I wrote what amounted to a message to myself in a way that was untypical of me. I have lost the original text but, with that insistently powerful drumming still sounding in my head, it went something like this:

They lined up in the street
Some twenty children in fair eastern dress
Welcoming a stranger with their flags and fruit,
Their smiles clean white against the Brick Lane sludge
And stinking rottenness.
Children, for you at least there must be time,
This much I promise you: together we will learn
And with your laughter and your skilful hands
And with a song that strides across the world,
We'll take these streets. And, soldier poet,
This time you must help to sweep them clean.

But I knew well enough that it was steady determination on the part of many people over several years, rather than violent resistance, that would improve the circumstances of Inner London's poorest and most disadvantaged children. But I would do whatever I could to help.

Only a small proportion of the daily interactions that occur in offices are written. Most are unrecorded and oral. I recall one such act of communication at some now unidentifiable date late in 1978. My secretary phoned me at my desk. She explained that someone called Barbara Cartland was insisting on talking to me but would not say about what. Apparently she was going straight to the Prime Minister if she was put off for another second. Would I take the call? Almost immediately, I was at the receiving end of an angry flow of words about the proposed closure of a small primary school of which I had never heard. Before this happened, I was told, I would be held up to public ridicule and might well find it prudent to resign. As the flow continued, it emerged that it was a village school that I was said to be closing. I then realised what had happened but was unable to insert more than an occasional 'but' or 'may I?' into the flow at the other end of the line. Eventually, there was a pause and I was able to produce a response that I had had ample time to prepare: 'Madam', I said with all the solemnity at my command, 'in the capacity in which you have been good enough to address me, I regret to have to inform you that I have been dead for seven years'. Leaving her to think this over for a few moments, I continued: 'I am not the late Sir John Newsom, the distinguished past Chief Education Officer of Hertfordsire, the county in which I believe the school you refer to is located; I am plain Mr Peter Newsam of the Inner London Education Authority'. There was a quasi-volcanic rumbling over the phone at this. Then silence. As no apology seemed forthcoming, I put the receiver down. Although two Chief Education Officers for Hertfordshire had succeeded Sir John, presumably his name had stuck in Barbara Cartland's memory and someone had been instructed to 'get Newsom on the phone' and had done his best.

Chapter 5: 1979

Early in January 1979, Alasdair Aston, inspector of English, entomologist and eight times winner of Cambridge University's Seatonian Prize for Poetry, put his head round my door, handed me this poem and disappeared before I could speak to him:

RESOLUTION

Today is another year,
Today is the time for clearing up gardens,
Today I shall visit Augustus,
Who is the manager of this whole section,
And ask him his plans for the future.
When we saw the way he set about the sprout stumps
We knew there was something in store,
The way he hacked and burnt and raked!
Yesterday, he will say, has gone into permanent retirement -
How did you do it, Augustus?
Permanent or premature retirement?
Has gone off for ever to get his advanced diploma -
Cannot now be expected to return -
His post is to be advertised shortly
And the new man, he will say with some pride,
Is Today!
Well! We knew that something was up:
All the digging, the dunging, the plans!
We will move all these over there
And replant that and chuck those
To make room for another like this -
All that digging, that raking, that dung
And today is another year
And here we are with such plans . . .
But, first, like a petal
Floats one and then all over the walls
And all round the world comes the snow.
Today there is much to be done.

Indeed there was. During 1978, there had been some time-consuming re-organisation of the ILEA's administrative structure. This had been unsettling for some individuals and a few had moved or been removed from their previous jobs.

The year began with unfinished business relating to the inspectorate. In the previous December, the Leader of the Opposition had publicly criticised the inspectorate. As he had not been specific about the cause of his displeasure, there had been some to and fro correspondence between us about this. The ILEA convention was that, if the Education Officer wrote or gave information to the Leader of the Opposition Party, it was on the understanding that anything said or written would be reported to the Authority's Leader. This was to prevent an ambush at a committee meeting at which the Leader might say one thing and be confronted by a statement from the Opposition to the effect that the Education Officer had told them something else the day before. So I sent a copy to Sir Ashley of this letter to Mr Vigars of 3 January in which I brought our correspondence about the inspectorate to an end:

> Thank you for your letter of 13 December about the inspectorate. As a general rule, I think it is wise to change the subject when the correspondence shows the gap between the correspondents is widening. So may I wish you a Happy New Year? For our part, in 1979, the Chief Inspector and I will continue to press for high standards. We will be urging the inspectorate, as always, to base their judgement of others on
> · fact and expert observation rather than on, to use Mill's phrase, 'the deep slumber of a decided opinion', or superficial prejudice. Taking your point about political hyperbole, I shall remind them that they must expect a few custard pies in the process. It is the season of pantomime after all!

Following this letter to Mr Vigars, my own concerns about the inspectorate were implied in a note to the Chief Inspector on 15 January:

> Inspectorate priorities
>
> This is just to confirm what I believe is happening:
>
> 1. Phase, Divisional and Staff Inspectors are being asked where their priorities lie over the next few years. What is it they want to see happening, in in-service training, curriculum development, improved premises and so on, and what we can do to help bring it about.
>
> 2. These suggestions are to be brought together and discussed within the inspectorate.
>
> 3. That which can be done as part of a coherent plan over the longer term will be put on paper by the beginning of May 1979 and submitted to the Senior Officers Group (SOG). That plan should be accompanied by any serious notes of dissent, i.e from inspectors who say the work for which they are responsible will suffer unless something that has been left out is put back in again.

4. The inspectorate document will then be costed and, between us, we will sort out the priorities for the 1980/81 budget. Evaluations will be built into the 1980/81 programme wherever this is appropriate

5. So the next thing I expect to see, by the beginning of May, is a document with a page or two from each of the leading inspectors on their ideas for the future. This would be accompanied by a paper from you, namely the plan for the future which I referred to in paragraph 3. above.

This note reflects a degree of frustration. Why wasn't the Chief Inspector banging on my door, wanting this or that to be done, predicting dire consequences if it wasn't and promising all manner of good things if it could be?

Interwoven with the day-to-day work of the ILEA's committees and visits paid to schools and, more rarely, colleges, the three main issues dealt with below are the planned reduction in the number of secondary schools in the face of falling numbers, the Authority's response to industrial action by teachers and a set of opinions I produced in a speech to the Secondary Heads Association about the way the education service of the country was being managed or, as I perceived it, increasingly mismanaged.

Dealing efficiently with providing, but not over-providing, school places had been an important function of any local education authority since 1944.

Now that selection at 11+ had ended, the ILEA had to respond to the predicted fall in the number of secondary school places needed and, in doing so, ensure that there remained sufficient schools in improved accommodation, distributed so as to be accessible to all. Hence this minute of 4 January on 'Secondary School Planning' to Trevor Jaggar, Staff Inspector for secondary education.

I attach a very rough note I have done on secondary school planning. The Leader is talking, in Islington and elsewhere, about secondary school planning problems. The point he has made to me, with some vehemence, is that he feels unsupported when attacked on this matter of school size. 'Why are we shutting these schools?' he is asked. 'What is the magic about a particular size?'

You will see the line of my argument, unworked out though it may be. It is that we are planning for the best, not the minimum. Now we have to make this stick. So could three things be done, please.

First, could my note either be rewritten or amended so that it can form the first part of a document to the Leader. Second, specifically, could Raymond Long's work on parental preference at the 11+ stage be properly incorporated into my final paragraph. Third, could a fairly simple account be given of why we want schools with an intake of 150 pupils a year or more.

To this needs adding the work Mr Rogers and others have done on the 90 pupil a year intake, noting some of the limitations. The one assumption that must not be made is that we keep to the present pupil teacher ratios. The Leader's point, a very fair one, is that if we could run a superb comprehensive system of small schools with a better pupil teacher ratio than at present, then that must be an option. This is a new thought from the one we had when we were developing the 90 a year intake. My argument would be, of course, that it is largely the number of pupils that determines what can reasonably be offered; but that is going to need some proving. As always, everything is in a tearing hurry so could you have a word with me about it as soon as possible.

There were two underlying problems here. The first was that, in arguing for the ending of selection, I had asserted that grammar schools with an entry of ninety could function well as comprehensive schools provided cooperative sixth form arrangements were in place. But here I was now reverting to Dr Briault's judgement that an entry of 150 pupils a year was far preferable. Why could schools suddenly not operate with an intake of ninety pupils? The answer did not lend itself to public explanation. The fact was, as Dr Briault had well understood, that many small secondary schools in London were, in practice if not in name, secondary modern schools. Good though the teaching was in a few of these schools and satisfactory in many others, few had a staff which could adequately teach pupils of high ability. That had not been their function. My earlier position had been, though I had never argued this publicly, that it was far easier for an academically well qualified grammar school staff in a small school to learn to teach less able children than they had in the past than it was for teachers, many of them college trained, in secondary modern schools of the same size, to provide a sufficiently demanding education for their ablest children.

The second problem was that, large or small, a number of schools needed to be closed, partly because they were or were about to become half empty, partly because they were in old and expensive to maintain buildings and partly because they were poorly led or in other ways difficult to improve. The notion was firmly held by some people in later years that a school with empty places provided parents with choice. As anyone who has taught or spent time in schools in that condition well knows, that is not so. Choice between several schools on the way to collapse is not worth having.

The opening paragraphs of my attached note put the issues in terms the Leader might want to use in his speeches, though he always prepared his own:

> **Secondary school planning**. The first principle is that we want to use falling numbers to improve the quality of what we can offer. The Authority is strongly committed to developing a fully comprehensive system of secondary education. It is worth spending some time on explaining what this means. Within a comprehensive system, either individually or in cooperation with others, all secondary schools should be able to provide

all that is needed for all children. The system is not to be described in negative terms; that is, we are not talking about a grammar school and secondary modern school system with the grammar schools eliminated and some minor adjustments made to what remains. We are talking about something positive. Area by area, school by school, it has to be asked whether the criteria are being met. This implies some harsh decisions. If there are individual schools which, on examination, prove to be unable to provide efficiently for one section of the school population, our first effort must be to improve or alter them so that they can so provide. If that fails and we are unable to bring a school up to a required standard, or prevent it from falling below that standard , by reason of falling numbers or some other cause, we have to consider whether we should continue to maintain it. The purpose of planning is to prevent a series of suddenly-taken decisions of this kind and, so far as possible, to anticipate them and take action several years in advance. It has to be remembered that teachers are being employed and children taught in the schools which are running down. Ideally, their personal and educational future needs to be settled at the start of the process rather than at the end.

One part of the improvement which falling numbers should bring concerns the quality of the premises used by our secondary schools. We still retain in use a number of poorly-housed schools. Over the next ten years, it should be possible to take out of use the worst of our premises. What it will certainly not be possible to do is to bring these up to standard. There is no question of national resources being allocated for this purpose. One would hope that there would be general agreement that no London secondary school child should be in substandard premises if alternative premises of a good standard are available within a reasonable distance. Over the past 25 years, the standard of accommodation has gradually improved and it would be unthinkable, at the very moment when it is possible to advance this process, to arrest it.

Caroline Benn, an added member of the Authority and a deeply-committed advocate of fully comprehensive, non-denominational secondary schools, now raised an important problem with the Leader about the increasing proportion of children going to denominational schools as pupil numbers declined. We had throughout been trying to retain something close to the existing proportion of children going to schools which were denominational and those which were not. This proportion had remained about the same since the 1944 Act but, as Mrs Benn had noted, was now slightly increasing. For County Hall administrators, concern about this did not arise from any hostility. It arose from the fact that if, for an increasing number of parents, the nearest school for their children was becoming a denominational one, to which they might have difficulty in gaining entry because they did not meet the school's denominational requirements, parental unrest could be expected. The wider issue was whether the ratepayers of London should be financing problems caused for parents in this way. Discussion with the Catholic secondary schools, though politely conducted, had reached a dead end. Dealing with this problem needed legislation rather than the further discussions with the catholic schools that Mrs Benn was suggesting.

> Note to the Leader (copy Mr Stubbs)   26 January
>
> Thank you for sending me a copy of your correspondence with Mrs Benn about voluntary schools. Frankly, I see little mileage in her suggestion. People do not abandon rights which ensure their continued prosperity as a consequence of meeting in consultative committees. I have talked long and earnestly to voluntary school heads, with and without county school colleagues. The former see the point precisely. They are generally sympathetic, for the most part, but why, they say, should they turn away appropriately qualified candidates who badly want to come to them (an educational good) in order to preserve or establish an apparently arbitrary proportion of places (of uncertain effect educationally) between county and voluntary schools? My own view, as I think you know, is that the way to deal with this issue is to make voluntary schools more like county schools. That needs legislation. For a start, the secular curriculum in voluntary secondary schools (which include disciplinary arrangements such as corporal punishment) should be brought under public control. With 100 per cent maintenance paid, what denominational objection could there be to that? I am sorry not to be more optimistic.

The problems arising from falling school numbers interacted with a second preoccupation during the year: industrial action by teachers. The ILEA broadly supported the teachers' case in relation to pay but was bound by national agreements which it had no power to vary. The pointlessness of attacking an Authority which supported them was not lost on most of the Union leadership; but they had to deal with militant groups to whom it was an article of faith that all local education authorities were instruments of oppression, whatever they said or did to the contrary. In dealing with industrial action in the form of pickets, it was essential to stand firm. Hence this letter to the Education Officer of the Association of Municipal Authorities (AMA), a past Under Secretary at the Department of Education:

> P.T. Sloman Esq.
> Education Officer
> Association of Metropolitan Authorities   25 January
> Dear Sloman, Industrial Action on 22 January
>
> In the midst of dealing with the immediate problems of picketing on Monday 22 January, it was reported to me that 'informal advice' from AMA was that teachers who declined to cross a picket line should nevertheless receive pay 'in the interests of good industrial relations'. I hope the report was mistaken. Just in case there is any doubt on the matter there are two points I must make. The first is that advice of this kind, whatever form it takes, is of crucial significance to local education authorities. I would therefore have expected, as an adviser to AMA, to be asked to express a view. One is asked for advice on comparatively trivial

matters and this must be one of the most important issues AMA will face this year.

My second point is that I believe the advice, if it was given, to be wholly mistaken. We will have one or two people standing outside a gate soon, perhaps a teacher or two, and be confronted by demands for pay from teachers who decline to walk past them. Such people are on sympathetic strike and the idea of paying them is ludicrous. If people are not prepared to lose a day's pay for their principles those principles cannot be worth much to them. We really must not collapse in the face of try-ons. ILEA teachers who do not cross picket lines, unless there is intimidation in which case the police are called in, will not be paid, I can assure you of that.

On receiving my note, Peter Sloman told me his remarks had been misunderstood. Perhaps so, but that 'good industrial relations' suggestion must have come from something said at the AMA.

Meanwhile, the day to day work of administration had to be dealt with. One of the criticisms of the published version of 'An Education Service for the Whole Community' had been that the picture on the front was of a white and, from the look of them, apparently middle class family near the entrance of a newish school building. To many of the people the Authority was trying to reach, this did not look like their sort of place or their sort of people using it. Conversely, why did we keep portraying Londoners with a different skin colour in the costumes of the countries their families had left, often many years ago?

> To Ted Enever, Editor of Contact   26 January
>
> About the front page of Contact, 26 January, can we contrive to have pictures of black people other than in native dress? Try suits occasionally.

At the same time that schools in Hackney and Islington were being dealt with, my colleagues were managing othe re-organisations that were taking place elsewhere in London. I kept an eye on these but only commented from the sidelines, as in this note to Mr Sawford, Divisional Officer for Greenwich of 8 February:

> Kidbrooke School
>
> One of the rather pleasing things apparent during discussions here has been the quality of the minutes I have just been looking through. I am not sure who is ultimately responsible for writing them, but I would be grateful if you could mention this to them.

Kidbrooke was one of London's first large comprehensive schools. It was a girls school. Falling numbers in the area led us to suggest that its best chance of survival lay in becoming a mixed school, thereby doubling the number of potential applicants for admission. At first, for understandable reasons, the proposal to admit boys to the school was resisted by governors and staff alike. Attitudes changed when the damaging effect on the size of its intake of remaining a school only for girls became apparent.

To return to the school places issue: secondary school re-organisation was requiring inspectors and administrators, within County Hall and locally, to concentrate their thoughts on the best way forward. The problem often was that administrators, accustomed to having to make up their minds quickly, were apt to do that well before inspectors were anywhere near making up theirs. Hence notes, such as the following on proposed changes in Hackney and Islington, with inspectors in the left hand column and administrators on the right. As with other re-organisations, it was left to one lead officer – in this instance me – to see it through. On the members' side, it was often Mrs Morgan who chaired the sometimes rumbustious local meetings as well as the Development Sub-Committee itself.

Note to the Chief Inspector from the Education Officer 12 February

Copy to Mr T. Jaggar Mr Stubbs
Mr D. Hicks DI/DO4 Mr Storr
Mr Mason Divisional Officer Hackney
Mrs C. Kisch DI/DO3
Mr E. Mercer
Mr R. Letheren
Mr PriceDivisional Officer Islington
Mrs E. Dunford
Mr L. Buxton

Secondary School re-organisation – Hackney and Islington

You will see from the discussion documents on Hackney and Islington that I have to report with recommendations on 28 May this year. Educational judgements must form an important part of that report. Obviously, the inspectorate will be closely involved with the discussions that are taking place but I want to be absolutely sure that anything I say in May is soundly based on educational principle and does not cut across anything for or against which we will be arguing elsewhere in the ILEA. I will leave it to you to see that I am in a position to put forward first rate educational reasons for whatever we decide to propose for these two areas. This means, of course, that the inspectorate must have a large part in deciding what those proposals should be. Would you consider this with your colleagues and come back to me on how you want this dialogue to take place over the next few weeks.

I wrote to our local HMI on the same day:

Miss Joan Cresserson HMI
Department of Education and Science   12 February

170

Hackney and Islington Secondary Schools

I enclose two discussion documents we have put together on the future of secondary education in these boroughs. We are sending separate copies to your administrative side. You will see from the opening page that I will be reporting on these two areas on 28 May. I shall want to be making some educational judgements at that time. This is really to let you know that there are some issues on which I would value a discussion with you before I set pen to paper.

These were the days when HMI saw it as part of their function to offer advice, when asked by local authorities to provide it, and saw no problem in reconciling that with their inspection of particular institutions or aspects of a local authority's education service. HMI knew more about what was happening outside London than we did and this national perspective was particularly helpful. Meetings and discussions with teachers, parents and the public about secondary education in Hackney and Islington continued in the following months and came to a head in May.

At the same time as the re-organisation of Inner London's secondary schools was taking place, a major restructuring of Adult Education Institutes was being managed by Peter Clyne and a small team of inspectors and administrators. I played no part in this. The new Institutes being created, replacing a number of smaller ones, needed governing bodies. Miss Elsie Horstead was the Labour Group's Chief Whip and had a no-nonsense approach to officers and elected members alike. She had a full-time job at the Cortauld Institute and delays developed in ensuring that sufficient local authority governors were appointed. For some reason, Miss Horstead became reluctant to deal directly with Peter Clyne, who needed governing bodies to be constituted so they could take over their new responsibiities. It was for Miss Horstead to supply Labour Party nominations for them but these were not forthcoming. Everything was being held up in consequence. It also seemed possible that someone had been unwise enough to make a disparaging remark about the delays being caused by Miss Horstead. That this had then been reported to her did not help matters. Hence this note to Peter Clyne on 13 February:

> You asked me what to do about the note from Miss Horstead of 23.1.79. I do not know the facts of the matter. If you are satisfied that none of our people criticised Miss Horstead, then you should say this (through me if you like) without further ado, and go on to say that this is something we will be vigilant about. If such a criticism was made, we owe her an apology. This had also better come from me. On the general point, I am out every evening and Miss Horstead is only in then; but I'm doing everything I can to get in touch with her to settle this AEI Governing Body matter.

The school support centres, established in the previous year, had been developing throughout inner London. Bill Stubbs was responsible for these and was keeping a close eye on what was happening. It was all being evaluated. The notion of 'permanent exclusion', as opposed to temporary suspension, was not part of the

ILEA's arrangements. All pupils of school age, however difficult to deal with, were entitled to the best education that could be offered to them, on or off the school site, so they had to remain on the register of an ILEA school and be dealt with by teachers employed by the ILEA. When passing by a support centre in Islington, I called in to discuss with the teachers there how they thought things were going.

Note to Chief Inspector (copy to Mr Stubbs, Mr Clyne)   16 February

I visited the Educational Support Centre in Islington and was most impressed by the general sense of people knowing what they were doing. It raises a general point. I know we are keeping an eye on these off-site units that are being set up to deal with disruptive children, but I hope we are systematically learning from the best practices. The particular point that stays in my mind, from what David Lane there was saying, was the necessity for young people to keep an actual link with the school from which they come; if only by attending there for one or two hours a week. Returning children who have retained that connection, in his experience, is incomparably easier than trying to get young people back who have severed their connection entirely. I leave it to you to see that, so far as humanly possible, we keep right away from this 'sin bin' nonsense.

A third theme for 1979 was my public expression of concern at the increasingly unfavourable political and economic climate within which schools in England were now having to work. In March, I delivered the opening address to the annual meeting of the Secondary Heads Association. My remarks constituted a personal account, developed over the previous ten years, of what was now happening. Later in the year, the Conservative Party won the general election. Arguably, 1979 was the final year of the last Labour government which, despite its precarious majority, genuinely believed in education as a public service managed by locally elected people. Extracts from my speech at Warwick University, on 26 March 1979, are below.

Speech to the annual meeting of the Secondary Heads Association

This morning, I shall be talking about the way the Education Service in this country is being run. It is an appropriate subject for a Monday morning. My purpose is to sketch the background against which you, the heads of the country's secondary schools have to work. I will then go on to describe how heads seem likely to be affected by forces at work outside schools. Finally, I shall put forward some suggestions about how heads, of independent schools as well as maintained ones, might respond to these forces. When I speak of heads, I must immediately admit, I speak as an outsider. I have never been one. I once reached the short-list for a middle-sized secondary modern school, but the governors' good sense prevailed.

Evidently, in talking of the government of education, it must be right to start with the House of Commons. There is no point in adding to the heap of generalisations about that institution so I will touch first on the progress of the present Education Bill. This, as you know, deals with important issues concerning governing bodies, admission limits to schools and a range of other matters.

So far, four features of the proceedings in the House of Commons Standing Committee considering the Bill have become apparent. I had better say at once that the Secretary of State is not a member of that Committee because the very next thing I want to say is that a disconcerting degree of ignorance is regularly on parade there. Here are two examples of what I mean, plucked out of a list of many others, with the Hansard references attached.

'Can the Minister say why it is not possible for a Local Authority to close a school, when that is manifestly the most sensible policy, and when the alternative is to put up with a slow haemorrhage of a school, which destroys the morale of the parents and teachers involved?' (Col. 579).

Animated talk then develops. Nobody points out that Local Education Authorities do not close schools. They may propose to do so, but schools are closed by the Secretary of State and by no-one else. No-one can even begin to understand the problem of planning a school system unless they have grasped this point. Again:

'I was saying that, under the present system, Local Education Authorities are able to reduce the size of schools. The Under-Secretary then said that I was quite wrong, that they are not able to reduce the size of schools, that they do not have the legal powers to do so, and that therefore Clause 6 is necessary' (Col. 497).

The speaker is then mercifully put out of his uncertainty. No, Local Education Authorities cannot enforce reductions in the size of schools, as the law now stands. But the Bill has had its second reading in the House and we have reached the ninth session of the Standing Committee. The clause has passed through all these stages without at least one of the debaters understanding what it is for. Some would argue that muddle of this kind does not matter much. Officials at the DES will make sure it all comes right in the drafting. But the problem remains. Our legislators appear strangely confident that they can change our laws for the better without being aware of what those laws are or how they operate.

A second feature of the proceedings is the constant disparagement of Local Education Authorities. Thick-skinned as ever, I ignore the fact that the references to my own Education Authority have been uniformly inaccurate; I mean something more serious. On the question of Clause 6, which concerns admission limits, how about the following?

'There should also be in Clause 6 and in the Bill generally the minimum latitude given to LEA bureaucrats . . . who may want to sacrifice the freedom of the few on the altar of bureaucratic convenience' (Col 492).

In the interests of decorum, I have omitted the political element that accompanied this remark. Really, though, what is one to make of it? The words need rolling slowly across the tongue to extract the full flavour of the clichés. Two points filter through. The first is the thought that Education Officers, the bureaucrats referred to, find it administratively convenient to frustrate the wishes of parents. How could anyone be so naive as to believe that? It is always 'bureaucratically convenient' to let things rip. What could be easier than sitting at home? The reason that, evening after evening, staff of Education Offices are working to try and ensure the run-down in numbers takes place without too much damage is that they have seen the consequences of standing aside and allowing what is administratively convenient to take place. It is time that point was registered in skulls everywhere, be they never so numb.

The second aspect of remarks such as the one I have quoted, which are liberally interspersed through the proceedings of the Standing Committee, is that they betray a deep and unthinking lack of trust in people working in local government. I say 'unthinking' because, if a phrase like 'bureaucratic convenience ' is repeated as often as it has recently been in the House of Commons, it is time to switch off the intelligence support system. Thought is clinically dead.

The third feature of the proceedings in the Committee can be described as euphoric irresponsibility. Here are two examples. We are to embark on new arrangements for governing bodies. The point at issue in this passage is not whether these arrangements are sensible but how much they are to cost. This is the way the talk went. One speaker said:

'We must realise that the £5 million which was mentioned by my Hon. Friend is probably another estimate. Whenever the Government estimates how much an Act will cost, one sees twice or three times as much when it comes into operation' (Col. 16). But how much more? No-one has the slightest idea or makes a serious effort to find out. Five,ten, fifteen million pounds a year? Does anyone mind which? This casual approach to the administrative and financial consequences of legislative decisions is not simply inept; it seriously depresses the performance of the whole Education Service, as I shall shortly demonstrate.

My second example is inserted as light relief. The danger has passed. But the suggestion was at one point made that entries to secondary schools be based on the 'realistic capacity' of each school. I quote 'Realistic capacity' is the phrase we sat cross-legged on for many hours and came up from as gurus.' (Col. 520). Now whatever the Hon. Gentlemen were doing crouching on the ground there, it cannot have been thinking. Realistic capacity? In whose opinion? Realistic as opposed to what? Idealistic? Phrases like that are pure High Court fodder. The observer marvels that anything so ill-considered could be put forward as a serious contribution to a matter of public concern. Fortunately, as I say, this particular absurdity had its neck rung somewhere off-stage; but with gurus abroad in the House of Commons it is hard for the rest of us to sleep soundly at night.

What does all this add up to? Anyone working in education must have a deep sense of unease about what is going on in the House of Commons. It would not matter so much if the present proceedings were simply an aberration. Unfortunately, they are not. The legislative track record of the past decade, so far as it affects education, is dismal. There is a long list of legislative measures which have acted as a dead hand on the education service. There was that local government convulsion in 1974, employment legislation, safety legislation and a whole barrowful of ill-considered and time-consuming bits and pieces with which the education service has had to contend. The result is that some of us working in education fear legislative change not because we believe it is not needed, it is, but because experience causes us to doubt the capacity of the House of Commons to change anything without making matters far worse than they were before.

One final point. In the past year or so, there has been a constant flow of largely unsubstantiated criticism of the country's education service. Some members of the House of Commons have been notably outspoken in their talk of falling standards. Perhaps it is time for a pause. My suggestion – and of course I tug at my forelock as I make it – is that our legislators should look carefully at their own proceedings. If those concerned about standards could bring themselves to do it, they might do worse than read right through the speeches made during the debates on the present Education Bill. Then compare them, for depth, understanding, and accuracy with the work of their predecessors. Start anywhere; maybe with Macaulay's speech on the principles underlying government's role in public education, delivered on 19 April 1847. Yes, read that. Then we might really have something to talk about when we debate collapsing standards.

So much for the House of Commons; now for the Department of Education and Science. First let me say that, in comparison with other departments of state with which the education service has to deal, the DES almost shines. But over the years the Department has been brushed aside on some key issues. It did not manage to salvage much from the local government re-organisation of 1974. One only hopes it can do better this time round in preventing a further bout of dismemberment, or of 'organic change', if that is what we are now to call it. Finally, the DES has difficulty with a fundamental contradiction. This country has a partially centalised and partially decentralised education system. In the past, this has been a source of great strength. It has allowed local enterprise to flourish. But now we have the worst of both worlds. In this country, the checks and balances now work to secure paralysis. The Secretary of State is charged with the duty of promoting the development of the education system and seeing that the local authorities do their bit. But how? Increasingly, demands are made upon the DES by outside bodies. Even by Prime Ministers. The cry for action grows louder and more insistent. But the demands far exceed the Department's power to move. It reminds me of the poor man in Baudelaire, under a great heap if bodies, 'qui meurt, sans bouger, dans d'immenses efforts'. In its frustration, the Department has learned what every teacher knows: that it is easier to ask questions than to answer them. The result is a flurry of questionnaires and consultative documents. But, as the DES well knows, this country's educational service needs more than debates. It needs action. Yet what the Department can do – and does well and conscientiously – is to prevent things happening. It is designed as a permission-refuser. No, you can't build that; nor shut this, nor open that. But on its own behalf, the DES can do little, to or for schools. Its creative ideas have to find expression through others, principally the Local Education Authorities.

Here I leave the DES and admit to being ambivalent about its performance. Its heart seems to be in the right place but it suffers from a touch of the Richard 111 complex: believing itself to lack horse-power and to be surrounded by hostile forces.

That brings me to the Local Education Authorities themselves. It may have crossed your minds that I have been cool towards other agencies governing education so that, in contrast, I can point to the virtues of local authorities. I only wish I could conscientiously do that. The story has been told before and this is not the time to repeat it at length. Briefly, since the local government changes of 1974, it has become unclear, in many Education Authorities, where educational decisions now rest. Corporate management has struck. Essentially, what this means is that many important educational decisions are taken within local authorities by people who have no knowledge of or direct concern with the education service and to whom the education service has no direct access.

Here are two tip of the iceberg examples of what this can lead to nationally. The first concerns local authority funding of national educational institutions. Two which directly affect schools are the National Foundation for Educational Research and the Schools Council. The total local authority contribution to these, to put the matter into perspective, is about one tenth of what my own authority spends on maintaining its premises each year. So the sums of money are not huge. Nevertheless, we have had the spectacle in recent months of local authority associations humming and ha'ing about whether they should support these bodies at all. Have the local authorities collectively any real responsibility for the NFER, it was asked owlishly. A great principle of local authority autonomy was held to be at stake. No individual authority is to be presented with a bill from any other. In fact, of course, the point of principle that this havering about the future of important educational institutions raised was whether those concerned should play any serious part in the education service at all. At some point, if this sort of thing goes on, a whistle will blow and local government will be sent off the educational playing field.

Again, with the Schools Council, there continues to be similar dithering. We should trust the reconstituted Schools Council to do its job. If, after three or four years, it is seen to be failing, it should be shot straight between the eyes.

What I have been saying can be summed up as follows: we have local education authorities of whom Parliament, central government and the Department of Education and Science are suspicious and even rather contemptuous. In their turn, the LEAs are suspicious of these other agencies. They fear central control. Two things follow from this. First, LEAs are so suspicious that they resolutely turn down gifts from the Secretary of State. The result is that central government offers money in less acceptable forms: through the Manpower Services Commission, through bits and bobs of urban aid, through weird and wonderful partnership arrangements, through arcane Section 11 schemes and so on. The distinguishing charateristics of all these offers is that they are uncoordinated, wasteful and require local education authorities to jump over portentously time-consuming hurdles to get at the money. But anything is to be preferred to money coming directly from the DES, the Department most concerned with and knowledgeable about education. It has led to my own authority now spending its own money in compliance with 41, I repeat 41, separate capital allocations by central government departments. It is a stupefyingly inefficient business.

The second problem is even more serious. I have not been describing fluff in the works; disarray can stop the whole machine. Here is an example of how major educational reform can be frustrated. As a nation, we want to see comprehensive arrangements for children under five, either in pre-school play groups, in day care, in nursery classes or schools. Everyone agrees on this. We want it but it does not happen. Why not? My answer is that we do not do what we want to do because a combination of the factors I have been describing stops us.

Let me list those factors: slack legislative effort by successive governments, mistrust between those who ought to be partners in the nation's education service and uncertain commitment on the part of some of those charged with educational responsibilities. These have led to a huge, continuing and enforced mismanagement of our resources. To be specific: in this International Year of the Child, with voluntary and other statutory bodies, my own Education Authority could offer to any child born in inner London this year the promise of access, in three years' time, to an appropriate form of under five care or education. We cannot make the offer because we have to mis-spend our money in other ways.

Let me prove this to you: a combination of legislation and its accompanying regulations will cause the ILEA to spend £690,000 in 1979/80 on measures to reduce fire risks in educational buildings.

Perhaps this is the point to mention that I can find no record of a child ever having been so much as singed in any day -I emphasise 'day' – school in London over the past fifty years by reason of anything that present fire regulations could have prevented. Then along comes the Health and Safety legislation. Again, my Education Authority has no intention of spending more than it has to. After a preliminary skirmish to acquire staff to enable the expenditure to take place, we find ourselves with an estimate of £650,000 to be spent in 1979/80. By legislative Act, everywhere seems to be in danger of something, apparently. So, fire precautions and health and safety measures together mean that we will be spending, from next year onwards, £1,340,000 a year, if we are lucky. All professional advice is that that figure will rise as various bodies become busy in an effort to push up our spending. Next year's nursery building programme for the whole country is £5.9 million, of which my own Authority is allowed to spend £490,000. To resume, if we could put these separate bits of money together we would have some £1.9 million to spend in each of the four years from 1979/80 to 1982/83, £7.6 million in all. A nursery place in a converted school cost about £1,000 to provide so, in one way or another, we could build about 7,500 places by early 1983. But we need fewer than 7,000 places to complete our present under-five targets and make good the promise to parents that I began with. Indeed, we could throw in an unnecessary extra staircase or two to please the fire people for good measure.

Would spending money on under-five places in this way put life and limb in hazard? On the contrary. Children between three and five are very vulnerable at home. A number of them daily get scalded, are hit by cars, or are subject to non-accidental injury. One London borough has had 145 children under five on its child abuse register since January 1975. So even in terms of human safety, more could be done by providing those under-five places, for all who want them, than by tinkering expensively with our school buildings. Day schools are about the safest place for anyone to be in. At least they were before we began to provide those fire doors that swing back and cause the unwary to lose teeth. To repeat my point: the enforced inefficiencies I describe are not trivial. They are sufficient to stop major educational reform.

How are you, as heads, affected by the way in which the government of education is now conducted? Those of you in the maintained sector will understand why people in County Hall too often have a preoccupied air about them. That may have its origin in a recent and wearisome corporate debate with an expert on traffic control about whether well-stocked libraries are, or are not, still really necessary in schools these days. Debates of this kind really do occur and are not always won. .

So these outside pressures I have been describing affect a Chief Education Officer's view of heads – and it is this view that I would like to end by putting before you. For my part, I start by accepting the fact that the job of a secondary school head is impossible. By this, I mean something quite simple; I mean there is a mis-match between the capacities of the ordinary, able, conscientious individual who finds himself or herself in charge of a secondary school and the range of skills and functions now ascribed to the task. These outside pressures, and many others I have had no time to mention, now bear directly on schools, just as heavily as they bear on officials working in education departments. Schools are at the receiving end of the mistrust, of the consequences of unsatisfactory legislation and so on. What is the response to this to be? One answer is for heads to become managing directors. There are courses springing up everywhere to enable heads to adopt this role. This is certainly one way forward and I would not wish to decry it; but, for the remainder of my time this morning, I would like to consider the implications of heads staying as heads. What does this look like from the outside?

Heads who succeed at staying heads do not ignore management principles but they start by grasping the two essential principles of administering something in a way that leaves time for more important matters. I define these principles thus. The first is to decide what you want to do and only then look round to see what is stopping you. That sounds easy but few people manage it. Most people start from what is stopping them and then decide what that leaves them free to do. That's hopeless. Of course, views and opinions will come into you from all sides and these will affect how you think and feel your way forward. But when the last Staff Working Party has submitted its report and the final ultimatum signed by absolutely everyone has been safely gathered in, you are left to decide. If you reach the point of deciding what you ought to do on the basis of what others think you ought to do, it is clearly time to move on.

So deciding what you want to do is the first administrative principle. That done, the second is to arrange, so far as possible, for someone else to do it. The art of delegation is to move from me to you through us as smoothly as possible. I recall Sir Alec Clegg achieving this in a note attached to one of those mountainously irrelevant documents that planning departments find it necessary to produce from time to time. Sir Alec's note to me ran:

'County Development Plan: Second Draft Report

I am terrified of this document, but I believe you know something about it. Is there something more we ought to know or do? If so, will you do it.'

'I am terrified' means, of course, 'make sure this document does not come anywhere near me again in any shape or form.'

The speech then deals with some of the ideas about schools that appear in the earlier West Riding section dealing with Edward Thring, Alec Clegg and others. In that section of my speech, I mentioned Thring's work, as a brilliant scholar, in the Ragged Schools of Gloucester and quoted his image of the teacher as a key. I added that, if the audience preferred immediacy, the points I was making all appeared in a study, published in the previous week, entitled 'Fifteen Thousand Hours', of twelve inner London secondary schools. The final words of my speech were Thring's. I concluded:

> These are not propitious times for education. We have a legislature that too often prefers easy speeches to applying itself with rigour to its legislative responsibilities. We have a Department of Education and Science with the brakes of a juggernaut lorry and a motor-bicycle engine. We have local education authorities that have been reorganised into a sometimes uncertain commitment towards the schools they maintain.
>
> Enforced waste of resources prevents important reform. This is accompanied by a restless desire, born of mistrust, on the part of all manner of people, some of whom are not performing their own functions with any particular distinction, to criticise or monitor the performance of those who work in schools or elsewhere in the education service.
>
> Schools are having to face these new and mounting pressures. Chief Education Officers know this and, believe it or not, mostly do what they can to protect schools, and even heads sometimes, from the worst consequences. But the pressures remain and they cannot altogether be managed out of existence. Some have to be resisted.
>
> So I have suggested that it is crucially important for heads to attend to the internal security of their schools. This security will ultimately rest on educational values which have not changed perceptibly over the years. If heads do not uphold these values, no-one else can. In their outward manifestation, heads will increasingly find occasions like today important for the opportunity it gives to argue for the healthy and confident school system the young people of this country deserve and against the dead hand, in whatever guise it appears.
>
> An infallible cure for the dead hand is intelligence, wit, a clear head, constantly renewed commitment, and professional unity. As I say that, you may detect a didactic glare in the eye of this ex-schoolmaster. I am determined that, when you have forgotten everything else that I have said, you will recall at least an echo of the words of Edward Thring, that great Victorian predecessor of yours. Here he is again, in words that bear repetition, referring to his work as a young teacher in the Ragged Schools of Gloucester and reminding us of the personal commitment that teaching or otherwise engaging in the work of education requires of us: 'There I learnt the great secret of St. Augustine's golden key which, though it be of gold, is useless unless it fits the wards of the lock. And I found the wards I had to fit, the minds of those little street boys, very queer and tortuous affairs. So I had to set about cutting and chipping myself in every way to try and make myself into the wooden key, which, however humble it might look, would have the one merit of a key, the merit of fitting the lock,

and unlocking the minds, and opening the shut chambers of the heart'.

The eagle eyed might detect in the written version of this speech that the first letter of each of the final five paragraphs were my way of thanking someone who had contributed to its content.

The reference to the Department of Education having the brakes of a juggernaut and a motor-bicycle engine indicates how far 1979 is from the present. My speech was followed by one from the Secretary of State, Shirley Williams. More prescient than I, she asked the audience: 'Well, which would you prefer, what you have now or a Department with the engine of a juggernaut and the brakes of a motor-bicycle?' This, of course, within a few years we got. My prediction that, if corporately managed local authorities did not take their educational responsibilities more seriously than some were doing, 'at some point, a whistle will blow and local government will be sent off the educational playing field' since proved correct.

One thing the Department did not do in 1979, perhaps it is worth recalling, was to spend much money on 'advertising, including press, television and radio'. In 1979–80, it spent £91,600 on those items, but in 1980–81 that went down to £8,900. Unbelievers can consult Hansard for 16.12.93 (Column 776) to verify that and note how that figure had risen to over £3 million within ten years. Such expenditure has since reached stratospheric heights.

A final point: the relevance of that last quotation from Thring, in which he explained the problem of getting into the minds of 'those little street boys', remains with us. The unwillingness or simple inability to grasp this point leads to excessive interest in the details of what and how elements of the curriculum are to be taught. That is as unhelpful as concentrating on the precise flow of water from the kitchen tap without detecting that the lid has remained on the kettle throughout.

After my speech, misreported as usual, I wrote to John Hudson, Deputy Secretary at the Department of Education and Science, to avoid any possible misunderstanding.

> Dear John,
>
> There have been some quotations in the press which imply that I have been critical of the DES. How could they suppose such a thing? I enclose the text of what I said and you will see that I was warily polite. My real point, which most people missed, was that, if local authorities do not re-establish greater comitment towards education, someone will have to move into the vacuum.
>
> Who else but yourselves?

In 1979, the weight of administrative work meant that I had fewer opportunities to visit schools than I had had in the past. But fresh in my mind when writing the letter that follows was an incident in a Wandsworth primary school. A nine-year-old was reading in a library corner. I asked him about the book he had nearly finished and he explained the plot in some detail. When had he started the book? Two days ago. What did he want to read next? He went to the shelf and pointed to a book. I asked him why he had chosen that one. He was beginning to tell me when he was called over to take part in one of those whole class 'how to read' activities that were popular at the time. When that had subsided, I asked the teacher how many books she thought the boy I had been talking to would read over the remaining six weeks of the term. After some thought, 'One, maybe two', she replied. My response, which I conveyed with all the tact at my command, was that, provided no one got in his way with too many lessons on how to read, he could probably manage closer to six. He could then be asked to talk about his favourite story to the rest of the class. He could write a different ending to one of them. The incident brought back for a moment memories of Cumberland and the West Riding and the love of reading generated by many of the teachers there. There must be many enterprising teachers in London also, but why were there not far more of them and where were they teaching? Michael Marland had written to me about English teaching and I replied to him on 2 April.

> Thank you for sending me that note on an overall language syllabus. Certainly, this makes the problem very clear. Apart from the matters raised, my own superficial observation suggests that there is a curious thinness about our English teaching in some primary schools. Teachers and children simply do not talk, listen or read enough. This is not a marginal matter. I am talking of children who have just acquired some skill in reading, to take one example, who read one book when I believe they could reasonably have read four or five. In some places the problem is of that order of magnitude. The whole operation, in some instances, needs to be lifted on to an entirely different plane.

A youthful Vernon Bogdanor, a member of the All Souls group that met regularly at Rhodes House in Oxford, sent me a draft of what he was writing on the balance of power in education. I sent him a copy of the speech I have quoted from above and commented:

> Vernon Bogdanor   Brasenose College   Oxford   23 April
>
> Dear Vernon,
>
> Here are a few thoughts on your article on the balance of power in education. I am enclosing some remarks I made recently on the same point, not in scholarly form but enough, perhaps, to indicate that I share much of your general approach. To be specific:
>
> Page 2. I am not sure why you say the Secretary of State cannot lay down policy by executive order. Certainly it is possible for legislation to have that effect in the lifetime of a parliament. My criticism of the DES is that they dither about for the first two or three years of a ministry, intentionally or

unintentionally, and then come with a rush of legislation at the end of it. This administration, for example, could have made in-service training for teachers, at some level, a right. After all, the government put the money into the Rate Support Grant. But the Secretary of State was allowed to go muddling on with notions of gentlemen's agreements, which require gentlemen, and the notion of specific grants, which, it should have been evident after one week, local authorities would not accept.

Page 4. It is interesting that innovation has tended to take place in largish county authorities but, as you say, longevity helps. Both Clegg and Mason were in post for over twenty years.

Page 8. I see no connection between reliance on central government activity and obtaining value for money. There is nothing quite as extravagant in local government as Concorde.

Page 10. I agree. Complexity is a great enemy of democracy. Only about 100 people in England think they understand the Rate Support Grant settlement and ninety of them (including me) deceive themselves.

Page 12. I rather disagree with this example. The resources were there, but there is now no way the Secretary of State can ensure they are used for the purposes for which they are provided.

Pages 13–15. Yes. Participation, when everyone affected is directly involved, it is not always recognised, is inimical to representative government.

Page 16. I am not clear why anyone should be consulting the House of Commons. Their business is to pass sensible laws or, more important, stop absurd ones getting on to the statute book. The first task of the House of Commons is, in some way or another, to become less ignorant. I am in some despair over how this is to be achieved.

Page 19. We have rather more information since 1976. The DES Primary Survey, a few months ago, clearly showed that the level of reading skills of 11 year olds has risen over the last twenty years.

Page 20. I am not sure why education is singled out in this way. Has the money been well spent on defence or social services? Save us from inefficiently applied direct funding systems. Legislation affording rights to individuals and imposing duties on, let us say, local authorities and/or employers is what is wanted.

Page 25. One problem at the moment is that major decisions affecting education, both locally and nationally, are increasingly taken by people with no knowledge of the subject or apparent desire to have access to those who can at least offer informed, but always rejectable, advice.

As I said at the beginning, I am sure your general thesis is right. We cannot get the education side functioning properly until government itself finds ways of arresting its own decay.

Later in the year, on 20 May, I responded to another suggestion Vernon Bogdanor was making.

My concern about local government's commitment to the education service, with newly empowered Chief Executives determined to act corporately while central government departments, such as the DES, remained firmly functional and were losing their direct connection with Chief Education Officers, had been expressed in that speech to secondary heads earlier in the year.

> Just on the point of a Select Committee on local government, I am not sure I can suggest much here. You may find it interesting, though, that Shirley Williams, Malcolm Thornton (then Chairman of the Association of Municipal Authorities and just recently a Conservative MP) and I met, with Toby Weaver, for an Open University broadcast. The Secretary of State commented that it was the first time she had really had a chance to talk informally with LEA people. This was only a few months ago, and it is incredible is it not? The meetings we have with ministers tend to be formal occasions with minutes and all the paraphernalia to prevent people saying what they think. Perhaps the All Souls Group should discuss whether education should stay in local government - that should get some discussion going at least.

May was a particularly busy month. While industrial action by teachers rumbled on, the work of relating the number, type and location of secondary schools to rapidly falling pupil numbers was being vigorously pursued. The notion was still being regularly expressed by some commentators that market forces somehow made planning in any form unnecessary. Quite how, was never explained.

For much of the year, industrial relations and dealing with falling numbers became related preoccupations

In May, industrial action by teachers was making life particularly difficult for headteachers. Hence this letter sent to the heads of all schools on 2 May:

> I am afraid we are not having an easy start to this term. It is not the purpose of this letter to express views on the various forms of industrial action you are having to deal with; but one consequence is that circular letters may descend on you from County Hall or Divisional Office, sometimes at short notice. These circulars may contain words like 'shall' or 'must' which are fortunately not customary in the ILEA's relationship with heads. The reason for these unfamiliar terms is that the Authority has certain statutory duties relating to the provision of education and, from time to time, has to make it formally clear that it is doing all it can to fulfill those duties.

The education service in London depends heavily on good sense and goodwill; and I have seldom been more conscious of the fact than at this moment.

An important problem that had arisen, during a year of sporadic industrial action by teachers, was how to decide when a school should close or, to some marked degree, alter its existing arrangements in a way that affected the education of its pupils. The 'must' referred to in my letter derived from the effort the Authority was legally required to make to see that heads did whatever they reasonably could – and be able later to justify it if they could not – to keep their schools open, at least for some of the time or for some of the pupils. It had also been necessary to remind the secretary of one of London's teachers' union of his members' contractual obligations. This reply to a letter to Sir Ashley came from me rather than from him, though of course I had discussed it with him. It was my name, not his, on the contracts made with teachers employed by the ILEA.

P. Herbert Esq. Secretary LNAS/UWT   10 May 1979

I am writing in connnection with your letter of 21 April to Sir Ashley Bramall informing the Authority that members of the NAS/UWT are being instructed to work a five hour day, starting from the commencement of the school day. As you will be aware, appointments of teachers to the ILEA are subject 'to the Authority's Standing Orders, regulations and rules in force from time to time' . Rule 39 (copy attached) concerning school sessions states that the normal school day shall be of five and a half hours duration. Consequently, if teachers in Inner London were to act in accordance with the instructions in your letter, I am advised that they would be in breach of contract. The advice I have received does not leave much room for doubt but, bearing in mind the importance of the matter, I am taking Counsel's opinion.

In addition, in relation to school hours, the Authority considers that a Head is entitled to require a teacher under the terms of the teacher's contract to attend school in time to receive the children when it opens or at the end of a session to see them safely off the premises. Consequently, any teacher who absents him or herself without permission during the normal school hours, as defined above, would be in breach of contract and deductions of pay may be made accordingly.

I am anxious to avoid any unnecessary disruption to schools in Inner London and to the Authority's normal good relations with its teachers. I shall be in touch as soon as I have the additional legal advice mentioned above and, in the meantime, hope that your members can be made aware that the proposed action could be in breach of contract. As there are matters here which I have discussed in a wider context with your General Secretary (Terry Casey), I am sending him a copy of this letter.

The additional legal advice being sought was not, as my letter might have implied, over whether the proposed action was in breach of contract. We knew perfectly well that it was. What we wanted was a second opinion on whether it could possibly be true, as the GLC lawyers had advised us, that the only salary we could lawfully deduct related to the half hour or so during which teachers decided not to work. This would make disruption virtually cost free. Hence the feeble-sounding 'pay may be deducted', until we could think of a better way of dealing with the matter.

The following, illegibly dated, draft was headed 'recommended action by heads in face of industrial action'. It included the following advice:

> If the Head or, in his absence, a member of staff authorised to act for him finds a school closed when children arrive in the morning, by any means available to him he is to open the premises. His first concern must be to ensure that he and his staff can bring the children off the streets and under cover.

The reference to a head opening a school 'by any means available to him' meant that, if this proved necessary, they were to get someone to use a sledgehammer. Divisional Officers still did not have keys to all schools despite quietly assiduous efforts to collect those keys over past months. So a threat made by schoolkeepers, who were inclined to associate themselves with industrial action, to close schools – by simply refusing to open the entrances to them – still meant that, at many schools, they could do just that.

Although relations with teacher unions or, more often with breakaway groups of them, were at times strained, annual union conferences almost always had LEA members present. I usually accompanied them and, without ILEA members present, spoke to the London delegation and answered their questions. The London delegation was large and influential nationally. In the photo, June Fisher is beside me. She was headmistress of a girls comprehensive school and a future President of the National Union of Teachers.

Michael Young, now in the Lords but without holding any official role in education, was one of the two or three most influential educators of the post-war years. His particular gift was to propose ideas which initially seemed impractical and then turned out to be brilliantly successful. In conversation and by letter, he peppered the ILEA with suggestions about how we could do things better. Here he is on alternative schools and the idea of a federal school that I had proposed for Hackney.

Lord Young at the Advisory Centre for Education (ACE)   31 May

Dear Michael,

Sir Ashley has sent on to me your report on alternative schools. I think I mentioned some of my worries when we met at the ACE Day Conference. In particular, I am concerned about the parents' contribution on what is or is not vocational. There are very few vacancies in London for the sort of skills which parents would like their children to be able to employ: engineering, metal, making things. Easily the best vocational preparation, so far as most London employers are concerned, is a reasonable level of general education, the ability to turn up regularly on time, a degree of honesty and so on. These are all very traditional accomplishments.

The particular point I derive from urban schools in the United States is that they tend to be very large. Within size one can achieve different forms of diversity and, like you, I was impressed by some of their mini-schools. What Hackney has above all else to avoid, it seems to me, is a whole range of small secondary modern schools. That may sound a very negative aim but it is certainly in my mind. Hence the idea of a Federal School, which has about two friends, so far as I can discern.

Soon afterwards, I spelt out the reasoning behind the Federal School idea.

To Lord Young at the Advisory Centre for Education   7 June

Dear Michael,

There is a misunderstanding about the Federal School idea. I do believe that such an idea would enable there to be considerable diversity within the comprehensive system. What I do not believe is that the idea has much support. People seem incapable of making the intellectual jump required. A study of theology would help, perhaps. I am thinking of the doctrine of the Trinity. It really is extraordinary that people can conceive of three separate schools: two 11–14 schools and one 14–18 school, each on separate sites. They can do this without any sense of stress. Suddenly to call that one school, with minimal movement of pupils or teachers between the sites, causes an extraordinary panic about giant split-site comprehensives. Of course, the purpose of making the change would be to enable internal rearrangement to take place as and when it seemed appropriate to teachers, parents and pupils. But all this will have been evident to you and came through in the excellent paper which Michael

Marland wrote on the matter.

The essential idea of a federal school was to keep the eleven to fourteen-year-olds in the most populous parts of a district in two fairly small premises and to have the fourteen to eighteen-year- old part of the school on a separate site somewhere between them. This would combine the intimacy of a small school for the younger pupils and the facilities and curricular advantages of a large school for the fourteen to eighteen-year-olds. The aim would be to develop in a school of this kind the all-encompassing curriculum envisaged in the London School Plan Michael Marland ran the first such school in Westminster. It began well but, when the ILEA was gone and Michael had left, it was no longer well supported and was later replaced by two newly-built and well-led academies.

The re-organisation of secondary schools remained a personal preoccupation throughout the year. My own direct involvement was with Hackney and Islington, two of the ten divisions of the ILEA. Elsewhere, Bill Stubbs, Don Venvell and, later, David Mallen, working closely with leading ILEA members and with divisional and inspectorate colleagues, took a similar administrative lead. As my involvement was frequently interrupted by commitments elsewhere, Chris Storr shared the work. Hence this note to him on 1 May:

> Hackney/Islington Secondary Schools
>
> I have inspectorate suggestions for both Hackney and Islington secondary schools. There seems to have been no reference to the FHE inspectorate. It is very important that they should be associated with any proposals I put forward. Could they be brought into things immediately please.

As the weeks went by, dates and the detail of arrangements to be made had to be constantly reviewed and elected members of both political parties kept informed, as in this note to Mrs Morgan, Chair of the Development Sub-Committee, of 1 June:

> Hackney and Islington re-organisation
>
> I have mentioned to Ron Brown MP the idea of talking to London MP's about secondary re-organisation matters generally. He thought this a good idea and is fixing a date some time before 10 July. I have undertaken to let him have a two page document of some kind which he could then circulate.
>
> I am arranging to discuss the Hackney/Islington proposals with Mr Pole (Conservative ILEA member) and have also mentioned the matter to Professor Smith (Conservative Party Leader of the ILEA), who said he would like to be there as well.
>
> I am arranging for you to have a set of all the comments made, either at Hackney or Islington and to receive any fresh comments as they arise. A

point occurs to me here. Would it be useful to do the same for members of your Sub-Committee? There would have to be an explanatory letter, of course, because some of the people who have sent in material may want to amend it or withdraw it in the light of the more recent papers. One way round this would be to wait and start sending the papers out in mid-June so people have a chance to absorb them fully. Would you let me know whether you think this sensible?

I am arranging for a full set of papers to be in the divisional offices and accessible to anyone who wants to go in and look at them. I am wary of agreeing to distribute copies on demand to all and sundry, even to entire governing bodies. Some of the material is virtually book length and we would have major reprographic problems.

The weight of documentation arising out of the Authority's consultative procedures was causing a variety of problems. A particularly severe one was the impossibility of any committee reaching a soundly based decision on the evidence before them if they had too little time to consider the papers in full. We made no attempt to summarise the array of representations received, sometimes amounting to several hundred pages; we had learnt that doing that always led to some people who did not like the decisions ultimately reached claiming that the committee had considered an inaccurate account of what they had put forward and therefore that the committee's decision was flawed to the extent of being invalid. In the days before email, this note of 12 June went to the Committee Chairman, Mrs Morgan, and to no one else. After summarising what had already happened, I suggested a variation to the previously agreed timetable that would follow the meeting to be held on 14 June:

14 June	Public Meeting (Mrs Morgan in the Chair)
29 May–22 June	Consultation on draft report
10 July	Development Sub-Committee

In my draft report of 22 May 1979 I said, para 1, that I did not recommend a change in the timetable proposed. I would now like to announce such a change at the public meeting on 14 June. The change itself would take the form of asking the Sub-Committee to receive all papers so far sent at their meeting of 11 July (not the 10th, so the meeting for that day can be cancelled). Consideration of these papers and of any others sent in could be deferred until the autumn. The autumn date I would propose for a meeting could either be 26 September or 10 October 1979. This would enable us to inform parents in reasonable time about the school they were choosing for September 1980. The Divisional booklets go to print on 20 June, but a suitable section could be included which would say that later information would be sent out on certain points. This later information could be inserted before parents receive the booklets in early November.

The reasons for proposing these changes are:

a. The weight of documentation is now too great to expect the Sub-Committee to deal with both Hackney and Islington in two successive days.
b. I simply cannot get to a meeting on 10 July and, in the circumstances, this would look very bad.
c. Opinion is plainly shifting in parts of Hackney. There will be a huge protest to anything recommended as early as in July.

It is for consideration whether the Sub-Committee on 11 July should also receive a paper from me with reasons for each of the proposals made. On balance, I am against this. There is no one correct solution for Hackney. A federal system or a system of amalgamations would work. So, if there is to be a postponement until the autumn, I favour a full-blooded EO's report which we have all agreed within this building. Never go out twice on the same limb is a sound administrative maxim!

An opportunity to escape from London suddenly arose in the midst of all this. Bill Stubbs and I paid a visit to Sweden. He had several contacts there and we had a chance to look at the way different elements of their education system worked. One feature of their system was a reminder of an earlier experience. In 1977, some Australian teachers had visited the ILEA. As I put it in a lecture later:

What particularly impressed us about them was a right they enjoyed to a term or more of sabbatical leave. Teachers in the UK have no such rights. They have to wheedle their way through interview boards to obtain, if they are lucky, what those Australians received automatically. How could this benefit be transferred to London's teachers? In Sweden, we found part of the answer: contractual arrangements which enabled teachers to build up their entitlement to sabbatical leave over a period of years in exchange for a few hours a month of non-teaching duties which, it immediately occurred to us, many London teachers already far exceeded.

So the essence of the proposed ILEA's Teacher's Contract would be that, in exchange for a commitment to undertake some non-teaching duties, including, for those who opted in this direction, supervision at lunch or at other times, teachers would receive leave entitlement equivalent to being able to take, after a number of years' service, a year off on full pay or, if they preferred, be able to add that year's salary to a lump sum on retirement; and so on. The aim was to make teachers' conditions in London the best in the country was genuine. But too much having to be dealt with in too much of a hurry defeated our efforts. As an administration, we did not have the time to explain to all the teachers what was intended and the almost lunatic suggestion that a plot against London's teachers had been narrowly averted was never decisively answered. The opportunity to provide, as of right, substantial improvements to the terms of service of London's teachers had, we suspected, been lost for ever.

There were two main ways to improve the quality of school education in London.

The first was to establish the appropriate structures within which teaching could take place. That we had set about doing. It became fashionable in later years to suppose that structure can be detached from standards: the quality of what is happening within a structure. That is a bad mistake. A good structure cannot guarantee good quality. There are hundreds of perfectly constructed but humdrum sonnets as evidence for that. Conversely, an inappropriate structure can virtually guarantee failure, as anyone who has tried to write something sad in the form of a limerick could testify. A good structure, of legislation or of schools, makes improvement possible; a bad one can make it impossible.

The second way to improve the quality of education in London was to recruit, retain and, when necessary, improve the skills of able and committed teachers, on whom the quality of what could be provided would ultimately depend. A new contract for teachers in London would have helped to achieve that. Fortunately, the large scale movement of teachers in and out of London had stopped and the Authority was now able to recruit fewer but better qualified teachers than in the previous decade.

I still managed to keep in touch with Alec Clegg but sometimes, as this note of 8 June explains, that couldn't be managed:

> Dear Alec,
>
> I am very sorry not to be able to be with you at the party on 22 July. I shall be somewhere over the Atlantic at the time and perhaps you will spare a thought for me, droning on in the dark, a regular feature of an Education Officer's life these days.

I found I was increasingly less free to attend appointments of senior staff. Hence this hurried note to the Leader about an appointment to be made on 12 June, the following day. On this occasion, I was able to be there:

> Chief Inspector (Schools)
>
> This is a particularly important appointment, in view of the fact that both the Chief Inspector and Dr Hayes will not be with us for more than a few years. The following are the points which seem to me important about the person we appoint. I use the word 'his' throughout to include 'her':
>
> Whether the individual has potential for growth. This may emerge from an enquiry into what changes he has successfully brought about in his present task in the recent past.
>
> Views on the nature of the inspection process. What are inspectors supposed to be doing and how do they reconcile their different roles of support and judgement?
>
> Views on the nature of in-service training. Nationally and in the ILEA there is considerable worry, justified in my view, about what we are getting

191

in return for the massive expenditure on in-service training. Does it do any good? How does one find out and has the applicant any ideas about how to develop in-service training in a way that really helps the schools?

Can the applicant bring new ideas into the ILEA? This can be done by people already here; but the difficult point to elicit is whether the individual both has the ideas and is the kind of person who can convince the inspectorate barons, if I may so describe them.

The major unresolved educational problem in ILEA is the way to tackle the 16 – 19 year olds. Obviously, outsiders will not have a clear understanding of our position but what general ideas have the applicants? Are they at home in the Further Education world as well as in the schools world? Can they get a discussion off the ground here with renewed vigour?

Other issues include their views on the different ways accountability works or should work into the 1980's. Who is accountable for what and to whom?

That 'we appoint' in the opening paragraph meant, of course, 'who is appointed by the Authority'. It was a committee that would appoint; my part or, in in my absence, that of one of my deputies, would simply be to advise. In practice, members never, in my experience, appointed anyone the administration did not want. How could the Education Officer be accountable for the performance of that person if they did? But they were certainly prepared to appoint any of the candidates the Education Officer and his colleagues had presented to them for interview, even though that person might not be their preferred candidate. For my part, I had reservations about the way members managed the actual appointments process but, as they had appointed my senior colleagues and me in that same somewhat idiosyncratic fashion, I was hardly in a position to suggest that their procedures were seriously flawed.

The minute to Sir Ashley quoted above related to an interview to be held next day, on 12 June. What I, for one, was supposed to be doing during that week appeared in a document that landed on my desk each Friday headed 'Education Officer's engagements':

Week commencing 11 June 1979

DATE	TIME	DETAILS
Monday	9.30	Senior Officer's Group Teachers Centre, LUNCH At Exton Street
	3.00	Professor Smith, Mr Pole Hackney/Islington re-organisation
	4.30	Education Committee Questions
Tuesday	9.30	Chief Inspector (Schools) Interviews Sub-Committee

	2.30	Education Committee
	6.50	CAR TO
	7.00	House of Commons Henry Pluckrose Group
Wednesday	10.00	AEO (Secondary) Officer Level Panel (Room 65a)
	12.30	Mrs Butcher for lunch at Highbury Hill School
	3.30	CAR TO
		N.West Quadrant meeting with Primary Heads
		CAR TO
	6.30	Dinner (if EO wishes to attend)
	7.30	Catholic Secondary Heads Conference at Allington
Thursday	10.30	Schools Sub-Committee
	11.00	JNC for Senior Officers
	1.45	CAR TO
	2.30	DES Multi-Ethnic Sub-Committee meeting Officer Level Panel (AEO) Special
	6.30 - 7.00	Hackney Downs School. Public Meeting
Friday	9.30	Mr Perkins, Mrs Grant ILFSA
	10.45	CAR TO
	11.00	Centre for Learning Resources.
	12.00	Cabinet
	12.45	Cabinet Lunch
	2.00	CAR TO
	2.30	Hollydale Primary School with Mr Hayling
	5.45	CAR TO
		Opening of More House, Osterley Middlesex (Cardinal Hume)

There is nothing unusual in this picture of the fragmented nature of the day by day activities in a large organisation, but it indicates how little time there was for reflection or carefully considered writing. Most of that had to be done away from the distractions and unpredictable interruptions that affected what actually happened during any given week. Diaries produced in advance predicted what would happen; what actually happened was often very different.

'CAR TO' had been put in capital letters ever since, to the understandable irritation of those involved, I had twice found my own way to wherever it was I was supposed to be and had forgotten about the car waiting for me somewhere else. On Wednesday, the reference was to the Catholic heads' conference at Allington Castle in Kent. This was an annual event to which I was always invited. It was an enjoyable social as well as an educational gathering. On Friday, Cardinal Hume, whom I had first met when he was Abbot at Ampleforth and I was in Cumberland, had invited me to a Club for young people that he was developing outside the ILEA. Some of the young people using it would be from inner London; otherwise I would have been trespassing.

The problem of too many meetings having to be attended by too few ILEA officials remained a constant problem. Mrs Chaplin, for example, had a strong, sometimes blisteringly forceful, interest in the museums for which the ILEA was responsible. She chaired their governing bodies and expected, but too seldom for her liking received, professional support from senior officers at their meetings. I found myself, as I had been since 1972, almost permanently on the defensive:

> Dear Mrs Chaplin, 26 June
>
> About the Horniman Museum; yes, but it's all go these days. I am in Brussels, Mr Bevan is at a Polytechnic Court; and the Chief Inspector and Mr Stubbs are interviewing for senior posts. So we have positively no face to show. This keeps happening and I am very sorry about it.

Early in September, several senior members of staff retired and reinforcements arrived in the form of David Mallen, Philip Hunter, Robert Harvey and Tony Cline, all from outside the ILEA's service. As the following examples illustrate, this left me more time to visit schools and, as tended to happen on my return to County Hall, to cause work for other people.

Note to Mr Storr   4 October

Thank you for your note about the heating problems at Hungerford. Infants School, I am deeply committed to seeing that the infants have an uninterrupted education this year. In my view, their interests must be put first and other people may have to budge a little. Please continue to keep me in touch, particularly if there is any real fear that they will be in trouble again this winter.

Note to Mr Chanin   16 October

Royal Visit to William Ellis and Parliament Hill Schools

Thank you for your note about these arrangements. In due course perhaps someone will let me know whether I am supposed to turn up. I note that the discussion may take place in the Girls Common Room. As I recall the place, it could do with a little tidying up but no doubt someone will see that there are pleasant pictures on the walls and so on. In general, someone from the schoolkeeping/architect side should take a fairly quick look at the proposed itinerary to ensure that if there are any graffiti at least the spelling is correct!

Sir William Collins was a boys school (later South Camden Community School) that we had decided to develop as a mixed school. It is not easy to attract girls into the first year group of an existing boys school, so it had to be in good working order when parents came to look at it. Bureaucracy consists of looking at a column of figures and deciding there is not enough money to do what needs to be done; competent administration consisted inn going flat out to find the money with which to do it. In this case, it only took a matter of minutes to transfer the necessary money from elsewhere.

Note to Miss McLaren P.E Inspector (copy to Mr Bradbury) 19 October
Sir William Collins School

I understand we are looking at the playing facilities at the school. In talking to the Head and Deputy one point does not seem to have been made clear. I assume we are designing something that will enable the school to timetable, say, the first two years so that they do not have to leave the school premises. Could someone ensure that this happens or let me know why not? At the moment, from what the people at the school said, we/they seem to be working from the other end; namely, starting from the amount of money they now have and then seeing what can or cannot be done.

I may have this wrong but my essential point is this: we must prevent young people from this school spending a quite unnecessary amount of time in buses when, in the long run, it would save money and be educationally preferable for them to play their games on the school site.

Lastly, no-one seems to have marked out the netball court, and this seems to be beyond the resources of the Area Architect system. May I beg someone to cut across all this and instruct any competent individual to put the paint where the paint is needed. We cannot open our doors at a mixed school without being able to deal with this kind of matter quickly.

The West Riding had taught me the importance of the caretaking staff. Mr Cook had no reason to reply to this letter to him of 29 October but, twenty years after I had left the ILEA, he reminded me of it when I was on the governing body of the renamed College.

A recent report on an inspection of North London College noted of the high standard of maintenance and cleanliness of the College. I would like to compliment you and your staff on the fine work you are doing.

Nearly all head teachers who end their careers with a sense of failure were once better than average classroom teachers. Otherwise, they would not have been appointed as heads in the first place. So, however things have ended, they should leave with thanks for what they have done during their career as teachers. On 20 October, I wrote to thank the Head of a school being amalgamated with another. He had not been appointed as headmaster of the new school, though it was to be developed on the site of his present school. I concluded:

> Finally, I would like to take this opportunity of saying how impressed I have been by the way you have, personally, handled matters in these last few months. It must have been a very difficult time for you and you have taught us all a lesson in magnanimity and true professionalism. With best wishes.

During 1979, I had still found it possible on visiting a school to bring back examples of what the young people had created. I wrote to Hydeburn School on 21 November:

> Dear Wayne,
> I am just writing to say that the bowl which you made is now in my room here and is about the best looking thing in it. It is an excellent piece of work and I congratulate you on it.

Meanwhile, towards the end of the year, the re-organisation proposals for Hackney and Islington were being implemented.

This major re-organisation of the schools there had belatedly attracted the attention of one of the Authority's most persistent critics. Hence this letter to The Times on 15 December:

> In his article, December 6, on secondary school re-organisation , Mr Ronald Butt fails to distinguish fact from gossip. Over the next few years, the Inner London Education Authority proposes to reduce sixteen secondary schools in Hackney and Islington to seven. As Mr Butt recognises, sharply falling pupil numbers argued for a reduction on this scale.
>
> The advice of ILEA officers to their Education Committee was that this process should take the form of amalgamations involving all sixteen schools, rather than by closure, which would involve nine. There can be argument about whether this advice was or was not sound, but it was based on hard-won experience. Whereas it has proved just possible to keep effective education going in one or two schools as they are run down to closure, to attempt this with nine schools in a comparatively small area was to risk educational collapse. On the other hand, experience of amalgamations shows that, despite the difficulties and stress that they cause, the results are good in two respects: the schools that result remain popular and effective and the depth of educational offer is, if anything, enhanced. I do not know why Mr Butt should suppose that amalgamation leads to reduced curricular opportunities. That is both untrue and irrational. I cannot debate the merits or otherwise of individual proposals

on which it is now for the Secretary of State to decide, but there are two points that I can properly make:

The first is that the schools suggested for amalgamation were put forward by me on the best professional advice available. Politicians then had to decide whether to accept that advice or not. No one from either political party asked me to include or exclude any particular school in my consultative document. Mr Butt may choose not to believe this, but neither political party in the ILEA behaves like that.

Secondly, it is a mistake to believe that inclusion in amalgamation proposals suggests disapproval of the schools concerned. The successful amalgamations over the past few years have all been based on highly regarded schools. The evidence is there if Mr Butt chooses to look at it.

So the sixteen secondary schools in Hackney and Islington, many on split sites and some poorly performing in impossible to improve buildings, became seven. They did that without any long-lasting objections from parents or teacher unions. One consequence of re-organisation on this scale was that Mrs Morgan, whose constituency was in Hackney, was ambushed by a politically active group of local teachers, bitterly opposed to change of any kind. She lost her seat and had to seek election to the ILEA elsewhere.

So ended 1979. Enter a Conservative government with which the ILEA had to learn to live. The 1979 General Election brought to an end what might be described as the thirty five years of the 1944 Act. From the perspective of the ILEA, the years that followed, particularly after 1981, led to a widening gap between the political leadership of the ILEA and that of the national government. As part of that process, the ILEA found itself increasingly subject to directly imposed financial pressures and, at times, to wildly inaccurate criticism from elements of the Press as well as to various forms of political attack.

Chapter 6: 1980

During 1980, three external factors indicated the nature of the problems the ILEA would be facing in the following years: in February, a report of a committee, chaired by Kenneth Baker MP, proposed the break-up of the ILEA and the creation of thirteen new Inner London Borough education authorities. The report was ineptly argued and swiftly withdrawn, but the thinking behind it was lodged in the minds of some leading Conservative politicians. The second factor was the increasingly strong move from government departments to fund education by means of formulas devised by officials in Whitehall. A formula is a useful device for avoiding the need for thought. It saves time, for example, when calculating the circumference of a circle. It can prove less appropriate, if strictly applied, when distributing money to local authorities. As a procedure, funding by formula left little room for the ILEA, a democratically elected body, to relate its expenditure to its detailed perception of the particular needs of Inner London. The third factor was a report by HMI on the effectiveness of the ILEA as an education authority. The report drew attention to a number shortcomings within the schools, of which the Authority was aware, praised other elements of the education service and was generally supportive of the action taken by the Authority to improve matters. This did not prevent some commentators, who plainly had not read the report itself, from asserting that the HMI report constituted an outright condemnation of the ILEA.

Before the Baker Report arrived in March, a variety of things were happening in January and February which are placed in date order below. They illustrate the fragmented nature of administrative work. On 8 January, I wrote to the Department's Permanent Secretary, Sir James Hamilton KCB, on a problem that was badly affecting head teachers and was concerning a number of Chief Education Officers:

> In connection with our meeting on Tuesday, 15 January, it might be helpful if I set down briefly what I see to be the main topic of our discussion. This is the need, which is now pressing, to secure general agreement to revised conditions of service for schoolteachers which will make explicit

the obligations on all teachers in connection with the running of schools. In particular, any revision should resolve the problem of mid-day supervision which now rests precariously and unsatisfactorily in a limbo- notwithstanding the theology of the Teacher' Associations that goodwill exists at all schools for the asking. The reality in many schools is different and leaves Heads with a burden which is quite unreasonable.

If it is accepted that a new contract is required, what are the opportunities for obtaining it? Until the last few months I would have found it difficult to see that many existed. But the climate seems to be changing. Negotiations in recent weeks seem to be giving grounds for hoping that most of the teachers are prepared to discuss possible solutions. The NAS/UWT are not, of course, by their own choosing, party to these discussions.

Doubtless it is no coincidence that this willingness of the Teachers' Associations to discuss topics which have hitherto been unthinkable, never mind negotiable, coincides with the deliberations of the Clegg Commission. There would seem to be a new acceptance, de facto if not de jure, that a correspondence exists between pay levels and contractual obligations. The question now arises – is there anything that could now be done, without by-passing the properly constituted machinery of consultation, which could ensure that this opportunity to resolve a major problem for the education service is not missed? That, I suspect, will prove sufficient to occupy us over lunch.

I have made arrangements for us to confer at the Teachers' Centre in Exton Street. It might be easiest if we were to meet outside the North Entrance to Elizabeth House. I am sending a copy of this letter to my local authority colleagues who will be present: Cunningham, Fiske, Gronow and Stubbs. On their behalf, I would like to thank you and Roy Walker for finding the time to meet us.

Unaware of what was to follow later in the month, I replied on 9 January to a letter from a retiring headmistress:

Dear Mrs Champagne,

A minor point of friendly disagreement: I do not think it has seemed in the least unambitious to have remained at Surrey Square since 1957. The point you make about the high turnover of staff is exactly the one that I would use to argue for stability at the head of things. I expect you could calculate the figures if you put your mind to it, but even I can see that many hundreds of children and a number of staff, probably in three figures, will have benefitted from your being in the best possible position to help them. No one could possibly do more than that. I shall have a chance to say so in other ways and at other times, but I hope you know how deeply your work for London has been appreciated.

Each year, all retiring teachers, several hundred of them, were invited to a gathering at County Hall. Wine, sandwiches and a thirty second speech of thanks were provided. It could be a moving occasion. Teachers who had taught together in the same school, sometimes nearly forty years ago, and had lost touch when they had gone their different ways, met each other again. There they were, hugging each other and exchanging addresses as they moved into retirement. To make recognition easier, maiden names were included on the lists of the marrried women attending. How were these details known? I once enquired. It was in the days before computers held this kind of information. 'Well, we have separate cards for the men and women teachers on which these details appear and the latter include their maiden names'. I was told. 'But how do we know which are the women's cards?' I asked. Yes, it was true; since 1904, it had been blue cards for the boys and pink ones for the girls.

Next day, on 10 January, still in letter-writing mode and oppressed by the weight of essentially unnecessary correspondence arriving on my desk, I had time to send a letter to the editor of *Education*:

> Differences of opinion are emerging about who causes administrative work. Some would have it that it is caused by administrators themselves. Others argue that much of the responsibility lies with legislation that is reckless in its disregard of its own administrative consequences. The latter view will be powerfully reinforced by the appeals procedure on school admissions which the House of Commons, full of good intentions, has just devised. But what of the general atmosphere within which public administration now takes place? Officials are so deferential these days. It was not always so. When, some time in 1894, the South Normanton Ratepayers' Association wrote to object to the dismissal of an attendance officer, they received the following reply from the Clerk to the School Board: 'We entirely ignore the supposed right anyone may think they have to demand to know from the Board their reasons for anything they do.' Presumably, that was that, but I do not believe the Clerk intended to be rude. I believe he thought in Latin and meant by 'ignore' that the Board simply did not know of, rather than paid no attention to, anyone's right to question anything the Board did. Anyway, that, presumably, was that.
>
> Nowadays, we order things differently. No self-respecting ratepayers' association would confine itself to one letter. They would write at least five: to the Secretary of State, the local member of Parliament, the local Councillor, the Chairman of the Education Committee and the Chief Education Officer. Further to confuse matters, there might well be no indication on any of the letters to whom the other copies had been sent. Whether they did all this before writing to the press and thereby cause deputations to eddy about County Hall would depend on local circumstances but, ultimately, most of the people concerned would write to the CEO asking for some explanation of his authority's behaviour. So far as administrative work is concerned, the peremptory response of 1894 would have to be multiplied many times over.

It would probably be too much to expect that everyone should think twice before causing other people work; but it would help if more people could be persuaded to think at least once.

From 1980 onwards, it became increasingly difficult for the ILEA to reach a decision on how much money it needed ask from London rate-payers to run the education service. Some of the Labour Group were determined, on the grounds of constitutional correctness and political prudence, to keep the Authority's expenditure within the limits proposed, but not as yet enforced, by central government; other elements were equally determined to carry out what they interpreted as manifesto commitments, even when these led to far greater expenditure than the government believed necessary. So it was important to establish the legal consequences of no decision on the amount of money the Authority needed in 1980/81 being reached by the appropriate date. Hence my note to Mr Lanham, the GLC's Principal Solicitor, on 14 January:

Budget Strategy 1980/81

It is just possible that the ILEA will find itself unable, on 5 February, to declare the amount for which the GLC should, on our behalf, precept on the Inner London Boroughs. Should that happen, I need to be clear on what would happen next, and would like your advice on the point. I shall therefore be grateful if you can manage a meeting with myself and some senior colleagues fairly soon, and will be in touch with your office about this.

After the meeting, Mr Lanham confirmed what he had told us and I wrote to Sir Ashley Bramall on 30 January:

I enclose the note from Mr Lanham to which I referred recently. There are three points I would like to mention about it:

i. You will see that 10 March is the last day on which, through the GLC, the rating authorities could be told what to do. The procedural and administrative difficulties referred to could, I believe, be overcome. That point has been discussed with representatives of the Director-General and the Treasurer.

ii. Mr Lanham went through in some detail with me the implications of Section 99 of the 1944 Act. Briefly, he does not consider that a writ of mandamus would in practice have force. This is a matter on which he would be prepared to speak to you directly, if you think this appropriate.

iii. The implication is that officers would be advising members on the consequences of not levying a rate at the appropriate time. They would be bound to record the nature of the additional expenditure that would be incurred if the Authority's expenditure had to be financed by loans. Even a rate which plainly could not meet the full needs of the Authority, for example, the same rate as in the present year, would reduce interest charges.

In the circumstances, I am not copying this note to anyone. Mr Lanham's note has been given to Mr Bevan, Mr Woodman and Mr Collins only.

In the days before email, it was possible to send a politically sensitive note to an individual without risking its unauthorized circulation. Under (iii) above, Mr Lanham's point was that if there was an argument going on about an additional ten million pounds over the previous year's budget of, say, £400 million, the interest payable on that ten million, if the four hundred million of the year was duly collected, would be far less than the interest on four hundred and ten million which would have to be borrowed if the Authority made no decision on what amount to precept. Members of the Authority failing to take advice on saving interest to that extent could render themselves liable for surcharge and would be told that in a document from Mr Lanham. Mr Woodman and Mr Collins were both GLC officials, operationally attached to the ILEA but professionally responsible to GLC Chief Officers.

While all this was going on, small but irritating administrative mistakes were being made. Apologies are best offered before anyone has time to ask for them, so I wrote to all members of the Education Committee on 22 January:

> I have an apology to make over the distribution of the papers relating to the Adult Institute boundaries. It had been intended that these papers should reach all members of the Education Committee as soon as they were produced. An unfortunate delay in distribution meant that they reached members a few days after reaching, amongst others, the Chairmen and Vice-Chairmen of governing bodies and of Consultative Committees.

> I very much regret this. The future of the AEIs is an important matter and I would have wished all members of the committee to see the discussion papers at the earliest possible moment.

The problem of persuading some headteachers about the need to be systematic about potential university entrants remained, as this response to Cathy Avent, Careers Guidance Inspector, of 29 January indicates:

> Thank you for your note about university entrance. I admit that I am beginning to despair slightly of some of the teachers themselves and wonder whether we would not do better to summon all potential university and polytechnic applicants together, in a series of meetings, and tell them directly what the score is. So few of them seem to know.

A particularly difficult problem was to persuade headteachers or senior staff to encourage very able pupils to apply for leading universities, such as Oxford or Cambridge, if they had themselves not been to such a university. These were seen as other people's universities. Cathy Avent, fervently Oxbridge herself, developed a series of programmes, including visits to Colleges, which had some success in increasing the numbers being admitted. But universities could not admit students who did not apply. Meanwhile, ideas needing a response flowed in from Michael Young:

> Lord Young of Dartington
>
> Institute of Community Studies   5 February
>
> Thank you for your letter of 30 January about the idea of a boarding school in Hackney. We are just establishing a boarding element - more of a hostel really – not far from County Hall, for the northern part of Southwark. It is an expensive business. As soon as LEAs move into this area, they are beset by regulations and standards and all manner of expensive requirements. So the idea of converting existing buildings doesn't usually appeal much. Fire regulations are about as expensive as a fire itself. The premises have to be gutted.
>
> On the educational side, I can see the arguments for providing residential experience, but we have thought of this in terms of short- stay help in cases of difficulty. This doesn't seem what you have in mind, and I would certainly like to be in touch about your ideas further. I will 'phone when I am out of immediate budgetary rush.

Michael Young's ideas, at first glance, often looked unworkable but then proved remarkably successful. The Open University, described at the time by Christopher Chataway as 'one of the Prime Minister's gimmicks', was just one example of that. But my experience of boarding schools run by local authorities, not least the two run by the ILEA itself, was that they tended to be far less flexible in their arrangements and in many ways less effective than those in the independent sector of which I had personal experience. Local authority conditions of service for staff, job descriptions, holiday entitlements and so on suited day schools reasonably well but not, in my view, the kind of boarding school that the young people Michael Young had in mind would require. But I could have been as wrong about that as Mr Chataway was about the Open University.

Enter Lord Butler. In a newspaper article of 10 February, he responded to research by Profesor A H Halsey and others. The conclusion of that research was that educational reforms since 1944 had made virtually no impact on Britain's class structure. In differing from that conclusion, Lord Butler wrote:

> I believe that the death of that (the 11+) exam combined with the birth of the comprehensive are the most significant developments in education in the past decade. I welcome both that death and that birth. In the 1943 White Paper, I stated that the three types of secondary school – modern, grammar and technical – might well be combined under one one roof, which is what the comprehensive is in effect. I think the comprehensives

– or at least the good ones – can give more of a chance to all children to reveal their developing skills and abilities. This would particularly be the case if the present government encouraged the amalgamation of grammar schools with comprehensives.

Putting all forms of learning under one roof was the principle behind the London School Plan of 1947. Amalgamating grammar schools with others or, in other ways, doing everything possible to avoid the dispersal of grammar school teaching staff, had been the ILEA's approach in the 1970s. Deciding, in areas where selection at 11+ still exists, to do nothing and therefore, as a direct consequence, requiring most children in that area to attend what amounted to secondary modern schools has been the policy of both Conservative and Labour governments from the 1980s onwards.

A particularly inaccurate article on examination result in the ILEA appeared in the Times Education Supplement on 8 February. Where had this misinformation come from? I replied on 11 February:

> The article on ILEA examination results began with a comparison between A levels achieved in schools maintained by the ILEA and 'the national average'. The latter includes independent schools as well as maintained ones. I suppose it would be possible to devise a more inappropriate comparison but, for the moment, I cannot think of one.

Rumours of plans to dismantle the ILEA began to circulate so, on 14 February, I wrote to Sir James Hamilton at the Department of Education:

> As you know, there have been several press reports recently on a suggestion from a number of MPs that the ILEA should be dismantled. This follows Wandsworth Council's declared wish to establish themselves as a local education authority. If this suggestion is to be considered by Ministers, no doubt there will be some opportunity to bring to their attention the educational, administrative and financial consequences of re-organisation on the lines suggested. No one qualified to do so appears to have considered these matters since Sir Frank Marshall reported in July 1978. Naturally this is a matter for you, but I would hope that there will be some opportunity for me to provide information which would be relevant to your own assessment of these issues.

> My particular concern at the moment is that the degree of confusion which attempts at restructuring would cause may have been miscalculated. This makes it all the more important for those of us who are trying to keep things on an even keel at a time of uncertainty to have, as soon as may be, some indication of what is being proposed and a timetable within which to work. If this at any stage would be appropriate, I am of course available to discuss these issues further with you.

On 22 February, with those press reports in mind, I wrote to Margaret Maden at Islington Green School:

I gather this Panorama business is still in train. My view, as I think you know, is that there is a risk, however slight, that the film will turn out not to follow the tidy form of any programme outline that may have been agreed with you. Such has been my melancholy experience.

The news value, just at the moment, of an attack either on comprehensive schools or the ILEA is enormous. The question is whether someone, somewhere is going to be able to resist the temptation. I say this without any disrespect to this individual producer; but matters do not always end there.

Kenneth Baker's 'Sherlock Report'

This letter was written just as a report, produced by a committee of London Conservatives that included a recently retired Under Secretary at the Department of Education, arrived at County Hall. The committee had been chaired by Kenneth Baker MP and was said to have been drafted by Stuart Sexton, an energetic but, on this occasion at least, particularly ill-informed political adviser. Versions of the document appear to have been leaked in advance for greater effect and had been circulated as the 'Sherlock' Report.

An immediate response to Kenneth Baker's report was needed. Two difficulties immediately arose in dealing with it. The first was that it was so full of factual, even arithmetical, errors that it seemed impossible to correct. When intellectual confusion and factual error are so inextricably entangled, any detailed response becomes unbearably complex. No committee could be expected to digest the catalogue of corrections with which they would find themselves confronted.

A second problem was that any report I produced would be to the ILEA's Education Committee. Both Conservatives and Labour members sat on this so anything that appeared as politically biassed remarks by ILEA's Education Officer would quite rightly be resented. But how could that be avoided? It was Philip Hunter who suggested what to do. The best way to demonstrate the ineptitude of Kenneth Baker's Report would be to get as many people as possible to read it. So my response would be in booklet form. The complete text of the Sherlock Report, page by page, would be on one side of A4 so that everyone could see it. On the opposite page, also on A4, would be a response, paragraph by paragraph, correcting the most obvious mistakes. After the opening paragraphs, the extracts that follow indicate the approach adopted.

The Sherlock Report arrived at County Hall on 22 February and the response to it was dated 26 February. In his autobiography, Kenneth Baker described his report, which was almost immediately withdrawn, as having been 'sandbagged' by me. Some of the comments on it certainly have a rather sharp edge to them:

> This report takes the form of a commentary on a document produced by the 'Committee on Education in Inner London'. The document itself

was released to the Press during the week beginning 19 February and was thereafter widely commented upon. The document was received in County Hall on 22 February through the courtesy of a journalist but not everyone who might feel entitled to see it may yet have done so. To avoid further uncertainty, it seems appropriate that the document should be given wide circulation.

The document, referred to in the Press as the 'Sherlock' report, is reproduced in full. It raises matters of accountability and other issues of a political nature on which it is not for me to express an opinion. But the document also puts forward arguments which are intended to have some basis in fact. As Education Officer to the Authority, I take it to be my responsibility to see that published information on the education service in Inner London is correct and that the interpretation of that information conforms to the ordinary processes of orderly thinking.

My comments appear opposite the text of the 'Sherlock' report but there are several specific points I wish to make at the outset:

The document proposes that the ILEA's functions should be transferred to the individual London Boroughs. It is evident that the pupil numbers on which the future size of the proposed new education authorities are intended to rest have been totally miscalculated. Unwittingly, therefore, twelve education authorities are proposed of which half would have, within six years, fewer pupils than any present local education authority in England, not excluding the Isle of Wight. Inevitably, this would mean a whole interlocking series of joint arrangements at different levels of administration and for different parts of the service.

 In the time available it has not been possible to cost such arrangements but they would certainly be complex, confusing to the public and expensive to run. Twelve new education authorities would need to set up twelve new sets of administrative arrangements. The fact that the extent of the fall in school population has gone undetected means that the planning implications of the arrangements proposed have also been ignored. In particular, there is no reference to the relationship between the ILEA and the Diocesan Authorities, whose planning arrangements cover wide areas of Inner London. There is no reference in the document to the future of the services provided centrally by the ILEA. For example, the future of the ILEA Inspectorate is nowhere mentioned.

In relation to the performance of the ILEA, the document relies on a selection of examination results. This is hardly an adequate measure but, even if it were, the figures provided in the body of the report are demonstrably unsound. Those in Appendix 3 are selected in an idiosyncratic manner. It has not been possible to study this document without contrasting its approach with that of other reports which have dealt with Inner London's education service. Irrespective of the conclusions reached, the decline in the quality of the information on which judgements in the present report rely is only too evident.

There were five principal criticisms made of the ILEA. The first was that the Authority was not democratically elected and thereby not accountable to anyone. It was contrasted unfavourably in this respect with, 'for example, Birmingham, Liverpool, Manchester' or the outer London Boroughs. The response to this was:

(a) The 40 inner London GLC Councillors are all members of the ILEA. As such they are the only directly elected members of an Education Committee in England. Elsewhere, elected councillors themselves select, from amongst their members, a committee to administer the education service.

(b) The distinguishing characteristics of the educational services of the three large cities referred to are that they are run, like the ILEA, as a single service. In this respect, they conform to the pattern of every large city in the western world. It is the suggestion that the education service of a major city should be fragmented that is unique.

The second criticism was that the 'ILEA prepares its own budget, determines its own expenditure and levies 'a precept which cannot effectively be challenged'. The response to this was:

The ILEA, as a precepting authority, is similar to the Greater London Council and every County Council in England. The inner London Boroughs, including the City of London, vote on the financial plans of the ILEA through their representatives on it.

The third criticism was that the ILEA was too expensive: 'the high unit cost per pupil when compared to either other metropolitan authorities or to Outer London Boroughs cannot be justified'.

It was certainly true that, as it had been since the early 1900s, London education was more expensive than elsewhere. But it was inappropriate to compare ILEA's costs with the educational costs, for example, of outer London boroughs. On that basis, other services in inner London, such as the social services departments of the inner London boroughs, were far more expensive than education. Inner London social services, for example spent £82 per head of the population; this was more than twice the average of £38 spent in the outer London boroughs. Unit costs of the ILEA were nowhere near double those of outer London education authorities. At £632 a head they compared with £557 and £497, the highest and lowest unit costs of education in those boroughs.

The fourth criticism was that 'the higher level of expenditure on education in inner London is not matched by higher academic achievement. Success in public examinations is consistently lower in inner London when compared to the average for England and Wales. The difference is in our opinion too great to be accounted for by the inner-city characteristics of inner London.' No evidence was provided on how this opinion of the effect of 'inner-city characteristics' was reached. One problem for the ILEA was the, seldom mentioned, increasing proportion of high performing London children, amounting to ten per cent in some districts, who were educated in selective. fee-paying, day or boarding schools. What was evident, however, was the inability of the Report's authors to manage simple examination statistics The response to the Report's mishandling of these was rather sharp:

> The examination results quoted derive from an incorrect numerical base and are used to make inappropriate comparisons:
>
> 1. Figures on examination results are nowhere published as a proportion of results 'per 1,000 children at secondary schools.' That would be a methodological absurdity. Some secondary schools, such as those in the ILEA, begin at the age of 11, others at the age of 12 or 13. Others taking exams are in VIth Form Colleges. Plainly this affects the proportion of passes per thousand. For this reason, results in national or ILEA statistics have to be related either to a sample of school leavers or to single age groups.
>
> 2. The figures shown for England and Wales, but not those for the ILEA, include pupils from independent schools, the former direct grant schools and some private and overseas candidates. Although the results from these sources are included, the school population base from which they derive, of some 350,000 secondary age pupils, is not. The figures are therefore doubly invalid. Even on the basis used, all the 'O' level figures are arithmetically incorrect.

The fifth criticism of the ILEA, again with no supporting evidence, was that it was not responsive to local needs by reason of its size. This criticism was made briefly and the response was equally brief. The point here was that many of the most important educational services provided in a major city, such as its adult education service, are used by people who work in inner London but do not live there. To that extent, they are not ' local'. Those that are require a local authority able, as I had put it in 1977, to 'mobilise precision' in order to meet their needs. It was issues of that kind which Sir Frank Marshall, with thirteen expert assessors, had recently examined and reported on in 1978.

The 'Sherlock' Report sank without any immediately visible traces, but some of its misunderstandings about education, in London and elsewhere, surfaced, uncorrected, a few years later. Kenneth Baker's own autobiography, The Turbulent Years, published in 1993 after a spell as Education Secretary, continued to indicate a depressing level of unchecked error. In that book, he refers several times to the 1944 Education Act and makes it clear he cannot have read it with any care. 'The Butler Act', he declares (p.164), 'had been based on three types of school – Grammar, Secondary Modern and Technical – with selection at the age of eleven as an essential part of this'. The 1944 Act does not mention selection at eleven anywhere, nor does it name any of these types of school. The Act simply required local authorities to provided education suitable to the 'age, ability and aptitude' of the children in their areas. The government of the day had earlier expressed its own preference for the tri-partite system but that preference had no statutory force. The LCC and several other local authorities had accordingly decided to provide comprehensive schools. Kenneth Baker also believed that section 76 of the Act 'boldly stated that pupils should be educated in accordance with the wishes of their parents' (p.210). It did not boldly state that. Section 76 says that all concerned with education should 'have regard' to the wishes of parents but went on to say that a local authority had also to have regard to other things, such as its duty to provide efficient education and to avoid unreasonable public expenditure.

By 1980, the Conservative government, possibly influenced by Schumpeter's theory of 'creative destruction', was already showing signs of what was to become its main contribution to the structure of English society over the next thirty years. From a restless desire to 'reform' an educational system which it showed little sign of understanding, successive governments set about the systematic destruction of any democratically elected agencies that acted as a check on government's own ability to govern as it wished. Hence this letter to Tyrrell Burgess, co-editor of the publication referred to, on 6 March:

> I wonder if it is worth while taking the idea, which appears in John Pratt's editorial in HER (Higher Education Review), a little further? He talks about the way that tyrannies set about controlling higher education and stifling academic freedom. It is also the case that tyrannies, usually in the form of people with bulging eyes, also start by attacking local government (Napoleon, Hitler, Stalin, Mussolini). You made the same point when you referred to a clause in Lenin's constitution.

> Is there not a theme here? Our experience of democracies has been with reasonably prosperous countries in a state of expansion. From the Greeks onward, expansion seems to have been a condition of freedom. Lose the expansion, take Rome, and you are into emperors, backed by the soldiery.

> Is there an example of a democracy, in anything like the shape that this country has known it, surviving decline? Faced by decline, everything becomes tidily centralised, and we know where that leads. My point is that the difference today is that our potential tyrants lack bulging eyes or any sense of purpose. It is all being done by accident, by people who think democratic institutions can work like the General Electric Company. What is wanted, it seems to me, is an article on the 'Conservative Road to Serfdom', standing Hayek on his head. We really are moving into very absolutist times, in which people with power are quite unwilling to see any serious part of it devolved to anyone.

Meanwhile, between March and October, when HMI produced their report on the

ILEA, the day-to-day work of the Authority continued. As always, it was essential to ensure that the administration did not ever-extend itself by taking on more than it could manage successfully. At the same time, it had to do all it could to retain its ability to manage its own financial affairs within the general guidelines set by the government. Some examples of the varied nature of that day to day work are given below:

> Mrs Barbara Chubb (Divisional Office 2) 21 April
>
> Dear Mrs Chubb,
>
> I am just writing to say that I have had a very pleasant letter from David Miles, the Chairman of North Westminster School, in which he specifically refers to the excellent work you have been doing over these past few months. I would like to add my own thanks and congratulations to you. I am sending a copy of this to Mr Bradbury.

One of Sir Alec Clegg's favourite quotations was from a long-dead HMI who spoke of the importance of giving individuals 'that recognition which our natures crave and respond to with renewed endeavour'. The clerks to governing bodies were members of the divisional office staff, in this instance Peter Bradbury's, and Mrs Chubb no doubt had several schools to look after in this way.

At County Hall, a major re-structuring of Adult Education Institutes had just been completed. The imminent retirement of a number of Adult Education Institute principals and the need to reduce administrative costs had made it necessary to develop fewer institutes, each large enough to provide the wide range of academic and other programmes able to meet the varying social, economic and community needs arising in different parts of London. Adult education included community-based family and parent learning, programmes for non-English-speaking immigrants, basic literacy and numeracy for adults, work in prisons and with recently discharged prisoners, one-to-one work with homeless people sleeping at the railway stations, pre-vocational courses for unemployed adults, learning programmes for adults in hospitals and residential homes as well as special programmes for adults with hearing impairments. Re-organisation led to a reduction of the number of institutes from thirty-one to nineteen rather larger ones. Like many other developments within the ILEA, I played no part in this important re-organisation, other than to help smooth occasional problems arising between those conducting it and the Chip Whip, Miss Elsie Horstead. The person responsible for this achievement was Peter Clyne, to whom I wrote on 1 May:

> Now that the re-organisation of the AEIs is through sub-committee, may I just repeat what I said to you earlier? After the initial hiccup, the whole exercise seems to me to have been carried out with outstanding efficiency: a combination of first-rate educational thinking, backed by excellently presented logistical argument. Add to that the necessary flexibility which

211

living in a political world requires, and we have this splendid result. I hope you will congratulate everyone on my behalf. Really, it has been, as I say, a quite outstanding achievement.

The ILEA was full of enterprising people, teachers, parents and governors, with ideas on how to improve what was being done. The question arose as to whether the idea of community schools could be applied in some areas of London. Ideas which I had seen working well in Yorkshire and elsewhere did not necessarily suit Inner London. Professor Harry Rée had been a good friend of mine from Yorkshire days and we met, more often socially than professionally, when he was working, as part of his 'planned demotion' as an assistant teacher in Hackney. He was a committed supporter of community schools, on the lines of those developed in Cambridgeshire by Henry Morris, whose excellent biography he had written. The following letter was sent immediately after a conference on the possibility of developing several community schools in London. The three headteachers at the conference were developing well-supported comprehensive schools and wanted to widen their scope to include the local adult community. The recently reorganised Adult Education Institutes were strongly opposed to further structural changes in the form of 'experiments', whereby the heads of the three secondary schools would add the education of adults from the surrounding community to their remit. Immediately after the conference, I wrote to those principally concerned:

Letter to: Mrs A. Jones Vauxhall Manor School 17 June
            Mr P. Mitchell Quintin Kynaston School
            Miss M. Maden Islington Green School
With copies to: Mr Harry Rée
            Mr David Miles Member ILEA
            Mr Stubbs Deputy Education Officer
            Mr Clyne Assistant Education Officer

Here are a few, post-Saturday, thoughts. I see the need to make sure you have a clear line to the ILEA on who is responsible for what, so far as your own new developments are concerned. I will see this is settled quickly.

I also see why there is some hankering after a policy statement, setting out a view of the nature of education in an urban setting and establishing the principles on which the education service should be responding to educational needs, in the widest sense. Nevertheless, I am against such a statement. Policy statements ought to be followed immediately by administrative action. Otherwise people become unsettled rather than inspired. But there are at least three reasons, which have nothing to do with the usual organisational inertia, why there will not be rapid or radical change in the way things are now run.

The first is that the AEIs are just being reorganised. A number of them are already carrying out effective and wide-ranging programmes within their communities. So no one will want to put all that suddenly into the melting pot.

Second, setting aside the voluntary schools, almost half of ILEA's secondary schools are in the process of some major upheaval: ending selection, being part of an amalgamation, or in some other way changing shape, size or function. A number of these schools are, as yet, insecurely established in public esteem. An expressed interest in the surrounding community does not necessarily lead to improved support for a school or to better performance within it. The response I have encountered from parents and the public in some parts of London over the past few months has made this very clear to me. The point has been forcibly put that the school should first of all put its own house in order before enlarging its scope of activity. It is no coincidence, if I may say so, that the schools now interested in putting into practice a wider vision of urban education have themselves had to battle their way through this first stage of being acceptable in their own terms as secondary schools. There are no short cuts to this.

Third, there is no possibility of guaranteeing the continuity of resources for widespread new developments. I do not believe the 'savings' argument. Minor administrative savings have to be set against the consequences of opening up fresh areas of educational need. But we do not know, from month to month nowadays, what financial arrangements may be imposed upon us. It is in that context that one holds back, for example, from negotiating Authority-wide arrangements to open up premises. Suppose it costs £1 million to achieve such arrangements? With the prospect of new cash limits, that £1 million has to be found elsewhere. That 'elsewhere' means people, because that is what we spend the money on. The risk is of establishing organisational shells into which we cannot afford to put the human resources.

All this may sound defensive. Part of my reasons for playing down the prospect, over the next few years, of some largely school-based transformation of our education system accord with points made by Chris Webb. What is needed in our inner areas, it seems to me, are risk-taking, open-ended, localised and flexibly arranged centres of educational enterprise. These are easier to establish in smallish towns or in defined areas, such as the Isle of Dogs or- well, this is the point you have to prove in your several ways.

Anyway, best wishes for such new developments as you can bring about. For my part, I will ensure that the administrative side of things is tidied up and made responsive to your needs. You will understand that the tensions and differences of view which you meet on the ground are precisely mirrored here in County Hall.

Chris Webb ran the Urban Studies Centre in Notting Dale. This was the form taken by the 'strong educational presence' I had mentioned to the Policy Committee in 1978. One major problem with community schools in inner London was and remains that many secondary schools attracted pupils from miles away and neither they nor their parents were, in any geographical sense, members of the school's local community. So, despite the efforts of able heads, such as the three to whom I was writing, widening the scope of the school in the way they wanted was never, other than exceptionally, going to be achieved in the near future.

The ILEA's Staff Inspector for science was Dr Spice, recently head of science at Winchester College. Whose advice on science laboratories were we to follow?

> To Mr Storr, Mr Claxton & Miss Clarkson. 4 July
>
> I must say I find it difficult to reconcile what HMI tell us about science provision and what we are told by our own Inspectorate. The gap between the two viewpoints is enormous and very expensive. For example, HMI suppose that an 11-18 five form entry school should have six laboratories. We think it should have nine. Would one or other of you have a word with me about this, please.

The problem of senior staff being regularly distracted from their work by unforeseen interruptions needed to be discussed. Hence this note of 29 July to the Senior Officers' Group:

> ILEA: Programme of Work
>
> 1. In looking at the programme of work for members of SOG over the next few months, I have had two points in mind
>
>> a. that we must not become so fully committed that we cannot deal with the consequences of major financial change (the block grant) or major constitutional changes (following the Young Committee).
>>
>> b. that individual members of SOG must be ready to take personal charge of some programmes which junior colleagues find difficulty in handling. There are jobs which are not ours but which no one else may be able to do.
>
> So we need to retain some spare administrative capacity in the system. In our different ways, our ability to do this is hampered by our national commitments. There are good 'political' reasons for being engaged on these at present but, as a group, we need to review what is happening here.
>
> 2. Apart from keeping the general ILEA and national work going, the main work with which SOG members will be directly concerned over the next six months appears to be:
>
>> a. the budget
>>
>> b. constitutional issues; the defence of ILEA interests

    c. the 16–19 complex of issues, including unemployment

    d. completing the review of secondary schools

    e. review of ILEA administrative structures and cost, including the relationship with the GLC

3. The list in paragraph 2 is by no means complete. To some extent SOG members will be involved in:

    a. getting the annual and quinquennial review procedures settled

    b. dealing with the ILEA's post- Warnock policies

    helping to advance the release of sites and premises at the same time as
    c. relocating badly-housed elements of the education service

At the same time, each of us will have a list of other programmes which need a watchful eye from SOG members: the multi-ethnic education policy and the disruptive units are two that occur to me.

Can we discuss please?

One thing this note illustrates is that, in 1980, the school curriculum was still perceived, throughout the educational system, as the responsibility of the schools, with such assistance as the inspectorate might be able to give. Politicians and administrators did not see themselves as qualified to impose their own ideas about the curriculum on schools.

Mr Greengross, a leading Conservative member of the ILEA, wanted me to prevent ILEA employees from putting 'Save the ILEA' stickers on ILEA vehicles. As Education Officer to the Authority, I could see that his point was a reasonable one, but it was not one that was easy for me to deal with, as I explained in a note to him of 1 August:

> You asked about stickers on ILEA vehicles. I have asked for this practice to be discouraged, though I would not wish to be too heavy-handed about it. We tend to look tolerantly on our employees who mount, for example, 'Save our School' campaigns, with banners all over the walls, in direct opposition to an Authority decision to close them. So it might look odd to jump on individuals who agree with the Authority's policy of retaining a unified education service in inner London.

The Inspectorate remained at the other end of numerous minutes:

> To Mr T. Jaggar (Senior Inspector Secondary Schools) 29 August
>
> The C.I mentioned to me your concern about the matter of access to myself. Briefly, I do not think the Senior Officers Group is a good forum in which to discuss educational ideas. It is very taken up with administrative matters and the C.I has a watching brief there. If we get tangled up with major educational issues, that should be the subject of a separate, inspectorate-based meeting.

215

The second problem is that we have a structure, rightly or wrongly, designed to pull me out of the day-to-day running of affairs. This was partly devised to ensure my own survival but the consequence is that there is a serious danger of misunderstanding if I deal too directly with educational issues. So there is a problem here. Why not drop in one morning and take it further? Nothing in the present arrangements ought to prevent colleagues talking to each other; or will be allowed to, may I add.

This was a rather better explanation of what ought to have been happening than of what actually was. Evidently, I was very involved in the day-to-day running of affairs but did try to engage with educational issues through the Chief Inspector or at meetings at which he was present. The relationship between us remained uneasy, as this note to him on 17 September indicated:

Inspectorate priorities

Thanks for the note on inspectorate priorities. I am concerned by what was said in the Primary piece. The Inspectorate must not make assumptions about what is or is not 'inexpedient politically'. What the administration needs to know is what the Primary Inspectorate think ought to happen about the size and disposition of the schools we maintain. If somebody really believes we ought to be going for primary schools with at least 150 pupils, I hope they will say so positively and with reasons, and leave others to worry about what we do with the recommendation.

Michael Young was critically supportive of the ILEA, constantly on the alert for an opportunity to sharpen up our thinking or to offer help whenever he could.

Lord Young Director Institute of Community Studies 2 September

Many thanks for your note about the future of the ILEA. I think this is in the lap of whatever the Conservative Party's equivalent of the Gods may be; so I am not sure there is much that can now be done. Of course, a letter to Baroness Young would always be useful. Whatever the outcome, the real factor which is oppressing us at the moment is the thought that all London services look likely to suffer under the present block grant proposals. These combine great ingenuity with damaging naivete: you take an average cost per client over the country, you introduce some factors for London, then you weight those factors. You then churn the result through a computer and, lo and behold, London is wildly overspent on everything. Not exactly a procedure to set against years of direct experience of meeting particular problems as and when they arise.

Funding education by formula

Funding education by formula had always been what elements in the Civil Service regarded as the best way to control expenditure and to distribute taxpayers' money equitably. The following letter, copied to Jack Springett, CEO of Essex, is to a DES Deputy Secretary on his draft proposals for reaching a funding formula that would apply nationally. Evidently, we had not yet stopped addressing people as 'Esq':

Edward Simpson Esq, CB,

Department of Education and Science   15 September

I understand that the Department has accepted that some of the assumptions on which the Block Grant calculations are based are still open to question and that you are prepared to discuss these further, both in deciding how to approach certain 'outliers' in existing exemplifications for the year 1981-82 and in relation to the method used in future years. If this is so, I am reassured, because I believe the arrangements now being devised are bound to affect the long-term interests of the education service in Inner London. Naturally, I do not wish them to do so adversely; yet I believe that this could be the result unless some of the assumptions at present being contemplated are modified.

My particular concern relates to the educational aspects of the assumptions underlying the 'weighted client group method'. This approach seeks to establish the size of the group of children, young persons and adults for which local authorities might reasonably be expected to make special provision; and the weightings to be assigned to each such person. I question the validity of the calculations made in respect of both.

So far as children are concerned, it is being argued that local authorities nationally might reasonably be expected to make special provision for 17.5% of their pupils. This figure is derived largely from the Warnock Report. This in turn relied, in considerable measure, on work carried out within the ILEA. I do not believe that the evidence can bear the great weight now being placed upon it, for it is no exaggeration to say that the level of education services in some parts of the country may depend heavily on that 17.5%. In any case, my own reading of the Warnock Report, taken with later ILEA surveys, points – as clearly as anything so fundamentally uncertain can do – to figures considerably higher than those now suggested. So, if an approximation has to be made, I would argue for 20%.

My second point, which concerns the size of the special needs group within ILEA, raises a familiar problem. The measures relate to what there are figures for rather than what is relevant. In this instance, particular weighting is given to people born outside the United Kingdom or who are from non-white ethnic backgrounds. These happen to be the figures obtainable from the National Dwelling and Housing Survey; but they do not in any way reflect the nature or scale of the educational problems in London. For example, considerable numbers of, in Survey terms, white parents arrive without a word of English. The ILEA has the figures for the children and adults for whom it has then to make special provision. These figures bear no relation to those now being used by the Grants Working Group. The latter reflect a serious underestimate of the educational job that has to be done.

I understand the difficulty of carrying through an exercise of the kind now being undertaken. There must always be a degree of arbitrariness. My concern is that a system is being devised in haste which will harden into a pattern that is impossible to shift in the future. I therefore must place on record my concern over the educational basis for the figures now being produced; they understimate the needs for which we provide and damage could be done to education in inner London if this is not recognised in the calculations finally approved.

Edward Simpson was one of an able group of DES administrators in the 1970s. He had a clear and directly acquired understanding of educational issues. His straightforwardness in his dealings with local education authorities made him, even when implementing policies they disliked, highly regarded as well as trusted. The problem for the ILEA, of course, was that basing grant on a formula related to the number of children thought to need help was a hopelessly flawed methodology. It did not take account of problems that affected London far more than anywhere else. Several thousand children in London, for example, had educational problems that did not arise from their personal characteristics. Their problems arose because they were in or having to move between schools with shifting pupil populations which themselves were affected by a damaging movement, in and out, of recently trained teachers. Meanwhile, we could at least do everything possible to improve the environment in which many London schools were still having to work.

To Mr Perkins GLC Valuations and Estates Department. 2 October

Just to confirm that I am anxious that the piece of land adjoining St. Matthias School, Bethnal Green, should be tidied up for use by the children, at least for the next year or so. I have had a look at it and it really is a tip.

In October we heard that a report by HMI on the ILEA was shortly to be produced.

It was the first report from HMI on a local education authority and we were not sure what form it would take.

Note to the Leader 21 October

We have heard that Her Majesty's Inspectorate are to produce a Report on the performance of the Authority over the past five or so years. At least part of the Report may already have been submitted to Baroness Young's Enquiry on the future of Education Services in London. My understanding is that HMI are sending the Report to us as they do for individual schools or colleges: it will be sent with a 'confidential' label to it.

I also understand that HMI would be prepared to join in a discussion with Members on the Report's major conclusions and that it would be open to us to seek the Secretary of State's agreement that the 'confidential' label be removed.

The Ministerial Enquiry referred to in the first paragraph was the one conducted, within the Department of Education, by Baroness Young, a Conservative minister with long experience of local government. I suggested to Sir Ashley that we should ask permission to make the HMI Report, whether favourable or otherwise, public. He agreed, so I wrote to Sheila Browne accordingly on 27 October:

Dear Sheila,

We have been considering how to handle the HMI Report on the ILEA. Subject to any problems at your end, we would like to be able to collect the Report (100 copies if possible) on Monday 10 November. On the same day I will deliver a letter to you asking permission for us to release the Report on Wednesday 12 November. On that day we would circulate the Report, with a covering paper by me, for a meeting at one of our Sub-Committees on the morning of Thursday 20 November. As soon as I send the papers out they would become publicly available to the press.

We would invite you to be represented at the meeting on 20 November to present the Report in a 'Part 2' discussion, to which no members of the press or public are admitted. This would be followed by a public 'Part 1' debate from which your colleagues, presumably, would wish to withdraw. I hope this timetable would suit your diary, if you are planning to be there. If not, perhaps you would let me know what other arrangements might be possible from your point of view.

In Stuart Maclure's book *The Inspector's Calling (*published in 2000) he suggests that I asked for the HMI Report to be published 'because he trusted the Inspectorate a great deal more than he did his Education Committee or the education ministers in the Thatcher government.' As indicated above, this was not correct. The Leader and I had agreed that the report should be published for two reasons. The first was that, with a hundred copies washing about County Hall, whether marked 'confidential' or not, the report would anyway soon reach the Press, who would simply pick out the bits they wanted to quote. The second reason was that, having seen many reports on individual schools, I was confident that HMI would point out the good things that were happening as well as to the unsatisfactory ones. The latter would be particularly important in alerting ILEA's inspectorate as well as the schools to what we needed to do better.

The Report by Her Majesty's Inspectors on the ILEA, as agreed, was released on

20 November. It was the first report on a local education authority and, although individual HMI had access to any documentation from the Authority they asked for, there was no systematic call for documents, designed to give an accurate picture of the Authorities activities. So I, for one, did not know what documents they had and which they were missing. Unfortunately, there was no opportunity for the Authority to correct statements of fact in the final draft though we had seen and commented on an earlier version.

HMCI Sheila Browne decided to present the Report in person. As she began to do so, there was an interruption. A group of school children were suddenly eddying about. In the midst of this disturbance was Ken Livingstone and a colleague. The report was declared to constitute some form of plot against a Labour-controlled education service. The interruption was itself interrupted by Sheila Browne at her most steely. Any more of that kind of thing, she remarked, and she would leave the meeting. She was assured by Sir Ashley, also at his most authoritative, that the Authority welcomed her presence and invited her to continue with what she had to say. Ken Livingstone and his entourage then left the meeting.

The HMI Report on the ILEA, like all Inspectorate reports, needs to be read in full. On the whole, despite a few errors of fact, it seemed to me to be, as I had expected, well-balanced and mostly fair. But when it reached the schools and colleges it was the source of considerable irritation, particularly amongst the secondary school heads. A group came to see me. Where was the evidence for these sometimes critical comments on their work ? they asked. The methodology, they argued, was thoroughly unsatisfactory. As the report itself stated, it had been based on only six full inspections of ILEA's 200 or so secondary schools. Those inspections had been spread over the past five years, during which time many secondary schools had been in the process of closing, ending selection or in some way changing their structure. There had also been a series of one day visits, by individual inspectors, to 55% of London'seprimary and secondary schools during the previous year. Which schools had been looked at and how had they been chosen? Most members of the deputation claimed never to have received such a visit from any HMI. Others acknowledged that an HMI had called in on a single day but had only looked round their school very briefly. The ILEA, they argued, should reject the Report on the grounds of its methodological inadequacy.

Arguing with the umpire is seldom sensible. As a general impression of how things stood in the ILEA, the HMI Report was, in the view of myself and my immediate colleagues, rather less warm than it had been in the early draft we had seen but constituted a not unreasonable, if necessarily impressionistic, assessment of the Authority's performance. A general problem was that there was little sign that the inspectors, almost all from outside London, had grasped the degree to which the decline, associated with huge population change in the late 1950s and 1960s, had been arrested, notably in the primary schools, and was slowly being reversed throughout the school system. Inspectors record what they see when they see it. Few had themselves had much experience of demographic turbulence on the scale that had affected such a large number of inner London's schools and was still affecting quite a few of them. Accordingly, when those inspectors detected what they saw as a degree of waste or over-generous expenditure they quite properly recorded a fact of which we were well aware. These were years during which the Authority had been consciously buying a degree of stability. The inspectors might have been unimpressed by this but had not themselves been faced, as the ILEA had been, week by week, with the prospect of serious disruption, caused by the enforced closure of schools through industrial action. The effect of this was to damage the day-to-day education of many thousands of children for whom the Authority had a statutory duty to provide.

To the irritation of some of London's leading secondary school heads, we did not advise the leadership of the ILEA to object to the HMI Report. It did, however, contain a few oddities. In talking of the way the ILEA's administration worked, to take one small example, the Report commented: 'There are, however, certainly instances when schools bypass the formal channels of communication and deal direct with senior officers.' That comment illustrated an attitude towards the administration of a public service which my colleagues and I did not share. If the education of children or students in any school or college was being adversely affected by some element of the ILEA's administration, we were in favour of the leadership of that institution telling us about it directly. It then became job of those of us who could deal with the matter quickly to do just that. What we disliked was a school telling the local newspaper about a problem before asking County Hall to deal with it. This was not regarded as helpful and could elicit a sharp response.

In his autobiography, *The Turbulent Years* (1993), Kenneth Baker stated that in 1980, 'following a devastating report by 200 inspectors on ILEA's inadequacies and failures', he had called for my resignation. I am not sure where the 200 inspectors came from – far fewer were actually involved – and, as I never learnt of the existence of the call for my resignation, it went unanswered. But where did the 'inadequacies and failures' bit come from? Mr Baker had presumably formed his opinions from one or two articles in hostile elements of the Press rather than from a reading of the report itself. In a brief covering report to the Education Committee, I noted that it had referred to weak points as well as to strong ones in what the Authority was doing, but that the overall message was one of an improving education service. Hence my comment: 'There is no need to devise strategies to deal with an imaginary decline in standards. The task now is for us to improve on improvement'.

Set out below are some pointers, in the order in which they appear in its text, to what the report had to say. It needs re-emphasising that, like any HMI report, this one has to be read in full to ensure that it is in not misrepresented in any way:

ILEA administration

The ILEA is well staffed by senior officers who are capable administrators and of a high intellectual calibre. They offer elected members sound, well thought out advice on policy options, and papers put forward to the Authority's committees are of a high standard. The planning and development of the education service in inner London has depended to no small extent on the quality of thinking and leadership they have provided. The Authority has clear policies on the major structural issue of falling rolls in primary and secondary schools and the arrangements for the education of 16–19 year olds. These have developed as a result of thorough documentation and careful consultation. In many respects the Authority's procedures at this level of policy making are exemplary. The Authority is well served by its Research and Statistics division which provides much of the necessary planning information and conducts many of the evaluation exercises.

Innovations

Some of its responses have necessarily been experiments which have added to the overall costs of the service without always producing the anticipated results or return on the expenditure. Nevertheless, other authorities have reason to be grateful to the ILEA for its readiness and ability to experiment. The decision to establish support units off the school site for disruptive pupils appears to have been implemented hurriedly and without detailed consideration of curriculum needs.

This last comment illustrates the difference between the point of view of administrators and that of inspectors, such as HMI. For administrators, the primary justification for the support units was to keep all young people under the care and control of teachers and to do this quickly rather than have them running loose one the streets on being suspended from school, sometimes for lengthy periods. Once in the unit, the task of the teachers there was to establish with each child, sometimes for the first time in that young person's life, a relationship within which that child would be valued and achieve, sometimes also for the first time, a degree of success. So far as this could be done through some elements of the normal school curriculum, well and good. If not, it was for those who knew the young people best to find other ways of developing in them the skills and sense of self-worth on which they could build a return to school or be encouraged and become able to enter some form of further training or employment on leaving school.

The Authority appears to be doing its best to give schools in the voluntary sector every chance, where necessary, to move into premises superior to those occupied at present.

The relationship between the Authority and the diocesan authorities, Church of England and Roman Catholic, was, with rare exceptions, good. The ending of

academic selection to the secondary schools, many of which were aided denominational schools, was greatly helped by the support of leading representatives of both
denominations. Their opposition would have been hard to overcome.

> The deployment of staff generally causes some concerns. On average,
> teachers in secondary schools in the ILEA are in contact with classes for
> one period less in a week of 40 periods than teachers elsewhere in the
> country (30 instead of 31); and there is no evidence that this extra time is
> used to prepare for better performance in the classroom.

The reference to an average class contact time of thirty periods each week was, like
most attempts to draw general conclusions from averages, misleading. In some of
the most difficult schools, far fewer than thirty periods a week was the norm. One
only had to visit the staff rooms of some of these schools to see that preparing for
the next encounter with their class was about the last thing on the minds of many
of the teachers, as it would have been in mine. Smoke hung heavy in the air, empty
coffee cups were everywhere and the whole place looked and felt like a recovery
centre. Few members of HMI had themselves attended, later taught in, or were
closely acquainted with schools where every lesson, in some schools in some parts of
London, could turn into a battle from which even the most effective teachers would
regularly retire defeated.

On the other hand, other schools managed well on class contact time at or even
well above the national average. I once tried to find out how a girls grammar school
managed to staff a small third-year sixth form. Lunch hours and a longer school day
for several of its teachers, with no extra pay, proved to be the answer to that.

> A significant development in recent years has been the growth in the range
> and standard of provision for the further education of low-achieving school
> leavers. This work has proved a sound base for courses provided within
> the Manpower Services Commission's Youth Opportunities Programme.
> Much sound and imaginative work of this type is being carried out in
> ILEA Colleges, reflecting the concerns of the Authority and its officers
> and the commitment of many of the staff involved.

The re-shaping of the Authority's Further Education Colleges, with its renewed
emphasis on recruiting and then meeting the needs of low achievers, was one of the
Authorities most important achievements during the 1970s. As I simply observed this
work, but played no significant part in it, I have few papers of my own to show for it.
Nor have I personal papers to illustrate the development of one year access courses
to Higher Education, initially to the North London Polytechnic. These courses
recruited members of under-represented groups, in this instance mainly students of
West Indian origin.

On primary education it was noted:

> There are many instances of classes in junior schools concentrating so

heavily on the basic skills that pupils receive too little encouragement to
develop initiative and an enquiring mind.

That observation confirmed my own concerns and I referred to this in my covering
report to the Education Committee. Concentrating on the basic skills was just what
ILEA schools were widely criticised in the Press, then and later, for not doing. The
point HMI were making, with which I agreed, had been made by HMI Matthew
Arnold a hundred years earlier: 'The schools in which the general instruction is best
are precisely those in which the elementary instruction is best also.' Ever since, the
evidence had indicated that excessive concentration on basic skills is not the best way
of improving them.

On secondary planning:

> In 1977 the Authority's development sub-committee adopted a standard
> policy for dealing with falling rolls. It is possible to argue that the Authority
> should have acted sooner.

It was not possible to argue that. The Authority had been reducing the number
of secondary schools well before 1977, by nineteen in 1975 for example. This was
before numbers began to fall. The facts could easily have been produced had HMI
asked for them. The 1977 statement, referred to in the chapter for that year, simply
gave formal approval to a methodology already in use.

On adult education:

> In summary, the ILEA adult education service provides a range of
> opportunities unmatched in any other part of the country.

On the Youth Service:

> The ILEA Youth Service is the largest service of its kind in the U.K and
> has developed characteristics which distinguish it from most other youth
> services in the country. Amongst these is the exceptional support given
> to voluntary youth organisations. The ILEA Youth Service has direct
> responsibility for 77 youth centres and 34 youth clubs, but supports no
> fewer than 650 voluntary clubs and projects with grant aid for salaries
> and maintenance, sometimes both . It is not so much the case that ILEA
> supports the voluntary organisations as that the voluntary organisations
> are a major part of the ILEA service.

Two hundred and forty thousand young people were members of ILEA or ILEA-
funded Youth Clubs, run by voluntary organisations. Their purpose was to provide
leisure-time or quasi-educational activities, in the evenings, at weekends and in the
school holidays. When told at a meeting with Ministers that the ILEA was spending
far too much on its youth service, I remarked that, though this was not its purpose,
that service constituted the cheapest and most effective police service in London.

Groups of inner-city youngsters clambering about in Wales on ILEA subsidised adventure holidays, for example, could not simultaneously be hanging about on London's street corners with nothing to do except get into expensive to deal with forms of trouble.

On multi-ethnic education, after references to the new team of multi-ethnic inspectors:

> Many children for whom English is not their native language need extra tuition in it. The Research and Statistics branch survey established the facts with a precision which no other LEA appears to possess.

The conclusion (pages 115–120) on ILEA schools:

> Nursery education is generally of a satisfactory standard and is improving.

> The range and quality of education in primary schools has also improved greatly in the last five years.

> Secondary schools, with help from many quarters, have mainly become quieter places than they were five years ago. Also on the credit side, there are many instances of notably harmonious relations between all sections of the school's community. But, as a very broad generalisation, too many secondary schools expect too little from their pupils at all levels.

> Finally: In the past five years, the Authority has given energetic and unremitting attention to a multiplicity of matters and to the deployment of considerable financial resources to counteract these problems. The picture that currently emerges is of a caring and generous authority with considerable analytic powers to identify problems, the scale of which is, in some cases, unique in the country.

The report added that the ILEA was the first education authority in England to have fully qualified librarians in every secondary school. The suggestion that too many secondary schools expected too little from their pupils was certainly true. Why did this problem persist? My own experience as a teacher had taught me that it is far easier to control a potentially difficult group of pupils by setting them to do routine and undemanding tasks than it is to engage with those same individuals in a lively and educationally more productive manner – and control, as many London schools understandably had been having to decide, had to be their first priority.

Two adverse comments were made in the conclusion that schools do not always deploy resources wisely and there are disturbing examples of waste and inefficiency. As examples of these defects were not given in the Report, it was difficult to respond to them but a comment also made, that improvements could be made without extra resources was one with which most of us in County Hall, then and later, would agree.

Given the haste with which it had to be put together and their lack of familiarity with some of the problems with which the ILEA was having to deal, in my view, HMI had produced a report which was in most respects supportive of the Authority. It had rightly pointed to two unresolved problems of which the Authority was well aware: the pervasive problem of under-expectation in too many primary and secondary schools and the fact that resources allocated to schools had too often been unwisely spent or inefficiently used by the schools. There was, however, absolutely nothing in the report that was, to use Kenneth Baker's term, 'devastating' and if he believed HMI had accused the ILEA and its officers of 'inadequacies and failures', he had plainly not read the report's references to the ILEA's administration.

Perhaps the last word on that HMI Report should be left with Carol Handley, the distinguished headmistress of Camden School for Girls. She was busy getting to grips with the first all-ability intakes to her school. Mrs Handley was a classical scholar, married to the Professor of Greek at London University. It was the summer school in Greek that the two ran each year that had so impressed me when I first came to London. I had recently sent her a copy of 'The Hill of Kronos' by Peter Levi to ask her what she thought of it. After commenting on its uneven quality, she ended her letter with a comment on the HMI Report:

> It sounds as if your own life is going to be even more stressful than usual during the next few weeks. Perhaps the Education Committee should reflect that their hysterical reaction to a balanced and tactfully expressed report shows that people do not always react rationally even to the most blandly expressed criticism – they should ask themselves if they think that annual reports on all teachers (disguised as career development) and quinquennial reviews of all secondary schools will really help London education. Teachers' confidence is always precarious because of the daily testing and under-mining it receives from teen-agers. It could collapse altogether if subjected to too much review.' She ended with 'the very best of luck – for all our sakes- in the coming months'.

In fact, the response of the ILEA leadership to the HMI Report, as opposed to that of some of its attention-seeking members, was far more balanced than Carol Handley had supposed. Unfortunately, it was the over-reaction of Ken Livingstone and later of Kenneth Baker, neither of whom had much understanding of education in inner London, that tended to interest the Press.

Just before the HMI Report on the ILEA was issued, television and the Press had become more full than usual of wildly inaccurate stories about ILEA schools. As part of this circulation-raising campaign, on 12 November the Islington Press printed excitable comments from a couple of teachers now, for reasons not here discussed, unemployed. Hence this letter to the Islington Gazette on 19 November:

> When I reported recently to the ILEA on the re-organisation of secondary schools in Islington, I remarked on the high standard of the debate that had taken place locally. I was a little premature. I am afraid that recently we have been treated to comments of uncertain quality about individual

secondary schools. Some of these comments have as much right to be taken seriously as Humpty Dumpty's advice on how to balance on a wall; but my serious point in writing to you is to remind your readers that, of course, all schools are capable of improvement. Islington Green, which seems to have been at the receiving end of much of the correspondence, is no exception to this but the considered view of those who have the experience and the professional competence to offer it is that the strong commitment on the part of the staff now teaching there is reflected in the standards being achieved in key areas of the schools' work.

As a general rule, which applies to all secondary schools in Islington, I hope that parents and others interested in the work of schools will form their judgements on what they see for themselves. As you know, parents are particularly invited to visit schools when deciding which school to choose.

So ended 1980. It was a year in which, with a new Conservative government in place, the ILEA had to learn how to pursue its policies with determination but to do so in ways that did not threaten its own survival. With Sir Ashley Bramall as its Leader and with the support of his experienced political colleagues, my colleagues and I saw no reason why this could not be managed. Part of our job was to ensure the Authority was not put on the defensive by having to explain away disasters at individual institutions or financial or other forms of mismanagement. Major or contentious structural change, unless absolutely unavoidable, also had to be put on the back burner. Major change in the structure of a public authority provokes the possibility of a complete change to that authority's structure; indeed, to its very existence. Prudence was essential. So far as finance was concerned, the ILEA never overspent its budget by as much as a halfpenny, nor were its accounts ever qualified by the District Auditor. As for institutions, there had been no more William Tyndale's to inflame the headlines of the national Press but that did not prevent hopelessly inaccurate Press articles regularly appearing and with equal regularity having to be answered. Meanwhile, standards of educational administration had to be maintained. Hence this letter to Arthur Cummings, Divisional Officer in Southwark, of 18 December:

> I have seen a copy of a letter addressed to Mrs Sofer by a school governor to the effect that the Education Welfare Officer is 'quite adamant that there is an impossible problem with the head's attitude to children from minority ethnic groups'. If it is the view of any ILEA officer that someone or other within the service is acting improperly, that view, with evidence for it, should be submitted to me through you. If there is no such evidence, views of this kind should not be expressed to third parties. The fundamental principle is that no one should be complained of without being made aware of the nature of the complaint and being given a chance to answer it. I shall be grateful if you will make this known to anyone who may need to be reminded of it.

Thirty years later, Ministers of both of the main political parties, either on defective departmental advice or on their own initiative, preferred to ignore this 'fundamental principle'. They became irritable when criticised for their failure to have regard to it, even after having to be expensively reminded of it in court .

Chapter 7: 1981

The main events with which I was concerned in 1981 were the ending of corporal punishment in secondary schools, responding to the unemployment of sixteen to nineteen-year-olds, financial pressures on the Authority from the Department for Education, the re-organisation of ILEA's divisional structure, dealing with the Press, the riots in Brixton and the change in the political leadership of the ILEA. As the dates attached to these events indicate, many were taking place at the same time. In that respect, heads of large organisations resemble chefs responsible for simultaneously supervising several main courses and the occasional pudding. It is when too much has to be done too quickly that things go wrong and custard pies start flying about in the kitchen.

The ending of corporal punishments in schools maintained by the ILEA was a lengthy business.

In the late nineteenth century, an attempt was made by influential members of the London School Board to ban its use. That failed. In 1905, the newly formed LCC's Supplies Department was offering schools infant canes for a penny farthing each and the more substantial ones for juniors at a penny half-penny. Corporal punishment in ILEA primary schools had been ended in January 1973. For ILEA secondary schools, the move to end corporal punishment began in 1978 and was completed in 1981.

Developments between these two dates have been collected together below. There was no commitment nationally to ending corporal punishment in secondary schools and there had been no reference to the possibility in either of the London Labour Party's 1973 or 1977 local government election manifestos. Nevertheless, dislike of the practice amongst leading ILEA members, notably Elsie Horstead, Harvey Hinds, Mair Garside, Anne Sofer and Sir Ashley himself, was intense.

On 26 January 1978, the Schools Sub-Committee called for a report on 'current trends' in the incidence of corporal punishment. On the following afternoon, the Conservatives responded by putting down a motion for debate which read: 'that this committee considers that head teachers in secondary schools should continue to use corporal punishment at their own discretion'. The deadline for submitting a counter-motion was noon on the following day. The Leader, who can have had little opportunity to consult anyone else, immediately proposed the following amendment: 'that for all the words after 'committee' the following be substituted: 'while recognising the present right of head teachers to use corporal punishment at their own discretion, within the terms of the Authority's regulations, expresses its hope that the Authority's proposals for dealing with disruptive pupils and consultations with the teachers' associations will lead to the elimination of this form of punishment'.

Sir Ashley's suggestion that the measures being taken to deal with disruptive pupils might be directly connected to a move to phase out corporal punishment took me by surprise. In discussions with head teachers and the teacher unions and in my report to the Education Committee on disruption, I had not made any such connection because the thought had never occurred to me. The Leader's sudden burst of lateral thinking caused trouble. It led one teacher union to suggest – and to keep on asserting – that I had been less than frank in my discussions with them and to declare that the whole policy for dealing with disruption was really an excuse to end corporal punishment. This it most certainly was not. The Leader's amendment was carried. So far, neither ILEA officials nor inspectors had been involved but, arising out of Sir Ashley's amendment, the Chief Inspector, in association with the Research and Statistics Branch, was asked to carry out a survey to determine where and to what extent corporal punishment was still being used. Hearing of this, the NAS/UWT immediately declared that 'compulsory abolition would bring the ILEA into direct conflict with NAS/UWT, whose members would not be prepared to accept additional burdens'. As the survey appeared to be taking far too long, at some point late in May 1979, Sir Ashley and his colleagues lost patience. They wanted action. It was pointed out to me and Bill Stubbs, with a degree of asperity, that ending selection at 11+ to secondary schools by a given date had got things moving. In the member's view, it was now time to set a date for a complete end to corporal punishment at any school; so it was for officers to put a paper to the Policy Committee with a series of options from which the appropriate executive committee would later be able to choose.

Members were understandably annoyed at the delay. Most ILEA administrators, myself among them, knew that corporal punishment was little used and believed it was gradually dying out. We were anyway unenthusiastic about tackling the problem at a time when persistent and difficult-to-deal-with forms of industrial action by teachers made it unwise to give one of the larger teacher unions an additional excuse to cause trouble. But the survey was showing that corporal punishment, though not widely used, was not dying out. The schools which had used corporal punishment in 1975 were still using it five years later. As the politicians had required, on 27 June 1979 a report with a several options was put to the Policy Committee. One option was, in effect, to leave things as they were; but the third option, later included in the report to the Schools Sub-Committee, read: 'Adoption by the Authority of a policy requiring the end of corporal punishment in secondary schools and the commencement of consultations with the various parties involved on the assistance required by schools to bring this about. At the same time it would be necessary to consider whether a date for implementation should be announced and, if so, what that date should be'. At the Schools Sub-Committee meeting on 18 September 1979, the various options were considered and the following motion was carried: 'That this Committee calls upon the Education Officer to initiate consultations with a view to corporal punishment being discontinued completely from February 1981'.

On 27 March 1980, there was a report to the Schools Sub-Committee on the results of these consultations. Inspectors had tried to persuade schools using corporal punishment to stop doing so but to little effect. 'It is a matter of judgement whether this would be changed by a general exhortation by the Authority', was the report's bleak comment. It went on to set out in full the amendments to the Authority's regulations that would be needed if corporal punishment was to end from 1 February 1981. These amendments were approved and, in April 1980, schools were notified of the new regulations that were to apply from February 1981. Nothing much happened immediately but, on 31 October 1980, Mr Herbert, the General Secretary of the London NAS/UWT, declared a collective dispute with the Authority. Sir Ashley had expressive hands. They needed to be observed closely. Hands raised near shoulder level meant that it was wise to develop some form of exit strategy. Arms and hands above shoulder level and that exit strategy needed to be implemented forthwith. The letter formally declaring a collective dispute with the ILEA led to arms and hands flying all over the place. Bill Stubbs and I, when called in, had taken a relaxed view of the matter. The Authority's policy had been clearly announced, well in advance. Consultation had been extensive. There was no need to be on the defensive or to hurry. When it wanted to be, the ILEA could be quite as sluggishly bureaucratic as any rule-book bound union official. So it was not until 18 November 1980 that we advised the NAS/UWT to raise their concerns at the next meeting of the Consultative Committee on Educational Matters, a formally constituted part of the Authority's consultative arrangements with teachers. They did. This got them nowhere because other unions, notably the NUT, were in favour of ending corporal punishment. On 18 December, the NAS/UWT repeated its request that the disputes procedure be activated. We had by then sought clarification from various sources, including the Secretariat of the Council of Local Education Authorities (CLEA), on the formal position. The Secretariat confirmed our opinion that the nationally agreed procedures did not provide for unilateral reference to the collective disputes machinery, either by a local education authority or by a teachers' association. That seemed to be that. All the Authority now had to do was politely to decline the invitation from the NAS/UWT to join them in activating the disputes machinery.

We had reckoned without Sir Ashley. Deeply committed as he was personally to ending corporal punishment, as a lawyer it seemed to him outrageous that both parties had to agree before a dispute could be put to some form of arbitration. Hands were raised and stayed high at a meeting he held with Bill Stubbs and myself. Eventually, he accepted that it should be left to the Schools Sub-Committee to decide what to do, under 'urgent business', at its meeting on 29 January 1981. This was cutting things rather fine for implementing regulations that were to end corporal punishment on 1 February, but the report to that committee explained the formal position and, with a potential visit to the High Court in mind, set out in full and answered in detail each of the points made in correspondence from the NAS/UWT. The committee, after considering the documents with care, decided not to refer the matter for conciliation. That decision was confirmed at the meeting of the Education Committee on 10 February, at which Sir Ashley made a notable speech, for once written down in advance and now with the documents at the Institute of Education.

On the same day as the Education Committee's decision, 10 February, the General Secretary of NAS/UWT, Terry Casey, wrote to invoke the national collective disputes procedure. The reply I sent to him on 12 February was on the dark side of obfuscation:

> Thank you for your letter of 10 February. I am sorry to learn that your colleagues are concerned over the exchange of correspondence with Mr Herbert on the collective disputes procedure and the subsequent decision by the Schools Sub-Committee not to refer the matter to a conciliation panel. The background is this. On receiving Mr Herbert's letters, as officers we had two things in mind. The first was to establish what it was that Mr Herbert, on behalf of the Association, was objecting to; the second was to ensure that, if a dispute was subsequently accepted under the terms of the codified conditions of service, there would be no delay. It was over this second point, the move towards convening a local panel, that I can see, with hindsight, that we should have more clearly described the position as we saw it.
>
> I see that it is your Association's intention to seek to refer the matter directly to the national collective disputes machinery. I am advised that such a reference can only take place with the consent of both parties to a dispute. This being so, I assume it would be necessary for the Secretariat of CLEA to seek the approval of the Authority to such a course of action. I should, therefore, let you know that the Education Committee

confirmed, on 10 February, the decision of the Schools Sub-Committee on 29 January that the matter be not referred for conciliation under the collective disputes procedure. I enclose an extract from the Committee Report for your information.

I am sorry it has not been possible to obtain the agreement of your Association to the Authority's revised regulations relating to corporal punishment in secondary schools in Inner London. I should, however, like to make it clear that I am available to discuss with you or your London colleagues any difficulties which have arisen in individual schools arising from the implementation of the revised regulations.

The reference to the Education Committee's confirmation of the Schools Sub-Committee's decision, one day before Terry Casey's letter had arrived, was important. There was always something of a grey area, including the possibility, however remote, of a Sub-Committee decision being overturned, until the Education Committee itself had approved the minutes of its sub-committees.

In the weeks that followed we received no evidence that ending corporal punishment was leading to an increased number of assaults on teachers or to other serious disciplinary problems. Schools were required to report any such problems to County Hall and none had been. Nevertheless, allegations to that effect kept being made. This caused irritation, as my note to Bill Stubbs of 28 April indicates:

Corporal Punishment and the NAS/UWT. Would you look into how things now stand with the NAS/UWT? I believe we left it that they would come in to talk to us about outstanding issues. You will have seen some of the things said about us at the NAS/UWT Conference and there is a particularly unpleasant letter in the New Standard of 27 April. It is about time, I believe, we forced the issue. I saw Casey yesterday and mentioned that I was getting tired of this public campaign. If teachers were aware of acts of violence and failing to report them they were seriously at fault. Casey's line is that that they would really like to pursue their claim that the ILEA should support the teacher in prosecuting the pupil, or his parents, when an act of violence takes place. I said that the ILEA was always prepared to consider this, but we had to look at the evidence first. The teacher might have been the cause of the problem. Would you take thought on these matters and have a word with me about what we do next?

The ending of corporal punishment in the few schools that used it had little effect, one way or the other, on the level of violence in schools. That remained a problem; but in dealing with really violent pupils, heads in the most difficult schools were aware that any attempt to enforce corporal punishment on some of the young people they had to deal with would almost certainly be anticipated by the pupil getting his retaliation in first. As it was, the ILEA was the first large local education authority to end corporal punishment in all of its schools.

Ending corporal punishment in secondary schools from 1 February 1981 had been a lengthy process. It illustrated the relationship between ILEA members, who were determined to end corporal punishment, and their officials, who appeared to them to be less committed to doing that. The administrative principle that applied within the ILEA will also be evident. Once a committee had decided that something needed to happen, it was for the administration, not elected members, many with day time jobs of their own, to ensure that it happened without unnecessary delay or the need for their further intervention. On this occasion, the administration, with so much else to worry about, had initially responded sluggishly. Parliament was even more dilatory. It was eight years later, just before abolishing the ILEA, that the government of the day passed legislation to end corporal punishment in all publicly-funded schools.

Early in January 1981, stresses were evidently developing within the ILEA's Labour Group. I was at a conference outside London at the same breakfast table as a senior DES official. He was reading The Times. Suddenly he remarked that it was reported there that the ILEA was proposing to reduce the price of school meals from 35p to 25p. Did I know anything about this? I did not. Hence the somewhat reproachful tone of the opening sentence of the minute I sent to the Leader on my return to London on 9 January:

> I note from a press release of 7 January that the Labour Group has decided to reduce the price of school meals from 35p to 25p. I have, as you know, been preparing a paper on school meals policy for the Schools Sub-Committee, with the intention of bringing it to their meeting on 15 January. The draft paper, which you have seen, shows for the purposes of illustration changes of price which would result in an alteration to the existing levels of subsidy. It does not follow that it would thought reasonable for the Sub-Committee to choose from the whole range and, in particular, the lowest price levels. I understand that you personally have doubts concerning a price reduction to 25p and have asked the Director of Legal Services for advice. This will no doubt take a little time and, as a consequence, my paper to Sub-Committee will be delayed.
>
> There are sound educational arguments for fixing the price of school meals at a level which attracts as many pupils as possible to stay in school at lunch time and eat a school meal. It is in the interests of the school to keep children off the streets during the lunch break and to have them properly fed for afternoon lessons. However, the marginal cost of attracting extra children to eat school meals can be very high. For example, I estimate that a reduction in the price of a school meal of 10p would attract an additional 10,000 children to stay for a meal. The cost to the Authority would be some £4 million (£3 million in reduced income from those now paying 35p for their meal and £1 million in loss of grant). This is equivalent to £400 for each extra child taking a meal.

Sir Ashley had probably been taken by surprise by this vote in the Labour Group. If the aim, reasonable enough in itself, was to induce more children to take a school meal, there were better and cheaper ways to achieve this. Subsidising large numbers of people who were already paying 35p for a meal was unlikely to go down well with the rate-paying public; particularly as those benefitting would include ILEA members and several Chief Officers, including Bill Stubbs and myself, with children in ILEA schools, who could well afford 35p for a meal. Nor did we think it likely that the courts would regard such a reduction as reasonable if the matter were to be taken there. The Labour Group could not, of course, itself 'decide' anything that required anyone to take any form of executive action, so my minute had been clumsily worded. Only an ILEA committee could do that and it eventually decided not to. The last paragraph of my minute indicated the nature of the report on which some executive committee would have to take a decision. In any report submitted to a committee, the full financial and legal implications of reducing the price of school meals would be set out and immediately become public. The word went round later that it was the Authority's officers who had called for legal advice. As my minute indicates, it was the Leader who had asked for legal advice, but he will have had his own reasons for being modest about that.

The unemployment of young people had become an increasingly serious problem.

ILEA politicians wanted to be absolutely certain that the Authority was doing all it could to respond to this, as my note of 4 February to the Chief Inspector, Mr Stubbs, Mr Bevan and Mr Hunter records.

> Education for employment (use of funds)
>
> The Leader had a word with me about what we are doing in relation to next year's budget. He wants a meeting to discuss how the fund is being used. His particular query relates to the accommodation needs of colleges. In particular, he wants to know:
>
> i. How colleges are to have access to the fund. He thinks some colleges have been told that they can only have money if the course they are providing is linked to one provided by a school.
>
> ii. What the capacity is of each of the colleges to expand the courses they run. Which need extra accommodation and which need some improvement to what they already have.
>
> iii. What the strength of that requirement for extra accommodation is.
>
> Members seem to be getting contradictory messages. From colleges it seems to be said that they cannot provide for the unemployed because they have no space; we appear to be saying that this is only a problem in one or two of them. Before any meeting (Mrs Ward, Mrs Sofer, the Leader and ourselves), I undertook to provide him with a note setting out briefly our answers to these three questions. Could we discuss please?

The Leader took a detailed interest in a wide range of issues. In this instance, he would be expecting a rapid and comprehensive answer to his questions. Several problems were, I believed, still having to be dealt with by 31 March, as this minute to John Bevan records:

> There are three matters on this 16–19 issue that need shifting:
>
> i. The accommodation needs of Colleges this September. I believe a list is/has been prepared but we will be in serious trouble if there is heavy unemployment of young people this autumn (which there will be), an increased demand for full or part-time Further Education (which there may be), coupled with an added readiness by the Authority to finance this (which there could well be). The trouble will come if we can't say what extra space we need, where, and what we have done to get it. Have we bid for MSC capital grants, for example?
>
> ii. Specifically, we need a paper on our Further Education presence in North Kensington. We have several sets of emptying premises there. We are committed to trying to do something there for young people. Who wants what space by when? This is becoming urgent.
>
> iii. The review of Lambeth schools is under way, FHE needs should be fed in at the outset so that Mr Mallen is aware of these. If FHE will look at the option papers they will see what is at issue. The related Southwark issue is also important. What are we able to do with Collingwood Girls School or Thomas Calton or Silverthorne premises? (ie schools closing but in solid School Board built premises).
>
> In the longer term, I believe we ought to be able to plan what FHE accommodation might be like at the end of the decade. Where are the big gaps? We ought to be able to fill some of them, but the secondary review will only keep the options open for a year or two longer.

Fortunately, John Bevan had already been shifting what I thought needed shifting and was able to produce costed alternatives for the use of premises for the Leader to consider.

Some good news had arrived early in February. The Secretary of State decided that the ILEA should continue to exist in its present form. That decision was a consequence of a report by a past Education Minister, Baroness Young, who had earlier been a Conservative chairman of Oxfordshire County Council. The report was unpublished but confirmed the findings of Sir Frank Marshall in 1978. It was evidently more convincing than Kenneth Baker's performance in the previous year. On 6 February I wrote to Contact accordingly:

> The Secretary of State has announced that the education service for Inner London should continue to be administered by a single authority. Much of the credit for this conclusion must go to all who have worked

hard – as parents, staff, governors or members of the public – in support of the Authority over this past year. Every thanks are due for that. The Government's decision places a responsibility on all of us to see that Inner London receives the education service it both needs and deserves.

Nevertheless, the pressure on the Authority from government agencies, principally directed at the level of the Authority's expenditure, and from hostile elements of the Press on almost any topic, intensified. On that same day, 6 February, the Department of Education had drawn attention publicly to the difference between what the ILEA proposed to spend in the following year and the formula used by the Department for arriving at its opinion of the Authority's needs. This issue became increasingly difficult to deal with from 1981 onwards. In previous years, decisions about what should be spent on education had been taken by the ILEA. The Authority included representatives from the City of London and of each of the London boroughs. Their decisions on what should be spent on education were ordinarily within the general limits set by central government, but increasingly, central government moved to determine precisely the amount that local authorities would be allowed to spend, even of its own money, and to make unlawful any departure from that amount. I found the Department's description of what the ILEA was doing both unclear and unhelpful:

J. R. Jameson Accounting Officer DES   11 February

ILEA BUDGET 1981/82
Maurice Stonefrost is replying separately to your letter of 6 February and I have no wish to add to the particular points he makes, with which I agree. In general, I am beginning to find this word 'volume' increasingly obscure in its application. Our 1981/82 budget provides for 62,661 staff, compared to 63,927 this year and 64,784 in 1979/80. In 'real terms' our demand for resources is being reduced, though not by as much as the government would like to see. Still, a reduction in real terms of 2% between this year and next in our main item of expenditure would seem to me to justify something slightly less cool than the epithets that have been applied to it publicly.

Jameson and I had entered the Civil Service in the same year but had not met in my brief stay there.

Letters hostile to the ILEA regularly appeared in the Press. The ILEA attracted the particular attention of one or two sincere but, from the ILEA's perspective, methodologically idiosyncratic educational 'experts'. In an article to the Times Education Supplement, I commented, shortly after its publication, on a pamphlet entitled 'Sixth Forms in ILEA's comprehensives: a cruel confidence trick?' At a time when only 11% of the national age group passed 'A' levels, the survey had considered results from ninety of the secondary schools the ILEA maintained in 1978; so a great deal depended on which schools they had chosen in their sample. Sixty-five ILEA secondary schools had fewer than 10% of their entry in the top 25% of the ability grouping at 11+; so they were hardly comprehensive in any meaningful sense of that term. On the other hand, there were still thirty schools which had more than 90% of their entry in that top group at 11+; in other words they were schools that had selected pupils at that stage. As I put it rather unkindly in the letter that follows:

> 'Examination results constitute ground where angels fear to tread so perhaps it was predictable that the Cox and Marks team would rush in. What was not predictable was that they would suffer such a complete intellectual collapse in the process.'

Error was everywhere. In describing the HMI Report on the ILEA, for example, they remarked:

> 'It is remarkable that this ILEA Report was originally to be kept secret and circulated only among officials and teachers. It was not even going to be seen by the elected councillors.'

My comment on this was:

> 'the truly remarkable thing is that anyone could believe this to be true. As the front page of the HMI Report on the ILEA, and every other HMI report on an institution, makes clear, it is supplied to the local education authority. That means councillors. As for making the report public, that was done at the ILEA's request.

In a Press interview on the Cox and Marks pamphlet, I had referred to it as 'buffoonery'. Hence the reference to this in a subsequent letter that included a comment on some remarks by Professor Flew, whose publications on philosophy were uniformly of high quality. I was regularly surprised by the way that, when dealing with education, otherwise perfectly sensible people often made not the slightest effort to check even the most easily checkable facts. I wrote to the *Times Educational Supplement* about this on 3 March:

> Professor Flew (20 February) believes that parent governors in the ILEA have no access to the examination results of their schools. That is not so. He also believes that there is 'total opposition' within the ILEA to the publication of results. That is not so either. It is just six years since the Authority's Education Committee decided to invite all schools to publish their results. What many people object to is the publishing of examination results in isolation and without relating them, as only the individual schools can properly do, in the fluctuating circumstances of Inner London, to the changing composition of the year groups from which those examination results derive.
>
> As for Cox and Marks (27 February), they must be about the only people in England who still have not grasped that, in a system with a high proportion of places in selective schools, the 'A' level results in the remainder will often

be poor. If they choose to call such schools 'comprehensive', I cannot prevent them but this leads them into absurdities. Here is an example. One of the three schools of which they give details appears to be identifiable by that 'A' level in Urdu. If so, the school in question was not 'comprehensive', it was designated 'other'. I say 'was' because Ministerial approval to close it was given in 1979. So when Cox and Marks, after referring to it as 'Comprehensive School B', suggest that parents would be sensible to avoid it, readers will see what I mean when I refer to their buffoonery.

Why are Cox and Marks so inaccurate? When they complain that I chide them 'for not consulting him and his experts before daring to interpret our data', they continue 'we did consult the ILEA and they sent us all the information which was publicly available'. I must make it clear to anyone who remains unfamiliar with the methods these people adopt:

i. that to this day they have never spoken or written either to myself or to the Director of our Research and Statistics Branch or submitted any data to anyone in the ILEA for checking.

ii. that 'we did consult the ILEA' just means that:

a. in the person of Dr Marks, last autumn they telephoned the Information Officer of our Research and Statistics Branch and asked for materials on examination results published centrally by the ILEA. These were sent.

b. Dr Marks subsequently telephoned the Information Officer for some published material on the ending of selection in the ILEA. In sending this material, the Information Officer wrote (27.10.80) 'If you want to follow up this information with more detailed accounts of individual schools, please let me know and I will arrange for the relevant papers to be sent to you.' There was no response to this.

c. in the only written communication addressed to the Information Officer or anyone in the ILEA, dated Thursday 29 January 1981 (I have your manuscript in front of me, Dr Marks), thanks were offered for the materials that had been sent and the letter went on:

'I am enclosing an advance copy of a pamphlet which is due to be published on Monday next, February 2, which I hope will be of interest.' The letter arrived on Tuesday 3 February. As the text makes clear, there had been no previous reference to the pamphlet whatsoever.

Readers must decide for themselves on the standards which Cox and Marks think it proper to apply when they say 'we did consult the ILEA'; but I, for one, have no more time to waste on people who operate in this way.

From early in the year, evidence of unrest amongst mostly black young

people in several parts of inner London, mainly over the behaviour of the police, was disturbing.

Note to Mr Osborn – Principal Solicitor GLC 17 March

> Arrests by police on ILEA premises. I attach notes on two recent incidents affecting ILEA pupils or staff on ILEA premises. May I have your observations generally and your advice on the following points specifically: is it in order for the police to enter ILEA premises on their own initiative, whatever the reason? In other words, is there a distinction between entering to investigate what is thought to be an indictable offence and entering for any other reasons?

> Given that the police enter our premises, have they any responsibility towards ILEA employees in charge of those premises and the people in them; for example the Youth Leader in the example I have enclosed? Conversely, what rights have our employees in relation to the police presence?

> Is there any assistance we can or, in your view, should give to an employee charged with obstruction who is acting in a manner which, on enquiry, the ILEA considers reasonable in relation to the duty of care she is required to exercise?

> What is the procedure for lodging a complaint in relation to actions by the police? Irrespective of the legal issues involved, I want to write to the Commissioner to express my concern at the probable consequences of police activity on ILEA premises. Have you any comments on my draft?

The draft letter to the Metropolitan Police Commissioner arose out of two events. The first was a recent meeting held with a group of secondary school heads. They had visited County Hall to express their concern at a number of incidents that had recently occurred in or near their schools, some of which they had themselves witnessed. Nearly all concerned the treatment of black boys. With their own concerns about ensuring law and order, heads were ordinarily strongly supportive of the police. The point they were now making was that, on the evidence of what was now happening to some of their pupils, they no longer had confidence in the way the police were behaving. It was this point that I was making in the draft letter to the Commissioner of the Metropolitan Police.

The second question to the Authority's lawyers related to a young, black, female, youth leader, paid to help at a youth club while preparing to become a solicitor. The police had arrived to arrest a youth on the premises of the club, attended by predominantly black boys. Any attempt at an arrest on the club premises could have led to serious disturbance. The youth leader had persuaded the boy in question to leave the club to meet the police. She followed him out to the police car and then wanted to know, as the person responsible for the club at that time, where the police were taking him. The police declined to tell her. She insisted. She was then arrested for obstruction and was later required to appear in court on that charge. My view, which Mr Osborn confirmed, was that she was carrying out her duty of care, as an employee of the ILEA, in trying to establish where the boy was being taken. As a potential solicitor, it would be particularly damaging if the charge of obstruction was upheld against her. Eventually, after I had spent a morning in a court in Lewisham, prepared to give evidence on her behalf, the case was dismissed without being heard. The police were unable to produce proper notes of the incident. The court was anyway unlikely to be convinced that a young woman of five foot three could seriously be supposed to have obstructed two largish police constables by asking them questions.

The timing of the approach by the secondary school heads was significant. Within a few weeks, riots broke out in Brixton. These were directly aimed at the police or at anyone with a camera rather than at anyone else. I happened to be in the area at the time and was able to walk about undisturbed as bricks and other material sailed through the air. I was encouraged by the fact that, unlike at similar disturbances in the United States, no schools were attacked, though I watched rather nervously as groups of youths, in pursuit or being pursued, swept across the playgrounds of the schools that some of them had only recently, if sometimes sporadically, attended.

How far was it the fault of the ILEA and the schools that rioting had occurred in Brixton? We had certainly been aware of the possibility of unrest in some parts of London. Poor employment prospects for young people, particularly black youngsters, was well documented; so too was the behaviour of some elements of the police about which I had recently written to the Commissioner. But there were also criticisms from within the ILEA itself, particularly from one warden of a Teachers' Centre, to whose opinions I responded in the following letter to The Times of 24 April:

> It was predictable that the recent troubles in Brixton would lead to a parade of hobby-horses. Those who dislike the police or believe there are agitators everywhere or think the unemployed are not trying hard enough or just resent the presence in London of its black citizens have rushed in to attribute blame to whatever it is they most dislike. Mr H. does not like what he describes as 'multi-ethnic education'. So for him it is this that is to blame. In particular, he suggests that black youths may be causing trouble because they are being given wrong information about the true nature of the slave trade. I do not myself want to comment on the plausibility of this thesis or fall into the trap of proposing what appear to me to be more sensible explanations for what is happening in Brixton. That is for Lord Scarman. But, from the point of view of the education service, over the past few years there have been three matters which have caused deep concern:

> The first is that, despite notable exceptions and determined efforts by many teachers, too many black pupils are doing less well, both in London

and elsewhere, than other members of the community. This remains true of those who have been born here and educated throughout in our schools. Second, at any given level of qualification obtained, it is proving more difficult for black school leavers to obtain jobs than others. This is not conjecture. We can compare the number of interviews and rejections with which different school leavers with similar qualifications are confronted. Third, the fact that the number of jobs for school leavers has dropped sharply has made the already difficult situation I have referred to considerably worse.

I, for one, look forward to the results of Lord Scarman's enquiry as a means of giving concerns such as these their proper weight and balancing them against others. Meanwhile, attempts to rush to judgement before the evidence is in seem rather foolish.

It was a few weeks after this letter that a, from my perspective, amusing incident, to some extent race-related, occurred at a public meeting in Camden. The origins of the incident lay in an encounter I had in 1979. I had been crossing Westminster Bridge after a meeting at the House of Commons. My way was barred by a large man, of Jamaican origin, looking displeased. He knew who I was, having previously attended some meeting at County Hall. He had a complaint to make. His son had special needs and required a place in a school that all were agreed he should attend. Unfortunately, no confirmation of that school place had yet reached him and the boy was still not at school. His father had then found that the person he had gone to see at County Hall was out. What, he enquired with a degree of hostility, was I going to do about it? I took down the particulars and said I would see what I could do. Rather reluctantly, he allowed me to go on my way. Back at the office, I had a few minutes to spare before my next meeting. With the person responsible now back in the office, I was able to write to confirm the place for Jason, the man's son, at the school he wanted. I apologised for any delay that had occurred. Now on a roll, I sent my best wishes to Jason at his new school and added that, if there was anything more I could do to help, I would. I then forgot all about the matter.

The crowded public meeting in Camden at which I was speaking in 1981 became fractious. A Bengali from Tower Hamlets, whose role as a full-time agitator will be known to many who worked in the ILEA in those days, was in full flow about the racist behaviour of the ILEA in general and of myself in particular. He was an eloquent speaker but had hardly got going on my failings when he suddenly sat down. He did so because two hands were pressing down hard on his shoulders. From the chair behind him had risen the huge figure of that Jamaican parent. He was very angry. He began to speak and, on each slowly spoken word, he gave his victim a violent shake. 'I-don't-want-to-hear-that-kind-of-talk-about-Mr-Newsam', he announced, looking round the hall as he spoke and shook. He then stopped shaking as he described the help I had given Jason. He gave a final, particularly violent, shake to his victim and, still standing up, looked round the hall and added: 'from this man or from anyone else'. After that the meeting went rather quiet. People soon began to drift away and I was able to stay behind and listen to how Jason was doing. Well enough, fortunately.

In my minute to the Leader at the end of 1976, I had said that the re-organisation of the Education department would be time-consuming. So it had proved. The changes within County Hall, from 1977 onwards, had been extensive. For example, at the LCC and since, the section of the education service dealing with property, the acquisition of school sites and related matters, had done this across the whole of inner London. Similarly, a section dealing with the building, maintenance and repair of schools also had London-wide responsibilities; so too had the section dealing with the planning of school places and the need to open, extend or close schools. This structure had remained in place for decades. But, since 1965, the inner London boroughs had become planning and housing authorities, so it was with their officers, rather than with other colleagues in the service of the London County Council at County Hall, that ILEA's administration now had to work. It therefore made good sense to re-shape the ILEA's administration so that each London borough had one ILEA team dealing with all matters where close cooperation on sites, building, planning and related matters was necessary. In practice, the necessary restructuring proved stressful and a serious distraction to staff during a period when so many changes to the organisation of the school system, the Authority's main concern at the time, were being undertaken. Experts on sites, for example, did not enjoy having to acquire and then have to use expertise in the complex regulations relating to school building at the same time as elected members were expecting them to help conduct the detailed review, earlier referred to, of every piece of land designated for future use by a school, college or other educational institution in the whole of inner London.

Towards the end of March, I reluctantly concluded that further changes needed to be made to ILEA's administrative structure.

In my perception, the need now was to deal with the longest delayed and perhaps most important change needed to improve the Authority's relationship with individual London borough councils: the decision to create, as vacancies arose in each of the Authority's ten divisions, publicly advertised posts for Divisional Education Officers. The problem had several parts to it. The first part was that, for most of the 1970s, the long-standing, matching, role of experienced Divisional Officers, promoted from within the Authority's service, and professionally qualified District Inspectors, many appointed from outside inner London, had worked well enough. The Divisional Officers were almost all highly competent administrators. The problem now was that most of them were nearing retirement. Their natural successors from within the ILEA came from a later generation. That generation, now nearly all graduates with good degrees, were confronted by opportunities outside education or London that had not existed for earlier entrants to Inner London's education service. Since the Bains report of 1974, all over the country well paid new posts for local authority

Chief Executives, their deputies and senior colleagues were being created. It was inconceivable that ambitious, academically and administratively competent, ILEA administrators would now be content to end their careers as Divisional Officers, fourth tier ILEA officials. Career development for most of these people lay outside the ILEA and they knew it. In that connection, John Harwood, Sir Ashley's personal assistant, within a few years became Chief Executive of Lewisham and then of Oxfordshire; Roger Brown soon went to the Cabinet Office and later became a professorial head of a college of Higher Education; Pamela Gordon became Chief Executive of Hackney and so on. On the other hand, ILEA administrative staff without these academic qualifications were almost all too young and inexperienced or too old and specialised in their administrative expertise to take on the responsibilities of a Divisional Officer. So there was no contradiction in saying, as I did at a meeting with the Staff Association, that ILEA's present County Hall staff were either too good or not well enough equipped to provide the Authority with suitable recruits to head its divisional administration.

For the inspectorate, a different problem had arisen. There were few opportunities within the ILEA for further promotion for most of them and their prospects of more senior employment outside the ILEA were also poor. A senior ILEA inspector of modern languages or drama, for example, would not find a better paid post outside Inner London and usually lacked the kind of generalist inspectorate experience that most other local authorities were looking for. Nor were other than a few ILEA inspectors particularly interested in or well suited to administrative work. Many had little experience of working with councillors or committees and lacked familiarity with the range of regulatory and other requirements needed, though it would be open to any of them to apply for the new divisional education officer posts now proposed. That there would even be such posts upset some members of the inspectorate. Although they did not want to have these jobs themselves, they saw problems in having to work with professionally qualified newcomers who did.

The final problem that I tried to explain, far too hastily for some long-serving ILEA staff to accept, was that the existing divisional structure was becoming almost unworkable. Since 1965, when important functions exercised by the London County Council were transferred to newly created borough social service and other departments, the relationship between the ILEA and the boroughs had been changing. Matters which earlier had been dealt with by LCC Committees in County Hall were now being dealt with by thirteen borough committees, each with its own group of officers and elected councillors. Senior officers from County Hall were increasingly now having to accompany elected ILEA members at meetings, mostly held in the evenings, with borough councillors or their chief officers. What were needed in each Division of the ILEA were professionally qualified administrators, who could talk on equal terms with professionally qualified and increasingly assertive senior borough officers.

The kind of issues a professionally qualified Divisional Education Officer would be able to discuss with his opposite number in a London borough, as the note below indicates, might appear rather trivial but were taking up far too much of my time and that of my senior colleagues. My note to Mrs Morgan about one at which I was having to accompany her indicates the nature of the problem:

Partnership meeting with Islington

I attach a note covering the points that we think may arise this evening. The three I would pull out, on the grounds that we should react firmly if they are raised today, are:

the notion that we should do more out of our main programmes, particularly on the capital side. We have explained our problem here – derisory building programme allocations – repeatedly. No one demurred at the Officers Steering Group meeting on 24 October when I explained, yet again, the point that Mr Storr has made orally and in correspondence. It should be a rule in this partnership that we do not have to explain the same things more than three times:

the nature of our consultative procedures. These are set out in the brief and any lecture from Islington is misplaced. Their proposals arrived just before that Steering Group meeting on 24 October so none of the partnership officers had a chance to look at them properly:

the whole business of one partner sniping at what another partner is doing. As I see it, the aim of the partnership is to align our programmes; to make sure there is a consistency of approach towards certain stated ends. It is not a matter of one partner thinking it can sit in judgement on the exercise of another partner's functions. No one can vote away our right to put a nursery class where we think fit. Similarly, I suggest we simply note such oddities as the Islington dog wardens. Their pavements may be cleaner but that success may have to be measured against the number of dog owners who now have to flee to Kensington and its parks to avoid the reproachful look on the faces of their constipated pets!

At a meeting with senior ILEA staff, my efforts to explain the need for a change to the divisional structure, arising from the changing political aspirations of the London boroughs and from what was happening to local government outside London, went down badly with some inspectors. It led to the manuscript letter from a Staff Inspector (personal and confidential) of 23 March:

Hoped to get to see you today but, as I shan't be in for a while, thought I had better write.

First – a pleasant thought – you will have been sent a copy of my book and I would like suitably to inscribe it. Secondly – and I have been fretting about this – I was very worried after the meeting of the Guild

> you addressed. It is not so much the issues, important though they are, but the impression created. There really was strong feeling against you in the personal sense. There is a strong sense of loyalty to the ILEA but it does need to be bolstered by personal respect for you. It would be better to say this to you face to face, for you know how much I personally like you – and have supported you.

Tut, I recall thinking when this arrived. Why was I thought to need the support of this individual? I was tempted to pursue the 'face to face' suggestion but decided that this might end badly, though perhaps not for me. So I did not answer the letter. Next day another letter arrived, not marked 'private', from a District Inspector. This one read:

> I recently sent you my formal minute about your inspectorate and administration proposals, with a copy to the CI. This letter is personal with no copies. I (and three others I happened to encounter on my way out of County Hall after your meeting with senior officers on 18 March) felt very much saddened by that meeting. While of course I accept that you believe in the validity of your proposals, I did not always feel that you were yourself convinced on specific points which you were defending. I found myself unable to reconcile your assertion that a significant number of promising young people have limited promotion prospects because they have been confined within the ILEA, with the statement that the ILEA/GLC is now too small to provide enough applicants for the top posts. I was surprised that you should hold out the carrot of career development to the young without any indication of what you had in mind. How could you expect people to accept a blank contract?
>
> Your very reason for instituting the title of Divisional Education Officer is to give them enhanced status in the eyes of applicants for the post and in the eyes of the boroughs and those outside the ILEA. Of course that new status will spread outside the ILEA. Clearly their duties, as you describe them, would carry greater responsibility than a merely co-ordinating Staff Inspector (Division). How can you pretend otherwise? I use the word 'pretend' after hesitation and with diffidence. But I really did not believe at the meeting that you yourself were always convinced of the points you were making. That is why I began this letter by writing that I was saddened.

On this occasion, I was particularly irritated by a colleague sending a letter to me of this kind that could be read by persons in my office other than myself. The word 'status', used twice in the final paragraph, had also jarred. For more than a year, the ILEA had been under sustained attack from certain political quarters, from elements in the Press and even from the Department of Education. County Hall administrators had been heavily engaged in dealing with this. Inspectors had hardly been affected; yet here, within the ILEA itself, were two of them, apparently unaware of the dangerous political climate in which the Authority was having to work and worrying about their status. Status? I certainly did not believe that the function of a Divisional Inspector, principally accountable for the quality of education in one of the LEA's ten divisions, was of lower status than that of a Divisional administrator, however entitled. But I had other things to think about so it was not until 3 April that I replied in a manuscript note. My response was unfriendly and I almost immediately regretted sending it:

> In your letter of 25 March, you say you use the word 'pretend' after hesitation and with diffidence. You are unwise to use it at all. You should certainly not do so in a letter addressed to me in a standard envelope not marked 'private' which, as you must know, is opened and read by persons other than myself. Please do not do anything of the kind again. Your points on the administrative side are so wide of the mark that, I must ask you to believe, I do not think I can help with them. If you want to talk to me about inspectorate matters, by all means arrange to do so.

This was not an appropriate way to address a long-serving inspector whose perception of himself had been hurt. Alec Clegg would never have written a letter like that but, I had also to recognize, he would never have received one like it either. These letters from inspectors indicated that I had badly underestimated the continued strength of the nearly eighty year old division in London between administrators and inspectors. It was still believed by some colleagues that these two functions had to be kept separate. When I arrived in 1972, the ILEA education service had had fewer educationally qualified administrators than the North Riding of Yorkshire or Cumberland, two far smaller education authorities. Since my arrival in London, I had found this absolute division between administration and inspection increasingly absurd. But there was an entrenched parochialism in some people working in County Hall who had never worked in- or had much understanding of- anywhere or anything outside London. With that in mind, I should have been far more careful to explain, what I had assumed everyone would by now have grasped, the increasingly difficult national and local circumstances with which the Authority was now having to contend.

Public advertisement for divisional education officers was an extension of a development that had already caused concern within County Hall. Traditionally, the ILEA and the LCC before it, like the Civil Service of those days, had rarely appointed outsiders to relatively senior administrative posts. Furthermore, neither the ILEA nor the LCC before it seemed to have sent anybody out to head a local education authority elsewhere. In 1972, my appointment as Deputy had been, in some quarters, an unpopular exception to the practice of promoting from within. Since 1977, the appointment of outsiders had accelerated and several future Chief Officers or heads of institutions had been recruited to the ILEA. These included Tim Brighouse, Bill Stubbs, Philip Hunter, David Mallen, Peter Mortimore and several others. Divisional Officer posts were one of the last preserves of promotion from within the ILEA's administration. Resistance to change was, to that extent, understandable. Less understandable was that objections to the proposed changes should be coming from inspectors, whose jobs would not be directly affected, rather than County Hall administrators, whose prospects for promotion might well be.

Preoccupied with all that was happening outside County Hall and to the political changes within it, I had recently been paying far too little attention to the mood within County Hall itself. Hence the note of 26 May to the Senior Officers Group:

> Some problems: morale
>
> 1. I am concerned about morale. Poor morale manifests itself in several ways; for example in:
>
>> a. exaggerated resistance to comparatively minor changes. Recent examples include the response to the changed DEO/Divisional Inspector designation and the general reaction 'we have not been properly consulted' to almost anything proposed
>>
>> b. failure of new ideas to surface or uncomfortable information to be reported; reactive rather than active intellectual habits
>
> 2. If – and this needs discussing – I am right in supposing morale is not good, we need to find out why and what we can do about it. Part of the reason may be a by-product of attacks on the ILEA and local government generally. Work in the ILEA, as a teacher or an official, at least in the upper reaches, tends to be fairly well paid but is not a high prestige job. The attacks will, of course, go on and will personally sometimes be very upsetting (e.g. on Gillian Klein at the Centre for Urban Education Studies). What can we personally do?
>
>> a. display a certain public optimism. We have often been forced into a defensive position.
>> b. improve our consultative procedures, informally as well as formally. I am personally conscious of having let this slip over the last year or two.
>> c. adopt a more positive approach to the media by speeches, writing and so on. Above all, our policies must be successful. We have got to have something good to say. This is my next point.
>
> Effectiveness of the ILEA
>
> Our general analysis, which needs challenging if it is wrong, is that most areas of the service are satisfactory to good. Our particular concerns at the moment are:

The next page of the note is missing but the persistent and most troubling problem, affecting too many primary and secondary schools, was under-expectation. HMI, our own inspectorate and any of us visiting schools were conscious of this. So too were heads, teachers and increasingly articulate parents. The fact seemed to be that there were still many teachers, when under varying forms of stress, who were finding it too tiring to move pupils out of what nowadays would be called their comfort zone. It was easier and sometimes essential to a teacher's own survival to allow a class, including individual pupils who needed stretching, to coast along on comparatively undemanding tasks.

Later in the year, one of the ILEA's ablest inspectors had gone a long way to sorting out the District Inspector/ Divisional Education Officer problems that had arisen.

Mr Jaggar (Personal)   10 August

> Many thanks for your note of 24 July setting out your arrangements for the Inspectorate re-organisation. I am very conscious of the amount of work, in human terms, that this has caused. The whole thing has been far more difficult than I originally supposed, but if some kind of administrative euphoria did not generally apply, who would ever do anything in this place? I am increasingly convinced that the changes are the minimum necessary to cope with the strains of the 1980s.

Later in March, in the midst of time-consuming administrative matters, a number of visits to schools had still been possible. I wrote to Mr Attwell, Headmaster of Baring Primary School, on 24 March:

> This is just to thank you and your colleagues very much for providing me with such a constructive and enjoyable morning. I was most impressed. Quite apart from the directly 'educational' aspects of the school, I liked the way adults and children spoke to each other, the way people moved about and so on. 'Ethos' is the word researchers have produced for this and, whatever that may be, I congratulate you on achieving such a pleasantly industrious one.

A few days later, I had another opportunity to see gifted teachers at work. I went to a schools concert at the Queen Elizabeth Hall. The instrumental and choral work, from a wide variety of secondary schools, was impressive. I was particularly struck by the performance of a group of girls from a Roman Catholic secondary school. On came the eleven and twelve-year-olds, with their teacher. After a brief look towards the audience, the teacher tidied the children into a semi-circle, smiled at them, raised a finger in a shushing gesture, smiled again, paused, and then they were off. The children sang beautifully. The applause for their performance was prolonged. As the applause continued, I noticed that the children had not turned their heads towards the audience. They were still looking at their teacher. She looked from left to right at each one of them, smiled again, and then put her hands together to clap them. As the children smiled back, the teacher turned briefly to acknowledge the applause from the audience and led the children off the stage. Some of the children, obviously delighted, were still smiling as they moved away. For my part, I left the concert conscious that I had been watching teaching of the highest quality. Those children sang well but what was also clear that, with such a teacher, they were not going to behave badly at school or fail to turn up there and that that teacher would be able to teach them anything she wanted them to learn and they would do their utmost to learn it. But did this teacher know what an outstanding teacher she was? I found out who she was – she turned out to be head of music at the school – and wrote to her to offer a few words of congratulation. She replied on a card that I kept:

> I was delighted to get your letter. I was amazed that you should have found the time – particularly when you must be even busier than usual at the moment. You tend to forget that the people at the top are human and it's a very nice feeling – particularly as the letter was addressed to me rather than to the Head. Probably sounds rather petty but officialdom often seems wary of recognising the individual. I was talking to trainee teachers at Goldsmiths last week – about relationships and new beginnings – and how the chain of need and help and encouragement goes on and on. I don't mean to embarrass you, but it was a lovely thought – we teachers aren't used to the personal touch; so thank you again.

Not used to the personal touch? I had learnt years ago that this was an essential part of the job I was supposed to be doing.

At the end of March I felt tired. Tiredness can have the same consequences as stress. Both can lead to displacement behaviour. This takes many forms. It causes apes to scratch and gibber and Department of Education officials to issue consultative documents that do not merit replies. My response had been to niggle about school notice boards. This was sometimes taken to great lengths. On two occasions, the Leader had mentioned to me that a notice board on premises now used by a College of Art still declared the presence of a school that had moved out of London three years earlier. I had asked for something to be done about this and nothing had been. I lost patience. I told the Architect's Department that, having invited the local paper to send a photographer, I intended to borrow a ladder from the College and take the sign down myself. That led to its removal; but on and on I droned and, on 31 March, I sent a note to Mr Claxton in Buildings Branch:

> To pursue my little fanaticism about notice boards, could something be done about the boards at Henry Compton School? As you know, there is considerable new building there and the first impression will be messy if we leave the existing boards up. One board elsewhere proudly declares that North Croft, a maladjusted school, belongs to the ILEA. The school closed some time ago, is boarded up and looks a mess for which we are responsible. The board needs removing.

Later in the year I was still at it, as this note to Chris Storr of 26 August indicates:

> You will know that I keep niggling about our signposting arrangements at schools and elsewhere. Recently, I visited some Careers Offices, for example the Southwark Careers Office on the Old Kent Road. I found a huge, battered sign declaring the presence of ILEA organisations which

had left some time ago. The Careers Service, inside the building, did not receive a mention. And the same was true at a number of other places. Could not one of those people in the Architect's Department take a look at the graphics of the matter? Individual Careers Officers find themselves tacking up notices with sellotape and it all looks a bit makeshift.

My prize for the worst school sign now goes to Acland Burghley. The head is making great efforts to build up public confidence in the school but a lop-sided sign still declares that Sam Fisher, who left nearly two years ago, is running the place. I know we have a programme to get these signs right but it should be someone's responsibility to prevent them getting into such a bad condition in the first place. Conversely, a good school notice gives an immediate impression of efficiency.

Sometimes my efficient office slipped up and Mr Jones, newly appointed Headmaster of Penbury Grove School, must have made fun of my warm, personal, but unfortunately unsigned, welcome to the ILEA. I replied on 3 April (File copy headed: please do not allow my letters to go out unsigned).

> This is just to congratulate you on your appointment and on your sense of humour. Long life to both.

As for the letter that follows, it was the settled conviction in some quarters, which no facts could disturb, that the ILEA censored the books heads chose to use in schools:

> The Editor
> The Daily Telegraph 1 May
>
> The logical force of your leading article on 1 May, linking the Law Commission's proposals on the law of blasphemous libel to a blacklist of racist children's literature, said to be circulating in London's schools, suffers from the fact that there is no such list; nor is there anyone authorised by the ILEA to produce one.

The Local Government elections in May 1981 require a thick, dark, line to be drawn under all I have written about my years at the ILEA.

Shortly after the election, Sir Ashley Bramall was voted out of the leadership of the Labour majority on the ILEA. Though it was not recognised at the time, it was probably at that moment that the destruction of the ILEA by the Conservative government in 1990 became inevitable. Even at the time, the loss of Sir Ashley's leadership was deeply felt by many of us, both personally and administratively. I wrote to him on 11 May:

> Dear Sir Ashley,
>
> There will be a proper time to write and speak, but I would like to convey, on behalf of myself and my immediate colleagues, our deepest appreciation for these last eleven years. When the achievements are

listed and attributed, as they will be, I hope the full extent of what you have done for London's education will be recognised. When I met the Divisional Officers and District Inspectors this afternoon, they asked me, with an unprecedented show of unity with their County Hall colleagues, particularly to associate them with the letter I told them I would be writing to you.

With my best wishes to yourself and Lady Bramall,

Sir Ashley replied in manuscript:

Dear Peter,

I am extremely sorry not to have been able to reply before to your kind and sympathetic letter following my 'deposition' as Leader. It is very cheering to know that my efforts over the last few years have been seen by those in the Service as having made a contribution to education. I only hope that recent events will not damage it.

I am sure you and your colleagues will not allow that to happen. I should like to take this opportunity to thank you personally and, through you, all your colleagues, for the enormous kindness, friendliness and help that I have experienced throughout my years as Leader. My most cherished memory of those years is of the partnership that we managed to build up between members and officers.

With best wishes,

So Inner London lost one of its most distinguished Leaders. It was a defining moment in the history of education in London. During Sir Ashley's Leadership the influence of elected members was direct and their decisions, with rare exceptions, well-informed and by no means always likely to gain them political advantage. Punch has a celebrated cartoon in which an elderly Bismarck is seen walking down from a huge ship on to a smaller one. Dropping the Pilot was the title given to it. So it was with the ILEA. What the ILEA most needed in the years that followed was consistency of well-informed political leadership, aware of the constitutional relationship between central and local government and intent on avoiding direct confrontation with the legislative provisions of a lawfully established government. That leadership was what Sir Ashley, perceived by the politically naïve as over cautious, had always provided. For the most part, his successors, though able enough in their different ways, proved unable to provide leadership of comparable quality. They failed to understand that when confrontational local government clashes with equally confrontational national government there can only be one winner.

At the elections, several very active members of the Education Committee, from both political Parties, lost their seats. One such was Mrs Patricia Kirwan, a forceful and ebullient Conservative member for Westminster. Mrs Kirwan had refused to be trampled on by Lady Porter and, despite the political advantage she could have gained by acting otherwise, had been steadfast in her support for the development of North Westminster School. Her manuscript reply to my letter of thanks to her for all she had done read:

> My dear Peter,   9 May
>
> Thank you so much for your very cheering note. I never really thought I would hold on to Paddington, but I was pretty miserable and your letter helped a lot; I remember the funny times, and the constructive ones, and how super you and your officers have always been – even when I was at my most disruptive! I hope to be back as an additional member – not simply because I have been enormously happy at County Hall but because I hope, on occasion, I've been constructive – remember North Westminster?! – and I am sure that if we stick together, we can still make sure that sanity prevails.
>
> Thank you for writing – and for all you and your officers have done to make life interesting, happy and instructive in the past four years.

It is difficult to give adequate weight to Sir Ashley Bramall's achievements as Leader of the ILEA. There was never any doubt that decisions made by the Authority, from whatever source they originated, rested with the Authority rather than with its officials; and that these decisions, at every stage, had depended on Sir Ashley being able to convince his colleagues that they were the right decisions to take. There can be arguments about the wisdom of particular policies implemented by the ILEA in the years since he became its Leader in 1970. What is undeniable is that, once the Authority had decided to do something, it almost invariably managed to do it.

So far as the political and administrative leadership of the ILEA was concerned, there were several reasons why this was so. Crucially, the decision-making process was clear. Ultimately, it was only formally constituted committees, on which both political parties were represented, that had the right to take decisions on which the Authority's officers were required to act. Individual politicians, however senior, other than in emergencies where what they had done was open to question at the next meeting of the appropriate committee, had no such right to initiate executive action. So the education service did not suffer from sudden bursts of any individual's initiative. The committees themselves reached their decisions only after having before them reports from two sources. The first source was the Education Officer, who was responsible for ensuring that the committee had all the information required to enable it to take a considered decision, with any advice for which he had been asked or thought it appropriate to give. The second source, usually added to the Education Officer's report, consisted of advice from the legal and financial officers of the Greater London Council. These officers, though operationally attached to the ILEA, were professionally responsible to the appropriate GLC Chief Officers. These in turn were not employed by the ILEA and were accountable only to the

Director- General of the GLC. This meant that legal and financial advice to ILEA committees, which they were free to ignore but seldom did, could not be directly influenced by anything officers or members of the ILEA might have preferred those GLC officials to say.

The responsibility for managing the Education Department rested solely with the Education Officer. It did not rest with the Leader of the majority Party or with any committee of elected members. This was made clear in the Standing Orders of the ILEA and Sir Ashley never sought to question it. He would and often did require something to be put forward for members to consider but did not involve himself in how and by whom it should be. Nor, other than in the form of a Christmas message, did he ever write directly to schools or to other elements of the education service on behalf of the Authority. That was for the Education Officer to do. The relationship, formal and personal, between the Leader of the Authority and the Education Officer was direct and close and there was no confusion about the separate roles. The Leader had to ensure the support of his colleagues for policies to be pursued and for any decisions that needed to be taken. The Education Officer, apart from putting forward his own suggestions, coordinated within the education department, for policies the Authority might or might not wish to pursue, had to ensure three things: first, with the Wednesbury principle in mind, that committees were in a position, before deciding what to do, to consider the full range options open to them, including the consequences of doing nothing, with the evidence on which to base a reasoned decision; second, that the policies the Authority eventually decided to pursue were efficiently implemented; third, that the Leader was quickly made aware of and therefore be in a position to respond to any problems arising, anywhere within the London education service or nationally, which might cause political or other problems for himself, his colleagues or for the ILEA itself. A further thing the administration was determined to do was never mentioned in conversation or in any other way. This was to ensure, unless elected members were acting directly against the advice they had been given, that they were extricated from any other than personal difficulties they found themselves in. The administration was not inclined to be over scrupulous about how it did that.

Sir Ashley and I got on well together personally. Proximity was also important. Our offices were close together, so it was easy for me to drop in to see him at short notice. It was an ILEA convention, instituted by Herbert Morrison at the pre-war LCC, that members did not visit officers in their rooms, officers always went to theirs. Crucially, there were no intermediaries. As communication was direct, there was little scope for confusion about who was supposed to be doing what as a consequence of any discussion held between us. It was sometimes suggested that the ILEA's procedures, though on a smaller scale, were similar to those of central government departments. There were some structural similarities, 'Question Time' at ILEA Education Committee meetings, for example, was particularly exasperating for officials charged with helping to suggest smart Alec answers to the opposition's questions; yet in the ways mentioned above, perhaps particularly in the total absence of intermediaries, so far as my experience of the relationship between Ministers and their Permanent Secretaries is concerned, lodged on separate floors as they usually are and each defended by a numerous staff of supportive assistants, they could hardly have been more different.

In October, 1981, I gave a lecture at London University's Institute of Education that was primarily intended as a tribute to Sir Ashley. The lecture was entitled 'Ten Years of Change'. Elsie Horstead was ILEA's formidable Chief Whip and it was prudent to clear any public reference made to elected members with her. Hence her, typically terse, manuscript reply of 5 October to the copy I had sent to her of the lecture I was about to give, drawing attention to the last two pages where I had mentioned the role of ILEA members:

> Peter,
>
> Many thanks for your lecture. The last two pages seem fine to me! I'll read the rest today or tomorrow and tell you at Policy if I think there is anything I'd like to discuss. Many thanks. Elsie.

The first part of the lecture dealt with a number of themes not reflected in any of the documents I have quoted elsewhere. For example, talking of consultation, I suggested that two problems remained unresolved:

> The first arises when the procedures adopted for consultation conflict with the political time-scale. Briefly, if an acceptably open system of consultation has been devised, whereby a variety of people or groups have time to consider and reflect on a complex issue and then give their views, this may prove wholly inconsistent with an externally imposed time scale. In the late 1970s, for example, the financial arrangements proposed by national governments sometimes changed even before the previous arrangements had been rendered intelligible by circular. In these circumstances, since 'proper' consultation was all that was acceptable and there was no time for it, often no consultation could take place at all. Hence the deliberate leak. An administration in a hurry has little inclination to incorporate the views of others. What it needs to know quickly is the strength of the reaction to its own. The leak is a device for measuring this.
>
> The William Tyndale affair (1973–75) illustrates a second unresolved problem of openness and the distributed decision-making that went with it. The collapse of this junior school was first of all seen as an example of poor primary education within the ILEA. Yet the truth was that, after an unsettled few years, ILEA primary schools were improving year by year. Despite diligent enquiry, the Press were unable to find another school like it. More accurately, the incident was seen as an example of the ILEA being indecisive when it should have been firm. In this there was some truth. The point universally missed, however, was how this indecisiveness came about. County Hall was inhabited by a number of strong willed people.

Why then the hesitation? The answer is that the people concerned were pulled by powerful and contradictory forces. The new policy, vigorously promoted, of devolving control to school governors was in conflict with the older and more authoritarian tradition of directing affairs from County Hall. In the report on the William Tyndale affair, which the Authority commissioned, Robin Auld QC put the legal point clearly. A public authority can devolve a function but cannot devolve responsibility for its proper exercise if it is the body to which that function has been statutorily entrusted. The law supports the old authoritarian position. So much for the legal point. The practical and political point this underlined is that the more a body with statutory functions decides, as it is entitled to do, to involve others in its processes who have no statutory powers or obligations, the more it has to be sure it knows what is happening and, if necessary, be prepared to intervene. So, beyond the legal problem, the wider problem remains. How is a freedom that can be withdrawn at will to be made genuine and how is that freedom to be reconciled with the accountability of those who enjoy it? These two problems remain to be tackled in the 1980s.

The second of those problems was dealt with later in the talk:

Later in the decade came the idea of self-assessment by each school, monitored by, in the case of the ILEA, the inspectorate. It would be for teachers, schools and colleges to examine themselves and for others to assess that examination. If the law locates responsibility precisely and hierarchically, an education service that wishes to retain its freedoms must devise systems which permit this. Externally monitored self-assessment is one such system and, far from being a passing fashion or an officious imposition on practising teachers, may prove to be the essential means by which freedom and accountability can be reconciled. One lesson of the 1970s is that, if they cannot be, it is accountability that will prevail at the expense of freedom.

On self-monitoring, it was Trevor Jaggar, Staff Inspector for secondary schools, who put together 'Keeping the School under Review'. This set out a list of all the things that a school might reasonably be expected to be doing or checking or planning to be able to satisfy itself and others that it was functioning as well as it could in the circumstances in which it was placed and with the resources at its disposal. The idea was further developed in the ILEA and by Tim Brighouse, when appointed Chief Education Officer in Oxfordshire. Unfortunately, externally monitored self-assessment of schools was not adopted nationwide. Had it been, many of the unsatisfactory aspects of school inspection which developed later might have been avoided. The prediction in that final sentence that accountability might well prevail at the expense of freedom proved correct. That is what later happened.

The final part of my lecture contained a personal tribute to Sir Ashley, on behalf of myself and my colleagues and of the many others who were aware of how much he had done for Inner London's education service over so many years:

> There is one feature of the political continuity of the 1970s on which it is appropriate to end this survey. Over the 110 years of its existence, the Inner London Education service has administered almost the same area. From its earliest days it has benefited from the work of many distinguished members. But in those 110 years only one such person has led it uninterruptedly for more than ten years: Sir Ashley Bramall, Leader of the Authority from 29 April 1970 to 9 May 1981. It is difficult to convey briefly the implications of this; but in those years the ILEA's Policy Committee considered more than one thousand reports dealing with every new development or controversial matter affecting the Authority. At 164 of the 165 Policy Committee meetings, which examined and refined the thinking behind those reports, Sir Ashley took the Chair. I have described this past decade as 'Ten Years of Change'. Yet if the continuity of the political leadership that shaped, directed and often had to fight for those changes is the criterion, it could justly be described as the decade of Sir Ashley Bramall.

In the memoirs of national politicians, the heroic efforts they tell us they had to make to get their civil servants to carry out their wishes is a constant theme. In my experience in local government, I was fortunate, except briefly towards the end of my career, to encounter political leaders that it was a genuine privilege to work for. None had seemed to find it necessary to quarrel with their officials or found it particularly difficult to get the things they wanted done. Since the creation of the London School Board in 1870, London education benefitted from a series of able political leaders, some excellent and a few of them outstandingly so. Of the latter, Sir Ashley was pre-eminently one.

Sir Ashley Bramhall, Leader of the ILEA from April 1970 to May 1981

Chapter 8: 1981-1982

In May 1981, the new leadership of the ILEA moved in. We had none of us heard of Sir Ashley's successor as Leader, Mr Bryn Davies, an able young actuary. It was as unlikely that he had heard of any of us. The immediate problem for ILEA officers was to establish a sound working relationship with the new political leadership. In working with Sir Ashley it had been unnecessary to explain how any of the ILEA systems worked or the implications of the statutory position of local government in relation to the national government. He was often better informed than we were on such matters. As for educational issues arising outside the ILEA, he knew a great deal about those also. He was, for example, the leader of the employers' side of the Burnham Committee, which then dealt with teachers' salaries. The new leadership lacked any established background in local government or in education. As happens on these occasions, elements in that leadership believed that the process of being elected automatically brought with it a form of wisdom which did not require much further effort on their part before important decisions had to be made or new policies promoted. Helping people to understand an organisation for which they are going to be responsible who are aware of the need for that help is one thing; trying to help people who see no need for it is quite another.

Almost immediately, I had experience of this. A newly elected member went to Tower Hamlets, unaccompanied. He came back convinced that the Authority had no idea what was happening there. He asked me to call in and see him. When I did, he produced the names of two people he had met in Tower Hamlets. They had told him how to improve what was being done there and that they needed financial support to help them do it. He had invited them to come to County Hall and wanted me to be there. I looked at the two names and gave him the bad news. The first name was on impressive notepaper. It belonged to a man and his wife who ran a society with an equally impressive title. This society, we had long ago discovered, consisted only of the two people named on the notepaper. There had been and remained no reason to fund them. The second name was of an individual who had been recently expelled, rightly in our view, from a group that we were already funding. So I had to tell the new councillor that I saw no reason to attend a meeting with either of these people. If he wanted to know what was happening in Tower Hamlets, I would ask someone who worked and lived there to accompany him. He did not pursue my suggestion.

Meanwhile, correspondence flowed between me and my colleagues. On 21 May I received a manuscript note from Peter Bradbury, Divisional Officer for Camden/Westminster. He had paid a visit to Sir Graham Savage, LCC's Education Officer between 1940 and 1951. Sir Graham was the person principally responsible for the London School Plan of 1947:

> Patricia Cocks and I spent a day with him on 27 April, exactly three weeks before he died. Although, as he said, he had 'gone down' physically a great deal in the previous few months, he was as alive intellectually as ever. He spoke for about one and a half hours about the early days and his beliefs, a virtuoso performance of utter clarity, full of cogent facts and figures, witty and urbane, the incisive intellect as evident as ever. One or two things may be of interest.
>
> We asked about the attitude of the LCC inspectorate and he replied with great force 'I cannot give you my opinion about them because I should make myself liable for a heavy libel action!' He had support from only four, he said. His own beliefs stemmed from his personal experience as far back, he said, as 1898-99, which was when he first went to secondary school. He always felt most strongly that the one day 11+ exam was uneven and the award of scholarships severely rationed by most authorities. These feelings were strengthened by his experience . . .

Unfortunately, no recording was made of Sir Graham's remarks and the next page of Peter Bradbury's notes is missing but may be buried somewhere in the archive. Sir Graham had come to the LCC from the post of Senior Chief Inspector at the Board of Education. The retirement age there was sixty as opposed to sixty-five at the LCC and the Education Officer's salary was twice that of the Board's Chief Inspector. Sir Graham's opinion of the LCC's inspectorate of his day was something of an eye-opener.

I was occasionally able to visit one of the sixth form summer schools that were now well established and enjoyed reading reports on what happened at them. In one report, I spotted that a soon-to-retire headmaster had been taking the lead in a course run on twentieth century poets, including T S Eliot. So I wrote to him on 20 August:

> I was cheered to see from the report on the Summer School at Beatrice Webb House that you are keeping your hand in with T.S. Eliot. Souls of so many of us are sprouting a bit despondently these days!

Back came the response on 25 August:

It was a nice gesture to write to me about the summer school and I appreciate it very much. Truth is that I was immensely sold on the whole thing; the atmosphere was quite electric in some respects as sixth formers actually wanted to sit down and debate pros and cons until the small hours of the morning. It was exhausting for the staff, I think, but immensely worthwhile. I loved every moment of it and found myself wishing for the excitement that often came with running an English Department. What a relief not to have to struggle to get the message across but merely to indulge in a debate with interested people.

I am sure that the Summer Schools are one of the best things that have happened recently. All my sixth formers have reported back most enthusiastically on them and have valued the opportunity to meet other students and other teachers. Just as an immodest aside, one of my herberts said to me afterwards: 'You know, Sir, we didn't really want you to come down but when you'd done we was really proud of you and the school.' As you know, I'm now off on my sabbatical thanks to your good offices, and I have fixed up to go to Thailand in October, visiting their school of dance and drama, a couple of village schools and a 'Government school', whatever that may mean. I'm not sure what benefit I will derive, but I'm greatly looking forward to it.

Actually, we had thought the school might benefit from the head's sabbatical as much as he would. I had expected sixth formers and their teachers, when a summer school was well run, both to enjoy and gain a great deal from them. I had not supposed that head teachers would take part, but it made good sense that they should. Teaching a subject that they had once taught well could usefully remind heads, now preoccupied with administration and other such distractions, why they had become teachers in the first place. This letter also reminded me that heads who may not be particularly successful towards the end of their careers were nearly all once excellent teachers.

Important educational outcomes are rarely predictable. This was certainly true of some of these summer schools for sixth formers. On one occasion, I was attending a display taking place some days after the end of a residential course run by one of the art colleges. As I was looking at some of the work, I was approached by a girl, looking pleased with herself. 'I want you to know', she announced, 'that this course has changed my life'. Anyone who has had similar responsibilities will recognise that these were alarming words for an official to hear from a seventeen year old girl at the end of a residential course with Art College lecturers on the prowl. 'Yes', she said, and I wrote her words down that evening, 'for the first time in my life, I felt near the frontiers of my self ' (clearly expressed as two separate words). 'And now', she added, causing me to look urgently towards the exit, 'here's my Dad come along to meet you'. But all turned out well. So had she decided to go to art school? Absolutely not, said her father. But before the course she had been dithering about whether she wanted to become a nurse. On her return, she had become absolutely sure that this is what she now wanted to do. And now here she was, up in the morning early, slogging away at her homework, bustling about; and even, her father told me wonderingly, helping with the washing-up.

The new leadership of the ILEA, like its predecessors, was strongly committed to improving conditions for the most disadvantaged members of society.

Members were particularly determined to tackle any form of discrimination against ethnic minorities, women or those with disabilities. They did not, however, know much about the day-to-day working of the Inner London education service or how its finances were dealt with. The scope for financial confusion soon became apparent:

Note to Mr Stead (cc Mr Bryn Davies, Mrs Morrell, Mr Herbert

4 September

1982/83 BUDGET

1. On 24 July, you asked Chairmen of Sub-Committees to be thinking about changes that would affect the 1982/83 budget. Subsequently, Chairmen have asked officers for suggestions. For my part, at this very preliminary stage, I have simply arranged for these suggestions to be in a common form. A set of them is attached to this note.

2. The items consist of matters which members might wish to consider further and which we think would benefit the education service. They are not recommendations because they have not been analysed or costed in detail, they have not been weighed against each other to see that the balance of development within the service is right, they have not been placed in any order of priority nor in the context of the Authority's likely budgetary position in 1982/83. All these things are for a later stage.

3. You may find it useful to have some general comments, on behalf of my immediate colleagues and myself, on how the ILEA service now stands in relation to its expenditure:

a. In any discussion on expenditure, we have found it useful to preserve the distinction between 'existing policies' and 'real terms'. In 1982/83 a budget based on existing policies would lead to a reduction in expenditure of several million pounds, excluding inflation, because falling numbers would be accompanied by reduced staff, capitation and so on. In our language, these would not be 'cuts', because the standard of staffing, for example the pupil/teacher ratio, would be maintained; though there would be fewer teaching and non-teaching staff overall.

A budget based on maintaining our expenditure in real terms would leave room for a considerable improvement in the service. We could re-use savings arising from falling rolls. For example, when numbers of pupils go down we could retain a given number of teaching posts, which would reduce class sizes, and still have money to spare for new developments elsewhere in the service.

b. My colleagues and I believe that the ILEA is well-resourced and, as we see them, the needs of the education service would not require us in 1982/83 to go beyond holding our expenditure at the 1981/82 'existing policies' level. We believe that many of the important suggestions attached to this note could be adopted within this level of expenditure. Obviously, the suggestions themselves exclude the financial consequences of any initiatives your colleagues will be proposing.

c. The remark 'the ILEA is well-resourced' relates both to our absolute and relative position. In relation to the former, our view is that the main improvements in the service are likely to come about by using our present resources more efficiently rather than by adding to them. As to the latter, our expenditure can be compared with that of education services outside Inner London and with that of other public services in Inner London. In relation to other LEAs, we are, in most areas of the service, the highest spending Authority, sometimes by a wide margin, and the gap between ourselves and others is tending to widen. In relation to the expenditure of Inner London boroughs on their services, comparisons are more difficult to establish. But our impression, derived from working alongside those services, is that over the last two or three years our standards of provision and our costs have risen in relation to those of the services administered by the boroughs (some of which, of course, have considerably reduced their levels of service), though these standards naturally vary from one to the other. Again, the gap seems to be widening. Hence the view that the ILEA is well-resourced both absolutely and relatively.

d. I have omitted from this note any reference to the Department of the Environment's view of the Authority's expenditure. This assumes, for grant purposes, sharp reductions in the level of expenditure that 'existing policies' would entail. Our concern here is a quasi-political one. The ILEA service does not absorb sudden changes easily. If marginal improvements made now had soon to be reversed and further reductions made, the consequences for the education service would be far worse, in terms of the dislocation caused, than if those improvements, particularly in staff numbers, had not been made in the first place.

4. All this will sound a little cautious. It springs from a genuine belief that the main way to improve this education service is to persuade the people in it to think harder and better about what they are doing on a wide range of issues, from multi-ethnic education and equal opportunities of all kinds to what is actually happening in each classroom. Spending more money can sometimes actually divert people from this process.

'You may find it useful', the first words of paragraph 3, were a first attempt to imply that it might have been better to ask me to put forward a range of costed options for the next year's budget, in some priority order. The Policy Committee, of which all chairmen of committees were members, would then be in a position to add, subtract and discuss options of their own and, in doing so, have an opportunity to interrogate officers on the full implications of whatever it was they wanted to see put before the various committees, ultimately for decision by the Authority. The last sentence would have been particularly unwelcome to the new administration. In suggesting that the best way to improve the service was for the people in it to think harder about what they were now doing, I was not excluding the new leadership itself, but I did not expect that point to register. Nor did it.

Eighteen years after the London Government Act of 1963, many people who ought to have known better still had not come to terms with the clause in the Act that read:

> Freedom of choice of schools – A pupil may not be refused admission to a school or institution maintained or assisted by a local education authority in Greater London on the ground that he is ordinarily resident in the area of some other local education authority if that area is within or contiguous with Greater London.

Hence the note to Philip Hunter on 8 September about a Chief Executive of an outer London borough who was unaware of this:

> I enclose a cutting to illustrate what happens when people who know nothing about a problem become involved in it. Is there anything for us to do here? If it is a question of telling the Chief Executive that Barnet parents are perfectly entitled to send their children to ILEA schools, perhaps you should take this on.

So Barnet children were as entitled to enter schools within the ILEA as the children of ILEA residents were entitled to enter schools in Barnet if there was room in them. This was news to at least one Chief Executive at the time and to almost the whole of the press forty years after the 1963 Act. Parents in the public eye, even Mr Blair as Prime Minister, were still being criticised for sending their children to a school in a London borough other than the one in which they happened to live. Borough boundaries had little relationship to distance or travel times on London transport and many thousands of London children crossed those boundaries to attend school every day. My own children went from Lewisham to a comprehensive school near a station in Greenwich. To be free to do that, so far as London was concerned, had been established as a parent's right for many years. The Greenwich judgment, on the break-up of the ILEA in 1990, simply confirmed the position that had existed within Greater London since 1963.

Consistently inaccurate letters about the ILEA kept appearing in the Press. These had to be answered, as in this letter to the Times Educational Supplement on 4 October:

Your issue of October 2 carried the headline 'Author claims ILEA blocked Thames TV's mixed race play'. What the author claims is one thing; the facts are another. The ILEA blocked nothing. We were asked to provide two facilities: a school building for location filming during the holidays and permission to film pupils in the last week of term for use as 'background' in the production. We simply pointed out that if children are to be filmed at an identifiable ILEA school for a dramatic production we expect parents to be asked whether they agree. That was the last we heard of it.

Remarks were sometimes made to me on visits to schools which needed following up. Hence this note of 11 November to Bill Stubbs and the Chief Inspector about the amalgamation of a boys school with a girls school to form a mixed one.

> Would you look urgently at the senior appointments being made or recommended by Governors at Hammersmith County/Christopher Wren? I hear that women candidates are being passed over – and that men are getting most of the senior posts. Is this correct and is there anything we could be doing about it?

And again in this note to the CI (copy to Dr Mortimore) on 3 December:

> Equal Opportunities for Girls: Are we or should we be monitoring what happens when we mix school science classes: for example, what is happening in different subject areas when single sex schools, such as Kidbrooke, John Roan's, Quintin Kynaston, Sir William Collins, develop as mixed ones? In general: what progress is being made within the scientific and technological areas to see that girls are at least holding their own?

A *cri de coeur* had landed on my desk from a recently married teacher whose happy day had been blighted by having her salary docked for suddenly moving her wedding day from a Saturday to the preceding Friday. Hence the note to Mr Naylor (Teaching Staff Branch) of 16 November:

> Surely we could allow this with pay? It is hardly this teacher's fault that registrars have suddenly stopped working on a Saturday.

Letter to Mrs Metcalfe (manuscript) Headmistress Haggerston School 18 November

> I've just been hearing from HMI about the inspection of your school. Amongst the many good things said about the staff – your caring and competent deputies for a start – there was one recurring theme: the straightforward, notable, profoundly influential, leading-from-the-front, unfussy, excellence of one particular individual. You.

> I am sure they said this to you directly but thanks are so rare these days that I would like to add mine to theirs.

All over England, local authority chief executives were emphasising the, in their eyes, subordinate position of the education service. The GLC's Director General,

Sir James Swaffield, through a GLC official, had asked me to supply a draft of a letter for him on an educational matter to send to the Chief Executive of a London borough. I did not think it was my job to do that. He had written rather sharply when I told him this, so I replied to him on 9 December to clarify my position.

Dear Jim,

Here are some thoughts on this general matter of letters from MPs and others on educational issues which reach you as Clerk to the Authority. First of all, may I say that I entirely accept the view that we should conduct our affairs in a civilised way. We are on the same side and should act in co-operation. That said, I do not accept that ILEA officers, including myself, should be asked to produce drafts on educational matters for others, yourself included, to send to whomever may have sent the original letter to County Hall.

May I take an example of what this leads to? I received from John Collins on 12 November a letter asking for detailed comments on one addressed to you by the Chief Executive of Lewisham. It is a lengthy letter and relates to the Authority's special education procedures. Had that Chief Executive consulted his Director of Social Services he would have discovered that the issue had been on the agenda for the Authority's meeting with the Directors of Social Services in Inner London, including his, held on 10 November 1981. For that meeting, we produced a note, which I now enclose, and at that meeting it was agreed that we should seek to intensify local involvement with our procedures and that Directors of Social Services would raise individual problems with our Divisional Education Officers. Recognising the problems arising from the 1981 Education Act, it was agreed that a small group of ILEA officers and representatives of the Social Services Directors would be set up to examine the financial arrangements relating to boarding provision. The first meeting will be held later this month with a view to producing a paper by the end of January 1982. In other words, I would have thought that the appropriate action here would be for the Chief Executive's letter to be answered directly, as it concerns the Authority's policy, by officers here after clearing the matter with your Secretariat. At a time when we are working quite unreasonable hours, the idea of producing draft letters for others to send causes a sense of stress here.

I am enclosing a spare copy of this for Mr Collins and hope he will accept it as a reply to his note to me of 12 November. Some polite way needs to be found to tell the Chief Executive of Lewisham that you understand that his colleague, the Social Services Director, has been involved in discussions with the ILEA on the matters he has raised and will be in a position to report to him about these early in the New Year.

Mr Collins, a member of the GLC Staff, serviced the Education and other ILEA committees. Sir James was Director General of the GLC and I was a member of the

Director-General's Board. But, as the GLC was not itself an Education Authority, I was not accountable to Sir James for any educational matter. His role in education was to be Clerk to the Education Authority. The distinction was an important one. Both Mr Collins and the ILEA's Chief Financial Officer were, in the phrase used at the time, operationally attached to the ILEA but professionally responsible to the relevant Controller in the GLC. The ILEA's Education Officer was not professionally responsible to anyone other than to the Authority itself. He, not the Director General of the GLC, was the Authority's Chief Executive.

Increasingly, notes to the ILEA's political leadership had two purposes: the first was to give accurate information and considered advice; the second was to ensure that that advice was placed on record. When ill-considered policies lead them into trouble, some politicians tend to argue that their officers never gave them the advice that would have avoided it. So increasingly it seemed prudent to provide written advice to elected members even when nobody had asked for it or, as in the example below about one of London's five Polytechnics, would be pleased to receive it. Hence this 'strictly confidential' note to leading members on 16 December. Rumour had it that unorthodox ways of getting rid of the Rector of one of the Polytechnics were being considered:

> My advice on this is:
>
> 1. The Court is responsible for the running of the Polytechnic, including the employment and functions of its senior staff.
>
> 2. The ILEA should not seek, or be publicly represented as seeking, to assume those powers; in particular in relation to the functions of any individual member of the Polytechnic staff, from the Rector downwards.
>
> 3. The ILEA is responsible for funding the Polytechnic and for assuring itself that the money it provides is properly spent. It is entitled to take such steps as it thinks fit to ensure that the Polytechnic keeps within the expenditure allocated to it. In the present circumstances, it seems to me proper to place on record with the Chairman and Rector, if these are the two persons you are seeing, that:
>
> > a. If the Polytechnic can find ways of dealing with its overspending that do not depend on the ILEA, then of course the Authority has no wish to intervene, other than by offering advice. The Polytechnic has an important part to play within London as well as nationally and the Authority wishes to see this continue.
> >
> > b. If the Polytechnic wishes additional funds from the Authority, it should know that the preliminary audit report indicates a disconcerting degree of what amounts to financial mismanagement by senior members of the Polytechnic staff. To be in any way effective, plans for restoring the financial stability of the Polytechnic depend on changes at this level

being quickly introduced.

c. the Authority will put no more money into the Polytechnic until it is satisfied that the Court has dealt effectively with this matter. By effectively, the Authority means that it would wish to see a recovery plan which includes accurate information on how, when and by whom the necessary action is to be taken or control exercised. Quite apart from the audit report, the experience of the past year has not been encouraging.

d. Finally, the Authority would emphasise that, like any other organisation in the position the Polytechnic now finds itself in, the Court should forthwith look closely at its top management structure and ask itself whether it has the right people in the right places. Decisions on these matters are for the Court but, bearing in mind the comparisons it can make with the four other Polytechnics aided by the ILEA, the Authority shares the concern expressed by the auditors and doubts whether it has.

Note – For the Authority itself to point to a particular individual within the Polytechnic whom it regards as unsatisfactory raises a principle of a far-reaching kind. Irrespective of the merits of the individual case, it would widely be held, in my view with justification, as unsatisfactory for an education authority to assert its financial power by seeking to dislodge a particular individual employed in an institution of Higher Education. So far as I know, there are no precedents for action of this kind and I hope the ILEA will not find itself trying to create one.

So ended 1981. The ILEA had survived a period of sustained attack and a change in its political leadership. I had worked in London for ten unsettled years and it was beginning to feel longer. Later in 1982, the examination results of the first year group entering inner London secondary schools after the ending of 11+ selection in 1977 would become known. I did not believe these would be very different from those of the previous year but what else was happening and where? It was already evident that most of the schools that had been selective were doing well, but I was aware of two that were not. In the past, children had travelled long distances to reach these schools but now their position in run-down parts of London meant that more easily accessible schools elsewhere were becoming preferred by parents. On the credit side, some ex Grammar schools were doing particularly well. Many years later, I read the history of the Cardinal Vaughan Memorial School . The effect of ending selection there was described as follows: 'In 1977, the intake of boys was divided into four forms instead of the customary three. This was made possible by the additional staffing the ILEA provided for schools during their transition from a selective entry . . . . it is a remarkable achievement that the comprehensive phase of the Vaughan's development has not only equalled the academic achievements of the selective period but, in many respects, has surpassed them. 1996 (the year before the book's publication) showed the best Advanced Level results in the school's history.'

Early in 1982, it became evident that action would have to be taken to avoid overspending the 1981/82 budget. Such a thing had never happened in the past and could not be allowed to happen now. It is sometimes assumed that, as individuals or collectively, people will not do something which it is not in their interest to do unless they are forced to do it. Asking them politely to do something that they can see that there are good reasons for doing can be quite as effective. Such was my view. The following letter caused a few bitten finger-nails in the Finance Department:

Letter to all Heads and College Principals 10 January 1982

Enclosed with this letter is a circular about the Authority's financial position in the present accounting year. This ends on 31 March, 1982. Briefly, our computer printout is telling us that we will overspend by £3 or £4 million unless action is taken now. I hope you will agree that this will not do. Of course, there are always those who argue that, with a budget of over £700 million, £3 or £4 million is not a significant amount. I take the opposite view. The larger the budget the more necessity there is for good housekeeping and for us to keep within the sums provided for us. Overspending is not arising from carelessness. It reflects higher than expected staffing costs: in particular, more supply teachers coming forward, lower vacancy rates, delayed moves of teachers to ensure they are appropriately placed and more overtime for non-teaching staff arising from community and other uses of the Authority's premises. So we have to reduce expenditure this financial year by £3 to £4 million. The circular describes how this is to be done.

The letter goes on to explain that savings originating in County Hall and not affecting schools or college allowances leave expenditure of £2 million for heads and principals to defer in the current financial year.

There are rather too many people these days telling schools and colleges how to manage their affairs so the circular does not propose a whole new apparatus of controls. We need to defer about £2 million of expenditure on school and college allowances between now and 31 March 1982. It can be done. I am relying on your common sense and managerial skills to see that it is.

It was. Meanwhile, internal disputes amongst the politicians on the Authority's proposed expenditure in the following year were eventually settled and I was able to congratulate the staff concerned.

Budget 1982/83

You will have heard that the Authority achieved a budget last night, no mean achievement these days. We will have to see what happens next but I am writing immediately to let you know how grateful I am for the prompt and efficient way that the administration has carried out the work to make this satisfactory result possible. It has been a notable achievement. For the future, there are a number of new developments which members of the Authority will want to see happen over this next year. They will cost money and we will have to find the money, within our existing level of expenditure, to make them possible. The ability to do this will be a test of our administrative skill. The review procedure which the Authority is establishing will itself mean more work for us but, as I say, it is essential that it should be well done if we are to provide the support to which members of the Authority are entitled. These last few weeks represent a notable administrative achievement.

Item by item, both before and during committee meetings, proposed expenditure had now to be checked to ensure that that it would not lead to a reference to the District Auditor or be subject to successful legal challenge. We had a GLC lawyer present at all meetings where expenditure was being approved. At each stage, the unhappy man was asked to confirm that, in his view, what the committee had decided did not conflict with any of the statutory requirements with which we were now required to comply. Some members found this fussy but, fussy or not, the lawyer's minuted acceptance of items as, in his opinion, lawful gave all members at the meeting personal financial protection against any subsequent challenge in the courts. Philip Hunter was primarily responsible for ensuring that we did not put a foot wrong during this process and we didn't. Hence this note to him of 10 February:

> This is just a word of thanks for all you have done over these past few weeks. If there were such things as ILEA medals, instead of brickbats, you would have one pinned on you for exemplary conduct under fire, persistence and valour in the face of the lawyers! Many thanks.

Several experience members of the Education Committee retained their positions under the new administration, so letters to them could accordingly be expressed briefly, as in the past. Miss Horstead, the Chief Whip, was one such person.

Note to Miss Horstead   12 February

Mr Bryn Davies has mentioned to me the matter of a letter to Sir Keith Joseph following our meeting of 16 December. We have not written. You will remember that, when we visited, we were costing government legislation which would restrict our expenditure. We argued with Sir Keith about the catastrophic effects of a reduction of about £90 million. This seemed to be the scale of reduction the government envisaged. Sir Keith was not impressed but we said we would produce supporting material. Next day it was announced that the government was dropping this legislation. There is now no direct control on ILEA's expenditure. These matters, it now appears, are to be decided in the law courts. In these circumstances, there seems little point in trying to convince Sir Keith of anything. His department will have our papers, cleared by the lawyers, I hope, and I think it would be unwise to put much more out in writing.

As this note of 17 February to my immediate colleagues indicates, we had been anticipating the need to produce a report on what the ILEA was already doing about one of the new administration's major policies. The draft referred to in the note that follows is missing but was no doubt incorporated in the report that went initially to the Policy Committee.

> Education in a multi-ethnic society: The next stage
>
> I shall be grateful if you will do two things: First, look through this draft to see whether anything you think important is missing or anything redundant is present. Second, in your own area of responsibility, please sharpen up the thinking in any way you can.
>
> As the introduction says, the report is intended as a reference point. It should bring together the bits of thinking or policy on which we will be acting or bringing forward further reports later this year. So it should be comprehensive. But it does not have to deal in detail with matters which are to come forward later.
>
> As to the conclusions, what are the things we would like to see happen immediately? You will know the financial position. There is no, literally no, money to spend on new ventures until we have identified the savings out of which the work is to be financed. So what should we go for in the first instance?
>
> I would like to get this report to Policy Committee on Tuesday 2 March, so I am afraid I need comments to Peter Clyne by the evening of 22 February.

No major changes to the Authority's administration occurred in 1982, the year in which I left. What follows illustrates some of the day to day actions with which I was involved. Establishing sound working relationships with the new administration, few with experience of public or any other form of administration, meant far more had to be put in writing than previously in order to avoid misunderstanding of a why-didn't you-tell-me kind. Mr Bryn Davies was the Leader of the Authority, but I consistently seem to have had difficulty in describing him as such. It was now necessary to keep telling the politicians in writing what we were doing and how and why we were doing it. The following three notes, written on the same day, indicate the nature of the problem that had arisen now that a few words exchanged with Sir Ashley were no longer sufficient.

> Note to: Mr Bryn Davies (cc Mrs Morrell, Neil Fletcher)   10 March
> Spring and summer 1982
>
> We hope that there will be no recurrences of the disturbances that took place in Brixton last year, but there may be. Without in any way wishing to cause unnecessary alarm, we have done three things:
>
> 1. Ensured that Divisional Education Officers are in touch throughout

Inner London with their borough colleagues to ensure that any action to be taken is well coordinated.

2. Ensured that all parts of the youth service have suitable programmes planned, including the extended use of premises, during the spring and summer months. Mr Bevan and Mr Stevens will be seeing Mr Fletcher about this directly.

3. Finally, we have asked both the youth service and our divisional administration to ensure that County Hall is informed immediately if any problems arise in providing what we believe is necessary. We also need to have news of any untoward incidents that occur; an isolated incident may have lessons to teach us.

Would you like to take this discussion further in some way?

So if things blew up again that summer, nobody could claim that members had not been given an opportunity to put forward their own ideas on how to respond to that possibility. On the same day, I had to return to the matter of the ILEA's administrative structure. None of the new politicians knew anything much about what the ILEA now did or had been doing in previous years, so anything I wrote needed to be in the nearest I could achieve to words of one syllable.

Note to Mr Bryn Davies   10 March

DEVOLUTION AND THE ILEA

1. At Policy Committee on 2 March, I was asked to let you have a note on this issue. The background, you will recall, was the discussion on the top administrative structure of the ILEA.

2. I attach a report on the organisation of the ILEA which I wrote early in 1977, immediately after becoming Education Officer. Mr Vigars, then leading the Minority Party, favoured a form of divisional executive, which is why the report spent some time (page 6) dealing with that idea.

3. In re-reading the 1977 report, two points occur to me:-

i. Given the threat to the future of the Authority (the Marshall Report was commissioned by the GLC in May 1977 and we had then to deal, in succession, with the Baker report and Lady Young's more recent one), I was cautious about proposing major changes. If major change was thought to be necessary, why not a complete change?

ii. I am even more conscious now than I was in 1977 of the diversionary effect of organisational change. I believe everyone now accepts that the restructuring of the Development Branch was necessary to enable us to carry out our sites review and school re-organisation; but the changes caused major problems and a good deal of ill-feeling over more than a year. You yourself have seen the consequences of comparatively minor changes, such as the decision to advertise publicly at divisional officer level.

4. I believe the 1977 report identifies what remain as two central issues:

i. The ILEA has to blend administration by areas with administration through functions. County hall is functionally organised (primary schools, secondary schools and so on). Divisional Offices are area based. Over the past five years we have experimented with extending the area basis of administration within County Hall itself. The reshaping of the Development Branch on a quadrant basis, within which separate boroughs are clearly identified, was one example. This was exceedingly unpopular with the Divisional Officers but, in my view, made, some of the re-organisations possible. The system worked well when we had the right individuals working it. As you know, our main way of seeking to improve our area thinking has been to develop the role of Divisional Education Officer.

ii. We have to be clear where political control is located. At present, we have two levels of political input: at County Hall and at the individual institutions we maintain, to which we have devolved a great deal of responsibility. As I argue in the 1977 report, I do not believe there is a place for an intermediate elected tier of any systematic kind. To introduce such a tier would be to introduce confusion. Nothing that has happened in these last five years has led me to revise that analysis. I believe we could run the ILEA from two places: County Hall, with its elected member committees, and a number of much smaller groupings, with real control over the resources at their disposal, dealing with all the educational issues in their area and supported by the administrative services of the Divisional Education Officers. Each Division would have from six to ten such groupings. Any parent or user of the Education Service would be within walking distance of the administrative centre of one such grouping.

5. Finally, a point I dealt with in the 1977 report. I believe we still need three people at the very top of the administrative structure. Until late in 1977 we had two and when illness struck one of them, as it did my predecessor, or when one became entangled in some full-time engagement (as happened to Mr Bevan early in 1977) the remaining officer was left with an impossibly difficult administrative load. In these circumstances, money tends to be wasted rather than saved. For example, we fought our way out of a commitment of about £500,000 a year to the Post Office for a cable link (used for the television service) because one of the top three took this on virtually full time, leaving the other two to share out his work. In the absence of concentrated effort of this kind, major savings tend to be delayed or even shelved altogether.

Paragraph 4 (ii) was the last gasp of the Education Officer's 'hundred flowers' notion of what genuinely local administration in inner London would look like. In the political climate of the time, there was no chance of any major restructuring of that kind. On restructuring generally, it proved difficult to establish what it was that the new administration wanted to do that it thought the existing structure could not or would not achieve. Not far below the surface seemed to be the wish to make the administration, as it is in the national civil service, directly responsible to the leadership of the majority party as opposed to the Authority as a whole.

Paragraph 5 made a point too often neglected. Senior local authority staff were too often simply seen as a cost. Ignorant management consultants made money from equally naïve Chief Executives in eliminating staff before properly calculating the cost of doing that. Savings are a local authority's equivalent of a private company's profits. In the instance quoted, a senior officer, at a salary of some £15,000 a year, succeeded in extricating the ILEA from a contract a year earlier than would otherwise have been possible. By so doing, he saved the Authority more than thirty times his salary for that year. On that same day, I again tried to explain the nature of the funding problems the ILEA faced:

> Note to Mr Stead (Copy Mr Davies, Mrs Morrell, Mr Hunter) 10 March
>
> The Chief Financial Officer is presenting a paper to the next Finance Sub-Committee meeting on 16 March. That paper fully discusses the impact of possible changes in funding on the education service and I see no reason to add to it. I would, however, emphasise the general point made in the paper that the present system of funding, confused as it is, has resulted in a level of resources for ILEA which more or less meets our needs. The CFOs paper rightly points out that the third option, some form of educational block grant could result in more grant to London as a whole. This is an important consideration but I think it is inconceivable that any such grant would benefit the ILEA itself. A block grant would be likely, under any government, to be closer to the 'Grant Related Expenditure' figure than our actual level of expenditure and the legislation would have to protect our right to raise the extra money in some way. I doubt whether there would be much enthusiasm for legislation which had this effect. The desire to keep local authorities on a tight financial rein is common to all political parties nationally. The specific ILEA interest is best served by methods of financing which are neither well-defined nor logical.

That last sentence anticipated a problem that was already causing serious financial problems. These became even more serious in later years. No funding formula, devised by statisticians in a Whitehall office, could possibly take account of the unpredictable and suddenly changing demographic movements that kept occurring in London. Detailed local knowledge was required to assess the nature of the educational problems arising from month to month and then to relate financial or other resources to wherever these new needs had arisen.

Problems such as these were soon to become someone else's. Towards the end of

1981, I had reminded myself that, shortly after arriving at the ILEA in 1972, I had concluded that ten years would be about the limit of my usefulness there. Shortly after becoming Education Officer in 1977, I had mentioned this time-scale to Sir James Swaffield, the GLC's Director General; so I now spoke to him again. What to do next was a problem. There was no likely job in local education authority administration for ex- Education Officers of the ILEA or of the LCC before it. Over the past eighty years, all except one had either retired or died in the job; and the one who had moved had only done so to be head of the LCC's administration. I do not know who said what to whom, but one morning I had a call from the Home Office. The Home Secretary, Sir William Whitelaw, wanted to see me. When I arrived, in those pre-Nolan days, after a brief discussion, he invited me to become the next Chairman of the Commission for Racial Equality. The Commission had recently run into serious trouble with a parliamentary committee and there appeared to be internal problems that need to be sorted out apart from positive things to do. After wincing at the salary being offered, I agreed to accept the job.

Why? I had become convinced that the most serious problems affecting the largest of the ethnic minority communities, Asian and African/Caribbean, certainly in London, were arising outside the schools. Discrimination in employment, housing and health and the behaviour of the police were just some of the areas where this was evident. Add to that poverty. Schools could only deal indirectly with these problems. They had to be tackled elsewhere and in other than educational ways. So far as education was concerned, I had served on the Rampton Committee and was still on its successor, the Swann Committee. This was dealing with educational issues, but not getting very far. There was a constant preoccupation about how we should think and talk about the consequences of demographic changes to our society, far less about what could effectively be done towards improving matters. Within ILEA, the new administration was deeply committed to equal opportunities of all kinds and there was little I could personally add to the structural, inspectorate and other changes that had already been made or were being proposed by the politicians in that direction.

There was another reason for me to move on. I had become aware that I was not getting better at what I was doing. Even comparatively simple tasks were becoming unusually troublesome to perform. I was becoming increasingly impatient, not with my immediate administrative colleagues, with whom I can recall only ever having minor differences of opinion, but generally. As for the ILEA's new political leadership, relationships had been civil but it was evident that, to them, I must appear something of a relic from the past. All my professional life, I had been younger, sometimes much younger, than those for and with whom I had been working. My four chief education officers had all been close to retirement: Frank Barraclough in the North Riding, Gordon Bessey in Cumberland, Alec Clegg in the West Riding, Eric Briault in London. The political leaders had mostly also been older or about the same age as myself. But here I now was, fifty three years old, probably perceived as wheel-chair material by ILEA's youthful new leadership.

There remained sound working relationships with elected members to be established. I would once have found it interesting to try and develop these. Now, I was not the right person to do it. What the ILEA needed in these dangerous times was mature, politically astute, political leadership. Instead, we now had a group of inexperienced politicians who believed that adroitness in winning battles amongst themselves was a skill that could be deployed against hostile forces outside the ILEA. These included the leadership of several London boroughs and influential elements within the national government itself. In believing that, the new ILEA politicians were seriously mistaken.

In 1977, I had been confident that I was the right person to be ILEA's Education Officer. In 1982, I was no longer sure of that. There were important educational issues, such as the whole issue of 16–19 education and training, that others were better equipped to deal with than I. It had been obvious for years that London needed to concentrate high level sixth form work in fewer places. Only by doing that could the best qualified teachers influence far more young people in more sensibly sized groups than were still to be found in many of London's sixth forms. The political climate now made it impossible to pursue the idea of inviting some leading independent school sixth forms to become publicly funded and open to large numbers of suitably qualified candidates from the maintained sector. So other ways would have to be found to achieve this. Furthermore, in theory I had twelve years to go before retirement. Long before then, my able and ambitious deputies, as well as other senior colleagues would have been promoted elsewhere and there would have to have been a series of fresh starts with new people. Now was as good a time as any for me to step aside.

There were no lame duck Education Officers under the Authority's Standing Orders. The Education Officer was personally responsible for anything that went wrong in the ILEA until the day he left. As Eric Briault had done before me, both I and the system had to go on working, as though I were not leaving, until I left at the end of August.

Once arrangements were well advanced for appointing my successor, the ILEA leadership returned to the ILEA's top structure. Yet again it proved difficult to establish what it was the politicians wanted me and my colleagues to do that, when asked to do it, we were not doing. Without that information, tinkering with the administrative structure hardly seemed sensible. The problem was, it became apparent, that the politicians were in the position of a family that cannot agree on whether it wants to go to Brighton or to Blackpool for their holiday. Unable to make up its mind, it tends to blame their car for any problems caused by their own indecision. My minute of 10 March on the ILEA's top structure had not resolved whatever it was that was worrying the new leadership, so I was asked to elaborate on what I had then written. After explaining the different changes that had been made over the past five years and the reasons for them, on 20 April I reiterated my belief that the Authority still needed three people at the head of its administration. I concluded:

> On general management principles, on grounds of economy and from the experience gained over the years, it seems right to have as few people as possible between the Authority's committees and the AEOs with direct functional responsibilities. Nothing is worse, in a large organisation such as the ILEA, than long lines of command or a proliferation of people with a co-ordinating function.

It was the latter I was concerned about. The immediate reaction of comparatively inexperienced politicians, intent on ensuring that their favourite policies are vigorously implemented, is to appoint extra persons, directly responsible to themselves, to hurry things along. This rarely works. The people appointed in this way find themselves working with limited success while the rest of the system sees little need to rethink its own attitudes or practices.

Another symptom of insecure policy-makers is their tendency to appoint assistants to comfort them with supportive opinions and to act as intermediaries. In my last few months I encountered one such newly-appointed individual. He began to tell me that Mrs Morrell wanted me to do something or other. My reply was that I was in the office and that, if Mrs Morrell wanted to say something to me, no doubt she would prefer to avoid any possible misunderstanding by saying it to me directly. That put an end to that conversation but some members of the new leadership found it difficult to accept that the best way to ensure that something got done in the ILEA was to make the Education Officer directly responsible for ensuring that it did. That only needed a few words but ensured that accountability was clear.

On 23 April, I was writing to Mrs Morrell to avoid a possible misunderstanding. The quite unfounded suspicion that officials were not fully committed to the Authority's new policies was still in the air, so it had to be clear that leading members and officers knew exactly who was supposed to be doing what at each stage of the policy process. Hence this note to Mrs Morrell on the follow-up to a series of conferences on equal opportunities. These had been addressed by Mrs Morrell, unwisely in my view. Teachers in London tended to respond politely but without enthusiasm to speeches by politicians on educational matters:

> 1. In response to your minute of 19 April, this is just to confirm how I understand the position:
>
> a. Dr Mortimore will be drafting the papers on multi-ethnic and girls' education as a follow-up to the conferences. In so doing, he will no doubt incorporate suggestions from a number of other people. That is what I meant by editing.
>
> b. The drafts that Dr Mortimore produces will go to Sub-Committee as draft publications. Thereafter the responsibility for authorising their

publication becomes that of the Sub-Committee itself.

c. The aim is to take the document on girls' education to the meeting of the Schools Sub- Committee on 22 July, but it must be possible that that date will slip. You will want to be absolutely satisfied that we are saying something first-rate rather than routine and that may mean waiting until the first round of Committees in September. My own view is that schools pay more attention to documents that come out early in the school year rather than late in the summer, when many teachers are reaching for their bucket and spade.

d. Consultation is in two parts. Consultation with members, I think we agreed, consists in the first place of Dr Mortimore and myself (or Mr Stubbs) discussing paragraph headings with you. If a general framework of the papers can be agreed, the next stage would be for Dr Mortimore to bring a first draft to yourself and the other members directly concerned. This would enable members' views to be incorporated into the final draft. On the officers' side, Dr Mortimore and I will be in close touch with colleagues throughout. This is important. Any document produced, if it is to be brought to life in the schools, needs to have as many people as possible, from the Inspectorate and elsewhere, associated with it at an early stage.

e. On girls' education, there are no separate budgetary items proposed in advance of the July meeting. Matters such as the Equal Opportunities Unit and teaching staff secondments for people engaged in consciousness-raising within the schools are either being dealt with as part of wider issues or can be dealt with within the Authority's main programmes.

f. I note that you want to write to the Community Relations Officers about a meeting before your Sub-Committee on 10 June. I will let you have a draft letter to them early next week.

2. I am sending copies of this note to the recipients of yours.

The recipients included eight members of Mrs Morrell's committee. It was becoming evident that the new administration's achievements, great or small, would require a great deal more paperwork than previously. Paragraph 1(a) in the minute illustrates another feature of the new administration: a suspicion that officials might be manipulating, 'editing', documents to prevent politicians getting at the full facts. Were Dr Mortimore or I trying to hide something? I later tried to explain a convention that was rigorously maintained in the ILEA. No alterations or amendments of any kind were made, by the Education Officer or by anyone else, to any report by the Research and Statistics Branch, the Finance Officer or the Legal Adviser. The Education Officer could add his own comments on these documents in a separate report of his own if he thought that necessary.

The advertisement for my successor as Education Officer went out soon after I sent in my resignation towards the end of March. Ordinarily – and I believe rightly – the holder of a post has nothing directly to do with the appointment of his successor. But for reasons that were never made clear, although I had nothing to do with the decision about who was to be interviewed, I was invited to attend the appointment itself. As the examples shown above indicate, leading members of the new administration were trying to get to grips with how the top administrative structure actually worked. At the appointments committee meeting, there would be people there, such as Sir Ashley Bramall and, on the Conservative side, Professor Smith, with detailed knowledge of the ILEA's structures, so it may be that the new leadership thought it better, if factual information was required, to turn to me. It was not proposed, nor would I have suggested, that I should offer advice on the merits of any individual candidate.

The interviews themselves were unremarkable. It was rapidly evident that there was one outstanding candidate: Bill Stubbs. At this point, a problem arose. There was some indication that Mr Bryn Davies, in the Chair, and the Deputy Leader of the Authority, Mrs Morrell, had another candidate in mind. This candidate had been anxious to agree, with a disconcerting lack of hesitation, that he would, in effect, do anything he was told. It was also obvious that he was so lacking in experience that he would be out his depth as head of the ILEA's administration. The Chairman and Mrs Morrell soon accepted this but now suggested that Bill Stubbs, although it was unanimously agreed that he was to be appointed and that he was an outstanding candidate, should be re-interviewed so that one or two matters, which there had been no time to deal with adequately, could be conveyed to him. What matters? Someone enquired. There was a certain rather irritable to-ing and fro-ing at this point until a Conservative member said that he was strongly opposed to any such suggestion. They had all agreed on the right person to appoint and, turning to me, asked whether there was a procedural point here to consider?

When asked a troublesome question, it had been my practice for many years to answer a rather different one; so I responded directly to the issues raised by the Chairman and the Deputy Leader. If there were matters to be clarified, as they had suggested, it was clearly important that this should be done. But re-interviewing was not, perhaps, the best way to do this. If the Committee wished, I would write a letter to Mr Stubbs, setting out the matters, in terms agreed with the Chairman and the Deputy Leader, which they thought needed to be clarified. At the same time I would confirm, as the Committee had already indicated, that no one had any doubt that Mr Stubbs was not only the best candidate but also one they were delighted to be able to appoint. Several of the members at the meeting had long experience of how to get decisions through committees. As soon as I stopped speaking, someone moved, 'that the Education Officer's suggestion be adopted'. This was immediately seconded and the motion was then passed. There was a general pushing back of chairs and that was that. My promised letter to the newly appointed Education Officer was composed with some care. I showed it to Mr Bryn Davies and Mrs Morrellbefore sending it; but they had lost interest in the matter by then:

Dear Bill,   April 1982

First of all, let me repeat my congratulations. I am pleased for you and delighted for the ILEA that you are to be at the head of its administration. Some points arose at the interview which I must pass on to you. This is not just because some garbled account of them may anyway reach you but also because these points are and remain important. At interview no one expressed any doubt about your ability or, a term never easy to define with precision, about your stature, either within the ILEA or nationally. The decision to appoint you was unanimous. But on the way to that decision, in amongst all the positive things said, two concerns were expressed. Both need thinking about carefully.

The first concern was that, as head of the service, you might seek to retain too much administrative control in your own hands. This is not an issue affecting the ultimate responsibility you will have, and could not shed even if you wished, for the way the service is administered. The point relates to the degree of freedom you are now prepared (and in future would perhaps increasingly have to be prepared) to leave colleagues to grow and develop ideas in response to the needs of the service, as these are expressed by the ILEA's committees and those who chair them. Since 1977, as you know, we have tried to move away from the strict hierarchical structures of the past. This has not been easy. But somehow the ability to give a decisive administrative lead, when circumstances require it, has to be combined with a relaxed, though wary, attitude towards the sometimes divergent administrative efforts of colleagues. I have no great success of my own to point to here; but the move away from hierarchy has been perceptible and the discussion at interview made it clear that members want that movement to continue.

The second concern expressed has to be balanced against the strongly positive things said at the same time. You are seen, as I said earlier, as a highly effective administrator. You get things done. This is particularly so on matters which you have, as it were, put your name to personally. We can all think of examples of this. The concern was whether you are as responsive to the priorities of others; in other words, whether you are fully prepared, in setting the administrative machine to work, to make those priorities your own. Once again, I have no great success of my own to point to here but I am clear on the nature of the problem. The ILEA is a large administrative system; its attitudes tend to be entrenched. In some way, its Education Officer has to become excited (or, to revert to an earlier point, to leave others free to generate the excitement required) by the new directions members set for it from time to time and to transmit that excitement and determination to achieve results to the service as a whole. No one doubts you can do this. You have all the skills. The concern was that you might hold yourself somewhat aloof from the process.

Such then were the two concerns expressed. I will have framed this letter badly if you are left with the impression that anyone at the interview was seeking to undermine you or in any way to depreciate you. The committee was unanimous about you and that expression of confidence in you is itself a rare compliment. As to this letter, I have shown it to Mr Bryn Davies and to Mrs Morrell so that they could assure themselves that it conveys the points the committee wished to explore further with you had they decided on a second interview. Again, with my warmest congratulations and good wishes for the future.

That 'hold yourself somewhat aloof from the process' meant, of course, 'concluding, possibly with good reason, that a proposed initiative was misguided and thereafter doing little to help it succeed'.

With a new Education Officer appointed the political leadership also changed within a few weeks. Mrs Morrell became Leader of the Authority in place of Mr Bryn Davies. A new era was to begin under her forceful, if at times somewhat erratic, leadership. 'Demob happy' is the expression sometimes used of people, such as myself, about to leave one job for another. Some of the notes that follow show signs of this condition. My visits to schools were still causing work for others, as this note to Chris Storr of 18 May indicates:

I know that everybody knows that the nursery at Redland Primary School is oddly placed, with the main corridor dividing its two spaces and thereby rendering one unusable when the second teacher is not present. Could it possibly be moved to the other end of the school? I know about lavatories but one really good nursery, which this can't be, may be better value than opening up another somewhere else. The child population is rising and, perhaps, the parents' room could be included in the under-fives' area. But the nursery really is bizarrely placed.

As retirement approached, at times I became somewhat frivolous, as in this manuscript note to Philip Hunter of 4 July:

I take it plans for producing the 1981/1982 annual report are now well advanced. In other words, please begin to start thinking about it.

But serious issues also arose; as in this note to him of 16 July:

I attach a copy of a document to the Director General's Board on GLC/ILEA vehicle fleets. You will see that our performance is slipping. Would you please ensure that those administratively in charge are once again made aware of the seriousness of the situation and of their responsibility for remedying it. If examples of negligence on the part of ILEA staff become apparent, the appropriate disciplinary action or warnings must be given and a note made that we have done this.

We cannot allow children to be conveyed in vehicles which are defective. I am particularly disturbed by the four ILEA vehicles which were prohibited (see Appendix 1). This compares most unfavourably with what GLC Departments have been able to achieve. Please deal with this issue firmly and, after recess, let Mr Stubbs know where you have got to.

After recess, of course, I would be gone and Bill Stubbs would be the Education Officer. But accountability in the ILEA was clear. Until the day I left, it rested with me. If there was an accident involving an ILEA vehicle, unless it arose from the negligence of the driver, who was to blame? If there was a mechanical fault behind the accident and the Education Officer knew that such problems had arisen and had done nothing about them, clearly he was to blame. He should have given or renewed instructions to a named person to deal with the matter. If that named person had not then taken rapid and efficient action, either personally or by a clear instruction to someone with the appropriate skills and responsibilities, then he was to blame. And so on. In this instance, the principle to be adopted had been set down in the original minute to Philip Hunter: 'We cannot allow children to be conveyed in vehicles which are defective.' Anyone told that by the Education Officer and in a position to act in accordance with that principle but then failing to do so would be in the firing line if anything went wrong.

The penultimate letter in the Black Books, on 25 August, was to a Miss Haythorpe.

> I am sorry you missed missed your 'A' levels and hope things go well for you next year. The fact that you have applied this year makes no difference to your application next year. Apply in the usual way. I hope you are not too discouraged.

This student had been ill during her exams; but why was she writing to me about it? Surely her school would tell her what to do? But that was now not for me to sort out.

The closure of a school can leave some members of staff adrift. Their past efforts seem to have been devalued and their future disrupted. At the end of the summer term, I had visited a secondary school which was closing. Nearly all the staff, teaching and non-teaching alike, had other jobs to go to. But even when they had, some had a sense of personal failure that they found hard to shake off. They had done their best as teachers, sometimes over many years. They had tried to save their school. They had failed. What was there for them to look forward to with any degree of enthusiasm? Hence: this note to Peter Clyne of 27 August:

> I attach a note from Mr D., with whom I have had a conversation. This is not to be taken as a complaint but I hope someone will talk to him about his future and, in particular, point out if there is anything he ought to be doing to improve his prospects. He seems very discouraged and that cannot be right.

That was the final letter in the black books. On 30 August, after the round of farewells customary on these occasions, I left County Hall. But it was not quite the end. Letters kept coming and amongst them, was one sent to me at my home address. This came from John Luzio, a teacher representative on the Education Committee. John was head of one of the first primary schools I visited when I arrived at the ILEA in 1972. It was in the White City and my visit had cheered me up. There he was in the middle of the children, quietly leading, encouraging, setting an example, in the way he spoke and listened to children and teachers alike. His school reminded me that initiatives come and go but that the most important things in children's education have not changed much over the years. Pride in their work was what the children in John Luzio's school had as they gathered round and pushed it towards me to look at. John was someone whose suggestions I was always inclined to adopt. He so clearly knew what he was talking about. As I particularly valued his opinions, personal or professional, I kept his letter of 27 August, written by hand:

> Just before you leave the ILEA let me say thank you for your many personal kindnesses to me but more so for what you gave to London children and teachers – care, concern and struggle on their behalf. Please accept my appreciation and best wishes.

At none of the local education authorities at which I had worked had officials spoken at meetings of their Education Committees, though they were always present. On this final occasion, I was asked to speak and did so briefly.

A few days later, Sir James Swaffield sent me a transcript of the remarks made at my last appearance at the Education Committee. Amongst the things said, two paragraphs from the remarks of Professor Smith, the Leader of the Conservative Opposition, illustrated the difference there used to be between the role of administrators in local government and those in the civil service. The lesson for Inner London, which Sir Ashley Bramall had well understood, was that once a Labour majority tried to establish one party rule, with officials behaving simply as agents of the majority party, the Inner London Education Authority, in which several of the thirteen boroughs were strongly Conservative, would be at risk. The Authority would be at risk even from a well-informed and fair-minded national government. So far as the ILEA was concerned, the Conservative government of 1988 proved to be neither. Professor Smith's remarks on my departure included:

> I would like to speak in particular on the relationship he has managed to develop with the Opposition. This is something that is often very difficult for chief officers in local government. In my experience not every officer is able to do this in quite as felicitous a manner as has Peter Newsam. He has certainly managed to excel in this, seeing himself as the Education Officer to all the Authority, and with responsibilities to all members, regardless of their political background.

> This has in no way compromised his relationship with the leadership of the majority party. He has, though, been able to discuss issues frankly with myself and with my colleagues on this side of the Chamber, and indeed has on occasion been able to modify our views – as I understand from the Leader he is able, on occasion, to modify the majority party's views. In this there has been no question at all that he has always had the interests of the education service within Inner London as his paramount priority.

I left a great deal for my successor to do, With series of new inspectorate and administrative promotions and appointments to be made, he set about doing that vigorously. As Education Officer, he inherited far less favourable financial and political conditions than, for my first few years at least, I had the good fortune to encounter. On leaving the ILEA, I was leaving an educational world, developed over more than a hundred years, in which teachers, locally elected people and their officials provided the public of inner London, of all ages and from cradle to grave, with an education service designed to meet needs expressed in countless public and other meetings. The final words of the London School Plan, published in 1947, still defined the way the ILEA saw its role as a local education authority thirty five years later. It saw itself as engaged in a process " which depends for its fulfilment on human effort and the working together in lively partnership of teachers, children and parents in close cooperation with the Council and its officers." From 1982 onwards, both in London and nationally, the destructive power of the Conservative Party and the detachment of the Labour Party from many of its core educational values changed that world out of all recognition. Some believe for the better. Others not.

Afterword

Educationally, the Britain of 2014 is a very different place from when I left school in 1947. Many of the changes that have occurred in those seventy years are referred to in this autobiography of an education. That account ends in 1982. This Afterword summarises those changes and then briefly describes what, in my perception, has happened since.

In 1947, victory in two wars had recently been enthusiastically celebrated. Britain was close to bankruptcy, with large parts of its major cities and industrial areas in ruins. India's independence had just been achieved and it was already evident that the further dissolution of the Empire, over which Britain had ruled and from which it had benefitted for many years, could not long be delayed.

In the immediate post-war years, Britain was led by people who had lived through a war against totalitarian government. Many had experienced the war at first hand. They did not intend their hopes for the future to be crushed by apparently insurmountable debt. Britain's successful staging of the 1948 Olympic Games was an early statement of that intent, followed by the Festival of Britain in 1951.

At school, we learnt of the proposal for a national health service and for an education system that would provide opportunities for all of the kind that we had taken for granted. There was a widespread feeling amongst many of my educated in war-time contemporaries that we had a duty to play an active part in our country's future.

So much for 1947. Seventy years later, England, though not the rest of Britain, has moved a long way towards nationalising its education system, without its electorate ever having been invited to say whether it wants that to happen. Any account of how this has come about begins with the Education Act of 1944.

The 1944 Education Act was a continuation of earlier thinking. The terms of the Act were devised by an able group of civil servants, working with a small number of politicians of outstanding competence. In its final form, the Act was warmly welcomed by all the parties involved: parliament, local authorities, teacher unions, the churches, the general public and even the Press.

The first of the 1944 Act's two main achievements was structural. It established a, subsequently abandoned, division between primary and secondary education. Primary schools would cater for children up to the age of eleven. Thereafter, all children would attend secondary schools up to the school leaving age, soon to be raised from fourteen to fifteen, and beyond. As part of that restructuring, the Act created a secondary school system out of two very different types of existing school. The publicly-funded elementary schools, which since 1870 had provided education for most of the population up to the school leaving age of fourteen, were combined with a group of mostly fee-charging secondary schools, provided by a whole range of denominational and charitable individuals or agencies, that educated children up to the age of eighteen.

Re-structuring led to many long-established and independently managed secondary schools, some denominational but many not, joining the national system as voluntary aided (VA) schools. As they brought their land, their school buildings and their teachers into the national system, these VA schools were allowed to retain important elements of their independent status. VA school trustees formed the majority on the governing body, retained the right to appoint their own staff, to develop their own curriculum and to decide which children to admit to their school. The incorporation of many of these essentially independent schools into the national system for England and Wales was a great achievement. It made possible a stated aim of the Act: secondary education for all.

The 1944 Act's second main achievement was to establish a school system that reflected the values of a democratic society. The Act had been drafted during a war against totalitarian governments in which institutions like schools and what was taught inside them were directly controlled by the government. The civil servants and politicians who developed the Act and the parliament that approved it were unitedly determined to create a structure which would make such a development in England impossible. To that end, the Act ensured that responsibility for the management of education in England and Wales would be shared between the government, elected by the national electorate, and local education authorities, elected by a local electorate. Accordingly, no publicly funded school could become wholly dependent for its wellbeing or its existence on either local or national government acting alone. Neither could open, close or change the character of any publicly funded school without the agreement of the other. Proposals for a new or significantly enlarged school had to be published locally, either by the local authority or by a group of proposers. Any such proposals were then subject to consultation locally. Proposals, with any objections to them, were then sent by the local authority to the Secretary of State. His role was to approve, amend or reject these proposals. For his part, the Secretary of State could not open, close or change the character of any school. He had to await a proposal to do that from the local authority that either already was or would be maintaining it. The 1944 Education Act made it impossible for any school in England or Wales to be directly controlled by an individual government minister or by any individual local authority because neither could act without the agreement of the other.

Parts one and two of this autobiography describe two of the many ways in which that partnership between central and local government worked. The 1944 Act placed a general duty on local education authorities to provide secondary education in schools 'offering such variety of instruction and training as may be desirable in view of their different ages, abilities and aptitudes.' The Act did not stipulate how this was to be done. It was left for local education authorities to submit their plans on how they intended to meet these requirements. The terms 'grammar school, 'secondary modern school' or 'technical school' do not appear in the Act but the government had made known its preference for a secondary school system consisting of these three types of secondary school. At a time of acute financial difficulty, this preference for what became known as the 'tri-partite' system was understandable. It broadly fitted the structure of schools already in use and was widely adopted. Existing secondary schools became grammar schools that selected their pupils as they left their primary schools; elementary schools, once primary aged children were provided for elsewhere, were adapted to become secondary modern schools. Technical schools were provided wherever that proved possible.

The preference of a government for a tri-partite system had no statutory force. Accordingly, several local education authorities, including the London County Council and the West Riding of Yorkshire, decided to meet the age, ability and aptitude criteria by combining in one school what the tri-partite system took to be three different types of pupil requiring three different types of education in three different types of school. Schools designed to meet the full range of the 'aptitudes and abilities' of pupils within one secondary school, rather than between three, became known as 'comprehensive' schools. The London School Plan of 1947, described at the start of Part Two, set out the London County Council's reasons for providing schools of that nature.

A second example of shared responsibilities between central and local government was the way in which school places were provided during the post-war years of sharply rising school numbers. Under the Act, the duty to secure sufficient and suitable school places was the responsibility of local government. Central government's role was to control the total amount of expenditure involved and to approve or reject major building schemes proposed by individual local authorities. Governments had to ensure that their own national priorities were met. The most important of these was ensuring that sufficient funds were available to provide 'roofs over heads', schools needed to cater for rising school numbers. Between 1947 and the mid 1960s, local education authorities and successive governments worked together to provide over five million school places within tightly controlled cost limits. The efficiency with which the Department of Education's Buildings Branch helped to make this possible was widely recognised within local government and nationwide.

A third aim of the Act had been to extend the amount and to improve the quality of technical and vocational education. In this, it failed. The cost of the school places needed to raise the school leaving age to fifteen meant there was little money left to spend on creating the technical schools required or on the system of national part time day release the Act had designed to provide continued training for those entering employment on leaving school. These constraints meant that the need to provide systematically for such training, first identified in the latter part of the nineteenth century and only partially developed following the 1918 Education Act, was still not dealt with successfully by the 1944 Act. Despite sporadic efforts to remedy this problem, notably by Kenneth Baker in 1988, it remains largely unresolved in 2014.

The 1944 Act deliberately did not deal with the school curriculum. It was not seen as the role of local or central government in a democratic society to require schools to teach pupils particular things in any particular way. Until the late 19th century, publicly funded schools in England had been required to work within a nationally prescribed curriculum. Teachers were paid on a set of measurable results achieved by their pupils. After some twenty years, there was general agreement that 'payment by results' had failed.

Under the 1902 Education Act, education became the responsibility of all-purpose local councils, as opposed to single-purpose School Boards. In 1904 the Board of Education issued a Prefatory Memorandum, setting out the general aim of the elementary school. The Memorandum contained the following paragraph: "The only uniformity of practice that the Board of Education desire to see in the teaching of Public Elementary Schools is that each teacher shall think for himself, and work out for himself, such methods of teaching as may use his powers to the best advantage and be best suited to the particular needs and conditions of the school." Subsequently, The Board provided a Handbook of Suggestions for Teachers in Elementary Schools. These suggestions covered all aspects of the curriculum and reflected an unchanged approach of successive governments to the role of teachers that lasted until the late 1970s.

Suggestions for teachers in secondary schools were not considered necessary. It was left for a variety of Examination Boards, working with universities and schools, to cause teachers to adapt their teaching, so far as they thought this necessary, to the questions posed by the examinations themselves.

The 1944 Act did not change the government's attitude towards the primary school curriculum. In 1949, the foreword to the Ministry of Education's publication, Story of a School, simply reproduced the words of the 1931 Consultative Committee's Report on the Primary School: "Instead of the junior schools performing their proper and highly important function of fostering the potentialities of children at an age when their minds are nimble and receptive, their curiosity strong, their imagination fertile and their spirits high, the curriculum is too often cramped and distorted by over-emphasis on examinations subjects and on ways and means of defeating the examiners. The blame for this lies not with the teachers but with the system."

In 1966, the Plowden Report on the Primary School broadly endorsed this approach to the primary school curriculum. Commentators with an insecure grasp of the history of English education interpreted what had been endorsed by successive governments since 1904, as an example of the supposedly collapsing standards of the 1960s. The evidence, contained in an appendix to the Plowden Report, of the marked improvement in reading standards over the previous twenty years was ignored.

The Department's circular number 10 in 1965 is an often quoted, but evidently seldom read, example of the relationship between central and local government under the 1944 Act. The circular took the form of a request to local authorities to submit plans for developing comprehensive schools. Requests by circular lacked the force of statute; so local authorities could not be required to respond to the circular. Most did, but others did not. Those that did could not be required to carry out any proposals they had decided to submit.

The twenty years between the 1944 Act and the early 1970s saw little substantial educational legislation but a succession of well researched reports on primary, secondary and higher education were published. These included the Crowther (1959), Newsom (1963), Robbins (1963) and Plowden (1967) Reports. The research appendices of these reports ensured that administrators and politicians alike did not lack facts, as well as opinions, on which they could base their decisions.

The 1944 Education Act had staying power. It was based on widely shared principles of the place of education in a democratic society. Its provisions under-pinned the expansion and improvement of the education service in England and Wales for some twenty five years and created, in the words of Sir William Alexander, a national system locally administered. It was not until early in the 1970s, at which point Part 1 of this autobiography ends, that this balance of responsibilities between local and central government showed the first signs of developing into a national system nationally administered.

Part Two of this autobiography concerns the years 1972 to 1982. It was during these years that the educational role of local authorities in England, either by accident or design, began to decline. The first stages of this process were described at the end of Part 1. In 1966, the government had established a Royal Commission on Local Government outside London. In June 1969, the Commission's Report was presented to parliament. So far as education was concerned, the Report made two crucial proposals and issued a warning. The first proposal was that, to be able to act as a full partner with central government, local education authorities needed to be much larger than many existing ones. The evidence from HMI, the Ministry of Housing and Local Government, local authorities and the Department of Education all indicated that large education services performed better than small ones, some of which were doing poorly. The Commission therefore proposed the creation of 78 education authorities, outside London, with a preferred population of 500,000 and a minimum size of 250,000. These 78 would replace 124 existing education authorities and the 156 other local government bodies with some responsibilities for education.

A second proposal was that, even with larger local authorities, some elements of education, such as further education, would need to be dealt with at a provincial level. The Commission suggested that the newly formed local authorities should, to deal with these issues, appoint some of their members to form eight provincial councils. The Commission did not recommend that a provincial council should be an independently elected body.

In 1970, the Government set aside the Commission's recommendations, notably on the need for some provincial local authority presence. Eventually, under the 1972 Local Government Act, 97 local education authorities were created instead of the 78 proposed. In Yorkshire thirteen local authorities, some of which have predictably since functioned poorly, were created in place of the five much larger ones proposed by the Royal Commission.

The Commission's powerfully stated prediction that, if local government was not reformed in the way it proposed, "local government will be increasingly discredited and will be gradually replaced by agencies of central government" has since proved correct.

A second development that substantially reduced the capacity, even the will, of some local authorities to carry out a full range of educational functions was initiated by local government itself. The Bains report of 1972 was produced by a group of local authority chief clerks. Historically, functional legislation was administered by functional government departments. So educational legislation was devised and administered by a national education department. Similarly, health, police, housing and so on were administered by separate government departments, each responsible for the legislation relating to their function. Until the 1970s, local government committees were organised in much the same way. Senior education officials in local government, working with their education committees, dealt directly with their opposite numbers in the national Department of Education. Similarly, political leaders of education in a local authority dealt directly with education ministers. Both had detailed knowledge of the legislation they were dealing with. Nationally, until the mid 1970s, leaders of local authority education committees and their senior officials formed the highly influential Association of Education Committees. For many of these years, Sir William Alexander, as its Secretary, was able to represent the views of local education authorities directly to senior officials in the Department and to its ministers.

From 1974, most local authorities outside London became corporately managed.

Once received by local government, money provided or expenditure authorised by central government departments was, to a varying extent, distributed in accordance with local government priorities rather than those of the government department that was its source. The managerial logic of corporate local government is indisputable; its practical and political consequences for the education service disastrous, culminating in 2010 by the government removing the word 'education' from the term 'local education authority'. Under the 1944 Act, the local management of schools was the responsibility of education specific local authorities with their own chief officer holding the statutorily required office of chief education officer. All that was set aside and the management of education no longer seen by politicians, few with any experience of either, as a specific function.

While local government became corporate, government departments stayed functional and could no longer rely on corporate local education authorities deciding to spend money on the department's national priorities. Having won money from the Treasury for one purpose, ministers and their officials were not content to see it used for some other purpose. As the Royal Commission had predicted, central government's reaction was to create organisations outside local government to perform educational functions that had hitherto been exercised locally. Combined with the failure to create local authorities of an appropriate size and in the absence of the Commission's proposed provincial arrangements, this led to the creation of government agencies such as the Manpower Services Agency, the Learning and Skills Council and later, Connexions and a series of funding and other such agencies created to do what had earlier been done by local government.

Within local government, newly appointed and corporately minded Chief Executives saw no reason for particular departments, of which education was by far the largest, to retain direct access to any functional government department. Many actively prevented it. From being a central element of the local authority system, education officers, almost all with teaching as well as administrative experience, found themselves spending much of their time dealing with issues that had little to do with their area of expertise. It was during the 1970s that the role of local authority education officer became less attractive as a career. With the decline of that career structure went much of the expertise and understanding needed to manage even a diminished set of educational responsibilities. In 1977, the authoritative voice for local government's education service ceased with the demise of the Association of Education Committees.

Part Two of this autobiography, as did my own direct participation in educational administration, ends in 1982. By the end of the 1980s, the role of local authorities in education and, in some of them, even their commitment to the education service itself had been further weakened. In a few urban local authorities, irresponsible behaviour had strengthened the government's general distrust of local government.

Between 1988 and 2014, two of the main changes to education in England have been the nationalisation of the school curriculum and, at an increasing rate since 2010, the nationalisation of its publicly funded schools. Nationalisation is here defined as a system under which all important decisions are exercised by a single government minister, accompanied by an actual or potential transfer of assets to the State. This process necessarily requires the elimination of local government and other independent institutions from anything more than a peripheral influence on decisions about the form and content of education, either locally or nationally.

The curriculum of schools in England was nationalised in 1988. This replaced the system whereby, since 1904, governments had provided advice on the curriculum which schools were encouraged but not required to follow. From 1963, under arrangements originating with the Department of Education, a wider range of advice than in the past had been provided by the Schools Council. The Council's members included representatives of teachers, local authorities, universities, officials from the Department of Education and members of HM Inspectorate. The documents the Council produced, its advice, the research it undertook and the experimental work it supported were designed to encourage good practice. Most of what it produced was of high quality.

In 1976, a speech at Ruskin College by the Prime Minister pointed out that the government had a legitimate interest in the curriculum of schools and that the balance between the role of local government and central government in dealing with this might well require adjustment. His carefully worded statement left open the question of how and to what extent this adjustment would be made. In the years following the Prime Minister's speech, elements in the Department of Education came to believe themselves better qualified to deal with the curriculum than the Schools Council. They openly expressed dissatisfaction with the Council's work and commissioned a report on its effectiveness. When the report recommended that the Council should continue, in April 1982 the Secretary of State's response was to stop financing it. That left the way open for the nationalisation of the curriculum in 1988.

During the creation of a statutorily enforceable national curriculum, advice from all quarters on its scope and content was, with rare exceptions, ignored. A complex set of curricular requirements, with an accompanying apparatus for ensuring schools were accountable for meeting these effectively, was given the force of statute. The national curriculum was poorly constructed and imposed in haste. It has since had to be regularly and expensively revised, with teachers having to be retrained to meet new requirements as these have arisen. In 2014, some schools are still required to comply with it while others are not. Its collapse has been gradual, in recent years punctuated by personal and often ill-considered interventions from government ministers.

The nationalisation of schools in England began, on a small scale, in 1988. Twenty five years later that process is well advanced. Nationalisation has gone through three stages, best identified by the ministers most closely associated with them. Each stage began with a good idea. The idea behind the City Technology Colleges (CTCs), promoted by Kenneth Baker, was admirable. New and forward looking sponsors, with a strong commitment to technical and vocationally relevant education, were invited to create and lead a series of enterprising and self-managed secondary schools. The sponsors of these schools would control the governing bodies, appoint their own staff, develop their own curriculum, decide on which children to admit and be responsible for the financial management of their school.

In creating these schools, Kenneth Baker was either unaware or deliberately chose to ignore the fact that schools with almost exactly the same degree of self governance as CTCs already existed as Voluntary Aided (VA) schools. Many of these had been developed as independent schools during the nineteenth century by City Companies, the Churches and by individuals such as Miss Beale and Miss Buss. To develop more of such schools with appropriate sponsors would not have been difficult. Two things had to be done. First, the 1944 Act requirement that proposers/sponsors of a new school of the kind required had to provide both site and buildings had to be replaced by the need to make only a token or even no contribution to the cost of the new school. Second, local authorities, in submitting their proposals for a new school in their area, as they had done since the 1944 Act, would have had to be required by the Secretary of State to include any proposal they received for a City Technology College. The Secretary of State would then have had to consider all such proposals on their merits and to decide which to accept, modify or reject. If he decided to approve a proposal for a CTC, it would then have been for the local authority to find the site and, as in the case of voluntary aided schools, convey it to the trustees. Within agreed cost limits, the trustees would then manage the construction of their school.

Kenneth Baker's decision to develop CTCs, in itself a good idea, as government schools instead of VA ones, maintained but not controlled by a local authority, was the first move towards replacing local government's role in education with control of individual schools in England by a government minister.

No Prime Minister since 1997 has been educated in a publicly-funded school in England or later had any personal association with the management of any such school. This lack of understanding has made it possible for unelected and inexperienced policy advisers to play an increasingly important role in formulating educational policy. One such adviser, Andrew Adonis, later ennobled as minister for schools, had an excellent idea. This was to encourage enterprising groups of sponsors to run independently managed and newly built schools in areas of poor performance. Like Kenneth Baker, he was apparently unaware that the voluntary aided model could provide the legally established independent trustees and status that he believed to be necessary. That is presumably why the existence of VA schools is not mentioned in the account Lord Adonis has given of his struggle to develop, against fierce resistance, a type of school that had existed since 1944.

In developing academies in the form of Kenneth Baker's CTC model of school governance, the Secretary of State was authorised, under section 65 of the Education Act 2002, to enter into a contract with 'any person' to 'establish and maintain' a school, at public expense. Contracts formed in this way are at the heart of the academy programme. As the governance structure of VA schools makes clear, academy 'freedoms' can be secured without any such contract. Although in themselves, contracts serve no useful educational or administrative purpose, what academy funding contracts successfully do- as they are clearly intended to do - is to place the minister concerned in ultimate control of the schools or groups of schools contracted to him. Contracts leave it to an individual government minister, the Secretary of State, to determine exactly how much money each school contracted to him receives to run itself each year. If the governing body of any school, wholly dependent on a single politician in this way, believes itself to be genuinely 'independent', it runs a severe risk of deluding itself.

Labour's enthusiasm for academies as essentially government schools, paved the way for Michael Gove. Rightly perceiving that good governance can do much to improve the quality of education a school provides, Michael Gove wanted to extend, as far as possible to all schools, what Kenneth Baker had provided for CTCs and, under New Labour, Andrew Adonis for a number of academies. This was a good idea. The decision to do this by means of funding contracts with individual schools, rather than by a version of the successful voluntary aided system described above, was a bad idea for three reasons. First, it is simply a fact that an equitably and publicly funded school does not require a funding contract with anyone. Whoever is responsible for distributing the money to a school simply pays it directly to the school. Second, although the declared purpose of a funding contract with a government minister is to fund, its intended effect is, rather obviously, to enable that minister to establish what, if he cares to exert it, amounts to something close to absolute control over the institution contracted to him. That is an unhealthy development. Finally, however unnecessary contracts may be, the many thousands of funding contracts between schools and a government minister that now exist need to be expertly managed. Unfortunately, for all their undoubted intellectual ability, the basic administrative, financial and managerial competence required to do that are qualities which Michael Gove and his chosen associates have conspicuously lacked. The result has been confusion. Too many of the many thousand funding contracts are evidently now being administered without anything approaching an acceptable degree of efficiency. In 2014, as a way of managing most or all of England's schools, the contract- based academy programme developed by Michael Gove shows unmistakable signs of quite rapidly becoming an organisational disaster

As an extension of its legislative approval of the Secretary of State's move to nationalise England's schools, parliament has further legislated to allow nearly all important decisions about education in England to be made by or on behalf of the Secretary of State without reference to anyone else, including parliament itself. Parliament is not a party to the contracts that it has allowed the Secretary of State to make with any set of trustees he or she finds acceptable. The only consistently applied criterion for establishing the suitability of trustees to run a school at public expense appears to have been that they have not been elected by anyone.

The Secretary of State's uninhibited control of education now extends to the examination system, the training or lack of it of teachers, the structure of the governing bodies of academies, including the right to decide whether any of which he disapproves are to be allowed to remain in office, where, whether and at what cost new schools are to be built, and so on.

Two consequences of this legislatively authorised control of education by an individual government minister have become evident. The first is that it is very obviously inefficient. Even the straightforward task of relating the number of school places provided to the number of school places required has been mismanaged. Public money is routinely spent on children and students who do not exist. Financial control of academies is defective. Schools are developed where new schools are not needed. This practice of creating extra school places where there are already spare places, apart from wasting money, almost always adversely affects what local schools with spare places can still afford to offer their pupils. Sixth forms are encouraged to proliferate at a time when sufficient teachers of high quality to teach a full range of subjects in many existing sixth forms are lacking. Narrowly defined systems of accountability are created which give teachers perverse incentives for teaching badly. Bad practices are routinely imported from foreign countries. Over the past few years, the list of poorly structured 'initiatives' and ministerial incompetencies has become long and is lengthening.

Control of education by an individual government minister is also leading to increasingly totalitarian behaviour. As Lord Acton put it in 1887, power that verges on the absolute corrupts. The symptoms are unmistakeable. Ministerial hostility to all forms of real or imagined sources of opposition is loudly proclaimed. Enemies of 'reform', a term used to describe any ministerial initiative however ill-considered, are said to be lurking everywhere. Local government, the universities, the judiciary, the churches, the BBC, non-conforming elements of the Press and any form of independent thinking or action from teachers or their unions are all perceived as inherently pernicious. All are treated with contempt. Disciplined conformity, within schools and by everyone connected with them is to be the order of the day.

The arbitrary and sometimes irrational behaviour of individual government ministers is just one instance of England's general retreat from its democratic past. Now that parliament, with the notable exception of some of its select committees, has legislated away its ability to exercise effective control of the Executive, parliament itself is widely perceived as little more than a noisy and largely irrelevant adjunct to the Executive. This has damaging consequences for England as a functioning democracy. It is becoming difficult for England's electorate to find good reasons to vote at parliamentary elections for individual members of parliament. Voters correctly perceive that few of the people they vote for have any influence on what the government of the day, once safely elected, then decides to do.

What next? Within narrowing limits, resistance to the government is still permitted but the form democracy has taken in England is increasingly reminiscent of the 'democratic centralism' proposed by Lenin in 1917. Under such a system, further developed in parts of Europe during the 1930s, people are still allowed to discuss issues and to march about with banners provided they behave themselves. But there is little room left for alternative sources of decision-making even on important local issues. All important decisions in England are now taken by the small group in charge of the government. Intervention from subordinate bodies such as local government, professional bodies, independent researchers or even, other than grudgingly, from parliament itself is rarely found acceptable. In the wings, another small group of much the same composition awaits its opportunity to replace the existing one.

Education in England has been particularly badly damaged by this nation-wide retreat from the widely shared beliefs in what constitutes a democratic society that underpinned the Education Act of 1944. As Friedrich Hayek put it in that same year "Nowhere has democracy ever worked well without a great measure of self-government". That measure of self-government is what the 1944 Education Act secured and has since largely been legislated away.

In 2014, one simple question about education needs to be asked: is England content to place a single individual, the Secretary of State of the day, in what is close to absolute control of all elements of this country's education system? If it is, no action is needed; that is what England's schools and other educational institutions are being frog-marched towards. If it does not, a second question arises. Is any political party prepared to put that question to the electorate? That is the question that hangs in the air awaiting an answer.